WINNING THE SILICON SWEEPSTAKES

ROB FRIEDEN

Winning the Silicon Sweepstakes

Can the United States Compete in Global Telecommunications?

Yale UNIVERSITY PRESS

NEW HAVEN AND LONDON

Published with assistance from the foundation established in memory of Amasa Stone Mather of the Class of 1907, Yale College.

Yale University Press books may be purchased in quantity for educational, business, or promotional use. For information, please e-mail sales.press@yale.edu (U.S. office) or sales@yaleup.co.uk (U.K. office).

Set in Scala Roman and Scala Sans type by Keystone Typesetting, Inc.
Printed in the United States of America.

Library of Congress Cataloging-in-Publication Data
Frieden, Rob.
Winning the silicon sweepstakes : can the United States compete in global telecommunications? / Rob Frieden.
p. cm.
Includes bibliographical references and index.
ISBN 978-0-300-15213-5 (alk. paper)
1. Telecommunication policy—United States. 2. Telecommunication—United States. 3. Information technology—United States. I. Title.
HE7781.F74 2010
384.0973′0112—dc22
2009046426

A catalogue record for this book is available from the British Library.

This paper meets the requirements of ANSI/NISO Z39.48–1992 (Permanence of Paper).

10 9 8 7 6 5 4 3 2 1

CONTENTS

PREFACE

As a university professor, I have a fly-on-the-wall vantage point from which to observe early adopters as they beg, borrow, steal, and occasionally buy new products and services in the information, communications, and entertainment (ICE) marketplace. I marvel at my students' hand-eye coordination and their ability to handle multiple tasks simultaneously. However, I am also amazed at their lack of sophistication regarding trends, the consequences of changes in ICE, and strategies for becoming smart consumers.

Most of my students offer limited support for government regulation of the ICE sector. Such a libertarian attitude may stem less from objections to government meddling in the marketplace and more from a sense that they can hack or evade any technological, regulatory, or legal restriction that they do not support. Many people appear to reject government oversight as unnecessary, ineffectual, or too costly, but they readily blame legislators and judges when the market fails to deliver what they want on terms and conditions they expect. For example, some of my students who bought Apple iPhones quickly objected to usage limitations imposed by AT&T and Apple, including a prohibition on using the phone to access competing networks.

Apple did not need to secure explicit user acceptance of its unilaterally imposed limitations on which formats the phone supports for music storage or which software applications the company permits users to launch. Even though students signed a take-it-or-leave-it contract, some of them have resorted to self-help to remove operational limitations. They "unlock" handsets to access other carriers' networks, and they "jailbreak" handsets to use unauthorized software applications. By taking the law into their own hands they risk "bricking" the phone—rendering it inoperable. They also void the warranty.

Rather than violate carriers' imposed locks and limitations, wireless subscribers could seek regulatory and judicial remedies, but few consider these options affordable or feasible. Ironically, just about every user of a wireline telephone readily assumes the right to purchase any type of telephone, to connect that handset to the telephone network without consent from the company providing service, and to use the handset on different telephone networks when relocating. While there are some technological differences between a telephone that acquires service using radio spectrum and one that acquires service via a closed-circuit wire, a consistent regulatory policy, together with consumer expectation, would establish the same usage and access freedoms for both types of service. Yet most consumers either resort to unlocking or jailbreaking their handsets or tolerate the limitations despite the inconsistency, unfairness, and possible illegality of carriers' rules.

Many of my students also know how to circumvent copyright protection software and technologies; they seem to consider anything available over the Internet free for the taking. They know how to "untether" music from services that tie content to a specific device. They can "rip" music by creating a copy on a compact disk, or they can change the format, making it possible to copy and distribute the content. Yet most of my students think nothing of paying three dollars for twenty seconds of a song converted into a mobile telephone ringtone, have no idea how assorted fees can add 20 percent to their mobile telephone bill, and have little sense of how digital technologies will change their lives as both consumers and citizens. They can spend countless hours surfing the Internet but have a hard time using the Internet for applied research beyond a Google search. They may read blogs, but they have not thought much about the impact of the Internet on politics, journalism, social cohesion, religion, race relations, sexuality, and the like.

In a course on ICE technologies that I teach at Penn State University I encourage my students to develop a template for considering whether and how use of the Internet as a medium for communications and commerce makes sense. What I encourage them to discover is that an Internet-mediated option will replace an existing option after the initial wonderlust fades only if and when the Internet-mediated option offers an experience that is faster, better, smarter, cheaper, and/or more convenient.

I would like for all telecommunications users, not just my students, to develop digital literacy and sophistication about ICE technologies, markets, and impacts. I would like everyone to understand how the regulatory process in the United States and in other nations largely fails to serve the national interest, because ICE ventures have mastered the art of gaming the regulatory process to their advantage. Few consumers share my outrage when the regulator agrees to tilt the playing field to the advantage of a particular company or technology, or when the regulator agrees to reduce or eliminate rules, basing the decision on bogus assumptions about how competitive markets have become. Consumers appear to lack interest or have little worry that eliminating government oversight can result in higher costs, fewer choices, greater intrusions on people's privacy, reduced innovation, and fewer of the social and commercial benefits that accrue from new technologies.

Consider this example. In an increasing number of grocery stores, consumers have the option of registering for a frequent shopper discount card that provides weekly discounts, other promotions, and the opportunity to pay for groceries using a check. Many consumers have jumped at the opportunity to save money, but they may not have considered the full consequences of having the bar code on their frequent shopper cards scanned. Most have not thought about what supermarket operators do with the data collected. They would not have to be alarmist, privacy-obsessed zealots to worry about the consequences of grocery store owners' ability to mine data acquired online via telecommunications links as consumers vote with their dollars at checkout.

Beyond the issuance of coupons based on individualized shopping behavior, might the grocery store owner share or market the data? Perhaps grocery store owners share data about personal tobacco, alcohol, and sugar consumption with insurance companies and others that might use the information to calibrate their next premiums. Even if I stood to save money with a card, I would not appreciate having proprietary information about my consumption patterns created and widely disseminated. Nor would most of us appreciate it if a car rental agency surreptitiously tracked the speed of cars to determine what rate to quote the next time a car was rented.

Both the supermarket and the car rental companies can justify their actions by saying that consumers consented to data mining and dissemination in exchange for possible discounts. I favor marketplace-driven transactions, provided both parties fully understand the nature and scope of the transactions. However, I suspect that few consumers completely understand the extent of the unregulated dissemination and analysis of consumer data. For a short period of time Amazon used data mining to estimate the price sensitivity of consumers. It offered the same book at different prices, based on a prediction about a specific consumer's willingness to pay. Amazon abandoned this pricing tactic when consumer advocates and individuals objected. Suddenly data mining became a means to discriminate on the basis of estimated price sensitivity rather than a new opportunity for consumers to save time and money.

When radio frequency identification (RFID) chips replace or become embedded in a shopper's discount card, making manual scanning unnecessary, consumers can check out of the supermarket quickly, but grocers can possibly acquire information about consumer behavior before the consumers arrive at checkout lines. In light of RFID mobility and data-processing speed, why not install them in passports to facilitate processing at national borders and to help with the accumulation of data? The law of unexpected consequences comes into play here—and everywhere in ICE markets. In the case of RFID passports, the possibility exists that terrorists could tune to the frequency used by RFIDs to identify American passport holders in a crowd.

Mining supermarket discount card data, tracking rental car speeds, and scanning RFID chips represent just a few of the challenges presented when information processing and telecommunications converge to offer faster, better, smarter, cheaper, and more convenient outcomes. But we need to consider whether and how these outcomes achieve sustainable benefits. Few consumers know that the self-scanning checkout process, on average, takes longer than relying on a cashier. Self-scanning might offer a better alternative if long lines led to the cashier and only short ones to a computerized voice prompt. But currently the scanner offers no discount even though in the long run the potential exists for the computerized option to reduce the number of employees. So the scanner option appears to offer more benefits for the grocery store operator than for the consumer, but the convenience factor and the length of the lines might shift the balance on any given visit.

I have written this book with an eye toward enhancing readers' digital literacy. Citizens need competency beyond the ability to make a gadget or service work. I believe that users of ICE technologies, such as cell phones, need to understand the impact and consequences of their use. I fear that most us do not fully appreciate the downsides and trade-offs presented by technological innovations, partially because we welcome novelty, new opportunities for personal expression, and faster and better options.

I also worry that we have become far too confident in the ability of unregulated markets to achieve an efficient and fair allocation of resources. Ventures that benefit from streamlined regulations and eliminated regulations have the financial resources and incentive to come up with both credible and false justifications. National regulatory authorities, such as the Federal Communications Commission, far too readily accept the wisdom of the marketplace despite ample evidence that in ICE sectors, markets can fail through manipulation and anticompetitive conduct and through resource allocations that do not provide as much access to ICE technologies and services as governments and their constituents might wish. Broad notions of democracy, citizens' participation in governance, and citizens' desire for free expression may support market-countervailing regulations in the ICE sector.

Digital literacy allows consumers of ICE innovations to understand the benefits likely to accrue to advertisers, information brokers, and vendors of equipment and services, among others. In addition to criminals, who can exploit enhanced access to private financial information, legitimate commercial players in the ICE economy stand to benefit from citizens' use of ICE technologies and services. That is fair enough, particularly because vendors broker access to many ICE services in exchange for an opportunity to expose consumers to commercial pitches. I am more than willing to trade my possible attention to commercial messages for the opportunity to view valuable content because in most instances I consume the content without buying the advertised goods and services—that is, I operate as a free rider.

Most consumers of ICE services, however, do not appreciate fully the expanded opportunities that Internet advertisers and ICE vendors have to reduce free ridership, to offer the same products and services at different prices, and to identify and target individual consumer's preferences and vulnerabilities. While Internet boosters herald unprecedented consumer "empowerment," I believe the Latin phrase *caveat emptor,* "buyer beware," applies as never before. ICE vendors do not operate as charities and have no desire to offer goods and service free of charge if they can realize and maximize profits instead.

Technological innovations make it possible, as never before, for ICE vendors to know individuals' buying habits and predilections. This knowledge, derived lawfully from data mining—to which we consumers have consented—and unlawfully by using various tracking software, helps ICE vendors pitch customized products and services. Viewed positively, this means that a book vendor such as Amazon can suggest additional book purchase options based on Amazon's analysis of a person's buying habits and the purchases of other people who have bought the same books. Hotwire, a travel vendor, once surprised me with an e-mail reporting that fares and hotel rates had dropped for a destination that I had previously searched. Viewed in a darker light, the availability of personal consumption data means that vendors can get a better sense of our intensity of preference, which economists call "demand elasticity," and calibrate prices based on that demand. ICE vendors capture the surplus that consumers otherwise would accrue when they buy a good or service below its maximum acceptable price. Here, the balance of power does not tilt to the consumers' side, although some economists argue that it inexorably will.

Digital literacy can provide a long-term opportunity for balance. If knowledge generates power, then a depth of understanding beyond making a gadget work will accrue ample dividends. To acquire digital literacy ICE users must become students and assume responsibility not just for mastering the intricacies of gadget use but also in fostering an awareness of how gadgets and the services they access function in society and affect the flow of ideas and commerce.

Suppliers of ICE equipment and services could make these tasks easier; so could governments. But perhaps all too predictably, vendors appear to sense the advantage of confusing consumers, while governments fail to appreciate the value of a level playing field to encourage competition. Telecommunications policy and practice currently favor one group of stakeholders who have managed to leverage lobbying, campaign finance, and ideology to secure an artificial advantage.

ICE convergence and the migration from analog to digital technologies has high-stakes consequences for every one of us, as I will explain. I will identify how and why many players want to thwart progress to preserve market share and safeguard existing revenue streams and market niches. Various incumbents lobby legislatures, litigate in the courts, and pester regulators to create unnecessary financial incentives for their reluctant and belated migration to digital technologies and markets. Telephone companies, for example, long hesitant to provide video services over their networks in competition with cable television operators, now seem to be making up for lost time by securing statewide or national franchises, as opposed to the municipality-specific franchises that cable operators had to secure. The telephone companies have successfully characterized the franchise process as a barrier to market entry and the consumer-welfare gains accruing from competition. But the franchise process also ensures that video content distributors pay attention to community needs and operate their networks in the public interest.

The digitally literate consumer understands that every stakeholder offers a distorted view of a public policy issue. Incumbent telephone companies, emphasizing the need for government-sponsored financial incentives to make long-overdue investments in next-generation infrastructure, have succeeded in forestalling investment ostensibly because of regulator-created uncertainty and their own duty to connect their networks with competitors' networks. But in reality these companies failed to predict the speed of consumer migration from wireline to wireless telephone options, as well as the speed of the reduction in margins for local and long-distance telephone service. Put another way, if regulators, legislators, and judges had not bought, hook, line, and sinker, the incumbent telephone carriers' argument that the government needed to "incentivize" network investment, these companies would have had to act sooner on the basis of self-preservation and competitive necessity instead of trying to make up lost ground now.

Instead of relying on market-driven ICE convergence, governments have become unnecessary underwriters of network investments by favored groups. Meddling in the marketplace, normally antithetical to many small-government advocates, has belatedly stimulated one group of stakeholders to make investments, but at the expense of several other groups, including ventures providing competitive alternatives to incumbents' local and long-distance telephone services.

Because of the government's ill-thought-through stance, I worry that the United States will lose its global ICE leadership. This nation can no longer serve as a proving ground for cutting-edge applications. Network access is inferior here, access to network features is locked down, and network operators are preoccupied with extracting maximum possible regulatory accommodations instead of working tirelessly to improve the value of their services.

Just as consumers need to understand how seemingly benevolent companies limit choice and limit the versatility of the devices they sell, consumers also need to understand how governments often fail to serve the public interest. My goal in this book is to enhance consumers' digital literacy both in the marketplace and in the halls of government.

ACKNOWLEDGMENTS

I wish to thank Professors Chris Sterling and Gary Madden, as well as several undisclosed peer reviewers, for their helpful suggestions and observations. Over the years, several colleagues have provided support and insights that have helped me prepare this book and other publications. I want to express particular appreciation to Yale Braunstein, Dan Brenner, Stuart Brotman, Jim Chen, Henry Geller, Hudson Janisch, Merehoo Jussawalla, Steve Kaffee, Kas Kalba, Bill Melody, Eli Noam, Anthony Oettinger, Jorge Schement, Ben Scott, Jim Speta, Richard Taylor, Robert Trager, and Kevin Werbach.

My thanks to the team at Yale University Press—Michael O'Malley, Mary Pasti, and Alex Larson—for their efforts to improve this book.

As always, I am grateful for the support of my wife, Katie.

CHAPTER ONE

The Law of Unintended Results

THE UNITED STATES has long led the world in telecommunications, specifically in information, communication, and entertainment (ICE) markets, as exemplified by its incubation and privatization of the Internet. Ironically, it does not lead in securing access to broadband wireline and wireless networks or in providing the government stewardship possibly needed to stimulate widespread installation of the infrastructure for these essential networks. It has lost much of its competitive and comparative advantage in ICE markets because limited efforts have been made to promote digital literacy and because ICE equipment and service providers have effectively thwarted necessary government oversight.

Other nations have understood better both the stakes in network access and the need for government involvement. Australia, Canada, the European Union, Japan, Korea, and other nations appreciate the benefits in having government involved in the ICE sector as an anchor tenant, loan guarantor, steward, and public interest advocate. Their governments do not seek to preempt market forces or private enterprise, but stand ready to underwrite projects that private ventures will not risk undertaking and to force cooperation and coordination among ventures that prevent or thwart competition to secure potential benefits.

In stark contrast to global best practices, the U.S. government, in particular the Federal Communications Commission (FCC), has contributed to a toxic environment characterized by game playing, partisanship, results-driven decision making, a short-term perspective, and corporate cronyism. Active players in the regulatory and judicial process understand the value of making sizeable investments in undisclosed sponsored research and in clever lawyers, creative economists, and ubiquitous lobbyists.[1] Far too many consumers fail to appreciate that they could get far more for their money than they currently do if they acquired digital literacy rather than relying on the generosity of the suppliers or the public interest safeguards provided by the government and by marketplace competition, which may not exist at the level claimed by either suppliers or the government.

Unprecedented technological innovation provides the potential for substantial enhancements to civil society and quality of life.[2] Yet at every turn, politics or pragmatism forges a policy compromise that makes it possible for stakeholders—particularly established telecommunications companies—to extract government accommodations that shortchange the public. At times it appears that two parallel but mutually exclusive ICE environments exist. In one, the FCC and various regulated operators claim that the ICE sectors operate competitively and effectively, so much so that the FCC should pursue additional deregulatory initiatives. Curiously, in this robustly competitive environment some stakeholders continue to secure government-sanctioned financial subsidies and clamor for more government initiatives to create incentives for investment in next-generation networks. In the other environment, recognized by only a few independent observers, the lack of significant competition supports the ongoing need for government oversight, targeted market intervention, and effective strategies to promote speedy progress in the installation of next-generation broadband networks.

The two worldviews clash abruptly in the arena of wireless telecommunications. If we accept the conventional wisdom, cellular telephone companies devote sleepless days and nights to competing and innovating and constantly sharpen their pencils to mark down rates. As cell phones increasingly provide a third-screen alternative for accessing content available via television sets and computer monitors, wireless carriers have extraordinary incentives to invest in next-generation networks that will expand the reach and scope of services, possibly increasing wireless carriers' average revenue per user (ARPU), a measure of the average monthly revenues generated by subscribers.[3] But the reality of the current cellular telephone business belies conventional wisdom. The industry has become so concentrated that in 2009 four national carriers shared about 90 percent of the market in the United States.[4]

The advertisements for these companies appear to show robust competition, but little difference exists in terms of actual cost per minute of use or in the terms and conditions of service. Indeed, most advertisements champion how the service actually works ("Can you hear me now?") or how new or existing subscribers can get a handset for little or nothing in exchange for a two-year service commitment, with early termination penalties reduced, if at all, by the magnanimous sum of five dollars per month. Remarkably, in the nation that commercialized the Internet and has exhibited best practices in many ICE market segments, wireless carriers derive most of their profits and comparatively rich ARPUs from providing telephone calls, ringtones, and text messaging.

Elsewhere in the world, wireless handsets have become much like a Swiss Army Knife, providing everything from electronic currency, high-speed access to the Internet, real-time videoconferencing, and location-based electronic commerce (e-commerce) applications, including scannable bar codes for admission into concerts. Yet cellular carriers in the United States have sold just about everyone on the wrongheaded idea that popularity, "free" handsets, and large minutes-of-use allowances mean a robustly competitive market having no need for government oversight or even recognized subscriber rights, such as the freedom to access or download any software, service, or content.

THE CURRENT ARRANGEMENT—AND SOME QUESTIONS TO ASK

In theory, companies and governments have to serve their consumers and constituents to survive in the marketplace and in the next election. With this assumption, we would expect the marketplace to reward innovators who offer the next "killer application" or device. But in far too many instances, innovation gets stifled, and a fair marketplace trial never occurs. Too often, a level playing field does not exist, largely because government institutions legislate, regulate, or pass judgment in ways that unreasonably favor one group over others.

Incumbent players—such as telephone companies that have been around for decades—typically benefit from this arrangement. As evidence of this perverse outcome, let us consider the following questions:

- Why does the United States demonstrate global best practices in some information and communication technology markets, such as software and computing, but woefully lag in others, such as wireless and broadband services?
- If the information revolution was supposed to "change everything," how did more than one trillion dollars in investment largely evaporate in three years?[5]
- How can incumbent telephone companies successfully argue the need for governments to create incentives for investment in next-generation networks and at the same time claim that the existence of robust competition eliminates the need for any other sort of government involvement?
- Why have nations failed to bridge the "digital divide"[6] despite having created subsidy mechanisms to invest billions annually in never-achieved solutions?[7]
- If the ICE marketplace has become so robustly competitive, where are the usual consumer benefits of lower prices, diverse choices, and responsive customer service?
- How can incumbent ventures regularly avoid the adverse consequences of failing to anticipate developing trends and serve new markets by belatedly acquiring or extinguishing most competitive threats through mergers and acquisitions?
- Why have some nations, including the United States, lost their comparative and competitive advantage in ICE products and services?
- Why does it look as though the next-generation Internet will be less open, less neutral, and less accessible, possibly turning the playing field into "walled gardens"[8] of content and services offered by incumbents keen on disadvantaging newcomers offering "the next best thing"?

Why does the United States demonstrate global best practices in some information and communication technology markets, such as software and computing, but woefully lag in others, such as wireless and broadband services? The digitally literate consumer can appreciate that the current ICE environment in the United States and elsewhere displays some best and some worst practices. On the positive side, the enormously optimistic projections that helped fuel the dotcom boom and the information revolution have become reality. Most people in industrialized nations and urban dwellers in many industrializing nations have access to, or will have access to, networks capable of supplying a broadband wireline or wireless pipeline to a cornucopia of content in text, graphical, audio, and video formats.

On the negative side, consumers in both industrialized and industrializing nations will continue to face unnecessary impediments to having access to cheap, reliable, and robust broadband networks.[9] They will have to pay rates well in excess of what a truly competitive marketplace would generate,[10] and they will have to tolerate inferior network performance. Having bought prematurely the view that a competitive marketplace exists and can self-regulate, governments, led by the United States, may lack the resources and lawful authority to provide industry-specific remedies in advance of adjudication by courts lacking specific industry expertise.

Irony abounds in the current and near-term ICE environment.[11] We would expect the United States to rank consistently at the top in terms of global best practices for ICE innovation, accessibility, and affordability. Yet ICE ventures in the United States have not leveraged superior performance in software and computing to achieve top rankings in terms of consumer access to networks, such as the Internet and wireless cellular telephone services.[12] The United States leads the world in ICE technology incubation and marketplace exploitation, but when it comes to basic infrastructure, where incumbents have repelled many of the competitive threats, the United States barely exceeds the third world in ratings: "American visitors to Asia often return with fierce technological envy over the whiz-bang handsets on display and the routine sight of nonchalant twenty-somethings updating Web sites from their cellphones. . . . References to the U.S. as a Third World country when it comes to wireless service now approach cliché."[13]

How can the United States not have multiple bests-in-class for wireline and wireless networks? Bear in mind that a significant portion of the one trillion dollars lost in the dotcom boom funded network infrastructure, particularly new underseas and transcontinental fiber-optic cables and local wireline and wireless technologies offering an alternative to the copper-wire technology that telephone companies had done little to upgrade. When the Internet promised to change everything, including basic laws of business governing such inputs as supply and demand, money flowed into the sector to fund even hastily drawn-up plans, with little regard for how and when the venture would turn cash flow positive—that is, generate more revenue than necessary to pay current liabilities. Even given overinvestment and excess capacity in the long-haul market and failed plans to offer alternative wireline and wireless networks, the essential first and last mile network access might have commanded attention and funding year after year. The wireline and wireless networks are essential for access to the Internet and for any service operating via the World Wide Web.

Incumbent wireline and wireless operators have conserved capital and limited their capital investment in next-generation networks. Only recently have these risk-adverse operators begun to think seriously about developing new markets. Incumbent operators have claimed regulatory uncertainty,[14] the necessity of leasing facilities to competitors at below market rates,[15] and immature technologies and markets as justifications for their reticence to invest, even though other operators scattered throughout the world have expedited network development and investment. Incumbent telephone companies belatedly have discovered the Internet and its revenue-enhancing potential, but their interest lies mostly in finding new revenue streams from video services, not in upgrading their networks for all types of broadband services. Looking back, we can see that incumbent operators have masterfully played the lobbying, regulatory, advocacy, and litigation games to thwart potential competitors while also delaying until the last possible date investment needed to upgrade networks. Incumbents would assert the prudence of conserving investment resources, particularly in light of the dotcom implosion, but the failure to plan for the future means that some nations, including the United States, suffer from a comparatively inferior telecommunications infrastructure, a condition likely to handicap native ICE ventures in the global marketplace.

Many consumers in the United States suffer the twin insults of limited broadband access and comparatively high prices for what they can get. Incumbent telephone companies, with the notable exception of Verizon,[16] seek to retrofit installed copper wire for broadband access.[17] This strategy limits upfront investment in next-generation networks and offers inferior service; the transmission speeds available from fiber-optic-cable links are much higher. Cable television companies similarly seek to stretch the usable life of their coaxial copper-wire plant. With rare exceptions, consumers in the United States have limited broadband options, despite claims by incumbents and regulators that robust competition already exists.

How can such a dichotomy exist between the perception of the ICE marketplace by incumbents and government officials, on one hand, and empirical evidence to the contrary, on the other hand? The answer lies in the measures used for defining success, as well as in the financial, political, and other resources a stakeholder has available for disseminating a preferred message. Incumbent cable television and telephone companies want to overstate the true degree of marketplace competition and facilities deployment to encourage legislators, regulators, and judges to deem unnecessary most, if not all, government oversight. Market entrants want government sanctions that help tilt the playing field in their favor. Relatively few industry observers exist who do not have a direct financial stake in the government's perception of the marketplace and the commensurate conclusions about the need for regulation. Even many analysts affiliated with universities and think tanks now offer their research and advocacy to the highest bidder, often without disclosing the scope of their financial sponsorship.[18] Likewise, public relations firms create many "AstroTurf" organizations that falsely claim to independently represent consumers' interests: they present purportedly grassroots reactions that are in fact propaganda funded by businesses or other organizations.[19]

Conflicting perceptions about the scope of competition and the need for government involvement have a profound and largely negative impact on the public. In the lingo of economists, stakeholders can extract "rents" —revenues and other types of advantages—that consumers otherwise would capture. In other words, consumers end up paying more for less, because government has not effectively prevented anticompetitive and other behaviors unfair and harmful to consumers. When government does not safeguard the public interest, individual consumers must individually and collectively resort to self-help remedies. "Self-help" refers to both lawful and unlawful strategies that minimize the harm caused by a government that is either deliberately inattentive or captive to the interests of particular stakeholders. Illegal practices, such as copyright piracy, can stimulate governments and the private sector to restrict network access, through the use of technologies that enforce intellectual property rights in ways that restrict or deny lawful and fair uses of content by consumers.

If the information revolution was supposed to "change everything," how did more than one trillion dollars in investment largely evaporate in three years? As the ICE industry recovers from a trillion-dollar reduction in value,[20] both incumbents and market entrants are understandably anxious about investing in telecommunications. This reticence contrasts with the often-reckless spending during the dotcom boom, which ended in 2000. A few highlights are worth pointing out here. The laws of physics, mathematics, the marketplace, and the business cycle apply to ICE industries. Blue-sky forecasters from Bill Gates on[21] bought the notion that the Internet would change everything, including the robustness of demand for products and services and the physical limits to meeting that demand, such as constraints posed by technologies that use radio spectrum—for example, satellites and wireless systems. Somehow demand would double monthly for the foreseeable future, and ventures could tap that demand with little regard for determining how to secure payment. The rising tide would raise all ships, regardless of how leaky or silly any given business plan was.

As with so many preceding economic bubbles—caused by everything from tulips in Holland[22] to real estate in Japan[23]—demand cannot rise without cyclical, sometimes dramatic downturns. Ventures aiming to tap demand for new telecommunications capacity, Internet services, and Internet-mediated content required a robust and ongoing source of funding to secure both customers and "shelf space"—a widespread marketing presence—to entice additional customers. Most ventures did not find sufficient numbers of paying customers, so what had constituted irrational exuberance became practical or excessive pessimism.

The trillion or more dollars invested in ICE infrastructure, goods, and services did not actually evaporate. Hard assets, such as servers, office equipment, transmission cables, and buildings, became someone else's property for pennies on the dollar. Many clever and creative business plans failed, but the best ones have survived. Indeed, the survivors may have acquired an extension of time to wait out pessimism and consumer reluctance. They have acquired failed ventures' assets, and out of those ashes of failed ventures have come ventures that consumers and investors now consider rock-solid companies, such as Google, Amazon, and eBay.

How can incumbent telephone companies successfully argue the need for governments to create incentives for investment in next-generation networks and at the same time claim that the existence of robust competition eliminates the need for any other sort of government involvement?

Contradictory appeals to the government to both create incentives for investment and eliminate its involvement in the marketplace point to the ability of some telecommunication companies to game the political system by creating divergent governmental perceptions of reality. No matter how inconsistent the arguments, stakeholders have convinced government decision makers to reach diametrically opposite conclusions even about the same marketplace environment. For example, incumbent wireline telephone company executives insist that they must work hard to survive in a cutthroat competitive marketplace, yet many of their companies receive subsidies from long-distance telephone subscribers based on the view that the marketplace fails to provide affordable telephone service to several different types of consumers.[24] Both the U.S. Congress[25] and the FCC[26] have reached the conclusion that the marketplace for plain old telephone service cannot function without government intervention,[27] including the subsidization of service, regardless of population wealth and density, to telephone companies operating in rural and high-cost areas so that they can reduce rates for poor and elderly subscribers.

Apparently the local telephone service marketplace is both robustly competitive and suffering from market failure by underserving or not serving citizens. Simple economics tells us that in robustly competitive markets the price for a good or service trends toward its marginal cost—that is, the additional expense incurred by a producer to generate one more unit of capacity.[28] Yet the local telephone service marketplace apparently has not reached marginal cost or anywhere near it despite its "competitiveness." Even if it has, that price remains prohibitively high to many consumers, and legislatures have decided to subsidize access. Until Congress chooses to revoke its mandate that the FCC pursue a universal service mission with billions of subsidy dollars, the so-called competitive marketplace for telephone service requires a monthly 11 percent surcharge on wireline, wireless, and Internet-delivered long-distance telephone services that access telephones connected to conventional wireline and wireless networks;[29] the intention is to help bring local telephone service within financial reach for millions of Americans.

Incumbent telephone companies would object to linking competitiveness to the universal service subsidy. Presumably a market can have robust competition but also generate high prices—consider, for example, the cost of a college education, even one subsidized by taxpayers. But in the case of telecommunications, stakeholders claiming marketplace competition argue for governments to abdicate responsibilities to serve the public interest. The unfettered marketplace, they say, can self-regulate. Incumbent telephone companies gladly accept government-mandated subsidies but reject government involvement elsewhere in the sector.

Why have nations failed to bridge the "digital divide" despite having created subsidy mechanisms to invest billions annually in never-achieved solutions? Although competition supposedly characterizes the ICE sectors, including telephone and cable television service, competition has not fully extended into digital markets; broadband access to the Internet is an example. Nor has the marketplace solved access problems for both basic and advanced ICE services. Again, some stakeholders and government officials reject these claims. Notwithstanding empirical evidence to the contrary, they fervently deny the veracity of statistics pointing to a poor record of achieving widespread access to the Internet and other digital services. To some, nations like the United States have a chronic and unresolved problem in achieving affordable and widely available access to broadband and other networks, despite competition, but to others, no such problem exists thanks to competition.

The agenda and perspective of the observer determine the degree of robustness and competition perceived in the ICE marketplace. When seeking financial support and incentives to invest in infrastructure, ICE ventures will point to market failure even as the same players point to competition as a better regulator than government.

If the ICE marketplace has become so robustly competitive, where are the usual consumer benefits of lower prices, diverse choices, and responsive customer service?

With all the alleged competition in the ICE marketplace, we would expect a consumer windfall in terms of price, diversity of options, and satisfaction. But what options in ICE equipment and services are readily available? In some sectors robust competition does exist, and consumers can walk away from poor service and high prices. Long-distance telephone service and wireline telephone handsets fall into this category. But in many key sectors there may not be many options at all. For broadband Internet access, few consumers have more than two facilities-based competitive options: (1) cable modem service[30] and (2) digital subscriber line (DSL) service.[31] Internet access via satellite requires the purchase or lease of costly equipment and typically offers lower bit transmission rates: fewer bits can be delivered per second, and at higher prices, than with cable modem and DSL services.[32] Terrestrial wireless service may constitute a cost-competitive option in urban and suburban areas, but vast regions of the United States lack high-speed wireless Internet access. Access using conventional cellular telephone networks constitutes a costly and slow option.[33]

Similarly, how many facilities-based options for basic telephone service are available? Consumers increasingly consider wireless telephone service a competitive alternative to wireline service, albeit at two to three times the price. Voice over Internet Protocol (VoIP)[34] and other Internet-delivered telephone services do provide a competitive alternative, but again, we must consider the actual out-of-pocket cost for such services. A $24.99 unlimited-use local and long-distance service package[35] appears both competitive and attractive as a wireline service. Some of the allure wanes, however, when we consider that most cable television systems do not offer telephone service on a stand-alone basis. You can get it only as part of a bundle of service that includes video and Internet access. Nor does the $24.99 plan factor in the cost of broadband access, which you also must have. If you add the cost of Internet access to the $24.99 service plan, you again reach a price point three times the conventional wireline rate.

How can incumbent ventures regularly avoid the adverse consequences of failing to anticipate developing trends and serve new markets by belatedly acquiring or extinguishing most competitive threats through mergers and acquisitions?

The more things appear to change in ICE markets, the more they stay the same. Incumbents seem to understand only belatedly the need to adjust to a digital future in which converging technologies and markets require single ventures to offer a combination of ICE services. Incumbents, particularly the ones with the deepest pockets and the most retained earnings, have proved adept at acquiring both failed and successful competitors and thereby coming out ahead. Critics of Microsoft, for example, accuse the company of executing an "embrace, extend, and extinguish" strategy vis-à-vis competitors.[36] They allege that when Microsoft finds itself behind the development curve, as occurred at the onset of the dot-com boom, the company can make up for lost time by exploring joint ventures with competitors, and then, whether rejected or welcomed, Microsoft can either buy out the company or devise ways to weaken the competitor—for example, by bundling as a free feature in its software the service offered for pay by the competitor. Microsoft allegedly extinguishes competition by having the financial staying power to offer as a free value-adding feature something for which a competitor used to charge.

Why have some nations, including the United States, lost their comparative and competitive advantage in ICE products and services?

Some, but not all, assessments of digital readiness and market penetration place the United States well below other nations in global best practices.[37] In a classic "shoot the messenger" strategy, U.S. government officials have challenged the negative assessments and the criteria used.[38] Few in government care to consider whether and how the United States has lost some of its competitive edge and comparative advantage in ICE sectors.

Clearly the United States remains ahead in many ICE markets. Silicon Valley and other commercial incubators for software, Internet services, and equipment attest to its ongoing global leadership. However, such superiority does not extend to the telecommunications infrastructure needed to switch, route, process, and transport bits via all the networks in the Internet cloud.[39] Will it continue to be possible for U.S.

ventures to retain global leadership in the devices and services that ride over wireline and wireless networks? Not too many years ago, Motorola dominated the wireless infrastructure and handset marketplace. Now this company risks a further drop in the rankings of companies that provide handsets for cellular telephone service, behind industry-leading Nokia, based in Finland, and Samsung, based in Korea.[40] Might a correlation exist between the robustness of a nation's telecommunications infrastructure and the global marketplace success of its native companies?

Why does it look as though the next-generation Internet will be less open, less neutral, and less accessible, possibly turning the playing field into "walled gardens" of content and services offered by incumbents keen on disadvantaging newcomers offering "the next best thing"?

As the Internet becomes the key medium for most ICE services, industry observers, academics, consumer representatives, and others have expressed concern whether service providers will manage their networks fairly. Advocates for "network neutrality" seek carriers' assurance and possibly regulator-established rules to ensure that the Internet continues to operate in a nondiscriminatory manner, both in terms of how subscribers access and receive Internet-transmitted services and how content and other service providers reach subscribers.[41] In all the phases of its development, the Internet has benefited from prudent decisions by governments to use a light hand when regulating and safeguarding national interests. Governments correctly recognized that they could rely on the motivations of mostly private stakeholders to build the telecommunications links and to diversify the services available from the World Wide Web. But as the Internet consolidates, the stakes have risen in terms of providing equal consumer access to the variety of services available via the Internet and equal service-provider access to consumers.

The Internet continues to evolve as it incorporates technological innovations and becomes a conduit for many services that previously traversed dedicated telecommunications networks. As the Internet begins to offer convergent services, such as VoIP[42] telephone services and Internet protocol television (IPTV),[43] some operators may perceive the opportunity to accrue a financial or competitive benefit by deviating from a plain-vanilla, one-size-fits-all Internet, characterized by nondiscriminatory, best-efforts routing of traffic,[44] and unmetered-use subscriptions.

Some Internet service providers (ISPs) seek to diversify the Internet by prioritizing traffic and by offering different quality-of-service guarantees. To some observers, this strategy constitutes harmful discrimination that violates a tradition of network neutrality in the switching, routing, and transmission of Internet traffic. To others, offering different levels of service provides the means for consumers and carriers to secure and pay for premium, "better than best efforts" service if so desired.

Little middle ground exists between net neutrality advocates and opponents, but practically speaking, the Internet will continue to deviate from a one-size-fits-all network. Accordingly, we should consider net neutrality in terms of a dichotomy between types of discrimination. Some nonneutral strategies make economic sense, will not harm consumers, and can enhance the Internet experience—for example, higher quality of service for "mission critical" bits. But other strategies mask unfair trade practices and other types of anticompetitive practices.

Opponents of network neutrality correctly state that external, non-market-driven constraints on ISPs, because of their ability to price-discriminate, can adversely affect the incentive to invest in broadband infrastructure and the ability to recoup that investment. ISPs have avoided common carrier responsibilities. Common carriers provide essential public utility services on a nondiscriminatory basis, typically subject to extensive economic regulation to ensure just and reasonable rates. Public utilities like telephone companies are required to provide services in a nondiscriminatory manner. The Internet, in contrast, largely functions as a product of countless interconnection arrangements flexibly negotiated and executed free of government oversight. ISPs correctly note that only in rare instances has an interconnection dispute triggered allegations of anticompetitive practices or resulted in consumers losing access to a content source or e-mail addressee as a result of network inaccessibility or balkanization.

On the other hand, network neutrality advocates have identified actual instances where ISPs have unilaterally blocked traffic to reduce subscribers' network demand, handicap a competitor, punish ventures for not agreeing to pay a surcharge, or stifle criticism about the ISP and its parent corporation.[45] Even if we were to dismiss such evidence as anecdotal or exceptional, an ISP's incentive and ability to discriminate in the switching and routing of bits seems to match or exceed the ease with which employees of electricity-generating companies have been able to create artificial congestion and false bottlenecks to accrue exorbitant profits. Employees of Enron and other electric utilities engaged in a number of anticompetitive practices that caused the spot market price for electricity to skyrocket because of tactics designed to mimic a dramatic increase in demand that the electricity distribution grid could not handle.[46] If Enron employees could manipulate the market for the switching and routing of electrons, then ISP employees might engage in similar tactics when switching and routing packets. Policymakers should seriously consider the potential for harm to consumers and content providers when ISPs deviate from network neutrality. Likewise, ISP should offer quality of service and other nonneutral service options in a transparent way that eliminates questions of intracorporate favoritism.

AN INDICTMENT: A GOVERNMENT PROCESS THAT DISSERVES THE PUBLIC

ICE policy, by its very nature, can trigger significant disagreements on how to proceed. Laws and regulations affecting this sector can affect citizens' rights of speech and expression. In addition, economic and political philosophies can suggest different preferred outcomes. Although ICE law and policy should not follow a political party line, most FCC commissioners seem to think they do. With increasingly regularity, FCC commissioners vote along party lines on ICE issues that have a profound national impact. The FCC's commissioners, and the presidents who nominate them, have made ICE policy rife with politics and partisanship. As a consequence, the work product of the FCC has grown increasingly inferior vis-à-vis other national regulatory authorities (NRAs). Such politically driven policies directly and adversely affect the degree to which the United States leads in ICE markets and policies.

With politics driving decision making, the commissioners review cases and controversies with predetermined assumptions and biases. Indeed, the FCC staff have become infatuated with the science of economics, including suspect new theories cooked up by sponsored academic researchers. Because the output generated by economic analysis requires assumptions, the assumptions become essential predicates for policy recommendations.

Long ago, commissioners who served on the FCC assessed issues based on the public interest and the facts presented, not on political grounds or self-serving assumptions. They did not write concurring statements in the form of a *Wall Street Journal* editorial, either. Now we have chairs and commissioners quite willing to use the political party registration of a fellow commissioner as reason for derision.

Until 2007, no official statement of a chairman or a commissioner preceded the name of a fellow commissioner with his or her party affiliation. But when a majority of the FCC commissioners conditionally approved AT&T's acquisition of BellSouth, FCC chairman Kevin Martin and commissioner Deborah Tate expressed displeasure at their "Democrat" colleagues for insisting on these conditions, as though their party affiliation was justification enough to disagree: "Importantly, however, while the Democrat Commissioners may have extracted concessions from AT&T, they in no way bind future Commission action. Specifically, a minority of Commissioners cannot alter Commission precedent or bind future Commission decisions, policies, actions, or rules. . . . [T]he Democrat Commissioners want to price regulate not only AT&T but also Verizon and Qwest."[47]

The FCC has sunk into a morass of partisanship, pseudo science, fuzzy math, creative interpretation of economic principles and legal concepts, selective interpretation of the facts, innovative collection of statistics, and flawed thinking. Partisanship at the top changes the behavior of civil servants, who hold important decision-making jobs, presumably without regard to which political party dominates Congress or the party affiliation of the president and individual commissioners.

In conjunction with party affiliation, FCC commissioners and staff increasingly rely on different baseline philosophies to drive policy outcomes. In other words, if a Commission employee embraces a pro-marketplace orientation, then that employee's recommendations will suggest deregulation regardless of countervailing facts. Similarly, a Commission employee predisposed to find regulation as a necessary safeguard will hold steadfast to this principle. We can readily appreciate that predisposition colors policy analysis. But predisposition has become bias. Couple bias with what comes across as a deliberate attempt not to acquire empirical data, and the FCC appears to engage in results-driven decision making.

For example, if a majority of the FCC commissioners believe that the broadband Internet-access marketplace has become robustly competitive, then they will make decisions predisposed to favor marketplace regulation. But what if the facts do not support the commissioners' assumptions and beliefs? Worse yet, what if the FCC shapes its empirical research and data gathering to support the false conclusion that robust facilities-based competition exists? A reasonable interpretation of the FCC's broadband market penetration statistics might support the view that such competition exists, but only because the FCC has used measures designed to overstate the case.

For more than a decade, the FCC defined broadband as the capability of delivering traffic at 200 kilobits per second (kbps) in one direction.[48] The Commission later deemed 200 kbps a broadband threshold rate.[49] However, at a time when consumers expect their broadband links to support full-motion video, 200 kbps does not constitute a minimally acceptable baseline rate, particularly since true broadband networks in the United States and abroad offer services with multi-megabits per second transmission speeds. The Commission totals the number of broadband providers without regard to whether they operate their own facilities or resell DSL and cable modem service. It adds up a single raw number of broadband competitors based on whether service is available anywhere within a zip code (a unit soon to be replaced by smaller census tracts).[50]

The FCC's performance in compiling broadband statistics supports the view that there are "lies, damn lies and statistics."[51] Embedded in the statistical compilation is the recognition that two types of facilities-based operators, cable television and telephone companies, provide over 88 percent of all broadband access in the United States. So is the market robustly competitive, as the FCC alleges and as countless sponsored researchers echo,[52] or is the market monopolized by two operators in most localities?

For example, the FCC states that a zip code area in a largely rural Pennsylvania location has eight broadband service options, down from nine in 2006.[53] But practically speaking, given price and performance considerations, only one real option exists for many residents. Despite close proximity to a major university, many residences do not have DSL service, leaving consumers with either cable modem service or a satellite service offering less than half the bit rate at twice the cost. Wireless data service providers do not yet offer a price-competitive alternative outside major cities; typical bit rates rarely exceed 500 kbps.[54]

In addition to using creative statistics, the U.S. executive branch has chosen to shoot the messenger when other statistical compilations do not show success. For the better part of a decade, the United States has lagged in broadband development. Incumbent telephone company managers have emphasized regulatory uncertainty and "confiscatory" FCC sharing requirements, but the fact of the matter is that investors lost over one trillion dollars in the dotcom bust, and a significant portion of that amount targeted burgeoning demand for telecommunications transmission capacity.

The FCC has also abandoned enforcement of a legislatively mandated unbundling strategy that required incumbent carriers to provide network access to competitors at below-market rates.[55] National regulatory authorities in many other nations have persisted in maintaining unbundling requirements, despite constant opposition from incumbents. In the United States no broadband carrier can credibly claim that regulatory uncertainty or infrastructure-sharing requirements have caused persistently poor broadband penetration rates. Nevertheless, both the National Telecommunications and Information Administration (NTIA) and the State Department have turned their attention to challenging broadband statistics that show comparatively poor performance. For example, the Organisation for Economic Co-operation and Development (OECD) ranks the United States fifteenth globally in broadband subscribers per hundred inhabitants.[56]

The State Department has made the issue something of a diplomatic affront to the United States, and the NTIA has offered explanations of why the scope of broadband access in such places as government offices and coffee shops means that the OECD ranking underestimates market penetration. So at first stakeholders could blame the government for mandating that wireline carriers unbundle network facilities and provide interconnection with the facilities of market entrants. Now the government can blame outside data collectors for underestimating the kind of success the FCC achieved when it used zip codes as the relevant market penetration measure.

In sum, the FCC has become captive to assumptions and political philosophy at the expense of common sense and empirical evidence. If the FCC concludes that competition exists, a conclusion no doubt upheld by stakeholders who benefit from this assumption, then at some point the FCC stops questioning whether the facts support the assumption.

AN INDICTMENT: STAKEHOLDERS SUPPORT FCC ASSUMPTIONS

Beneficiaries of the FCC's deregulatory policies recognize the need to shore up the Commission's decision making with science, albeit fuzzy science. Far too many academics and think tank affiliates contribute to the public policy debate thanks to undisclosed benefactors who surely expect something back for the hundreds of thousands invested. The concept of plausible deniability allows a sponsored researcher to state with a straight face that he or she does not receive any direct financial support for the white paper, law review article, or legislative testimony that just happens to offer unqualified support for a particular stakeholder's or group's viewpoint.

Not only does the money go unacknowledged but it gets laundered. A stakeholder supports a think tank's general mission with a sizeable grant. In turn, the think tank's staff or affiliates just happen to come up with creative thinking about a public policy issue that resonates with the stakeholder's political and public relations agenda. Since the stakeholder's grant helps pay for the employees' or affiliates' income, though indirectly, there is no direct quid pro quo.

It strains credibility to accept that so many initiatives in ICE policy, first announced through the writing of an academic or think tank affiliate, arose completely unsolicited. For example, we can thank undisclosed but sponsored research for innovative rethinking of economics and the law that supports the view that the interconnection responsibilities compulsory for a common carrier "confiscated" incumbent carrier property.[57]

Managers of commercial ventures invariably have to decide the proper balance between making investments in new ventures and infrastructure and concentrating on finding ways to secure more benefits (rents) from various government programs. For example, a professional sports team might put forth the possibility of leaving a city if the local or state taxpayers do not underwrite construction of a new stadium. In telecommunications, incumbent carriers have engaged in similar leverage: limiting investment in next-generation networks unless and until the government creates financial incentives or other inducements to invest, by, for example, removing "regulatory uncertainty," which might just mean unfavorable and costly regulatory obligations. For example, a telephone company might not build a fiber-optic network capable of providing video competition with incumbent cable television ventures in a particular state or region unless and until the prospective market entrant can avoid having to secure operating authority (a franchise) from each and every municipality within which the newcomer wants to operate.

The tension between rent seeking and profit seeking has adversely affected the pace of next-generation network deployment. Too many actual or prospective investors recognize the benefits of seeking government-generated incentives to invest. It becomes difficult to determine when competitive necessity would have forced an investment without government assistance and when incentive creation was necessary. This problem will become even more acute for nations that target economic development through taxpayer-funded subsidies of telecommunications infrastructure projects.[58]

The recent substantial infusion of capital investment by incumbent carriers into next-generation networks may evidence a healthy response to the elimination of unbundling and below-market access pricing regulations. But it also may evidence the disappearance of core and previously captive revenue streams that incumbent ventures, cable television and telephone companies alike, expected to remain unthreatened. How much longer could the incumbent local-exchange telephone companies see declining local voice service revenues before they had to find and serve new profit centers? When stakeholders demand government incentives, it probably makes sense to ask whether the stakeholders would make the investment and take the risk without special accommodations.

The public, as consumers and voters, are not blameless for the pitiful state of affairs in ICE law and policy. Far too few people appreciate the stakes involved when the national regulator acts; far too few understand what the public loses when special interests get preferential accommodation. Acquiring digital literacy takes time and effort, but the investment is well compensated by cost savings and other benefits. To make the effort, however, citizens need to appreciate the costs of laziness and the risks of blindly expecting governments or corporations to serve the public interest.

Consider the monthly rental cost of the cable television set-top converter, a device that consumers think they must have to qualify for access to digital cable television content. It is simply not true that they need it. Cable television subscribers can eliminate the set-top box rental by substituting something called a CableCard,[59] provided they have television sets that contain a slot for the card. CableCards substitute for most functions performed by set-top converters at a fraction of the cost. Acting on a congressional mandate to provide consumers with an alternative to compulsory rental of set-top converters supplied by cable television companies, the FCC has directed the companies to support CableCards or other downloadable copyright protection and service-tiering functions.[60]

It has taken ten years for the FCC to get serious about mandating the CableCard and other options. During this time cable operators have accrued countless extra revenues by not having to do so. It should come as no surprise that the cable companies have no enthusiasm for widespread use of these cards, because that will force the companies to find new ways to offer on-screen navigation, copyright protection, and security functions. Had more consumers demanded the cheaper CableCard option, it might not have taken ten years for the FCC to force cable operators to support this option and complete two-way interactivity between the cable operator and subscribers.

In many instances, by excessively accommodating particular constituencies, the FCC has failed to serve the public. But in many instances consumers have accepted restrictions and inferior service or resorted to self-help to compensate for their abandonment by the FCC. Americans, as consumers and citizens, can do a great deal more to acquire digital literacy and possibly establish a level telecommunications playing field.

CHAPTER TWO

Feast and Famine in the Information Age

TECHNOLOGICAL INNOVATIONS offer unprecedented opportunities for consumers to achieve faster, better, smarter, cheaper, and more convenient access to information, communications, and entertainment services. In light of the extraordinary U.S. success in commercializing the Internet, as well as its best-practices leadership, spanning many years, in computers, data processing, software, and other ICE industries, we would expect the United States to have achieved equally stellar achievements in building the infrastructure to provide and access ICE services. Remarkably, the United States has failed in that respect, despite being the location for much of the investment made during the heady dotcom boom of 1998–2000.[1] To understand why, it will be useful to compare and contrast the costs and benefits resulting from U.S. government polices, and the U.S. approach more generally, with the often more productive strategies of other nations.

On the supply side, the United States has achieved only lackluster broadband market penetration with comparatively high Internet-access costs, particularly in rural locales. On the demand side, consumers find that the convergence of ICE technologies and markets has not made all technologies more user friendly and competitive. That is partly because the major players in the United States prefer to game the regulatory process to secure more deregulation or to reduce their regulatory burdens vis-à-vis competitors, rather than deal with a level playing field, just as many would rather litigate than compete in the marketplace. Lax enforcement of antitrust laws and generous assessments of ICE market competitiveness make it advantageous for incumbent ventures to buy market share through mergers and acquisitions. Although the legal and regulatory process allows litigation and other stalling tactics to predominate in the United States, other nations, such as Korea and Japan, as well as nations with large hinterlands, such as Canada, provide best-practices leadership in making the Internet and next-generation telecommunications services widely available at affordable rates.[2]

HOW THE UNITED STATES LOST ITS ICE LEADERSHIP

Operators in the American ICE marketplace have reduced consumer expectations and have largely failed to meet even these diminished performance standards. From Wall Street to Main Street, from Capitol Hill to the Supreme Court, a variety of stakeholders resist change, tilt the playing field, and take advantage of deep pockets to confuse consumers and decision makers. Even with the debut of Apple's iPhone, most American consumers cannot use cutting-edge handsets to access next-generation wireless network services equal to what carriers in Asia and Europe offer. American carriers have yet to complete upgrades to their networks, and remain stymied by a technical standards battle over which format to use when providing high-speed services capable of delivering full-motion video content. Likewise, few consumers know that they pay some of the highest rates in the industrialized world for wireline broadband access and, with rare exceptions, receive inferior bandwidth.[3]

Despite remarkably poor performance with respect to global best practices, stakeholders have mostly succeeded in convincing regulators, legislators, and judges that the ICE infrastructure marketplace is working just fine. Consumers apparently do not know what they are missing, particularly given the relentless advertising and public-relations campaigns that tout what is available. The fact that the Apple iPhone cannot operate at true broadband speeds and therefore cannot fully exploit all features of the Internet attests to how far below global standards U.S. ventures have fallen. Advertisements for wireless carriers typically pitch how often the service actually works and what new handsets the carrier has available, not lower prices or new services.

Carriers in the United States have a woeful record in terms of providing the telecommunications infrastructure that carries the bits representing ICE content. They mostly blame applicable law, the FCC's implementation of the law, and the lack of government-created incentives to invest in infrastructure upgrades. Yet representatives of these carriers have had direct involvement in legal, regulatory, policy, and judicial forums and have often enjoyed a privileged role in forging compromises, accommodations, and rule exceptions. Federal and state governments act as though they have forgotten what affirmative steps they can take to facilitate progress beyond accommodating a particular stakeholder's self-serving requirements. Other nations have pressed carriers to adopt a long-term perspective when investing in infrastructure rather than make such expenditures only if near-term profitability appears certain. These nations shore up private investment with public expenditures and other fiscal incentives. At the risk of appearing to be socialistic central planners, many governments assume a vigorous role in articulating a national broadband infrastructure policy that anticipates coordination between the private and public sectors and requires ICE ventures to temper private gain with public interest considerations. In most countries facilities-based carriers have to share rights of way and network facilities and often have to provide access at below-market rates for newcomers.

Perhaps the best way to understand how poorly the United States has performed in establishing a telecommunications network infrastructure is to examine how it has excelled in other ICE markets. We need only take a drive along the crowded highways of Silicon Valley, California, to see American excellence. How does the United States excel in the products and services generated in Silicon Valley and in other technology hotbeds? The authors of *The Silicon Valley Edge* suggest ten factors:

1. Favorable and transparent rules of engagement—there are laws, regulations, and standards for securities, research and development, taxes, accounting, corporate governance, bankruptcy, immigration, and development designed to support entrepreneurship and risk taking.
2. Knowledge intensity—the region has achieved a critical mass of ideas for new products, services, markets, and business models. Silicon Valley serves as a magnet for entrepreneurs, educators, venture capitalists, and people with vision.

3. A high-quality and mobile workforce—talented, educated, and motivated people seek to make a home and a fortune in the region.
4. A results-oriented meritocracy—talent and ability accrue rewards in Silicon Valley without regard to race, ethnicity, or age.
5. A climate that rewards risk taking and tolerates failure—the region supports a high-risk, high-reward calculus but also makes it possible for entrepreneurs who have experienced failure to regroup and try again.
6. An open business environment—the region supports robust competition as well as knowledge sharing. This win-win environment results from the frequent formal and informal interactions among people with similar interests and objectives. Social networking and relationships matter as much as technological innovations.
7. Universities and research institutes that interact with industry—major universities like Stanford, the University of California at Berkeley, and Santa Clara University foster exchanges among academics and entrepreneurs, as well as prepared students to become innovators, leaders, and risk takers.
8. Collaborations among business, government, and nonprofit organizations—the region houses universities, trade associations, labor councils, service organizations, and companies, all of which collaborate and network with an eye toward a successful future.
9. A high quality of life—despite traffic congestion, extremely high housing prices, a relentless pace of work, and even power outages, Silicon Valley offers proximity to open spaces and urban amenities.
10. A specialized business infrastructure—the region provides access to specialists needed for economic development, including consultants, lawyers, venture capitalists, and executive recruiters.[4]

While not all of these factors can apply to ICE infrastructure development, they provide a basis for comparing and contrasting the rights and wrongs in Silicon Valley ICE development with what happens in Washington, D.C., state capitals, and corporate headquarters outside the entrepreneurial, incubating environment of Silicon Valley.

Favorable Rules of the Game

Sometimes the rules of the game favor one company or group to the detriment of others, including consumers, often through unequal, asymmetrical deregulation. The favorable rules for ICE development in Silicon Valley apply fairly and equally to all, so a level playing field exists for market entrants vis-à-vis incumbents.

In the overall American ICE infrastructure environment, the rules attempt, but fail, to establish parity of opportunity, primarily because laws and regulations have to achieve two potentially conflicting objectives. Ideally, facilities-based competition would evolve between two or more operators who have invested in their own facilities. But given the high cost to enter a market and given the large market share held by incumbents, laws and regulations also must promote competition, or at least ubiquitous access to networks, in the absence of robust competition. The second-best strategy requires incumbent operators to provide market entrants with cost-based access to their facilities. Such compulsory interconnection and cooperation trigger many problems, including how to determine a fair price for access by a competitor, how wide to make the scope of such compulsory cooperation, and what impact such regulator-imposed access has on the incentives of both incumbents and newcomers to invest in new facilities.

For the first objective—promoting facilities-based competition—to have any prospect for success, legislators and regulators have to work on the second objective, allowing market entrants to access incumbents' networks, because newcomers cannot quickly establish a complete alternative network even if they have ample financial resources. The second objective requires cooperation among competitors and all but guarantees disputes over the terms, conditions, and quality of interconnection, despite the obligation of telecommunications service providers[5] to cooperate as regulated common carriers.[6] If the law, as implemented by regulators, mandates interconnection at below-market rates, incumbents will claim that their property has been confiscated and that the confiscation will result in a reduction—if not an elimination—of their incentives to invest in next-generation infrastructure. Incumbents, claiming that the rules of the game have so changed as to tilt the playing field in favor of market entrants, can forcefully argue in courts, regulatory forums, and federal and state legislatures that government has fostered "artificial" or induced competition.[7] Incumbents also will argue persuasively that market entrants, having secured the right to lease access to competitors' facilities on favorable, regulator-created terms and conditions, will never have the incentive to build their own networks.[8]

Incumbents have successfully argued that stimulating competition requires them to make illegal or unwarranted sacrifices in order to jump-start competition. Yet most of the so-called sacrifices represent fundamental responsibilities that commercial ventures assume when they acquire favorable legislative and regulator-conferred rights. For example, telecommunications service providers, such as wireline and wireless carriers, operate as common carriers, a classification that requires nondiscrimination in the provision of services, mandates, accessibility, and prohibits unreasonable practices that stifle competition or disserve the public interest. In exchange for these obligations, common carriers accrue ample regulatory benefits, including the right of eminent domain—that is, the opportunity to install wires and towers on both private and public property, typically at below-market rates and often at zero cost. Facing the obligation to provide market entrants with access to their networks, incumbents complain about the unfairness of such interconnection obligations even though they have accrued ample financial benefits from the rights to install network infrastructure across (over and under) private and public property.

When incumbent carriers effectively game the administrative and judicial process and achieve delays and official decisions absolving them of the duty to interconnect or to price their facilities at fair rates, market entrants face a playing field tilted against them. Under these circumstances, governments cannot know whether market entrants can wean themselves off competitors' networks, because the market entrants eventually fail, having exhausted all startup capital before turning cash flow positive. This scenario has played out in the local telecommunications marketplace, where most recent market entrants, commonly referred to as competitive local exchange carriers (CLECs), have gone out of business. Likewise, the first objective will never be achieved, and we will never know whether the lack of progress in fostering competition results from incumbents' anticompetitive practices and stalling tactics because the market cannot sustain competition or because market entrants were poorly capitalized and otherwise ill suited to survive in the long term.

Does the ICE infrastructure provide the competitive, or potentially competitive, open market with low barriers to entry that incumbents and others have claimed? The rules of the road in ICE infrastructure development have to straddle a fuzzy line between promoting competition and creating a fair opportunity for market entrants, on one hand, and forcing incumbents to accommodate, if not promote, competition through mandatory interconnection, on the other. National regulatory authorities in many nations require incumbent-entrant interconnection in the markets at regulator-determined rates that fall below what the incumbent thinks is fair and what it would attempt to charge in arm's-length negotiations with competitors. Neither incumbents nor market entrants can have rules that accommodate all their interests. Incumbents want market entrants to fail, yet be able to state that competition exists or that all competitors have a fair marketplace trial. Market entrants want guaranteed success and market share.

ICE infrastructure stakeholders can and will dispute whether the rules favor or harm them. But collectively they all can claim that the rules are not clear, uniformly enforced, or designed to establish a fair marketplace trial for competition. For now, suffice it to say ICE infrastructure competition at the local wireline and wireless level, for narrowband voice and broadband data, has not thrived in the United States. Regardless of whether CLECs could cherry-pick the most profitable customers of the incumbent local exchange carriers (ILECs) and otherwise acquire market share unfairly, as claimed by incumbents, the CLEC competitive threat has come and gone, as have billions of dollars invested in CLECs.[9] Likewise, the wireless marketplace has become dominated by four carriers, two of which (AT&T and Verizon) also dominate wireline market share.

Remarkably, while ILECs claim that the regulatory environment has created disincentives for the multibillion investment in next-generation plant, market entrants have succeeded in attracting billions of dollars for just that purpose. Yet after a few years of increases in market share, most CLECs have gone out of business, the result of poor business practices on their part—for example, emphasizing geographical reach without regard to profitability—but also ILEC litigation and other strategies designed to disadvantage CLECs or to reduce their regulator-conferred marketplace opportunities.

Knowledge Intensity and Other Human Resources

Knowledge intensity refers to the level at which a region attracts individuals and institutions having the qualifications, skills, and resources needed for successful development. High knowledge intensity results from cerebral academics combined with applied smarts, raw intelligence coupled with entrepreneurism, and other qualities not easily taught. Silicon Valley rewards innovation, creativity, leadership, and entrepreneurship. In contrast, success in ICE infrastructure may include crafty lobbying, tireless lawyering, and the power of incumbency.

Variable levels of knowledge intensity do not suggest that the United States leads in ICE hardware and software because its stakeholders are smarter, or that ICE infrastructure operators suffer from comparatively lower intelligence. The difference in knowledge intensity refers to the synergistic effects of having a critical mass of like-minded people with shared objectives even as they aggressively compete for market share. In Silicon Valley, hostile competitors can share views about the need for national policies promoting ICE development without losing any of their entrepreneurial or competitive vigor. Because ICE infrastructure development takes place in dispersed geographical locations, the key players may not have operated in the superheated environment of Silicon Valley. Nor do the skills needed to thrive in the Washington policymaking and legislative environment closely match what Silicon Valley requires.

Few would dispute that a robust ICE infrastructure can help reduce the comparative and competitive disadvantages suffered by regions lacking the critical mass of resources available in regions like Silicon Valley. Telecommunications can reduce the comparatively higher costs incurred by ICE suppliers and consumers located in remote locales, particularly if carrier-pricing policies average costs nationally. By carrier choice and regulatory policy, telecommunications carriers typically offer "postalized" rates for service, that is, rates set regardless of the actual distance traveled by any single transmission. A single postage rate covers mail delivery across the street and across the nation. Similarly, a postalized telecommunications rate offers a single per-minute charge regardless of whether a call links next-door, intrastate, or interstate parties.

Another common pricing strategy, "all you can eat" (AYCE), provides opportunities for users in remote areas to reduce their competitive disadvantage. AYCE makes it possible to stimulate demand for ICE services by offering a single rate regardless of amount of usage. Users in remote locales would doubly suffer if they had to pay a per-minute-of-use rate coupled with a high mileage charge reflecting their distance from urban areas that already have reached a critical mass in knowledge intensity. Distance- and usage-insensitive rates disproportionately benefit ICE suppliers and consumers located in remote areas with high rates of use. Although remote users cannot generate the same critical mass of resources as urban users can, they can mitigate somewhat their comparative disadvantages, particularly for telecommunications-intensive applications.

Unlike distance-insensitive pricing, which may become a permanent choice for some telecommunications service, such as local telephone calling, AYCE pricing may last only for the short term during which ICE infrastructure providers perceive the need to stimulate and promote network usage or during which metering costs exceed the benefits for Internet access or other services. As ICE markets mature, AYCE pricing may overstimulate usage, leading to congestion and the need to raise prices to accommodate the volume of traffic generated by the heaviest users. Economists typically reject AYCE pricing because it fails to offer efficient pricing cues, can trigger excess consumption, and can force low-volume users to subsidize high-volume users. Currently, Internet service providers have begun to experiment with two-element pricing that combines a fixed monthly usage allowance with a variable rate based on usage above a download allowance.

The pricing decisions made by early Internet carriers and service providers helped increase the knowledge intensity and aggregate utility derived from the Internet. Economists term as positive network externalities the increase in value or utility accruing from networks that have rising usage and subscriber populations. With distance-insensitive rates, ISPs eliminated financial disincentives to use networks that traversed the globe. To some observers, the Internet heralded the "death of distance"[10] as a cost or other impediment, even though on a route-by-route cost analysis, a longer link, across a continent or ocean, still costs carriers somewhat more to provide than a short link. But in the initial years of Internet development ISPs forecast more gain in stimulating usage and selling subscriptions than in tracking the distance of each link. Similarly, positive network externalities accrued when ISPs decided to charge a flat monthly subscription to attract subscribers. The collective value of the Internet increased both in terms of the number of discrete links to individuals and content sources and in terms of the number of times such links could be established.

Collaboration with Universities

Another key advantage available to Silicon Valley ICE ventures lies in the mutually beneficial collaboration between universities and commercial ventures. Academic institutions, such as Stanford and the University of California, Berkeley, generate research that can translate into commercial opportunities. These institutions also prepare students for careers, including ones that exploit research they conducted in school.

ICE infrastructure ventures take comparatively less advantage of synergistic opportunities with universities, possibly because of the lack of close proximity and shared perspective. However, some ventures recognize the impact of academic research and opinion on the regulatory and policymaking process. Some professors have developed a major sideline in offering expert testimony and research as sponsored and funded by industry. Academic papers and consultations come from research centers and think tanks, many located in Washington, D.C., to exploit the opportunities available from proximity to national government bodies. Sponsored research can have a direct impact on the regulatory and policymaking process. But too often the authors of such research do not disclose their receipt of direct or indirect financial support. In addition, this type of research too often accommodates the sponsor's requirements, including the expectation that the research be used to support a particular position. Sponsored and undisclosed research often finds its way into prominent law reviews and other publications.

THE ICE CULTURE WARS

ICE technological and marketplace convergence has triggered a clash of cultural identities and regulatory philosophies among the many providers and users. The culture, mindsets, folkways, and knowledge base of people involved in telecommunications do not readily mesh with what people involved in the Internet and other ICE ventures know and think. Because stakeholders do not come close to a shared perspective about the role of government, the marketplace, and collaboration, the synergies created in a place like Silicon Valley cannot readily accrue elsewhere.

If the Internet ever stood separate and apart from its telecommunications transport roots, it has now become a fully integrated and multifaceted ICE marketplace. The convergence of telecommunications markets and technologies has proven disruptive to preexisting concepts used for categorizing, using, and regulating ICE services. Just as we can no longer think of content access solely in terms of a channel or network affiliation, so, too, must we stop compartmentalizing ICE services into separate legacy classifications, such as television, broadcasting, regulated telecommunications, and unregulated information processing. Market-defining service classifications cannot work in a convergent world where regulated telephone companies offer access to unregulated video and data services and unregulated companies offer services that compete with those of regulated telecommunications carriers. For example, ISPs now offer the functional equivalent of incumbent telecommunications services—for instance, Internet-mediated voice telephony,[11] commonly referred to as Voice over Internet Protocol (VoIP) or Internet telephony.[12] For their part, telecommunications service providers, such as the incumbent Bell Operating Companies, AT&T, Qwest, and Verizon, now offer Internet-mediated services as transporters, processors, repositories, or creators of content.

Such a proliferation of services and expanded coverage challenges tactical, business, operational, legislative, and regulatory assumptions. ISPs initially offered unregulated, non-common-carrier ICE services carried over the telecommunications transport facilities of unaffiliated, regulated common carriers. Telecommunications service providers initially considered the Internet primarily as a vehicle for expanded telecommunications line sales and not as a threat to voice-service revenues, a core offering and a major revenue generator. ISPs and other Internet-based ventures could largely operate free of regulatory oversight. Given the lack of regulatory oversight, even though governments helped incubate development of the Internet, and given the largely libertarian attitudes of most Internet stakeholders, a "Nethead" culture developed that was substantially different from the "Bellhead" culture of telecommunications service providers.[13] These cultures derived from the perspective and orientation of the people involved in the telecommunications and data-processing worlds. In the non-convergent past, Netheads and Bellheads worked in substantially different environments.

Most content creators, in the current convergent environment, as in the previous non-convergent environment, have generally operated without much interest in the Nethead and Bellhead clashes. Satisfied to live in a creative and often glamorous world, the "Contentheads" realize the importance of their product and the need for independence in the creative process. This independent streak pervades the Contenthead attitude toward technology except when Contentheads affiliate with downstream distribution companies, such as a broadcast network. Contentheads have a neutral or agnostic attitude toward technology except where it affects distribution revenues, as occurs through piracy. Digitization enhances piracy opportunities and creates pressure on the Contentheads' preferred ways to make content available, by establishing windows of exclusive distribution rights—for example, first-run theatrical displays followed by pay-per-view on cable television and at hotels, followed later by cable and broadcast television. In a convergent digital environment, various technologies and media display the same content at the same time—for example, DVDs for viewing on a television set and video files for downloading and viewing on a computer monitor.

Regulatory dichotomies exacerbate the clash between cultures. Having initially operated in data-processing markets, which qualified for little, if any, regulatory oversight, Netheads assume that they can foreclose government intervention in perpetuity regardless of the markets they enter and regardless of the potential for adversely affecting preexisting regulatory programs, such as the annual multibillion-dollar universal service program funded by customers of long-distance telephone services. Some Netheads have deluded themselves into thinking that mediation via the Internet can largely insulate any transaction from governmental oversight, even if the transaction had triggered government involvement in a direct, non-Internet-mediated environment. Regardless of how integrated information processing and telecommunications might become, some Netheads extend their assumptions about nonregulated markets to new markets. Similarly, some Bellheads have ignored the need to respond to changed circumstances by thinking that the status quo will persist and existing regulations will extend to new circumstances, largely insulating telecommunications service provider incumbents from Internet-mediated competition.

With all the buzz and hype surrounding the Internet's ascendancy, we can easily conclude that a new world order will offer services that incumbent players somehow cannot or will not offer. Slogans like "Faster, better, smarter, cheaper, and more convenient" describe the characteristics of what new out-of-the-box thinking generates, the product of a mindset largely lacking in the regulation-numbed and competition-insulated world of incumbent telecommunications operators. Conventional wisdom largely relegates telecommunications service providers to the low-margin transmission of bitstreams generated by others who add value and accrue greater profits. Nethead information-economy players apparently have the mental nimbleness and other skills to thrive while their Bellhead counterparts only can muddle through.

Pity the Netheads, however, who underestimate the Bellheads' ability to exploit their market dominance in facilities ownership at the local and long-haul level and their ability to game the legislative and regulatory system to thwart change, or dominate large, convergent ICE markets. Netheads offering "the next best thing" typically fail to appreciate fully the role of telecommunications in making or breaking their business plans. While the Internet creates many new market opportunities, laws and regulations have yet to diminish the powers held by enterprises providing the underlying bit transmission, particularly where traffic must traverse different networks, which requires the physical connection of facilities and often triggers payments from the customers of bit transport to the carrier providing the delivery service. When a carrier controls access to the first mile of a telecommunications or Internet link to and from residences and businesses or else faces limited competition, the carrier can unilaterally establish take-it-or-leave-it terms and conditions.

While Bellheads may bank too much on their continuing ability to maintain toll booths along the information superhighway, Netheads largely fail to appreciate that unless and until they integrate throughout the service chain, they must rely on Bellheads who are ready, willing, and able to take advantage of the limited competition and their superior expertise in working the regulatory process. Indeed, the Nethead managers of major Internet service providers, many of which incumbent telephone companies own, recognize the value of controlling gateway access and have adopted some of the pricing and interconnection tactics of their Bellhead counterparts.[14]

Bellheads and Netheads do not understand each other, largely because they speak different languages, operate from fundamentally different assumptions about their businesses, and have generated substantially different cultures. Few in either camp realize that success depends on the acquisition of skills resident in both groups—the Netheads' keen interest in competing and embracing change; the Bellheads' ability to attend to details, including cost recovery and management of complex networks requiring customer care, accurate billing, and maintaining high quality of service. Because of the distrust between Bellheads and Netheads, perhaps both camps should work harder to understand each other. Technological and marketplace convergence means that different types of people will work within a single company or have to reach consensus in the joint provisioning of a service.

The Bellhead Persona

For more than one hundred years Bellheads have dutifully worked inside the system to provide public utility services. By operating "businesses affecting the public interest"[15] they executed a public compact: trading off pricing flexibility and accepting unprofitable service commitments in exchange for significant insulation from competition and application of a regulatory process designed in part to ensure their ongoing financial health. No wonder Bellhead stocks historically have offered rock-solid investment opportunities for widows and orphans: these companies have generated substantial, predicable cash flows and dividends. At the risk of resting on their laurels, Bellheads could afford to move incrementally. Prior to the onset of technological innovations and new pro-competitive regulatory policies, Bellheads enjoyed the ability to manage change and to plan for the future at a leisurely pace.

As much as they might disparage regulation, Bellheads actually have benefited far more from it than they have suffered.[16] Government served as guarantor of a stable revenue flow, even when insisting on long depreciation schedules and prescribing rates of return. Regulation pervades the Bellhead mindset as a necessary evil, but also as a mutually beneficial mechanism for both regulator and regulated. Regulation offers a check against some of the most perverse marketplace forces, making it possible for Bellheads to live in a safe and largely predictable environment. Professional money managers and individual investors historically have not rewarded cautious conduct with speculative valuations based on future performance and prospects. Bellheads have offered continuity, predictability, and safety. In the process they have generated reliable and effective billing and customer service systems, as well as a complex set of operating rules, including complex revenue-sharing arrangements when handling the traffic of other carriers.

Even without aggressive and creative marketing, incumbent telephone companies have managed to generate billions in revenues, with plenty of retained earnings to fund acquisitions of ventures that operate in converging markets.

The Nethead Persona

Netheads, who work in the information-technology world, make vastly different assumptions about the role of government, the nature of markets, and role of businesses in society than their Bellhead counterparts. Netheads view any government involvement with suspicion and claim that much of the Internet's success results from the government's hands-off approach. Netheads thrive on a competitive, no-holds-barred environment and have great confidence in the marketplace's ability to reward innovation. Netheads rarely assume social responsibilities beyond considering that their innovations will make life better for everyone. With the rise of Internet-mediation, Netheads have achieved substantial marketplace success and influence. Many of the leading Internet firms did not exist ten years ago. Until recently, the highest stock appreciation and capitalization have been accrued by information-hardware, software-processing, and e-commerce ventures, not telecommunication incumbents.

Netheads often think out of the box, given their nonconformist, libertarian bent. They generally deem any form of government involvement as anathema because they operate on Internet time—they count the microseconds—and have no patience for external forces that might cause delay. If Bellheads thrive on continuity, Netheads find chaos stimulating, and they embrace uncertainty and risk rather than trying to control them. Netheads may risk reinventing the wheel or having to learn lessons the hard way. They could not tolerate the sleepy and measured life of most Bellheads. Netheads typically take high risks and hope for high rewards. They take as a given the absence of barriers to market entry.[17] They expect to build the proverbial better mousetrap, which not too long ago attracted ample venture capital funding.

Bill Gates could serve as the archetypical Nethead: he was able to achieve incredible accomplishments and attain fantastic wealth but was unwilling or unable to avoid legal and regulatory quagmires. A less doctrinal Nethead might have found ways to avoid having to defend his company (Microsoft) from an antitrust suit brought against the company by the U.S. Department of Justice and many state attorneys general.[18] Yet the sense of purpose and relentless pursuit of a vision foreclosed reticence or discretion. Netheads would rather shoot first and aim later. They are not afraid to fail, but are surprised when failure occurs, because they truly believe they have created the next best thing.

The Contenthead Persona

Contentheads would like to avoid clashing or perhaps even having to deal with Bellheads and Netheads. The Contenthead world has little in common with either. Contentheads look, act, work, relax, and consume differently. They correctly know that without content, Bellheads and Netheads have nothing more than a distribution infrastructure of limited value. Contentheads know that bit creation generates more value than bit transport, even though individual Contentheads may so emphasize the creative process that little time remains for mastering the business side.

Convergence has forced Contentheads to recognize that the future requires their collaboration with wireline and wireless telephone companies that previously operated as neutral conduits for transmitting content. With Bellheads and Netheads moving into content creation and active distribution, Contentheads must partner with strange bedfellows. Think of Stephen Spielberg or George Lucas forming a venture with Bill Gates and the heads of Verizon and AT&T. Such mixed collaborations will become a frequent occurrence.

NETHEAD DOMINATION OF EARLY INTERNET DEVELOPMENT

The short history of the Internet evidences little ongoing management and planning by either governments or incumbent telecommunications carriers, even though governments underwrote its development and incumbent carriers engineered and provisioned the telecommunication networks that provide the Internet's bit transport.[19] Netheads point to this hands-off approach as a primary reason for the Internet's success. They may infer that they alone possessed the skills needed to provide light-handed governance in the limited areas requiring coordination—for example, establishing and fine-tuning technical standards, including the domain name registration process and the Transmission Control Protocol/Internet Protocol used to manage traffic across disparate networks and to route traffic based on World Wide Web letter addresses.

During the Internet's incubating years, when governments and academic organizations served as anchor tenants, a loose set of voluntary standard-setting and coordinating bodies benignly offered nonbinding recommendations for optimizing connectivity.[20] Operating in a generally noncommercial environment, Internet stakeholders emphasized ease of use, coordination, and consensus building. Most ISPs agreed to connect their networks at centralized locations known network access points.[21] An ISP agreed to handle another ISP's traffic on a settlement-free, zero-cost basis, commonly referred to as peering. The emphasis on building the Internet and making it work predominated over such commercial issues as determining whether ISP A caused ISP B to incur costs to accommodate the traffic requirements of ISP A. Accordingly, most ISPs agreed to a "bill and keep," "sender keep all" financial arrangement,[22] on the possibly erroneous assumption that outbound and inbound traffic flows were roughly symmetrical, which obviated the need to meter.

Achieving global connectivity and promoting the Internet could be emphasized when the financial underwriters did not expect near-term profitability. These goals also promoted a democratic philosophy of welcoming the participation of anyone other than government officials. Most volunteers serving on the nonbinding standard and policymaking forums represented Internet stakeholders and expressed Nethead views. Telecommunications service providers had little to say outside the technical realm.

Vounteerism and participatory democracy waned as the Internet privatized and became more businesslike. In 1995 the National Science Foundation (NSF) largely withdrew from financially underwriting Internet development, drawing to a close the U.S. government's Internet incubation and promotional activities.[23] Telecommunications service providers, which had served as contractors to NSF, assumed responsibility for operating the backbone networks that provide much of the long-haul transport between network access points. Unlike the federal government, these carriers realized the potential upside and downside financial stakes involved. On the upside, becoming a major Tier 1 ISP provided telecommunications carriers with the opportunity to lease substantial bandwidth and to serve an increasingly important data-communications market. On the downside, telecommunications carriers quickly saw the need to determine who was causing expanded network upgrade requirements and to charge them for the expanded capacity and services these ISPs required.

Managers at telecommunications carriers also recognized the financial importance of Internet line leasing, particularly in light of a substantial growth in data communications demand and relatively flat growth in voice communications demand. Even before a data-centric Internet-based telecommunications marketplace was envisioned, telecommunications carrier managers sensed the Internet's ascendancy and the need to control it. As lessors of both local and long-haul bandwidth, Bellheads easily assumed control of the Internet and replaced ambiguous Nethead policies with specific telecommunications rules, responsibilities, and rates.[24]

BELLHEAD DOMINATION OF THE CURRENT INTERNET

We should not underestimate the consequences of having incumbent telecommunications carriers dominate the Internet, particularly if regulators continue to abstain from subjecting the Internet to close scrutiny. Ironically, incumbent telecommunications carriers can achieve much of their hotly contested deregulatory agenda by concentrating on Internet market-entry initiatives in lieu of seeking relief in courts and regulatory agencies. An information services "safe harbor"[25] provides a largely unregulated classification in most nations. An information service is defined in the United States as the "offering of a capability for generating, acquiring, storing, transforming, processing, retrieving, utilizing, or making available information via telecommunications."[26] Incumbent telecommunications carriers can qualify for this category by offering services that arguably subordinate the telecommunications element and make it an inseparable transport component of an information service.[27]

Incumbent local and interexchange carriers can extend their market reach throughout Internet market segments. Better yet for these carriers, the substantially unregulated Internet provides an extraordinary opportunity to offer cheap and unregulated services that constitute functional equivalents to regulated telecommunications services. Incumbent telecommunications carriers have begun to exploit this opportunity because they recognize that they could expand the array of services they offer that qualify for the largely unregulated information-service classification.

Despite the information service safe-harbor opportunity, however, incumbent telecommunications carriers continue to expect regulation to occur and continue to find ways to secure competitive advantages by gaming the process to secure comparatively fewer regulatory burdens. Similarly, Netheads cannot avoid regulatory issues relating to interconnection and cooperation. They consider such issues to be subject to Internet "governance"[28] and may not see links to telecommunications rules of the road. The parallels do exist, and they grow stronger and more obvious as telecommunications carriers consolidate ownership and control over many Internet market segments. For example, the requirements imposed by the major Tier 1 ISPs that interconnection, transit, and delivery be paid by smaller ISPs enable us to closely track how telecommunications carriers interconnect lines and who has to pay for access to other carriers' networks. Applying a telecommunications interconnection regime to Internet facilities access would affect the debate over network neutrality. We would have to ask, What nondiscrimination rules must ISPs follow when providing access to subscribers, content providers, and other ISPs?

Telecommunications carriers own just about all of the Tier 1 ISPs, which operate the Internet's backbone networks.[29] These carriers establish the terms, conditions, and payment requirements for internetworking—administering a collection of networks operating as one network—and they operate from a telecommunications perspective. These Bellheads understand the role of regulation, as well as ways to evade, thwart, or dilute regulations. In one future scenario—possibly the worst case for Netheads—telecommunications carrier managers and their ISP colleagues establish telecommunications rules of the road, ostensibly subject to government oversight but amounting to regulations in name only. Under this regime, Netheads both lose control of the Internet and lack an effective forum for redress.

Consumers may also face a worst-case scenario if the Bellheads consolidate control of the Internet, further develop Internet-mediated telecommunications services, and manage to qualify these services for the largely unregulated information-service classification. Some may find the prospect of nonregulation attractive, particularly Netheads. But a prematurely unregulated telecommunications services marketplace offers Netheads and consumers alike no accessible forum, outside a costly courtroom, to resolve issues like predatory pricing, the deliberate underpricing of services with an eye toward driving out competition, discriminatory interconnection policies, violation of network neutrality rules, and refusals to interconnect. The incentive exists for both Bellheads and Netheads to restrict access and to favor affiliates in terms of what content subscribers can easily access, as in walled gardens, and in terms of what rates affiliates and competitors have to pay for network access. In the Bellhead world, compulsory interconnection responsibilities, imposed on telecommunications common carriers, limit the potential for corporate favoritism and other types of anticompetitive conduct. In the Nethead world, no such safeguards exist, and the conduct of a dominant player, Microsoft, demonstrates the potential for abuses.

Regulators, legislators, and judges will have to watch out for loopholes and arbitrage opportunities in the unregulated Internet for carriers to evade regulatory responsibilities or to exploit differences in regulatory treatment that translate into financial or operational advantages vis-à-vis competitors who bear more extensive and costly regulatory burdens. A telecommunications common carrier providing a telecommunications service should not be able to rebrand the service as an information service and thereby qualify for limited or no regulation. We have not yet seen the telecommunications marketplace become so competitive as to foreclose the need for government oversight, nor has Internet mediation yet become the primary conduit through which every type of ICE service travels.

So long as a regulatory dichotomy exists between the Internet and telecommunications, ISPs will avoid being classified as telecommunications service providers even when providing functionally equivalent services. Similarly, telecommunications service providers have every incentive to migrate services to the unregulated Internet category if little cannibalization of revenues results; with cannibalization, the new service would trigger customer migration and access to lower rates. Much attention has been focused on ensuring that legacy regulations do not extend to include Internet markets. Equally compelling but largely ignored is the need to ensure that Bellheads do not use Internet mediation as a way to avoid regulations still needed because of the current level of competition and consumer choices.

AN OPEN VERSUS A CLOSED BUSINESS ENVIRONMENT

Favorable rules of the road apply both to dealings with the government and to business transactions. Because ICE development requires substantial investment, the business community must believe that the investment will accrue sufficient returns. Until an increase in volatility, characterized by increased risk and reward, the telecommunications portion of the ICE marketplace demonstrated ample, if not spectacular, returns on investment. An open business environment matches sufficient upside profit potential with the resources to exploit such opportunities.

Netheads expect to operate in a free and open marketplace with little or no government oversight. Bellheads might similarly resent government intrusion, but they expect it to exist in the form of regulations, and they have learned how to exploit them. Major Nethead companies, such as Microsoft and Google, have belatedly recognized the importance and permanence of government oversight. These companies have paid a high price for not fully understanding the role of government, particularly its competition laws in the case of Microsoft and its intellectual property laws in the case of Google.

The American ICE infrastructure marketplace does not operate in a fully transparent environment primarily because a small number of ventures have dominant market share and make decisions largely free of government oversight. In other nations, carriers and government collaborate and coordinate, bearing in mind the possibility that infrastructure projects will begin even if the carrier cannot assume that a certain profit will accrue. ICE infrastructure ventures require enormous capital to operate because infrastructure typically involves sunk investment—the installation of costly equipment and facilities before the company can earn revenue. Unlike ICE markets that can operate on a shoestring and ramp up if and when demand grows, ICE infrastructure requires the initial installation of large chunks of business-handling capacity regardless of initial demand. Wireless and wireline networks require a substantial labor force and investment in plant. Regardless of whether the government creates regulatory barriers to market entry or attempts to reduce or eliminate barriers, the start-up costs for these types of ventures constitute a major barrier to entry. Accordingly, only a few well-funded ventures can hope to secure necessary loans and issue stock during ordinary times, when prospective investors look closely at business plans and anticipated revenue streams.

In light of the need to sink substantial capital into the ground or the sky, it follows that additional facilities-based competition most likely will come from incumbent ventures that find ways to use existing sunk investment for added types of services. Such competition occurs, for example, when cable television ventures can retrofit their networks to provide competitively priced telephone service and when telephone companies can retrofit their networks to provide competitively priced video-delivery services. Incumbents can exploit technological innovations that bring together previously stand-alone markets. These ventures can retrofit their networks at a lower price than if a new venture started from scratch, and in the closed business environment, their incumbency and proven profitability make it easier for them to qualify for loans to make network upgrades.

We need not conclude that ICE infrastructure markets lack the potential to operate in a robustly competitive environment to agree that a closed business environment exists. Even with technological innovations that can significantly reduce the costs of operating and even serve additional customers, initial market entry may have substantial limits. Most ICE infrastructure markets have low incremental costs, with few, if any, costs to serve additional customers. But these ventures have high initial fixed costs to cover before they can exploit these low marginal costs.

The ICE infrastructure business requires ventures to have sizeable initial capitalization and staying power if they are to compete successfully with incumbents that have massive capitalization and sizeable market shares. Nevertheless, a major debate, which affects how regulatory policy should proceed, focuses on whether the ICE infrastructure marketplace is or could be competitive. Despite high financial barriers to market entry, advocates say that a competitive marketplace exists and point to reduced regulatory barriers and FCC statistics as supporting further deregulation.[30] They also allege that even if a market does not yet operate competitively, the possibly that it will become competitive in the future warrants deregulation now. Opponents of reduced regulatory safeguards dispute the FCC's statistics and the conclusion that the ICE market has become or will become competitive.[31] Just as Bellheads and Netheads appear to operate on different assumptions, the camps that claim robust competition exists and those that reject that assertion appear to operate in separate universes.

CHAPTER THREE

How the United States Lost Its Digital Advantage

BASED ON REALISTIC measures of ICE infrastructure installation and market penetration, the United States lags behind many industrialized and even industrializing nations in market penetration, costs, correlation with per capita gross domestic product, annual growth, deployment of fiber-optic links, and average speed.[1] Why these shortcomings? Government ICE policymaking has become politicized, distracted, and ineffectual, and ICE ventures have effectively deflected complaints about performance, price, and business practices. While the United States falters, other nations recognize how a robust ICE infrastructure can prime the pump in many aspects of commerce and social interaction.[2]

The United States has a long and successful record of creating government incentives in combination with commercial entrepreneurship to ensure near-ubiquitous access to such elements of basic infrastructure as canals, roads, electricity, water, and communications services, including telephones, broadcasting, cable, and direct broadcast satellites. In the telecommunications sector, the government requires all long-distance telephone subscribers, including VoIP users accessing conventional wireline and wireless networks, to pay about an 11 percent surcharge to subsidize basic telephone service access by poor people, rural residents, and people with disabilities. An "E-Rate" program subsidizes broadband services to schools, medical facilities, and libraries.[3] Despite these subsidies and a record of successful infrastructure development, the United States has failed to keep pace with other nations in installing and providing access to next-generation networks.

Instead of conscientiously examining this failure, both the government and the major broadband service providers deny that a problem exists. In fact, the Departments of State and Commerce in 2008 attempted to discredit market penetration studies undertaken by the Organisation for Economic Co-operation and Development as underestimating U.S. levels by, for example, failing to include widespread broadband availability in business locations and libraries.[4] On the other hand, public and private officials regularly cite unquestionably flawed FCC studies on broadband market penetration to support the premise that robust facilities-based competition obviates the need for most regulations.[5]

John Kneuer, former assistant secretary for communications and information and administrator at the Commerce Department's National Telecommunications and Information Administration claimed that the United States "has the most effective multiplatform broadband in the world."[6] On the contrary. If we were to measure broadband effectiveness as penetration per one hundred residents and assess price, bit rate, and number of facilities-based competitors, the United States does not come close to global best practices.

The United States has relatively shoddy and expensive broadband access, because government agencies do not hold carriers accountable for delivering on promises made in exchange for deregulatory concessions and other incentives to invest in next-generation physical plant. Nor, apparently, can government officials say no to mergers and acquisitions that further concentrate ICE industries, or acknowledge that various markets require vigorous and effective oversight in light of insufficient competition and market-driven self-regulation. How can anyone declare a market robustly competitive when four carriers control 90 percent of the wireless telecommunications marketplace and carriers using one of two technologies serve over 90 percent of the market offering true (one megabit per second [Mbps] or higher) service?[7]

In the United States, wireless carriers spend millions in advertising but engage in little price competition, only infrequently changing their prices, terms, and conditions of service. While wireless carriers in most places aggressively introduce new third-generation services, U.S. carriers appear content to squeeze out profits from a handful of services highlighted by first-generation voice and second-generation messaging, music downloading, and ringtones. The United States does not have widely available broadband competition at comparatively low prices, because telephone and cable companies considered it prudent to postpone network upgrades for several years after the dotcom implosion. In addition, incumbent telephone companies sought to reduce or eliminate interconnection and facilities-access requirements, despite their common carrier regulatory status and, in the case of the Bell Operating Companies, their opportunity to provide long-distance telephone service in exchange for offering more expansive and lower-cost facilities access to competitors.[8] Now that the FCC has eliminated most facilities-access requirements,[9] incumbent telephone companies, facing a static or declining market for core services, have discovered that they can capture market share and higher revenues by offering "triple play" bundles with Internet access and video and telephone services. Cable companies now offer similar bundles.

To conserve capital needed to upgrade and retrofit networks, both cable and telephone companies initially offer attractively priced packages to residents located in the wealthy neighborhoods of cities. Less well-to-do urban areas and rural localities do not yet have robust facilities-based broadband competition, and they may never have them unless and until a third wire enters homes or wireless broadband services of three or more carriers extend into the hinterland using next-generation (3G) technology.

Having one or two broadband options does not trigger the kind of competition, downward pressure on rates, service diversification, and consumer focus as would occur if a real third or fourth option became available. The FCC and others can tout statistics claiming to show one half-dozen or more broadband providers in a particular region corresponding to a single zip code,[10] but the true level of price and service competition typically does not correspond to the FCC reported number, because the Commission considers ventures serving at least one location within a zip code as functionally serving the entire geographic expanse represented by the zip code. Similarly, the FCC makes no distinction between resellers and facilities-based carriers, or between differences in the price of services. Far too many players find it beneficial to cite the FCC's statistics regardless of whether the actual scope of competition corroborates the collected data. The policymakers and public relations experts can state without reservation that the United States enjoys a robustly competitive marketplace for broadband cellular telephone and other advanced telecommunications services.

SUPPLY-SIDE DECEPTION

From Wall Street to Main Street to Capitol Hill and in the FCC and reviewing courts a variety of stakeholders seek to alter perceptions about the state of competition, tilt the playing field, exploit deep pockets to confuse consumers and decision makers, and generally resist change. Creators of the laws, regulations, and policies and their interpretations join with suppliers of ICE infrastructure services to accept mediocrity and to ignore inconvenient facts about the true condition of the American ICE infrastructure. Although these participants do not acknowledge its shortcomings, consciously or otherwise, they benefit from the current regime that rewards incumbency, allows incumbents to reduce risk, and refuses to scrutinize incumbents' assertions about how intense the competition is.

The current efforts to maintain the status quo can be contrasted with previous efforts to promote market entry, innovation, and service diversity. Perhaps at the risk of overstimulating market entry, in 1996 Congress enacted sweeping amendments to the nation's basic communications law, enacted in 1934 and rarely amended since then. The Telecommunications Act of 1996 ordered the FCC to promote competition among companies that provide telecommunications links directly to businesses and residences. In exchange for having to cooperate more extensively with competitors, the Bell Operating Companies (BOCs) received legislative authority to pursue lines of business that they were prohibited from entering when they were spun off from AT&T. The BOCs avidly grasped the opportunity to provide long-distance and other telecommunications services free of entry restraints. In exchange for the removal of these restrictions, the BOCs had to cooperate with market entrants in ways that all but guaranteed lost market share and revenues in core markets, including plain old telephone service and other local network services that provided first- and last-mile access to long-haul services.

The BOCs soon realized that markets for long-distance telephone service did not have extraordinary margins that would offset their lower revenues from having to provide regulator-mandated interconnection with competitors at below-market rates. Representatives of the BOCs had participated in the negotiations among stakeholders that were needed before Congress could craft and pass the Telecommunications Act of 1996. But having agreed to offer unbundled access to local exchange service elements, which jumpstarted reseller competition, the BOCs quickly realized their mistake and undertook a decade-long campaign to reduce their interconnection obligation to competitors and raise their rates, making resale competition unsustainable.

The BOCs' playbook and their interactions with financiers, lawyers, academics, regulators, and the courts provide a case study in how to game the system. Checkbook research, flawed jurisprudence, and results-oriented policymaking have combined to thwart competition and disserve the national interest. Many of the FCC's policymaking failures, including the failure to promote ICE infrastructure competition, stem in particular from the Commission's willingness to embrace sponsored research as irrefutable science. Stakeholders in the FCC policymaking process typically seek to legitimize their positions with endorsements by prominent academics, most notably economists. Economists' sponsored research can provide regulators with "evidence" of the rationality and public interest benefits of a desired policy outcome. The creative economist and the clever attorney can fashion new rules of economics and interpretations of laws and congressional intent that ignore available empirical evidence but appear rational, prudent, and persuasive to a willing recipient.

For example, when incumbent telephone companies grew weary of the duty of offering local exchange network access to competitors on favorable terms, they bought the services of economists to declare the irrationality of the pricing regime that their clients had accepted earlier. Armed with white papers, journal articles, and affidavits, the incumbent telephone companies claimed that the regulator-endorsed pricing methodology robbed the companies of incentives to invest in next-generation networks and forced cooperation on confiscatory terms. The FCC's pricing methodology used long-run incremental pricing as a baseline above which some contribution to total service costs was added. This method comports with the long-standing mainstream economic theory that prices in competitive markets will trend toward marginal cost, that is, the additional cost to provide the last unit of capacity required by consumers. To jumpstart competition, the FCC, as mandated by Congress in the Telecommunications Act of 1996, ordered incumbent telephone companies to interconnect with competitors[11] using a long-run incremental cost methodology and to assume that incumbent telephone companies would quickly install new technologies offering cheaper and more efficient access.[12] The rates derived from this pricing model were designed to exceed the incumbent carriers' break-even costs but to fall below—possibly well below—the rates that incumbent carriers would seek to charge in tariffs filed with the FCC or in commercial arm's-length negotiations with new carriers.

Incumbent telephone companies have a legal duty as common carriers to interconnect with other telephone companies on fully compensatory rates.[13] This means that the BOCs had a legal duty to interconnect even in advance of the more specific duties identified in the Telecommunications Act of 1996. Fully compensatory rates mean that a regulator cannot confiscate common carrier facilities by ordering compulsory interconnection at rates below carrier costs. But it also means that the FCC violated no economic principle or law when it mandated compulsory interconnection at rates below what the incumbent carrier might want to charge and might otherwise secure in the absence of the FCC's orders as directed by Congress.[14]

In other words, incumbent carriers have specific rights and responsibilities as common carriers. On the benefit side, these carriers can acquire rights of way to install towers, poles, and conduits, often without compensating the property owner at market-based rates. Incumbent local exchange carriers receive generous subsidies to provide service to rural locales and to offer reduced rates to low-income subscribers. Furthermore, incumbent carriers have satisfied most of their radio-spectrum requirements without having to pay the government. On the detriment side, these carriers have to interconnect their facilities with the new and usually incomplete networks of competitors, sometimes using rates that might fall below a market-generated price. The BOCs, notwithstanding their long-standing free or below-cost access to land, rights of way, and spectrum, have retained the services of countless economists and other consultants to claim that having to provide analogous access to their property constituted an unlawful taking and violated sound economic principles. While the very same economists might endorse in theory the premise that price should equal marginal cost plus a reasonable rate of return and profit, they found ways to object to interconnection pricing using this fundamental principle.

In earlier interconnection disputes, even before the Telecommunications Act of 1996 was passed, sponsored economists created a new interconnection "rule" that would deem fair only compensation paid to the incumbent carrier that covered all of the carrier's opportunity costs—that is, all lost revenues and profits that the carrier might have generated if it used the facilities leased to a competitor for the carrier's own services, provided sufficient demand existed. The so-called efficient components pricing rule (ECPR)[15] ignored the fact that having to interconnect with a competitor typically does not crowd out or foreclose service to a customer of the interconnection-providing carrier, nor does it typically force the facilities-based carrier to install new equipment to handle the aggregate demand generated by its customer base and by new ventures. Likewise, this rule required full compensation for costs that the interconnection-providing carrier would no longer incur and could avoid because a user of its facilities had sought interconnection without the need for marketing, advertisements, and other promotion.[16]

WALL STREET AND THE POWER OF THE PURSE

Because many ICE industries require substantial sunk investment in physical plant that cannot generate revenues until complete installation, ventures need long-term financing. Venture capitalists will loan or invest in ICE ventures if forecasts confirm ample demand and plenty of upside profitability. During the dotcom boom, both incumbent and start-up ventures had easy access to capital. Such readily available money drove the perception that the ICE marketplace defied the business cycle and other rules of economics and that the Internet changed everything. When irrational exuberance quickly changed to irrational pessimism, capital became far less available.

Regardless of where in the business cycle a venture operates, access to capital remains essential, because few, if any, companies can finance all capital requirements internally. Accordingly, financiers have a major impact on the ICE marketplace in determining which ventures qualify for short-term and longer-term funding. When a market has easy access to capital, it may appear increasingly attractive merely because of the perception that professionals with successful track records have targeted this sector for lavish investment. When a market lacks easy access to capital, managers may have to devise creative ways to secure funding. After the ICE industry faltered in the dotcom bust, some managers resorted to illegal tactics to shore up their companies by overstating earnings and by securing loans based on false reports of major capacity sales that actually involved a swap of lines, resulting in transactions that netted no additional revenues.[17]

Until the onset of market volatility and disruptive new digital technologies such as the Internet, the ICE infrastructure business could moderate the impact of the business cycle's upturns and downturns, primarily because ICE companies had enormous scale and self-financing capabilities. But during the dotcom boom, even established companies assumed greater-than-usual risk and debt in their quest to tap new markets. Senior management may have perceived the need to take on greater risk to capture the greater potential rewards. But not all ventures, established or new, successfully executed their business plans. The losers in the dotcom financial sweepstakes either went bankrupt or became targets for leveraged buyouts or other types of unanticipated or emergency acquisitions. Satellite telecommunications provides a case study.

A Satellite Case Study

Operating a constellation of satellites represents one of the most capital-intensive sectors of the ICE marketplace. Managers in this sector have to think twice about taking on even more debt for growth and diversification, given the requirements of their core business. It costs roughly three hundred million dollars to construct, insure, launch, track, and manage a single satellite.[18] To provide adequate service with backup capacity in the event of a launch or in-orbit satellite failure, operators typically deploy two or more satellites in each region where they do business. Because of the cost and risk presented by satellites, governments underwrote most of the initial research and development.

Until such time as private ventures could handle the risk inherent in satellite service, governments throughout the world served as the primary investors in organizations providing the service. Even when satellite technology matured and offered the prospect of participation by private ventures, the initial commercialization occurred in a hybrid model with the government still involved as investor, benefactor, or both. A cooperative model was used to create an organization for providing international telecommunications. In the United States, a single venture, created by an act of Congress, participated in the cooperative. Nations agreed to a treaty-level document creating the International Telecommunications Satellite Organization (INTELSAT). By agreeing to insulate the cooperative from competition, specified as "significant economic harm," nations throughout the world reduced INTELSAT's cost of capital and operating risk.[19] On the domestic front, Congress similarly reduced the cost of capital and operating risk for INTELSAT's sole American investor, the Communications Satellite Corporation, later known as Comsat.

Both the international and the domestic satellite marketplace evolved to such a point that protecting INTELSAT and Comsat became unnecessary and anticompetitive. In time, both markets became competitive with the entry of a few facilities-based competitors. Nevertheless, even in the best economic times, the business remained capital intensive and risky, particularly because, on average, one out of three satellite launches fail, and even operational satellites may suffer premature reduction in their usable lifetime of about ten years.

Despite the risk and capital requirements, venture capitalists helped fund the entrepreneurial visions of a few would-be satellite network managers. During the dotcom boom the expectation that demand for the Internet would double monthly also created the expectation of similar pent-up demand for satellite capacity. Venture capitalists anticipated high rewards from tapping the market behind the significant barriers created by huge capital requirements, as well as by the administrative requirements of registering orbital parking places for the satellites with the International Telecommunication Union and securing a license from the FCC.

Suddenly satellites became such a hot and attractive industry that they attracted venture capital in the form of privatization of INTELSAT and hostile takeover bids for one of INTELSAT's major competitors, PanAmSat. Before INTELSAT could secure funding through an initial public offering of stock, a team of private venture capital firms acquired it.[20] INTELSAT never got around to an initial public offering of stock, and it became an easy mark for private equity investors who were able to cash out their $515 million investment in a $6 billion sale. Along the way, INTELSAT lost its blue-chip risk status, because the private equity players saddled the venture with $11 billion in debt. PanAmSat, which had become a publicly traded company, also became privately held by venture capital firms. These firms generated extraordinary profits by substantially adding to the already sizeable debt carried by the satellite operators even as the firms pulled out millions of dollars in management fees.

We can conclude that the privatization of satellites signaled the successful completion of government incubation of nascent technology followed by appropriate commercialization. But the satellite ventures as now constituted operate with far greater debt than they did previously, even though some operated as publicly traded companies at one time.[21] Because of the essential contribution to global accessibility and commerce made by satellites, the firms that own and operate them might not have the immediate capability to respond to a spate of satellite launch failures. Should a worst-case scenario play out, governments might have to step in and bail out private ventures in this now-private industry because of the national security interest in having multiple fully operational satellite networks. Even today, some island nations and countries far from a coastline do not have access to fiber-optic submarine cables. Without retention of a core-service mission to these countries, which the privatized INTELSAT has agreed to sustain,[22] parts of the world would not have reliable telecommunications access.

INTELSAT, PanAmSat, and other privatized satellite ventures remain solvent, although they are not the cash cows they were expected to become. The risk/reward profile for satellite networks has changed in part because of the added financial risk generated by borrowing to pay the billions of dollars in fees extracted from the numerous transactions that reshaped the ownership composition of companies such as INTELSAT and PanAmSat.

Capacity Swaps to Generate Fake Revenues

After several years of blind-faith belief that ICE infrastructure demand sparked by the Internet was doubling every month, reality started to take root. Some senior managers of ICE ventures considered it necessary to perpetuate now-discredited assumptions about demand and growth. Their stock options, bonuses, and reputations depended on increased revenues to satisfy Wall Street expectations and continue to boost stock prices.

It became clear that carrier-to-carrier capacity transactions could provide a plausible way to boost revenues. Historically, carriers acquired capacity from other carriers if and only if they needed the extra capacity in the near term to satisfy actual consumer demand. Carriers also swapped capacity in one ocean region, where they had an excess, for capacity in another ocean region, where they lacked sufficient capacity. Because a small group of carriers, often owned by or affiliated with a government, operated international telecommunications facilities, the parties could devise mutually beneficial models for handling adjustments in capacity occasioned by slight miscalculations in how much capacity to acquire in a new cable. The phrase "indefeasible right of use" (IRU) refers to the conveyance of capacity in an underseas telecommunications cable from the owner to a lessee who would acquire the right to use the capacity without actually owning it.[23]

Transferring IRUs became a way to create the appearance of revenue generation without actually having the commensurate near-term demand to load traffic on the newly acquired capacity. Unscrupulous carrier managers, desperate to claim still-robust traffic growth and demand, engaged in sham IRU transactions with other equally desperate managers.[24] With a swap of IRUs, each manager could claim to have generated millions in revenues despite having received no money. For example, a representative of carrier A might agree to sell IRUs worth ten million dollars to carrier B in exchange for which carrier B would sell IRUs in another cable worth ten million dollars to carrier A. Both carriers A and B would announce the sale of an additional ten million dollars in capacity, and their accountants would consider the entire amount as current revenue. In reality, even if carrier A were to receive ten million dollars from carrier B, carrier A would have to make an identical ten million dollars payment to carrier B. And because an IRU applies to using a transmission facility for a number of years, both the payments and the actual accrual of revenues typically should occur throughout the usable life of the cable.

Capacity swaps became an increasingly important and false part of some ICE infrastructure companies' financial statements. Ventures such as Worldcom, Asia Global Crossing, and 360 Networks declared bankruptcy.[25] Some officers of ICE infrastructure companies, most notably Bernie Ebbers, CEO of Worldcom,[26] and Joseph Nacchio, CEO of Qwest Communications,[27] were convicted of engaging in securities fraud, orchestrated primarily through the IRU swap scam that provided the basis for claiming financial health despite severe losses.

CREATIVE INTERPRETATION OF THE CONSTITUTION AND LESSER LAWS

In the United States the ICE policymaking process relies on an independent regulatory agency that combines its in-house expertise with expertise provided in comments and other filings submitted by interested parties. But the FCC has not always engaged in rational decision making based on the facts; instead it has occasionally relied on political ideology and instincts to shape its perception of economic and legal principles. Just as sponsored academic researchers help shape the FCC's perception of economic principles, lawyers representing various stakeholders help shape the FCC's interpretation of applicable laws and case precedent.

Administrative law requires the FCC to establish a factual record, solicit and consider the views of interested parties, fashion reasonable policies, and avoid engaging in arbitrary and unlawful decision making.[28] The Commission cannot abuse the discretion accorded it by law and betray the deference it receives from reviewing courts inclined to respect its expertise.[29] Clients' desires are in conflict with that requirement. Stakeholders want the FCC to embrace politics, novel legal and economic concepts, and a biased or selective interpretation of the facts when rational decision making would establish unfavorable policies.

Regulation imposes costs on the regulated party and forces it to do things or to refrain from doing things that it otherwise would prefer to do. Regulated enterprises predictably emphasize the burdens of regulation while ignoring or downplaying the benefits that accrue—for example, government-conferred privileges, such as the telephone and cable television companies' ability to use the property of others as rights of way for transmission facilities, and incentives that convert into financial rewards (tax savings).

When regulation compels behavior that the regulated party considers too demanding, economists and lawyers are readily available to claim that the regulation imposes an unlawful burden. The burden often becomes quantified in financial terms and is deemed an unlawful taking or confiscation of property by government. For example, lawyers for incumbent telephone companies executed such a game plan when they asserted at the FCC and subsequently in judicial hearings that the FCC had exceeded its lawful authority when it ordered compulsory interconnection with new carriers on financial terms designed to stimulate, if not guarantee, profitable market entry.[30] The incumbent telephone companies launched a twin attack on the FCC by (1) using economists to reject the FCC's interconnection policy as irrational and inconsistent with long-standing or newly crafted economic principles and (2) using lawyers to challenge the policy on the grounds that it violated the Constitution's prohibition on the government's taking of property without adequate compensation.

The Telecommunications Act of 1996 ordered incumbent local exchange carriers to unbundle their networks as one of their common carrier interconnection responsibilities. The unbundling requirement forces carriers to separate the multiple elements of their networks used to switch, route, transmit, and process traffic. Unbundling a McDonald's Big Mac would require the company to offer individually one or two all-beef patties, the special sauce, lettuce, cheese, pickle, onions, and a sesame-seed bun. But unlike McDonald's, which would have to offer all the elements that make up its special hamburger, competing telecommunications service providers might need to offer only a few elements. Forcing competitors to lease all combined elements would handicap competition by imposing unnecessary leasing costs.

Specifically, section 251 of the Telecommunications Act requires all carriers to bear the "duty to provide, to any requesting telecommunications carrier for the provision of a telecommunications service, nondiscriminatory access to network elements on an unbundled basis at any technically feasible point on rates, terms, and conditions that are just, reasonable, and nondiscriminatory in accordance with the terms and conditions of the agreement and the requirements of this section and section 252. An incumbent local exchange carrier shall provide such unbundled network elements in a manner that allows requesting carriers to combine such elements in order to provide such telecommunications service."[31]

Incumbent carriers have claimed that the FCC's implementation of this requirement resulted in a taking or confiscation of their property. The Supreme Court on two occasions rejected this assertion and endorsed the FCC's implementation of a congressional mandate to promote competition. In *AT&T Corp. v. Iowa Utilities Board,*[32] the Supreme Court upheld the Commission's implementation of the congressional mandate contained in section 251 of the Telecommunications Act of 1996 as a reasonable exercise of its rule-making authority, including its requirement that incumbent local exchange carriers unbundle network elements and offer the competitive local exchange carriers the opportunity to pick and choose from an à la carte menu or platform of elements. But the Court also ruled that in identifying which network elements incumbent carriers should unbundle, the Commission did not limit the set of network elements to those necessary to promote competition, elements whose absence from the list might impair the new carriers' ability to compete. This lack of specificity and granularity ultimately forced the FCC to reduce and later eliminate most of the congressionally sanctioned interconnection requirements.

The Supreme Court did not deem unconstitutional the congressional mandate to unbundle. Indeed, the Court initially deferred to the FCC's determination of how to price these unbundled elements. In *Verizon Communications, Inc. v. FCC,*[33] the Court rejected the arguments of the incumbent local exchange carriers that using a theoretical most-efficient-cost model, instead of actual historical costs, constituted a taking that violated the Fifth Amendment.[34] The Court noted that no party had disputed any specific rate established by the FCC-prescribed pricing model and concluded that "[r]egulatory bodies required to set [just and reasonable] rates . . . have ample discretion to choose methodology."[35] In addition, the Court stated that the Telecommunications Act of 1996 did not specifically require historical costs, particularly in light of its explicit prohibition on the use of conventional "'rate-of-return or other rate-based proceeding'... which has been identified with historical cost ever since [a previous case] Hope Natural Gas was decided."[36]

Arguably, a credible taking argument might have been made if the interconnecting carrier ended up having to invest in more facilities to accommodate the aggregate demands of carriers requesting interconnection using unbundled network elements. Likewise, an argument might have been made that interconnection foreclosed other, more profitable undertakings, a type of opportunity cost. But neither worst-case scenario ever occurred. Using the FCC's statistics, at the high point of having to accommodate competitive local exchange carrier unbundling requirements, the incumbent carriers had to release 13.5 percent of their lines to competitors.[37] The most recent figure is 8.2 percent, and it is declining further.[38]

The incumbent carriers did receive compensation for leasing lines. They disputed the rate of compensation because pricing that uses forward-looking replacement costs or long-run incremental costs falls below what the incumbent carrier would demand in commercial negotiations or what it would file as a tariff rate at the FCC. If unbundled network elements were provided for less than an incumbent carrier might have received but for intervention by the FCC, the incumbent carriers surely had ample capacity to satisfy a lawful mandate while also seeking higher profits from their own retail and wholesale customers.

SCHIZOPHRENIC JUDICIAL RELIANCE ON FCC EXPERTISE

Many FCC decisions trigger a judicial appeal. Courts frequently affirm the FCC's decisions, but the very same courts also reverse its decisions with some regularity. The Commission does not have a good record of having its policies, rules, and regulations pass muster with reviewing courts. When a court reverses the FCC, the court has determined that the Commission has not engaged in rational decision making. The FCC acts irrationally when it establishes rules based on doctrine, politics, or unproven assumptions instead of a complete evidentiary record. Case precedent favors judicial deference to the expertise of the FCC and other administrative agencies, however. Judges typically lack any particular knowledge of ICE industries, which makes them ill suited to decide matters involving both technical complexity and high stakes. The engineers, economists, lawyers, and other experts at the FCC and other regulatory agencies generally qualify for deference because they presumably have the necessary expertise to make reasoned decisions, supported by the facts and designed to serve the public interest.

That FCC decisions trigger court reversals might mean that the FCC has acted in such a manner as to lose judicial deference. Alternatively, a court reversal might have less to do with the FCC's actions and more to do with the standard used by the court to review the lawfulness of the FCC's actions. A particular judge, or the judge's staff of law clerks, might second-guess the FCC's interpretations of law and economic doctrine, the factual record, and the public interest. Reluctance to defer could legitimately catch the FCC in unlawful or flawed decision making, or it could show that a particular judge is an activist, willing to intervene to right actual or perceived wrongs.

Regardless of the cause, a judicial reversal typically forces the FCC to engage in further deliberations. This process injects more time and uncertainty into the policymaking process, two factors that stakeholders do not want to face. Indeed, these factors, caused by the FCC or the litigiousness of stakeholders, can contribute to an ICE carrier's claim that it cannot make sizeable infrastructure investments until definitive regulatory rules exist.

The Standard for Deference to Agency Expertise

The Supreme Court's current model for evaluating whether courts should defer to decision making by a regulatory agency uses a two-step process. Under the *Chevron* test,[39] a court first should examine the legislative basis upon which the agency based its decision making. The court should assess whether the regulatory statute was silent or ambiguous on the precise question raised by the agency's decision. If the legislation offers an unclear directive, the court should then consider the reasonableness of the agency's interpretation of the law. In later cases the Supreme Court fine-tuned this assessment by holding that such deference applies only where "it appears that Congress delegated authority to the agency generally to make rules carrying the force of law"[40] and that if an agency issues an interpretation of a statute without seeking public comment, then courts should apply a less deferential standard.[41]

The Supreme Court's standard looks first to whether the applicable law specifies a mode of analysis and whether the regulatory agency complied. Where the law directs a regulatory agency to implement policies that lack specificity on exactly how to proceed, a reviewing court will assess the reasonableness of how the agency responded to a congressional mandate. A reasonableness standard invites parties to explain how the regulatory agency did or did not apply best practices in its implementation of a congressional directive. "Best practices" here refers to whether and how the regulatory agency formulated policies, rules, and other decisions that reasonably comport with applicable economic, legal, and regulatory principles.

Of course, reasonable people, including hired advocates, can disagree on what constitutes proper application of principles in an interpretation of what a law requires. When a court reverses a regulatory agency, the judge concludes that the agency did not act consistently with congressional intent, typically by acting without authority or by reaching an unreasonable decision on how the agency applied the facts and interpreted the law.

Examples of Non-deference to FCC Expertise

In a number of cases, courts have rejected the FCC's decision making on the grounds that the Commission exceeded its lawful authority, that the facts did not support the Commission's decision, or that the Commission failed to justify and support the basis for its decision. These cases are important to note because they demonstrate an important check on the FCC in instances where it seeks to achieve a preconceived policy outcome without regard to what it can legally do and what the factual record showed. Although in many instances, courts have accepted the FCC's policy rationale or opted not to second-guess the Commission, the examples below show that some courts will not tolerate unprincipled and unlawful decision making.

In *MCI Telecommunications Corp. v. American Telephone & Telegraph Co.*,[42] the Supreme Court held that the Communications Act of 1934 did not give the FCC authority to exempt designated "nondominant" carriers from the act's requirement that all carriers file a public contract, known as a tariff, specifying the terms and conditions of service. In essence, the FCC jumped the gun on deregulation, based on its perception that marketplace competition supported the elimination of requirements established by Congress and still in effect. Section 203 of the Communications Act required telecommunications service providers to file and comply with tariffed rates.[43] Although Congress eventually did authorize the FCC to eliminate the tariff-filing requirement, the Commission could not order this unilaterally.

The MCI case provides an example of unilateral FCC decision making: it decided whether and how to reduce a regulatory requirement that Congress had not yet rescinded. In *American Library Association v. FCC*,[44] the Commission unilaterally attempted to extend its jurisdiction and expand the scope of regulation. The District of Columbia Circuit Court of Appeals reversed the FCC's decision to extend its jurisdiction to include television sets located on consumers' premises and to regulate what this equipment can do after a broadcast television signal has reached it. The FCC sought to require manufacturers of television sets to include the capability of processing "broadcast flag" instructions, designed to guard against piracy of televised content through interconnection with television sets and other receivers by non-television devices capable of recording and disseminating the content.

The court decided that the FCC had no regulatory authority over equipment located on consumers' premises or over the behavior of consumers who had already received broadcast content. Although the FCC has authority over licensed broadcasters and television broadcasting, the court determined that the FCC could not extend that authority to regulate what consumers can do with digital equipment at home after receiving video programming. The court's decision frustrated an attempt by the FCC to require television set manufacturers to help support digital rights management by processing broadcast flag instructions.

A more concrete example of judicial non-deference to the FCC's expertise occurred when a court rejected the Commission's evaluation of the factual record generated in a proceeding where the Commission solicited public input before it revised its rules and policies. In *Prometheus Radio Project v. FCC*,[45] the Third Circuit Court of Appeals reversed the FCC's decision to expand the maximum permissible market share available to any single owner of television stations from 35 percent to 45 percent. The court rejected the FCC's decision as arbitrary and capricious under the Administrative Procedure Act[46] because the Commission did "not provide a reasoned analysis to support the [relaxed] limits that it chose."[47] The court also ruled that a "diversity index" used by the FCC to assess how much single-company ownership of radio, television, and newspapers to permit within the same local market relied on several "irrational assumptions and inconsistencies."[48]

The *Prometheus* case provides an example of a court plainly unwilling to allow the FCC to decide that marketplace conditions supported relaxation of media ownership controls designed to promote diversity. While many courts do not second-guess a decision on whether and how to respond to perceived changes in marketplace conditions,[49] the *Prometheus* court rejected such changes in the absence of new legislation.[50]

In two instances, the District of Columbia Circuit Court of Appeals rejected the FCC's decision to cap the national market penetration of a single cable operator at 30 percent.[51] In what it considered egregious disregard for changed circumstances, such as the onset of substantial competition from direct broadcast satellite (DBS) operators and fiber-optic video providers, the court vacated the rule, rather than remanding to the FCC a requirement that it reconsider the rationale and evidentiary support for the rule.

The court determined that the FCC did not have evidentiary support for the Commission's assumption that the two largest, vertically integrated cable operators, each having up to 30 percent national market share, would collude and refuse to carry programming from new programmers. The Commission's "open field" analysis assumed that for a competitive video programming marketplace to function, new programmers need to have access to the 40 percent of the market not controlled by the top two cable operators.

The court also rejected as "feeble"[52] the four "non-empirical"[53] reasons the FCC used for largely ignoring the competitive alternative provided by DBS operators: (1) high consumer costs in switching to DBS; (2) the attractiveness of non-video services, such as broadband Internet access, provided by cable operators; (3) the inability of consumers to know the attractiveness of alternative video programming packages before consuming them; and (4) the inability of DBS to support new programming networks lacking financing.[54] The court noted that 50 percent of all DBS subscribers had previously subscribed to cable television service and that the Commission did not provide evidence to support the conclusion that offering non-video services conferred a competitive advantage on cable operators, particularly in light of the fact that the two DBS operators have partnered with telephone companies to provide bundled services. The court also refused to agree that consumers do not know the nature of the content and new networks offered via DBS.

The court noted the significant increase in the number of cable networks and the fact that the percentage of networks affiliated with, or owned by, a vertically integrated cable operator had declined since 1992, when Congress enacted the Cable Television Consumer Protection and Competition Act that authorized FCC-prescribed market penetration caps.[55] The court concluded that "the Commission has failed to demonstrate that allowing a cable operator to serve more than 30% of all cable subscribers would threaten to reduce either competition or diversity in programming. First, the record is replete with evidence of ever increasing competition among video providers: Satellite and fiber-optic video providers have entered the market and grown in market share since the Congress passed the 1992 Act, and particularly in recent years. Cable operators, therefore, no longer have the bottleneck power over programming that concerned the Congress in 1992. Second, over the same period there has been a dramatic increase both in the number of cable networks and in the programming available to subscribers."[56]

Examples of Deference to FCC Expertise

Many cases show the courts' deferral to the FCC's expertise, particularly when the Commission was pursuing a deregulatory agenda with some linkage to a law. Even when offered evidence of extraordinarily high interconnection rates, a court opted to refrain from second-guessing why the FCC would refrain from investigating them. The court stated that its "task on review is therefore limited. We review the FCC's action in this case only to ensure that it is not 'arbitrary, capricious, an abuse of discretion, or otherwise not in accordance with law.' That standard is particularly deferential in matters such as this, which implicate competing policy choices, technical expertise, and predictive market judgments."[57]

Even the Supreme Court frequently defers to the FCC's expertise. By a unanimous ruling, the Court further reduced the opportunity for a carrier competitor of an incumbent to seek an FCC or judicial remedy to pricing strategies arguably designed to eliminate competition by offering retail prices below that charged to competitors for similar services.[58] In 2003 several Internet service providers (ISPs) filed suit against Pacific Bell Telephone Company, contending that this incumbent carrier attempted to monopolize the market for digital subscriber line (DSL) broadband Internet access by creating a price squeeze, with ISP competitors obligated to pay a higher wholesale price than Pacific Bell offered on a retail basis. Both the district court and the Ninth Circuit Court of Appeals agreed that the ISPs could present their price-squeeze claim, despite a Supreme Court ruling in *Verizon Communications, Inc. v. Law Office of Curtis V. Trinko, LLP*,[59] that limits antitrust claims against common-carrier telecommunications service providers and further restricts what remedies a court can provide in lieu of what rights the Telecommunications Act of 1996 provides market entrants.

The Court assumed that Pacific Bell had no antitrust duty to deal with any ISPs, an assumption based on the Court's blind acceptance of the FCC's premise that ample facilities-based competition existed.[60] But for a voluntary concession to secure the FCC's approval of AT&T's acquisition of BellSouth, the Court noted that Pacific Bell would not even have a duty to provide ISPs with wholesale service.

This decision evidences great skepticism about whether the ISPs had any basis for a claim, because in the Court's reasoning, the ISPs failed to make a claim that Pacific Bell's retail DSL prices were predatory, and the

ISPs also failed to refute the Court's conclusion that Pacific Bell had no duty to deal with the ISPs, that is, to provide wholesale service.[61]

Remarkably, the Court did not seem troubled by the possibility that all ISP competitors could exit the market, an event that surely would enable the surviving incumbent carrier to raise rates: "For if AT&T can bankrupt the plaintiffs by refusing to deal altogether, the plaintiffs must demonstrate why the law prevents AT&T from putting them out of business by pricing them out of the market."[62]

In *National Cable & Telecommunications Association v. Brand X Internet Services*,[63] the Supreme Court affirmed the FCC's decision to classify cable modem access to the Internet as a lightly regulated information service and not as a more extensively regulated telecommunications service. Even though information services use telecommunications to link customers and suppliers of content, the FCC crafted a distinction between telecommunications provided as an integral part of an information service and telecommunications services offered to users. The Supreme Court accepted this distinction largely because it lacked the expertise to question the FCC's rationale and evidence that the FCC could plausibly deem cable modem service an information service using definitions contained in the Telecommunications Act of 1996.

The FCC's classification of Internet access as an information service will make it hard for it not to classify as information services other software applications that need Internet access to function. For example, most Voice over Internet Protocol services combine Internet access and software to provide users with the capability of making local and long-distance telephone calls. Some VoIP services compete with, and constitute a functional equivalent to, regulated telecommunications services. Although the FCC wanted to deregulate Internet access, it now has to find ways to regulate aspects on VoIP, even though it will find it difficult to deem VoIP anything other than the information service on which VoIP software rides.

The FCC's goal of deregulating Internet access has created new problems in finding rational and lawful ways to regulate some types of information services, such as VoIP, which the FCC believes should be subject to government oversight.[64] Subjecting VoIP to government oversight, even though the FCC sought to decline oversight of the bitstream transmission link needed to provide VoIP, presents an intellectual inconsistency that will challenge the creative lawyering expertise inside the FCC and within the law firms that will participate in FCC proceedings.

So far, the FCC has managed to achieve the twin goal of not boxing itself into a corner by having to classify VoIP as an information service yet managing to impose regulatory burdens on VoIP service providers. In *Vonage Holdings Corp. v. FCC*,[65] the District of Columbia Circuit Court of Appeals affirmed the FCC's decision to require VoIP service providers to contribute to universal service funding, a contribution previously required only from conventional wireline and wireless telephone companies. The court concluded that the FCC could expand the set of universal service contributors beyond telecommunications service providers, a classification the FCC could not readily apply to VoIP service providers in light of the decision to deem Internet access provided by cable television and telephone companies and used to provide access to VoIP to be an information service. Section 254(d) of the Telecommunications Act allows the FCC to require universal service contributions from "[a]ny other provider of interstate telecommunications . . . if the public interest so requires."[66] Even though VoIP service providers arguably do not offer retail telecommunications services, their use of telecommunications as a component or integral element of their service permits the FCC to include them as universal service contributors.

To reach such an outcome, both the FCC and a reviewing court must delve into the meaning of the words "offer" and "provide." Ventures offering Internet access provide a telecommunications link that combines seamlessly with an information service. Such integrated service qualifies for the unregulated information service classification. Only when a venture retails telecommunications services will it become a regulated carrier. Both the FCC and the Supreme Court accepted the rationale that VoIP service providers use telecommunications as a building block in combination with software and other applications to deliver information services. They chose to ignore the Commission's previous determination that the telecommunications component that VoIP service providers use, typically cable modem lines or DSL lines, is part of a composite information service. Notwithstanding a previous conclusion that the FCC could ignore the telecommunications component in an information service, a conclusion that supported deregulation of cable modem and DSL service, the very same telecommunications component now serves as the legal basis for regulating VoIP services. Here a court endorsed the FCC's interpretation of telecommunications use as triggering a regulatory requirement even as another court has endorsed the FCC's interpretation of telecommunications use as insignificant and not triggering a different set of regulatory requirements applicable to retailers of telecommunications services.

The FCC has managed to interpret telecommunications usage as the basis for regulation in one instance, but for deregulation in another instance. Two courts have accepted this semantic sleight of hand that the FCC used to achieve two outcomes: (1) it found a way to ignore or downplay the significance of telecommunications when telecommunications are used as the medium for providing access to the Internet, which means that the link constitutes a largely unregulated information service; and (2) it found a way to emphasize the use of telecommunications as the trigger for regulatory responsibilities when doing so achieved a desired policy outcome—shoring up funding for universal service by expanding the set of mandatory contributors.

FEDERAL PREEMPTION

In many nations, national regulatory authorities (NRAs) work with governments at the state, provincial, and local levels with an eye toward promoting harmonized and progressive regulatory policy. NRAs may perceive other regulatory agencies as threatening a single, consistent national policy. However, the concern about fragmented (balkanized) policy may also obscure more pedestrian concerns about competition over policy leadership and the potential for other regulatory agencies to pursue conflicting objectives.

When the FCC undertook a significant change in regulatory policy with an eye toward promoting market entry and competition, some state public utility commissions objected. At that time, the FCC successfully persuaded courts of the need for a new, uniform regulatory regime. Courts affirmed the lawfulness of preempting state regulatory policy with federal regulatory policy[67] and a related principle, that the FCC had primary jurisdiction to resolve telecommunications policy disputes, even to the point of postponing judicial review until after the FCC had completed its administrative proceedings.[68]

Case precedent supporting deference to FCC jurisdiction and the power of federal preemption now works against having independent review by state regulators and courts. The prospect of fragmented and inconsistent telecommunications regulatory policies lends support to the idea of a single FCC determination, even though the Commission might emphasize partisan objectives, consistency with questionable economic doctrines, or unreasonable reliance on marketplace solutions. Rather than allow states to provide a guard against excessive deregulation, the FCC seeks to preempt state safeguards. For example, the FCC has claimed the lawful right to preempt state consumer protection laws and regulations as applied to wireless telephone services.[69] The FCC would like to prevent state forums from resolving disputes over allegedly deceptive billing practices, over financial penalties for early termination of service, and over compulsory and binding arbitration requirements. Putting federal preemption in its best light, we could say that the FCC wants to fashion an equitable national remedy. Less charitably, we would say the FCC simply wants to prevent consumers from seeking and receiving possibly more accommodating responses from state regulators and courts.

Absent a parallel state judicial and regulatory review mechanism, the FCC has largely unchecked discretion. While states may once have attempted to thwart deregulatory initiatives, the FCC's federal preemption campaign now appears designed to thwart consumer safeguards and fair procedures that consumers deserve.

CHAPTER FOUR

Case Studies in Wrongheaded Policymaking

POLITICS, ECONOMIC DOCTRINE, and expediency appear to have overtaken reason in ICE policymaking in the United States. Though obligated to uphold the public interest, fairly interpret statutes, and generate a complete factual record before making decisions, FCC commissioners, with increasing frequency, consider policy issues from a political perspective. Partisanship can create incentives for individual commissioners to seek predetermined policy outcomes regardless of the factual record that the Commission staff generates—or could generate if the FCC would conscientiously seek public participation. No matter what the commissioners read and hear in testimony or what actual empirical evidence and statistics the Commission could collect, the FCC has come to many unproven and overreaching conclusions.

The FCC has stated often that all ICE markets are robustly competitive, except for cable television and wireline telephone services to rural locales. Ironically, even as the FCC tirelessly asserts the existence of ample marketplace competition, it also expresses the need to create incentives for increased investment in the ICE economy. The FCC has also concluded that the public typically benefits more by paying for access to spectrum configured by professional license holders than by sharing unlicensed spectrum. This conclusion motivates the FCC to limit the amount of radio spectrum it will make available for free, unlicensed use in lieu of specifying uses often linked with efforts to auction off spectrum to the highest bidder. With a bias favoring allocated use for pay, the FCC also accepts the view that spectrum licensees deserve substantial freedom to use the spectrum as their own property; they may, for example, impose rules and regulations on use by subscribers, including limitations on their freedom to access and use the spectrum. The FCC responds to the duty to update Congress on deregulation and incentive creation with creative collection and interpretation of statistics, novel interpretation of economic theories and "rules," and self-serving statutory construction. The FCC managers understand the beneficial budgetary and congressional relations arising from reports of good news, such as evidence of increasing competition, construction of infrastructure, and enhanced consumer welfare. The FCC also has concluded that it should err on the side of deregulating or not applying regulations to new technologies, even when a powerful incumbent diversifies into new markets.

The FCC wants to create the impression that it can migrate from extensive heavy-handed regulation to progressively declining light-handed regulation. However, in contradiction to this posture, it also sees the need to regulate heavily in some ICE sectors. For example, the FCC increasingly subjects VoIP service providers to many elements of wireline telephone regulation because VoIP threatens the financial well-being of politically connected, incumbent wireline and wireless telephone companies.

The FCC also infers the political and public relations benefits in making quick deviations from previously factual conclusions and policy prescriptions. Its managers regularly test the political waters and willingly change policies and factual or statistical determinations if smart politics requires such a shift, regardless of whether empirical evidence supports the conclusion that significant changes in the competitive marketplace require commensurate changes in policies and rules.

The FCC comes across as either pragmatic or expedient when it changes course in policy and deviates from consistency. Even though the FCC has come to favor deregulation, in plenty of instances it has opted not to deregulate competitors or to subject competitors to unequal regulatory burdens. The FCC apparently has concluded that having at least one technology or category of ICE service provider to target for aggressive and unbalanced regulation will demonstrate its commitment to consumer protection. This retention of a heavy-handed regulatory policy seems at odds with the prevailing view that the FCC should err on the side of concluding that competition exists so that it need not promote market entry or prevent incumbents from acquiring spectrum and other publicly owned resources that could preempt new or additional competition. Finally, the FCC has developed a record that shows a remarkable willingness to approve any merger or acquisition. Its (faulty) assumption here is that industry concentration will promote competition and benefit the public interest rather than reduce competition, limit diversity, and raise prices.

There is plentiful evidence that the Commission has ignored the facts, engaged in results-driven decision making, played partisan politics, accepted questionable economic doctrine as gospel, and falsely perceived market conditions in reaching its conclusions. In some instances, the Commission can justify its actions to the public and, perhaps more importantly, to Congress and reviewing courts on the grounds that reasonable people might legitimately disagree on findings of fact, conclusions of law, and policy prescriptions. But in other instances, the FCC has acted so arbitrarily and with such obvious bias and disregard for the truth that even deferential courts cannot ignore such egregious violations.

In the quest to find global best practices for ICE regulation, reviewing FCC cases provides numerous examples of what *not* to do. National regulatory agencies throughout the world cannot ignore politics, the incessant lobbying pressure of deep-pocketed stakeholders, or the uncertainty caused by technological and market convergence. However, the FCC's inferior performance shows what happens when expediency dominates principled decision making and when a regulatory agency ignores the facts to achieve a predetermined outcome.

Before considering numerous case studies that give rise to questions about the fairness and veracity of the FCC's policymaking process, let us review what the Commission specifically, and other NRAs in general, are supposed to do. The FCC operates as a quasi-independent regulatory agency that receives operating authority from laws enacted by Congress.[1] It has ample latitude in determining how to interpret and apply statutes, but it cannot operate too far from the will of Congress, because its decisions are subject to judicial review. The FCC receives funding from the legislature and must participate in congressional oversight hearings. In addition, the FCC must comply with rules enacted by Congress to ensure fair hearings, due process for stakeholders. and opportunities for the public to participate in the policymaking process.

Courts review the FCC's decision-making process to ensure that the Commission compiled a complete evidentiary record and reached a rational decision. When the FCC cuts corners—whether out of expediency, partisanship, laziness, or reliance on doctrines not corroborated by the evidence—a reviewing court can prevent it from achieving its preferred outcome. Reviewing courts can determine that the FCC failed to demonstrate how the record it generated supported the outcome it sought to achieve. Courts can question the adequacy of the record and whether the FCC complied with all administrative rules. If the court identifies a deficiency in the FCC's work product, the court can determine that the FCC acted arbitrarily or capriciously or otherwise abused its discretionary powers and failed to comply with applicable laws.[2]

Courts reviewing an FCC decision that crafted a new rule, regulation, or policy typically accord the Commission ample discretion. Most judges lack the expertise to make industry-specific decisions and have a general disposition not to intrude on the administrative process, to legislate from the bench by assuming the role of the legislature or executive branch. The *Chevron*[3] standard, articulated by the Supreme Court, supports deference to administrative-agency decision making that reasonably interprets and implements statutory language. A court's prior judicial construction of a statute trumps an agency's construction otherwise entitled to *Chevron* deference only if the prior court decision holds that its construction follows from the unambiguous terms of the statue and thus leaves no room for agency discretion.[4]

The FCC typically has little trouble qualifying for judicial deference when it can identify a specific statute and explain how it reasonably interpreted the ambiguities contained in the law. The more technical or complex the issue, the more likely it is that a court will rely on the Commission's expertise to reach conclusions and craft appropriate policies. But even if the FCC cannot directly link a policy decision to a specific statutory mandate, the Commission's decisions may still pass muster with a reviewing court. Title I of the Communications Act of 1934[5] confers broad, "ancillary" regulatory authority[6] for the FCC to serve the public interest.

The FCC's statutory analysis of definitions and the scope of its Title I authority have generated mixed results when subject to judicial review.

Some courts accord the Commission extraordinary latitude using the *Chevron* analysis, perhaps augmented by a reluctance to second-guess an expert regulatory agency on highly technical matters, on its conclusions about how robustly competitive broadband and other markets have become, and its analysis of economic policy. Other courts, which have reversed FCC decisions, and judges filing strong dissents have refused to defer to the Commission notwithstanding great complexity in the subject matter.

THE PRESUMPTION OF ROBUST COMPETITION

In policy pronouncements and statistical compilations, the FCC has concluded that robust competition exists throughout the ICE marketplace with the exception of cable television services and some services to rural areas, such as voice telephone service. When the FCC can identify a competitive market, credibly or not, it can act on its predisposition to deregulate, unregulate, and otherwise abandon regulatory oversight. Concluding that robust competition exists serves the twin objectives of confirming that it made the right call both in previously reducing the scope of its oversight and in pursuing further deregulation over time. Credible evidence of competition refutes the view that market failure exists; that is, lack of competition would mean that the Commission must intervene to remedy a situation where the price, quantity, quality, or availability of a service lies at a level below what the Commission considers adequate to serve the public interest.

Ironically, the FCC used to be accused of regulatory lag, of failing to modify or eliminate regulations when circumstances changed.[7] Sponsored researchers used regulatory lag and the prospect of future competition to claim that "contestable markets"[8] obligated the FCC to start the administrative process for deregulation or streamlined regulation in anticipation of future increased competition. Now the FCC assumes that because competition exists with few barriers to market entry, it should further reduce regulations. In this current regulatory environment, the FCC can state that because competition already exists, it need not take steps to promote market entry. In application, this approach allows incumbents to acquire most of any newly available spectrum, thereby reducing the prospects for market entry and additional competition. For example, in the wireless market, the FCC has abandoned caps on spectrum acquisition by any single firm,[9] even though this allows incumbents to acquire spectrum that might have provided the medium for new competitive wireless services. Next-generation wireless services offer the promise of true broadband access to the Internet, but instead of promoting competition by making additional spectrum available only to newcomers, the FCC has allowed incumbents to control most wireless broadband spectrum. Accordingly, companies with dominant market share in both wireless and wireline telecommunications services can calibrate their broadband services in each industry segment to forestall significant cannibalization of revenue streams. In other words, companies such as AT&T and Verizon will offer true wireless broadband in ways that neither harm their wireline broadband services nor generate robust competition between their wireline and wireless services.

Evidence of competition is the supreme validator allowing the FCC to reduce or eliminate its regulatory oversight and increasingly rely on market-driven self-regulation. Adam Smith's concept of an invisible hand refers to the ability of the marketplace to respond to consumer requirements and to reach an optimal equilibrium that matches supply and demand. Competition occurs when two or more ventures have invested in facilities and equipment to provide service. With facilities-based competition, two or more ventures operate separate networks that can each provide a stand-alone service without requiring cooperation with a competitor. For example, direct broadcast satellite (DBS) consumers can access ample video programming from either the satellites owned and operated by DirecTV or by Echostar. Neither competitor needs to access the other's satellite or inventory of programming. The Sirius and XM satellite ventures provided facilities-based competition in the market for premium satellite-delivered music and other audio programming before the FCC concluded that their merger would serve the public interest and improve odds that the merged company would remain a viable competitor with other audio content sources.[10]

But even if competition exists in ICE markets, a regulator will still have job security, because the public interest, convenience, and necessity may require the regulator to ensure that competitors cooperate on such essential matters as interconnecting their separate facilities to ensure that subscribers of one network can communicate with subscribers of other networks. Normally, competitors do not have to cooperate with each other, nor should they. Consumers want competitors to compete aggressively and to work tirelessly to expand markets and to acquire competitors' market share. But in some ICE markets, such as telecommunications, the regulator may have to ensure that subscribers of carrier A can access the subscribers of carrier B without having to become a subscriber of both carriers' services. Such compulsory cooperation constitutes part of what it means to be a common carrier; the existence of competition should have no impact on whether the FCC should exercise its statutory authority to require cooperation and to monitor how such cooperation occurs, regarding, for example, the terms, conditions, and performance of the interconnection between carrier A's and carrier B's facilities.

Market advocates might make the argument that competing carriers would voluntarily cooperate and provide interconnection between their networks even in the absence of a statutory or regulatory mandate. Connectivity between the networks that make up the Internet corroborates this view. But the issue of whether network operators will agree to interconnect does not address how they will interconnect, nor does it guarantee that they will also agree to do so on fully transparent, nondiscriminatory, and reasonable terms, conditions, and prices. An additional question is whether the public might want connectivity between networks even if a number of commercial and strategic reasons motivate the parties not to interconnect. For example, an Internet messaging network operator might not want to facilitate interoperability, even though that would enhance the reach, utility, value, and convenience of online messaging for users.

When the FCC lets marketplace forces remedy network access disputes, it may woefully disserve the public interest in two ways: (1) by manipulating data and opinions to establish that robust competition exists where it might not be as vibrant as the Commission assumes and (2) by concluding that its inference of competition justifies a nearly complete abdication of regulatory responsibilities.

Competition, like beauty, lies in the eye of the beholder. Where the FCC sees a political or public relations benefit, it will often assume, despite limited empirical proof, that competition exists, using internal statistics or anecdotal information to confirm the veracity of its findings. The FCC readily ignores the fact that establishing the existence of competition depends on more than the compilation of the number of potential competitors operating in a particular locality. For example, the Internet offers a lot of news, but quantity does not guarantee that a variety of news sources compete. In rejecting some of the FCC's decisions to relax the rules about media concentration, an appellate court noted that while the Internet and cable television supplement viewpoint diversity, they do not constitute complete substitutes for the content provided by newspapers and broadcast stations, nor do these options always generate independent local news. With respect to the Internet, while some evidence on record in the *Prometheus* case indicated a negative correlation between respondents' reliance on broadcast television and the Internet as news sources (suggesting that people who use the Internet for local news do so at the expense of television), the Internet was also limited in its availability and as a source of local news. Therefore, according to the court, the FCC can rely on cable or the Internet to mitigate the threat that local station consolidations pose to viewpoint diversity, but only to a limited degree.[11]

Competition occurs when two or more service providers offer functionally equivalent services and use price and other enhancements to acquire market share and to expand the size of the market. Under this definition, competition might not exist even if the FCC identified a dozen potential competitors, particularly if they did not operate stand-alone networks and simply repackaged the services of another carrier or content provider. If these ventures engaged in price fixing or "consciously parallel" conduct, consumers would have little benefit accruing from the ability to select from twelve operators all offering service on the same terms and conditions. So price, or—in economists' lingo—cross-elasticity, matters in an assessment of competition.

A market might be robustly competitive if it has two vigorous facilities-based operators who regularly lower prices, introduce new services, and innovate. A market would not be competitive even if it had plenty of operators who advertised aggressively but who targeted different types of consumers and rarely changed prices for service. The FCC simply counts the number of Internet-access providers without acknowledging that some ventures can carve out a profitable and uncompetitive market niche. For example, subscribers of satellite-delivered broadband service tolerate higher prices and slower bitrates because they probably do not have access to cheaper terrestrial options, such as DSL and cable modem service. In the FCC's results-driven world, the Commission can infer competition from the use of a technology that few would choose if cheaper and faster alternatives existed. In reality, satellite-delivered Internet access and most terrestrial wireless options do not yet provide a competitive alternative; rather, they serve as carriers of last resort in regions where DSL and cable modem service options do not exist.

The FCC infers robust competition in the wireless telephone marketplace even though its own statistics show that four national carriers share about 90 percent of the market and offer nearly identical and rarely adjusted prices. The FCC also infers ample competition in the broadband Internet access market even though its statistics report that two ventures control nearly 90 percent of most local markets in what amounts to "a series of non-geographically overlapping duopolies," to quote one industry observer.[12] For wireless service, the FCC has abandoned most common-carrier telecommunications service regulation of cellular telephones, and for broadband Internet access, it has applied an information services classification that qualifies the duopolists for a deregulatory safe harbor. In both instances, the FCC assumes that robust competition exists, and has expressed confidence in a marketplace solution to any public interest shortfall.

The FCC typically concludes that competition exists when it can count two or more competitors in a locality or when it can generally identify two or more service alternatives available to the same consumer. So in the wireless telephone service and Internet-access markets, the FCC can attempt to corroborate that robust competition exists by referring to other services and technologies that these services compete with. True, Internet consumers might consider as a partial Internet-use substitute the content available from radios, television, newspapers, magazines, DVDs, and books, but to infer competition from that observation requires quite a stretch. Nor should the FCC infer that wireless telephone service providers compete with wireline options, because some consumers have begun to treat wireless as a complete alternative to wireline service.

THE PRESUMED NEED FOR INCENTIVES TO INVEST

Remarkably, even as the FCC touts statistics showing an impressive take-up of new technologies, it also frets over whether it has done enough to stimulate investment in next-generation infrastructure. If it can point to world-class market penetration for both wireline and wireless broadband service, why should it have to offer additional financial incentives for incumbents or new ventures to invest in services for which consumers apparently have robust demand? A new word has entered the regulators' lingo in the United States: "incentivize." Aside from being another perverse creation of a verb from what used to be a noun, this word provides a snapshot of how the political process works.

Stakeholders perceive a benefit from simultaneously pushing parallel, though inconsistent, policy outcomes. A venture wanting relaxation of costly regulations will seek to provide confirmation that deregulation has stimulated market entry and competition, as confirmed by the FCC's own statistics or statements. But because the federal government often offers generous financial inducements for ventures to invest in preferred projects, parties that might otherwise make such investments without any need for the government to create financial incentives for them to do so nevertheless will devise strategies to secure additional government funding or tax relief. So apparently there is no inconsistency in a venture touting competition as the remedy or substitute for regulation even as the same venture proclaims the need to be incentivized by the FCC to make the necessary investments.

Incumbent telephone companies have mastered the art of simultaneously invoking competition as a panacea even as they claim the need for the government to create incentives for investments that can sustain or enhance competition. Both Congress and the FCC appear eager to offer such incentives without even considering whether existing competition and the need to remain competitive obviate the need for additional incentives. Facilities-based competition for basic voice telephone service has increased with the onset of service provided from cable television companies and ventures that offer telephone service via the Internet. Wireless telephone service provides an alternative and sometimes a substitute for some consumers, including college students and other temporary residents.

The statistics of incumbent telephone companies, provided to the FCC and to Wall Street financiers, confirm declining revenue from conventional wireline telephone service.[13] Facing such a decline in fortune, would it not make sense, based on competitive necessity, for the incumbent telephone companies to find new markets to serve? Wouldn't competitive necessity and the expectations of owners of stock in these companies require them to reorient the companies to markets with growth prospects? If so, where is the need for the government to offer further inducements for investments that these companies have to make if they are to survive in an age of technological and market convergence?

THE FCC'S EMPHASIS ON POLITICS, DOCTRINE, AND EXPEDIENCY

The FCC has managed to avoid making decisions based on a complete record in a number of cases. Politics, confidence in debatable economic theories and doctrines, and results-driven decision making have created the wrong policies, rules, and regulations. The FCC makes statutory interpretations guaranteed to achieve outcomes that do not promote global best practices but instead favor particular stakeholders or groups. Because regulation increases an ICE venture's cost of doing business, it has become standard operating procedure in the United States for ventures to invest substantial sums of money into strategies aiming to reduce or eliminate regulatory costs or to have competitors incur comparatively greater regulatory costs. Stakeholders consider lobbying, litigation, and aggressive participation in the FCC's notice and comment rulemakings and other proceedings a wise investment. If such activities can encourage the FCC to make a decision that favors one party or group of stakeholders to the detriment of others, then the regulatory process has tilted the playing field, possibly insulated a venture from competition, helped a firm save money, disadvantaged a competitor, or created incentives for a firm to make an investment in ICE infrastructure and services, which it might have made even without such incentives.

Far too often the FCC does not do its homework. It has a legally enforceable duty to generate a record based on collected evidence. Too often it articulates a policy direction based on an assumption that it never gets around to corroborating with empirical evidence. For example, the FCC can point to the Internet as evidence that the marketplace for ideas and ICE services has so expanded that it can relax rules designed to curb the concentration of media ownership and control. Of course, it is entirely plausible that widespread access by consumers to Internet-mediated sources of news, information, and entertainment offers competitive alternatives to incumbent media such as radio, television, cable television, and newspapers. But the FCC has cited the *availability* of Internet-mediated options as sufficient proof that the time has come to relax limits on media ownership by a single firm. The Commission should have assessed whether and how Internet-mediated options actually *provide* competitive alternatives to the status quo. In reality, many of the most popular Internet sources of news are produced or owned and operated by incumbent media that "repurpose" content, created by affiliated broadcast, cable television, and newspaper companies.

Had the FCC done its homework, it could have determined that incumbent mainstream media ventures provide many of the Internet-mediated sources of information, communications, and entertainment that consumers access. In other words, availability of a new medium for the distribution of ICE content does not by itself confirm that the content traversing the new medium is new and different from that available via incumbent media, or that new and different ventures have become the major suppliers of such content. But if the FCC wants to achieve a preferred outcome—to approve a merger, justify the relaxation or elimination of regulatory safeguards, or to rationalize an assumption about marketplace conditions—it will concentrate on the theoretical possibility that competition exists rather than provide verifiable proof that it does. On some occasions, reviewing courts have detected the FCC's failure to conduct verifiable empirical research and have overturned its decisions, but in other instances, overly credulous courts have refrained from second-guessing the FCC's "findings."

Few would dispute that reasoned decision making requires verifiable research—findings of fact, statistical compilations, and policy recommendations that others can confirm as true and legitimate. If an NRA wants to justify a deregulatory initiative, approval of a merger, or relaxation in rules that will result in further industry concentration, it should conduct empirical research to prove that the public will not suffer in terms of higher costs, fewer choices, declining innovation, and an artificial competitive advantage given to a venture that gamed the regulatory process. Fundamental consumer protection requires that a regulatory agency undertake transparent data-gathering and subject its work product to peer review, that is, to examination by independent experts to confirm that the process used and results generated are legitimate, verifiable, and uncontaminated by ulterior motives.

Only in rare instances does the FCC encourage peer review of its work product and that submitted by interested parties. Worse yet, the FCC provides ample evidence of worst practices in its fact finding and statistics compiling. Some examples are the way it measures national progress in broadband market penetration, the way it completely reversed a finding that consumers would not benefit from per-channel access to cable television programming, and the way it seems unable to determine the level of national market penetration by cable television. In each case a credible argument can be made that the FCC had a policy outcome it wanted to achieve and that senior management had made it clear that facts and statistics had to support that outcome.[14] But even without evidence that staff had been told to cook the books, the FCC's woefully inadequate work product points to a process designed to reach outcomes that outside researchers cannot corroborate.

Broadband Market Penetration Statistics

Section 706 of the Telecommunications Act of 1996[15] requires the FCC and the states to encourage the deployment of advanced telecommunications capability to all Americans.[16] In conjunction with this objective, Congress instructed the FCC to conduct regular inquiries concerning the availability of advanced telecommunications capability. In response the FCC seeks input from interested parties as well as requires reporting of statistical data. Had the FCC intended to make the process transparent and fair, its staff would have constructed a questionnaire or similar data request with an eye toward acquiring and disclosing data sufficient for Congress, the Commission itself, and other interested parties to determine the actual national, regional, and local market penetration by broadband service providers, such as the incumbent telephone and cable television firms that offer DSL and cable modem access, respectively.

Instead, the data request appears to have been intentionally designed to overstate market penetration. Furthermore, the FCC has agreed to treat the data as trade secrets deserving protection from public disclosure, as though the decision by a venture to serve or not serve a locality would have the same business impact as the loss of control by the makers of Coca-Cola over their recipe for the soft drink.[17] The FCC has received justly deserved criticism for the way it has compiled statistics of broadband market penetration and the inferences it has derived from the collected data.[18] For more than a decade, the FCC considered broadband to mean any service transmitting more than 200 kilobits per second in one direction. It used zip codes as the geographical measure of broadband penetration and considered the entire zip code served if one user existed, regardless of circumstances and prices paid. This measure overstated the degree of real competition for broadband services, particularly in light of the Commission's own data showing cable modem and DSL carriers having nearly 90 percent national market share.

The FCC offered some acknowledgment that its statistical compilations may overstate the true level of access, particularly in rural locales: "In sparsely populated rural Zip Codes this could mean that a given provider has just one broadband subscriber who is located in a small town or at some other location convenient to telephone or cable facilities. Broadband 'availability' could be non-existent for that carrier's other customers located a few blocks or many miles away from that single customer. In other words, and notwithstanding the value of data currently submitted on the Form 477, there is more precise information that we could gather to give us a more accurate picture of current broadband deployment."[19] This candid acknowledgement or afterthought never gained much traction, because the FCC and parties benefiting from a finding of robust competition and market penetration heralded the finding whenever possible. Despite ample evidence to the contrary, the Commerce Department stated unequivocally in 2007[20] that the United States had achieved the mission of cheap and ubiquitous broadband access articulated by President Bush in 2004.[21] The Commerce Department used the FCC's flawed statistics to confirm its "mission accomplished" conclusion. Had the Commerce Department chosen to subject the FCC's findings to critical review, ample evidence existed that challenged the FCC's findings. But evidence to the contrary only provided fleeting dissonance to the message that the United States has retained superiority in market penetration by next-generation networks.

The FCC's statistics also provided the basis for comments filed by interested parties with the FCC corroborating its view that robust competition existed and that the deregulatory process should continue. Remarkably, the mere presence of conflicting statistics triggered official government opposition. Both the National Telecommunications and Information Administration and the State Department challenged as flawed the statistics complied by staff of the Organisation for Economic Co-operation and Development that showed the United States in the middle tier of nations, not the first, in having market penetration.

It apparently matters little that the FCC has belatedly recognized the need to achieve a more granular and locality-specific assessment of broadband penetration. In 2008 the FCC made improvements in its broadband data collection with an eye toward increasing the precision and quality of information about broadband subscribership.[22] Rather than generally report on market penetration by any broadband service that offers transmission at 200-plus kilobits per second in one direction, the FCC expanded the number of speed tiers for reporting purposes to capture more precise information about upload and download broadband speeds. The Commission now requires broadband providers to report numbers of broadband subscribers by census tract, broken down by speed tier and technology type, instead of by the much larger geographical region represented by a zip code. The FCC also expects to improve the accuracy of the information that it gathers about mobile wireless broadband deployment.

Despite recognizing the need for better data, the FCC and other interested parties have relied on the existing statistics as proof positive that the United States has not lost its competitive edge in information and communication technologies (ICT) infrastructure. The FCC has made no official statements that would certify an assumption that the United States has evidenced global best practices in broadband access. In its reports to Congress on the subject, it offers nothing but breathless optimism about technological, deregulatory, and marketplace improvements that have already delivered broadband "in a reasonable and timely fashion."[23] The Commission's *Fifth Report* to Congress, released in June 2008, identifies numerous technologies that can offer broadband services, as well as spectrum allocations whose licensees have the option of providing such services. The report also showcases deregulatory initiatives that create incentives for next-generation investment—for example, abandoning requirements that incumbent carriers unbundle network facilities and make them available to competitors at favorable, below-market rates,[24] classifying broadband access as an information service, imposing deadlines on consideration of franchise applications by cable television competitors,[25] and requiring incumbent local exchange carriers to offer market entrants access to wholesale services.[26]

Reading the FCC's reports to Congress, we can easily conclude that all of the technologies, spectrum allocations, and deregulatory initiatives identified by the FCC have achieved a direct and positive impact on broadband access. In reality, the Commission has identified several technologies that might provide additional broadband services in the future, such as transmitting broadband over electric power lines, but which currently constitute no competitive alternative. Likewise, the Commission has identified numerous spectrum allocations whose licensees do not provide broadband services and who would face extraordinary opposition at the Commission and in the courts if they tried to offer competitive retail broadband services. The FCC also conveniently fails to disclose that incumbent carriers have acquired the vast majority of prime spectrum suitable for broadband services, including former ultrahigh frequency (UHF) analog television bandwidth.

Until it gets around to providing better, more granular statistics, the FCC is simply listing numbers that ostensibly represent how many separate broadband options exist in each zip code in the United States. The number for a zip code offers scant evidence that a locality actually enjoys significant facilities-based competition. Even if a school, library, clinic, or hospital acquires broadband services on a subsidized basis, the FCC can inflate the number of broadband options to include such site-specific services. An aggregate number provides no evidence of price competition, nor does it offer assurance that American consumers are adequately covered by numerous broadband options.

However, the FCC's current collection of broadband options by zip code does provide incumbent wireline and wireless carriers with some justification to press for greater deregulation. Taking an offensive posture, incumbents can argue that broadband statistics prove the virtue of marketplace resource allocation, competition, and deregulation.[27] When countervailing statistics spoil the positive picture, incumbent carriers and their sponsored researchers have to take a more defensive posture to explain any deficit in light of negative demographics and computer illiteracy or in light of inadequate efforts by Congress and the FCC to create even more incentives for infrastructure investment.[28]

The impact of defective statistical compilations at the FCC becomes more extensive and harmful when interested parties get their hands on the data and use them to support policy initiatives. Because the findings can help support arguments for deregulation, mergers, and relaxed consumer-protection safeguards, stakeholders quickly incorporate the Commission's findings into advocacy documents filed with the Commission. To add gravity, legitimacy, and the appearance of widespread agreement on the wisdom of a public policy change that happens to benefit a specific party or group, external research papers are appended to an FCC pleading or filing. This external research, generated by consulting firms, affiliates at think tanks, and individual academics, offers the appearance of independent, third-party analysis. Nothing could be further from the truth.

Many academics and think tank affiliates contribute to public policy debates because undisclosed benefactors invest substantial sums of money in their research and writing—presumably in return for some benefits. The concept of plausible deniability allows a sponsored researcher to claim that he or she has not received direct financial support for the research and advocacy that uphold a particular stakeholder's or group's viewpoint. However, the author indirectly benefits financially, because a think tank disburses honoraria and other sorts of compensation from the stakeholder's grant. Think tank staff and affiliates generate creative ideas about a public policy issue that resonate with the stakeholder's political and public relations agenda. The stakeholder's grant helps pay for the employees' or affiliates' salaries, albeit indirectly. So there is no direct quid pro quo, but no one can believe that so many public policy initiatives in telecommunications policy, first appearing in the work product of an academic or think tank affiliate, arose completely unsolicited. With no need to pass the rigor of peer review and apparently without the need to disclose financial support arriving directly or indirectly, sponsored researchers readily use the FCC's flawed statistics to support a shared policy outcome.

Academics, foundations, and think tanks that generate advocacy documents supporting a stakeholder's public policy agenda are well rewarded because both the FCC and individual companies benefit if advocacy documents submitted for inclusion in the public record—for, say, a deregulatory broadband policy—corroborate the FCC's inferences and assumptions about competition as supported by the FCC's statistics. The think tank experts rarely compile their own statistics; by using the FCC's compilations, they endorse and validate the FCC's conclusions. Challengers to the validity of the FCC's statistics do not appear to get much of a hearing, primarily because the FCC wants its statistical compilations to support the inferences being made by politically connected stakeholders.

À la Carte Access to Cable Television Programming

The FCC has developed an inconsistent record on whether and how access to individual channels on cable television would save consumers money in lieu of the current business model, where cable operators package programming tiers containing many channels. The Commission initially concluded that à la carte program access would not save consumers money, based on research conducted by the Media Bureau and most of the sponsored research filed with the FCC. In a November 2004 report, the FCC's Media Bureau estimated that the impact on retail rates of optional or mandatory à la carte sales would benefit only those consumers who would purchase access to fewer than nine programming networks.[29] Because most consumers watch seventeen or more channels, most consumers would probably incur an increase in their monthly bills if they paid on an à la carte basis. The Media Bureau concluded that a seventeen-channel à la carte purchase would trigger a monthly rate increase of between 14 percent and 30 percent.

The Media Bureau report included several policy recommendations that Congress and the FCC should consider as possible ways to enhance consumer choice, foster competition, and provide consumers with the tools to prevent objectionable programming from entering their homes. Among these recommendations was promotion of competition in multichannel video programming distribution (MVPD), which would generate downward pressure on rates, as occurred with aggressive marketing by direct broadcast satellite operators and the video service providers of such wireline telephone companies as Verizon and AT&T. The Media Bureau also suggested that policymakers consider creating incentives for operators to provide consumers with more control and access to programming, like that provided by pay-per-view and video-on-demand services. Another suggestion was rapid deployment of broadband networks to create additional content access options for consumers, such as access per game or by subscription to Major League Baseball game coverage via the Internet. The Media Bureau noted that many retransmission consent negotiations between content providers and cable systems may bundle less-desired channels in exchange for a lower carriage rate for more-desired channels. Such bundling may crowd out desirable programming and possibly raise both public-interest and antitrust concerns.

In a stunning reversal of its previous findings, the FCC later asserted that à la carte access to cable television programs could save many consumers money and would not result in a reduction of television viewership. In *Further Report on the Packaging and Sale of Video Programming Services to the Public,* made available in February 2006,[30] the FCC reexamined the conclusions and underlying assumptions of the earlier Media Bureau report on à la carte programming. The FCC reported that previous calculations of per-channel cable television costs submitted by sponsored researchers failed to net out the cost of broadcast stations and overstated costs by as much as 50 percent. It also abrogated its previous finding that à la carte access would cause consumers to spend nearly 25 percent less time watching television, or two-plus fewer hours of television per day. According to the *Further Report,* there was no reason to believe that viewers would watch less video programming simply because they could choose the channels they found most interesting. The FCC concluded that "many consumers could be better off under an à la carte model."[31]

The FCC did not revisit à la carte pricing because it unilaterally detected flaws in its internal calculations and doubted its reliance on analysis by sponsored researchers. Rather, it acted at the behest of several representatives and senators. Given the complete reversal in its findings, either the Commission previously engaged in shoddy research and sloppy review of sponsored research, or it subsequently responded to a shift in the political winds and changed its interpretation. The economics of cable television program creation and distribution did not dramatically change in two years. However, the politically wise position did change, making it prudent to support à la carte program access.

More Regulations for Cable Television

In light of the FCC's relentless confirmation that competition is ascendant, it comes as a surprise that it is apparently hell-bent to broaden the scope and reach of its oversight of cable television. The FCC can point to statutory authority that confers broad flexibility in formulating a regulatory campaign for cable television. Section 612(g) of the Communications Act, as amended in 1984, provides that when "cable systems with 36 or more activated channels are available to seventy percent of households within the United States" and when 70 percent of those households subscribe to them, "the Commission may promulgate any additional rules necessary to promote diversity of information sources."[32]

Prior to 2007, the FCC determined that the first benchmark of the so-called 70/70 test had been reached and suggested that the second benchmark may also have been reached. In 2008 it determined that the second benchmark of the 70/70 test had indeed been reached, but based this conclusion on the 71.4 percent market penetration rate reported by Warren Communications News, not on data compiled by FCC staff. In light of growing market penetration by direct broadcast satellite and telephone company services, one or both of the 70/70 test criteria may no longer be satisfied. The recent refusal of an appellate court to accept the FCC's rationale for capping market penetration of single cable-television ventures corroborates this.[33] However, the FCC appears intent on assuming that it has grounds for extending cable television regulation, the grounds being anecdotal, third-party evidence not subject to notice and comment or review by the public or other interested parties. In any event, the FCC's reliance on third-party statistics to justify a substantial increase in regulatory oversight for cable television is inconsistent and procedurally suspect, especially since it uses the assumption of increased competition and its own statistical compilations to justify less, not more, regulation for broadband, wireless, and incumbent wireline carrier services.

To gather data for its annual assessment of competition in video programming, the FCC ordered all cable operators to disclose the total number of homes the cable operator currently has the ability to serve; the total number of homes to which the cable operator currently can offer thirty-six or more activated channels; the total number of subscribers; and the total number of subscribers with thirty-six or more activated channels.[34] The FCC widely disseminates these statistics if the data confirm its policy objectives. If not, it might not disseminate the results and might even treat the data as confidential or proprietary, which is how it treated broadband market penetration data.[35] Evidence of where cable television ventures operate and what their subscription rates are arguably have the same trade-secret value as broadband market penetration rates. Alternatively, neither should be hidden from public scrutiny.

THE FCC'S DOUBTFUL COMMITMENT TO CONSUMER PROTECTION

If we were to extrapolate from the FCC's cable television regulations, we could infer its objective: to protect consumers from ventures having both the incentive and the ability to harm the public. Apparently, it perceives the need to target cable television for especially aggressive regulation while letting other ventures, such as cell phone and incumbent wireline carriers, enjoy unprecedented regulatory laxity and forbearance. The Commission attempts to justify this lack of oversight parity by pointing to prices: increases in cable television rates regularly exceed general indices of price increases, whereas competition in other markets prevents gouging.

In 2006 the FCC reported that average monthly rates for basic and expanded cable programming services continued to exceed overall cost-of-living measures, increasing by 5.2 percent over the twelve-month period ending on January 1, 2005, from $40.91 to $43.04.[36] Remarkably, the FCC reported only minor cost differences where cable television systems faced significant competition from satellite or other wireline operators. For the same twelve-month period, the average monthly rate for basic and expanded cable programming services increased by 4.9 percent for cable operators in communities not protected by basic tier rate regulation (the effective competition group) and by 5.2 percent for the group of cable operators without a finding of effective competition. As of January 1, 2005, cable operators without a finding of effective competition charged an average of $43.33 per month for basic and expanded programming, which was 7.9 percent more than the $40.15 charged by the group of operators with a finding of effective competition. The Commission concluded that DBS competition did not appear to constrain cable prices, for average prices were the same or slightly higher in communities with DBS (i.e., a cable operator was relieved of rate regulation because of the presence of DBS) as in noncompetitive communities. The FCC apparently concluded that facilities-based competition between DBS and cable would not adequately protect consumers from price gouging—and it reached this conclusion even though it still seems to assume, without quantitative proof, that this type of facilities-based competition adequately protects consumers of all other telecommunications services.

An alternative interpretation to the statistics shows that expanded inventory of content, which might have shown a reduced cost per channel, forced cable operators to raise prices. So for cable television the FCC seems ready to punish price gouging with expanded regulatory safeguards while for other services the FCC does not devote much effort to collecting pricing data on the assumption that competition automatically forces pricing discipline.

Cable Television Regulation Revisited

Although the FCC regularly approves mergers and acquisitions that make the telecommunications services ever more concentrated, it has extraordinary concern about the potential for large cable television firms to dominate the market in both the creation and the distribution of video programming. At a time when the FCC aggressively dismantles regulatory safeguards for telecommunications services and has determined that it need not bother regulating information services, such as Internet access, it retains and in some instances has expanded its regulation of cable television. In fact, the market penetration of cable television has started to decline in light of true facilities-based competition from the satellite and video-program-distribution services of incumbent telephone companies. Absent occasional disputes over access to regional sports networks, satellite and telephone company competitors rarely complain to the FCC about their inability to acquire programming, even from ventures owned in part or in whole by cable television companies. Nevertheless, in the past few years the FCC has affirmed the need to scrutinize how vertically integrated cable television companies, which own both content production and distribution ventures, provide their services.

The Commission also requires cable companies to offer subscribers an alternative to mandatory rental of cable set-top boxes for accessing content and for safeguarding intellectual property rights,[37] even though cellular companies have no similar obligation to allow subscribers to use a handset that the cellular company did not sell them. Recently the FCC established mandatory timetables for state and municipal franchising authorities to satisfy when considering the applications of telephone companies to provide competing video services.[38] It prohibits franchising authorities from requiring telephone companies to comply with many of the burdens imposed on cable television companies; for example, it prohibits cable television companies, but not telephone companies, from redlining —targeting wealthy neighborhoods for service while refusing to serve poor neighborhoods. But perhaps the high-water market of regulatory intervention, not applied in other ICE sectors, is the FCC recent decision to revoke contracts voluntarily reached between cable television companies and owners of multiple dwelling units (MDUs), such as apartments and condominiums, which represent 22 percent of all housing units.

Abrogation of Exclusive Service Contracts in MDUs

The FCC has declared that distributors of multichannel video programming (MVPDs) cannot negotiate exclusive service agreements with owners of MDUs[39] in light of the requirement in section 628 of the Communications Act that proscribes "unfair methods of competition or unfair or deceptive acts or practices, the purpose or effect of which is to hinder significantly or to prevent any multichannel video programming distributor from providing satellite cable programming or satellite broadcast programming to subscribers or consumers."[40] The Commission concluded that exclusive service contracts prevent 22 percent of the population from having potential access to multiple video programming options: "[E]xclusivity clauses bar entry into MDUs by new providers of multichannel video service. It also shows that, in reaction to the recent competitive challenge posed by LEC [local exchange carrier] entry into the video marketplace, incumbent providers (chiefly incumbent cable operators) are increasingly using exclusivity clauses in new agreements with MDU owners to bar the entry of their new rivals and potential rivals."[41]

While acknowledging that exclusivity might provide a strong inducement for investment in MDU video programming distribution plant, the Commission concluded that the harms clearly outweigh the benefits, particularly in light of recent market entry by incumbent telephone companies: "[A]lthough exclusivity clauses may in certain cases be beneficial, at least in the short term, to consumers, the harms of exclusivity clauses outweigh their benefits. The evidence described in the preceding paragraphs demonstrates that exclusivity clauses, especially when used in current market conditions by incumbent cable operators, are a barrier to new entry into the multichannel video marketplace and the provision of triple play offerings. Such exclusivity clauses inhibit competition in these markets and slow the deployment of broadband facilities. In doing so, exclusivity clauses deny MDU residents the benefits of increased competition, including lower prices and the availability of more channels with more diverse content, as well as access to alternative providers of broadband facilities and the triple play of communications services their facilities support."[42]

Stating that exclusive service contracts constitute an "unfair method of competition or an unfair act or practice proscribed by Section 628(b),"[43] the FCC announced that "no cable operator or multichannel video programming distributor subject to Section 628 of the Act shall enforce or execute any provision in a contract that grants it the exclusive right to provide any video programming service (alone or in combination with other services) to a MDU. Any such exclusivity clause shall be null and void."[44]

The Commission summarily rejected the view that its intrusion into private contracting constituted an unconstitutional taking of property. Using the three criteria established by the Supreme Court for assessing whether a regulatory taking has occurred,[45] it concluded that "[n]one of these factors counsels in favor of finding a regulatory taking here."[46]

Leased Commercial Access

In a report and order and proposed notice of rulemaking in 2008, the FCC expanded the nature and scope of its requirement that cable television companies lease channel capacity to third parties.[47] Ostensibly to promote competition in video programming by lowering the rate paid for access channel capacity in cable systems, the FCC in effect told cable operators what they can charge. The FCC modified the leased-access-rate formula to a rate of approximately ten cents per subscriber, adopted customer service obligations that require minimal standards and equal treatment of leased-access programmers vis-à-vis other programmers, eliminated the requirement for an independent accountant to review leased-access rates, and required annual reporting of leased-access statistics. It also adopted expedited time frames for resolution of complaints and improvements to the evidence discovery process.

The current rules authorize the FCC to establish different formulas for full-time carriage on programming tiers and for occasional à la carte services. The former requires a calculation based on an "average implicit fee"—the amount that other programmers are implicitly charged for carriage to permit the operator to recover its costs and earn a profit—while the latter uses the "highest implicit fee." Cable operators may not unreasonably refuse to cooperate with a leased-access vendor in order to prevent the leasing of channel capacity.

The recent order facilitates the use of leased-access channels by adopting more-specific leased-access customer service standards and increased enforcement of those standards, faster cable operator response times to information requests, and "more appropriate" leased-access rates. It also expedites the leased-access complaint process and improves the discovery process related to leased-access disputes.

The FCC also requires cable operators to submit, on an annual basis, information about their leased-access rates, usage, channel placement, and complaints.[48] In response to claims that setting leased channel rates confiscated cable operator property, it noted that a court has affirmed the lawfulness of the provisions of the Cable Act of 1992 that establish the general basis for compulsory capacity leasing.[49] Remarkably, as the FCC imposes incredibly complex and expansive capacity-access requirements for cable television operators, it has abandoned all network-access requirements imposed on incumbent telephone companies. Apparently, ample competition exists among local telecommunications services, but the facilities-based video programming provided by telephone and satellite companies apparently provides no major competition for cable monopolists.

A Market Penetration Cap

Even as the FCC tries to find ways to relax market penetration caps and cross-ownership limitations on broadcasters and other convergent media operators, it has decided that national market penetration rules for cable television remain necessary. In 2008, acting six years after a remand in *Time Warner Entertainment Co. v. FCC*,[50] the FCC again proposed a cap on attributable ownership interest in cable systems serving more than 30 percent of multichannel video programming subscribers nationwide, as it had initially done in 1993.[51] It reiterated the need to cap ownership interest so that no single cable operator or group of operators could leverage size and market power to impede unfairly the flow of programming to consumers as mandated in section 613(f) of the Cable Act.[52]

The Commission sought to remedy the defects in its previous order that had triggered a reversal; the argument then was that it lacked evidence to conclude that cable operators would collude and coordinate their behavior in an anticompetitive manner. The Commission had justified a 30 percent cap on the assumption that the video marketplace could function well if 40 percent of the market constituted an "open field," with 60 percent captured by the two largest multiple system operators, Comcast and Time Warner. In repeating the proposal the FCC also responded to the court's admonition to consider both market share and the nature and type of competition when establishing a percentage cap on attributable ownership interest. The Commission sought to shore up the record with an analysis of bargaining theory, monopsony (single buyer) behavior, and empirical and survey data identifying the contractual relationships between programmers and cable operators, compiled "in order to establish the extent of cable operators' market power and the effects of market power on the quantity and quality of programming, as well as the effects of market power on the programming costs of smaller MVPDs."[53]

The Commission concluded that even one powerful Multiple System Operator (MSO)—a company with two or more cable television systems—could have sufficient market power to thwart the successful debut of a new programming network: "Most importantly, we do not believe that a single new programming network, having failed to gain carriage on the largest cable operator's system, would have a good chance of both gaining carriage on other MVPDs and then induce enough of the large cable operator's subscribers to switch to the other MVPDs either to allow the network to gain sufficient subscribership to be financially viable, or to place substantial pressure on the large cable operator to carry the network within a reasonable period of time."[54] The Commission noted that "without an open field that is large enough, many new programming networks might not even attempt to enter the market without a contract from the largest cable operator."[55]

The District of Columbia Circuit Court of Appeals again reversed the FCC's 30 percent ownership cap and dismissed as bogus the seemingly scientific analysis that it had undertaken.[56] This time the court vacated the rules, deeming them instantly nonapplicable in light of "feeble"[57] analysis that failed to factor in the competition generated by direct broadcast satellite and video services provided by telephone companies.

Streamlining Video Franchising

To expedite competitive market entry by wireline telephone companies into the MVPD marketplace, the FCC has established rules that limit the scope of local franchising authority (LFAs) jurisdiction.[58] Ostensibly to provide guidance for the implementation of section 621(a)(1) of the Communications Act of 1934,[59] the Commission acted in 2005 to prevent LFAs from failing to grant additional cable service franchises to telephone companies in a timely manner or from requiring the new franchisee to meet costly conditions.

The FCC concluded that the operation of the franchising process obstructed competition and investment in broadband infrastructure: "We find that the current operation of the local franchising process in many jurisdictions constitutes an unreasonable barrier to entry that impedes the achievement of the interrelated federal goals of enhanced cable competition and accelerated broadband deployment."[60] After identifying several methods used by franchising authorities for unreasonably refusing to award competitive franchises—protracted local negotiations with no time limits, unreasonable build-out requirements, unreasonable requests for in-kind payments that attempt to subvert a 5 percent cap on franchise fees, and demands relating to public, educational, and government-access services—the FCC concluded that it was "now appropriate . . . to exercise its authority and take steps to prevent LFAs from unreasonably refusing to award competitive franchises."[61] But the FCC never provided evidence that LFAs regularly use such tactics. In other words, the FCC assumed market failure, a counterintuitive conclusion given its determination that just about every other ICE market operates competitively.

The Commission justified intervention based on its conclusion that Title VI of the Communications Act of 1934 generally, and section 621(a)(1) in particular, granted it broad rulemaking authority. It bolstered this assumption of jurisdiction by referring to section 706 of the Telecommunications Act of 1996, which directs the FCC to encourage broadband deployment by removing barriers to infrastructure investment.[62] The Commission determined that if an LFA denied an application based on a new entrant's refusal to undertake certain unreasonable obligations relating to public, educational, and governmental (PEG) and institutional networks (I-Nets), the LFA's refusal to award a competitive franchise was unreasonable. The Commission also stated that it had statutory authority to preempt local laws, regulations, and requirements to the extent that they imposed greater restrictions on market entry than the rules applied to cable franchise applicants did.

The FCC summarily rejected the notion that its initiative overstepped its statutory authority and adversely affected the ability of LFAs to administer their franchise assessment.[63] The FCC's specific safeguards for entrants to the video programming market evidences great concern that incumbent cable television operators might try to use the local franchising process to thwart, delay, or set conditions for entry into the competitive market. Such activism by the FCC on behalf of market entrants juxtaposes a willingness to fetter new local and long-distance VoIP service providers with the same sorts of regulatory burdens that incumbent telephone companies bear, and an interest in eliminating interconnection regulations designed to promote local telecommunications service competition, despite ongoing statutory mandates to promote competition. Senior management at the FCC apparently consider the marketplace for video program delivery insufficiently competitive, despite facilities-based market entry by incumbent telephone companies and satellite carriers; or else it considers the telecommunications services marketplace robustly competitive, despite having two or less facilities-based operators—the telephone services provided by incumbent telephone and cable television companies—in most localities.

Requiring an Alternative to Set-Top Box Rentals

By law, cable television companies cannot offer set-top converter boxes that combine security functions (limiting channel access to what subscribers have ordered) with other navigation functions (program guides, channel changing, and content selection). Furthermore, cable operators must allow subscribers to use alternatives to set-top boxes rented from the cable operator. Section 629(a) of the Communications Act of 1934,[64] as amended, requires the FCC to "ensure that consumers have the opportunity to purchase navigation devices from sources other than their multichannel video programming distributor."[65] The primary alternative to the set-top box is a CableCard modular security component, also known as a point-of-deployment module,[66] which can be inserted into most recently manufactured television sets. Although a competitive market for such devices has not evolved and few consumers even know about the CableCard option, recent innovations in digital video recorders and in two-way interactivity in television sets may incorporate many of the features provided by the cable operators.

Cable operators do not want to lose control over content access by subscribers or any revenues from either subscriber-initiated on-demand service requests or set-top box rentals. Indeed, current alternatives to set-top boxes provided by cable providers do not support two-way features available with cable systems, including electronic programming guides (EPGs), video on demand (VOD), pay-per-view (PPV), and other interactive television (ITV) capabilities. Subscribers may benefit from having a CableCard monthly lease rate lower than a set-top box lease rate, but the inconvenience of not having immediate access to on-demand services may dampen their enthusiasm for such services.[67]

The FCC appreciates the current limitations of CableCards but also recognizes that technological innovations will provide options for downloading security and digital-rights-management functions to devices leased by the cable operator or secured independently by consumers, such as next-generation television sets. Such bidirectional compatibility of cable television systems and consumer electronics equipment eventually will solve the problems with alternatives to set-top boxes supplied by cable operators. However, negotiations between cable operators and manufacturers of consumer electronic devices have not generated a single equipment standard. The cable industry favors the OpenCable Application Platform (OCAP) as the foundation for two-way, ready-to-use (plug and play) products.[68] As the FCC noted, "While the cable and consumer electronics industries agree that OCAP should be part of the solution for two-way plug and play compatibility, the industries appear to disagree on how an OCAP solution should be implemented."[69] The FCC also implied that it did not want consumers to lose the opportunity to purchase competitive devices while representatives of the cable and consumer electronics industry dither. Eventually most or all television sets will have the set-top-box functions built in. Until then, although the FCC seems to have consumer protection concerns about sole-source rentals of set-top boxes, it appears unable to prevent that outcome.

THE FCC'S REGULATORY UNCERTAINTY: WIRELINE VERSUS WIRELESS

Although the FCC has rejected requests by cable television operators to combine the delivery of video service with the lease of set-top boxes that integrate security and navigation functions, it has allowed wireless carriers to severely restrict subscribers' ability to use handsets not sold or sanctioned by a particular carrier. More than forty years ago, when wireline carriers claimed that they could not possibly separate the installation of premises wiring, the leasing of telephone handsets, and telephone service because of the potential for harm to company personnel and facilities, the FCC rejected those claims. The FCC's *Carterfone* policy[70] established the right of wireline telephone subscribers to buy telephones and to attach them to any carrier network, subject to a straightforward certification process to ensure technical compatibility.[71] Since 1968 the FCC has extended the policy of separating equipment from service in other instances to give consumers the opportunity to access only the devices, services, and content they need and want.

Remarkably, the FCC has not established a wireless *Carterfone* policy on its own initiative or in response to an invitation to do so by interested parties such as Skype,[72] a provider of VoIP services, and Google.[73] This reticence to act has generated regulatory uncertainty and has frustrated ventures from offering new and innovative services that consumers could access only from unlocked handsets.

The Commission has evidenced no such reticence vis-à-vis cable television operators. In fact, it explicitly linked this consumer right to attach navigation devices with its previously articulated *Carterfone* policy: "Subscribers have the right to attach any compatible navigation device to a multichannel video programming system. We conclude that the core requirement, to make possible the commercial availability of equipment to MVPD subscribers, is similar to the *Carterfone* principle adopted by the Commission in the telephone environment. The *Carterfone* 'right to attach' principle is that devices that do not adversely affect the network may be attached to the network."[74]

Yet for wireless service the Commission has no problem allowing wireless carriers to couple their delivery of telephone service with the sale of handsets. The carriers have successfully touted the benefits accruing from subscriber opportunities to use increasingly sophisticated handsets at subsidized sale prices to access a blend of ICE services. But in exchange for accepting two-year service contracts, subjecting subscribers to a significant penalty for early termination, subscribers also agree to significant limitations on the versatility and functionality of the handsets they own.[75]

Even though wireless subscribers own the handsets they use to access network services, carriers control and limit the handsets in several increasingly significant and frustrating ways: by locking handsets so that subscribers cannot access competitor networks (by frequency, transmission format, firmware, or software)—in the United States carriers even lock handsets designed to allow multiple carrier access by changing an easily inserted subscriber identity module (SIM); by using firmware "upgrades" to "brick" the handset—render it inoperative—or disable third-party firmware and software; by disabling handset functions, such as Bluetooth (short-range wireless connectivity), Wi-Fi (wireless networking) access, Internet browsers, GPS (satellite navigation) services, and setup for e-mail clients; by specifying formats for accessing memory—for example, music, ringtones, and photos; by creating walled-garden access to favored video content of affiliates and partners; and by using proprietary, nonstandard interfaces making it difficult for third parties to develop compatible applications and content.

Cellular service subscribers increasingly recognize how carrier-mandated limitations on handsets have little to do with legitimate network management or customer service objectives.[76] When handsets provided access primarily to voice telephone calls, text messaging, and ringtones, subscribers may have ignored limitations that block access to more sophisticated functions and access to third-party software, applications, or content. Only recently have cell phone subscribers begun to identify the forgone or limited options resulting from this decision. For example, a significant percentage of Apple iPhone purchasers[77] have risked loss of warranty coverage and the possibility that their handset will be bricked and thereby turned into an expensive paperweight in order to evade limitations on which wireless carrier, software, applications, and content they can access. Apple and its exclusive U.S. vendor, AT&T, emphasize that their handset users can access more than one hundred thousand applications, with flexibility and options far exceeding what other handset users have. But consumers would object vigorously to having any software or content access limitation imposed by an Internet service provider, wireline telephone company, or computer manufacturer.

As a result of the FCC's *Carterfone* decision and its subsequent orders, wireline telecommunications services have no direct control over what devices subscribers can acquire and connect to the telephone network. Telephone companies used to bundle telephone handset rentals, installation and maintenance of inside wiring at customers' premises, and telephone service. Consumers had no way of knowing the actual cost of each item, nor could they opt out and procure and use their own telephones and arrange their own wiring. When the FCC ordered the unbundling of telephone service from wiring and accessing devices, a competitive market evolved for both the installation of premises wiring and for devices that attach to telecommunications networks.[78] Consumers now take for granted the legally enforceable right to possess and connect their own telephones, facsimile machines, modems, and computers to wireline telecommunications networks and to use the same phone when changing carriers and locations.

The FCC never has stated that its *Carterfone* policy applies equally to wireless carriers when providing telecommunications services. Absent such an affirmative declaration by the FCC, most consumers accept the default option of buying handsets from wireless carriers and "big box" stores when they acquire or renew cellular telephone service.[79] Wireless carriers currently offer no discount-service plans for subscribers who bring their own handsets and do not trigger any subsidy requirements. Without such a discount on service, consumers have no incentive to make do with older handsets, because they cannot secure cheaper monthly service rates if they do use them. Accordingly, consumers regularly renew service when they replace their handsets, and the contract for such bundled service includes language permitting the carrier to disable equipment features and limit the manner in which subscribers access third-party content, services, and applications.

The FCC has articulated a long-standing concern about vertical integration—the combination of separate market activities by a single enterprise[80]—when undertaken by video content creators and distributors in light of the likelihood for harm to consumers. Because cable television companies and their corporate affiliates generate the vast majority of desired video content and control the major medium for distributing the content, the FCC worries that they can stifle competition, extract rates above competitive levels from subscribers, favor affiliated content providers, and retard development of new content sources. This concern for the consumer and worry about market failure in connection with cable television companies contrasts with the Commission's lack of concern in connection with similarly integrated providers of mobile telephone service, despite documented proof that cellular telephone companies have blocked access to competitive services.

The FCC recently released a report and order[81] that extends the ban of exclusive contracts between vertically integrated programmers and cable operators to October 5, 2012.[82] It determined that vertically integrated programmers still have the ability[83] and the incentive[84] to favor operators with whom they have a corporate affiliation over competitors.[85] Given the FCC's determination that vertically integrated ventures still control "must have" content, for which no viable substitute exists,[86] it retained the prohibition against contracts for exclusive content distribution from ventures that vertically integrate content production and distribution to consumers.

The FCC recognizes that vertical integration in video content creation and distribution requires regulatory intervention. Wireless operators operate in a similarly integrated mode. The top two carriers, AT&T and Verizon, control over 55 percent of the wireless market[87] and are owned by the ventures that have substantial market share in broadband wireline access, by, for example, DSL[88] or fiber-optic cable links, and wireline telephone services. In addition to the possible market power accruing from commanding a share of the wireless industry, AT&T and Verizon, in conjunction with many other wireless carriers, vertically integrate by securing exclusive content distribution rights for carriage via their wireless networks. They horizontally integrate[89] by bundling triple-play[90] and quadruple-play service packages[91] combining wireless service with wireline telephony, Internet access, and wireline video program access.

As the Internet increasingly becomes the focal point and preferred medium for all ICE services, ventures such as AT&T and Verizon have great opportunities to leverage their size, vertical integration, and horizontal integration to offer competitive facilities-based alternatives to incumbent providers such as cable television operators. On the other hand, these carriers currently face none of the structural safeguards that the FCC has appropriately placed on vertically integrated cable television ventures such as Comcast and Time Warner.

Nothing prevents any wireless operator, including AT&T and Verizon, from engaging in the anticompetitive practices that the Commission seeks to prevent in the cable television marketplace, a plausible outcome given the strong incentives for major telephone companies to find and dominate new markets to compensate for declining revenues from core wireline telephone markets. The FCC apparently assumes that having four wireless operators in a market prevents any single carrier or group of colluding carriers from harming consumers by favoring owned or affiliated content providers. Likewise, the FCC appears unconcerned about the ability of companies having a dominant market share in wireless telephony, broadband Internet access, and wireline telephony to leverage bundled service packages into market dominance in most ICE markets.

TILTING THE VOIP PLAYING FIELD, FCC STYLE

The FCC has made a plausible case for deregulation based on existing or prospective competition and the ability of the marketplace to self-regulate. But for this campaign to pass muster with reviewing courts the FCC must offer more than rhetoric and questionable statistics. Actual market entry and marketplace success by new ventures would help corroborate the FCC's theoretical arguments and assumptions. Accordingly, we would expect the FCC to make a special effort to incubate new technologies and provide a nurturing regulatory approach, one that avoids imposing unnecessary regulations, particularly since market entrants start with no market share.

The FCC typically avoids regulating enterprises with little market share and no market power—that is, those without the ability to affect the price or supply of a service. Yet when it comes to Voice over Internet Protocol service, the Commission appears to go out of its way to impose regulations as though VoIP operators had extensive market share and provided the functional equivalent of telephone service. In fact, VoIP service offered on a stand-alone basis by companies unaffiliated with incumbent telephone and cable television ventures has an insignificant market share. The largest independent VoIP operator had 2.6 million subscribers, out of a total 118.2 million telephone subscribers, in 2007[92] and had a subscriber-discontinuation-of-service (churn) rate of 3.3 percent.[93]

Nevertheless, the FCC has imposed a variety of regulations on VoIP service that can connect with traditional wireline telephone lines. Rather than treat VoIP carriers with the same sort of regulatory forbearance that it applies to wireless telephone service providers and increasingly to wireline service providers, the FCC has saddled VoIP service carriers with regulatory burdens that make VoIP service more like conventional telephone service at the expense of reducing its competitive cost advantage.[94] VoIP service providers, which offer subscribers telephone-calling access to the conventional wireline public switched telephone network (PSTN) or to wireless networks, must contribute to universal service funding[95] and reconfigure their service to provide wiretapping capabilities to law enforcement authorities,[96] caller location identification and emergency-911 access,[97] and service to disabled users.[98] Despite extensive rhetoric about refraining from imposing regulation on both emerging technologies and competitive services,[99] the FCC has chosen not to allow the marketplace to determine whether considerable service discounts available from VoIP service providers outweigh the risk in an emergency and the inconvenience for some users.

The FCC has imposed costly market-countervailing public-interest obligations on VoIP operators because it believes that inadequate public-access issues warrant speedy administrative remedies. VoIP service providers must reconfigure their networks to provide additional types of services and access that they had not contemplated or had not wished to provide. Regardless of whether they want to position their services as the functional alternative to existing wireline or wireless services, the FCC has imposed a number of requirements that force closer equivalency. It made no assessment of the financial costs incurred by VoIP providers or the potential adverse impact on competition and service rates borne by the public. It seems to have elevated regulatory parity concerns over its general concern to avoid imposing regulatory burdens on market entrants having a minor market share. Such intervention must have occurred because the Commission identified several instances of market failure, instances when market forces were unable to generate outcomes that it considered essential for the public interest. VoIP service providers must adjust their business plans to accommodate the FCC's regulatory requirements.

THE RADIO SPECTRUM SWEEPSTAKES

Both Congress and the FCC have discovered the value of the radio spectrum and its ability to generate billions of dollars for the national treasury. The FCC used to give away spectrum in exchange for licensees' agreement to serve the public interest, an ambiguous criterion that made it possible for the FCC to serve as a traffic cop—allocating and assigning spectrum licenses primarily to avoid spectrum interference—and to regulate the content carried over the airwaves. The FCC continues to assign some licenses for allocated spectrum uses when it believes that the public interest payoff of free use exceeds what the Commission could generate in cash for the national treasury.

Using that calculus, the FCC always offers broadcasters spectrum free of charge, presumably because the public greatly benefits from commercial, advertiser-supported media that offer content free of charge. Viewers and listeners of broadcast television and radio can consume without buying the products and services advertised. This "free rider" principle and the assumption that broadcasting promotes civic engagement has provided the basis for access to free spectrum. In the transition to digital television, broadcasters had the opportunity to use a second six-megahertz channel to simulcast both a digital and an analog signal. Having established a 2009 deadline for the conversion to all digital television,[100] the FCC has reallocated some broadcast television spectrum for nonbroadcast services. It generated more than nineteen billion dollars when it auctioned off the rights to use the "reharvested" spectrum. Verizon and AT&T acquired most of the auctioned licenses, thereby foreclosing prospects for wireless broadband market entry by one or more ventures.[101]

In addition to broadcasting, other licensed services qualify on public interest grounds to be excluded from having to bid money for the right to use radio spectrum. These special users include most satellite operators, public safety users such as police departments, and a variety of public and private network operators, such as microwave carriers that deliver telephone calls and video programming and handle Internet traffic.

The FCC also has the option of offering spectrum primarily for private use without a license, on a shared basis. Unlicensed users incur the risk of having to share spectrum, which could lead to harmful interference that prevents successful use of the spectrum. Despite this risk, shared use of unlicensed spectrum offers individual users an opportunity to extract the value of spectrum. Unlicensed spectrum is used by Wi-Fi networking, baby monitors, cordless telephones, low-cost and low-powered voice communications using spectrum allocated for the Family Radio Service, and garage door openers, among others.

Because of the potential to accrue billions of dollars by licensing spectrum to the highest bidders, the FCC has a strong motivation to auction spectrum to individual licensees. Nor do those with licenses to bid want the FCC to allocate or reallocate spectrum that can be used by unlicensed individuals who otherwise would have to pay for retail services offered by a licensed spectrum operator. For example, cellular telephone service carriers, which had to bid for most of the spectrum they use, would object if sufficient numbers of unlicensed Wi-Fi service users accessed free or inexpensive voice telephone and Internet service. Even though most consumers would prefer to pay for a reliable and professionally provisioned service, cellular companies would not want to risk losing any revenues to consumers willing to tolerate inferior and potentially unavailable voice communications service via Wi-Fi. Manufacturers of cellular radiotelephones have introduced models capable of accessing Wi-Fi networks, but because cellular telephone companies sell most handsets in the United States and, as major buyers, have substantial clout with handset manufacturers, most consumers do not have the option to buy Wi-Fi compatible handsets, and some wireless carriers disable the Wi-Fi access function in the handsets they sell. Even the widely loved and flexible Apple iPhone can access the Skype VoIP service only via local Wi-Fi islands and not via AT&T.[102] Unlike some carriers that disable Wi-Fi access via cell phones, AT&T could not block Apple's interest in making handsets operate more like wireless computers than like simple phones. But the financial stakes were too high for AT&T to allow its subscribers to substitute cheap Skype international long-distance minutes for expensive AT&T minutes that combine airtime with substantial surcharges for international calls.

However, when handsets help sustain market share, some wireless carriers embrace conditional use of unlicensed applications. For example, a new type of handset will be able to access equipment installed by cell phone companies and located in subscribers' offices and residences. This "femtocell" will operate as an interface with the cell phone company but within the users' premises, making it possible for subscribers to use handsets that access both femtocells and conventional cell phone towers. The femtocell might operate on the cellular company's licensed spectrum, or it might use Wi-Fi frequencies to provide access to the cell phone company's local and long-distance telephone services without accessing the cell phone company's towers.

The main point here is that spectrum has value, sometimes substantial value. Who can extract that value and how much they have to pay for the privilege will vary greatly. Licensees, particularly those who have paid for spectrum or who view unlicensed operation as a potential competitor, will use sponsored research, lobbying, litigation, and other strategies to keep the FCC from expanding the amount of unlicensed spectrum. The latest battle over whether to allow unlicensed access to spectrum involves unused broadcast television frequencies. These so-called white spaces offer a large amount of bandwidth at frequencies likely to enable reliable short-distance transmission of voice and data traffic without causing interference to licensed operations.[103] Predictably, broadcasters, who have failed to identify any real potential for interference, want the FCC to prohibit such access. Broadcasters want to prevent any undermining of their exclusive right of access even to spectrum allocated for broadcasting but not used by broadcasters.

THE FCC'S LAX SCRUTINY OF MERGERS AND ACQUISITIONS

Over the past few years the FCC has rarely confronted a merger or an acquisition that it could not find a way to approve. The FCC has approved multibillion-dollar mergers that have reduced the number of major wireline and wireless telephone companies, satellite carriers, and independent content providers.[104] It typically rationalizes the merger as a way to promote competition and serve the public interest, even though the merged company, created when one company acquired another, has a larger market share than either single company, and the market has one fewer competitor.

Mergers and acquisitions can make business sense and not harm the public interest, particularly if substantial competition remains. In an age of converging technologies and markets, ventures may need to get larger to achieve the kind of scale and operate with the kind of efficiency that current conditions require. On the other hand, a merger makes it possible to buy market share and to eliminate a pesky competitor.

Yet again the FCC appears disinclined to conduct rigorous, empirical research to determine whether a merger will result in harmful concentration of ownership and control or whether it represents a prudent business decision to acquire scale efficiencies. Time after time, the FCC resorts to the same bromides about enhanced efficiency and competition without harm to the public interest. To assuage stakeholders with legitimate concerns about dangerous concentration and diminished competition, it manages to secure "voluntary" concessions from acquiring parties that mitigate some anticompetitive impact. Below are summaries of two blockbuster mergers and the concessions that the FCC secured from the acquiring companies.

AT&T and BellSouth

The FCC approved AT&T's merger with BellSouth in light of significant voluntary concessions made by AT&T to break an impasse between Republican and Democratic commissioners.[105] The Commission concluded that significant public interest benefits would accrue from this $84.5 billion merger based on the following consumer benefits: deployment of broadband throughout the entire AT&T–BellSouth in-region territory in 2007; increased competition in the market for advanced-pay television services due to AT&T's ability to deploy Internet Protocol (IP)–based video services more quickly than BellSouth could do so without the merger; improved wireless products, services, and reliability due to the efficiencies gained by unified management of Cingular Wireless, a joint venture operated by BellSouth and AT&T; enhanced national security, disaster recovery, and government services through the creation of a unified end-to-end IP-based network capable of providing efficient and secure government communications; and improved disaster response and preparation from the companies because of unified operations.

Despite unconditional approval of the merger by the Justice Department, the FCC's two Democratic commissioners opposed the merger without binding conditions imposed by the FCC or similar conditions voluntarily imposed by AT&T. In a letter to the FCC on December 28, 2006, AT&T committed itself to such conditions; it promised to make available broadband Internet access service by December 31, 2007, to 100 percent of the residential living units in the AT&T–BellSouth service regions and to roll out unregulated fiber-optic-based facilities reaching at least 1.5 million homes, caps on prices, and discounting of high-speed data transmission services. AT&T also conditionally agreed to provide neutral, nondiscriminatory Internet access.

The latter two commitments warrant closer scrutiny for two reasons: (1) the unprecedented statement by the FCC chairman and one of the Commission's Republican commissioners that neither they nor the FCC should hold AT&T to its pricing commitments, which they considered the reimposition of price regulation, and (2) the selective nature of AT&T's commitment to neutral Internet access. On the matter of AT&T's commitment to refrain from exercising the deregulatory pricing flexibility that it had previously secured from the FCC, the Republican officials stated that "even when AT&T attempts to fulfill its merger commitments by filing tariffs, the Commission is not bound to approve these tariffs. Indeed, consistent with the Commission's prior policies and precedent, we would oppose such discriminatory practices and would encourage such tariffs to be rejected."[106]

AT&T's commitment to Internet neutrality appears generous until we consider its practical ramifications. AT&T committed itself to "conduct[ing] business in a manner that comports with the principles set forth"[107] in the Commission's statement of the principles of network neutrality policy for thirty months running from the merger closing date.[108] However, AT&T limited its neutral network operation and routing commitment to its wireline broadband Internet access service, that is, DSL service, and not to the fiber-optic network that it will emphasize in the future for video and higher-speed broadband service. In addition, AT&T limited its commitment to network neutrality to the pathway linking end users to the closest location where it receives and hands off Internet traffic with other carriers. These reservations provide AT&T with the means to operate next-generation Internet networks with no network neutrality obligations.

Adelphia Assets

The FCC approved letting Time Warner Cable and Comcast Corporation acquire assets held by bankrupt Adelphia Communications Corporation.[109] The transaction involved an exchange of certain cable systems and assets between affiliates or subsidiaries of Time Warner and Comcast, the redemption of Comcast's interests in Time Warner Cable and Time Warner Entertainment Company, and compliance with several FCC-imposed conditions designed to prevent anticompetitive practices.

In reaching its decision, the FCC found that the transactions, as conditioned, would serve the public interest and would comply with all applicable statutes and Commission rules. It determined that subscribers would benefit from the resolution of the Adelphia bankruptcy proceeding in the form of new investment in and upgrades to the network. The FCC also concluded that the transactions would accelerate deployment of VoIP and other advanced video services, such as local video-on-demand programming, to subscribers.

To guard against the potential for harm to the sports-programming marketplace, the FCC imposed "remedial" conditions on Time Warner and Comcast ownership and operation of Regional Sports Networks (RSNs). These conditions match the safeguards imposed by the commission on News Corporation when the company acquired the direct broadcast satellite operator DirecTV.[110] The FCC also imposed conditions to safeguard the supply and accessibility of other video programming types to multichannel video program distributors. Unaffiliated RSNs unable to reach a carriage agreement with Time Warner or Comcast and unaffiliated programmers unable to reach a leased-access agreement both have the FCC-prescribed right to seek commercial arbitration.

CHAPTER FIVE

Best and Worst Practices

DESPITE CONFIDENT assertions about a robustly competitive ICE marketplace, state and federal telecommunications regulators in the United States still maintain a complex, expensive, and woefully flawed mechanism to subsidize access to basic, "lifeline" telephone service and, in limited instances, broadband access to the Internet. Residents in remote areas and Indian reservations, poor people, schools, libraries, and rural medical facilities qualify for subsidized access on the grounds that market failure has occurred in terms of both geographical penetration and affordability.

As articulated in section 254 of the Telecommunications Act of 1996, the FCC and a Federal-State Joint Board on Universal Service, composed of representative commissioners, must find ways to ensure that "[c]onsumers in all regions of the Nation, including low-income consumers and those in rural, insular, and high cost areas, should have access to telecommunications and information services, including interexchange services and advanced telecommunications and information services, that are reasonably comparable to those services provided in urban areas and that are available at rates that are reasonably comparable to rates charged for similar services in urban areas."[1]

The U.S. Congress has explicitly stated that the FCC must mitigate differences in market-driven costs of service and access between densely populated and remote areas and between regions where telephone companies incur high costs and areas where they can operate more efficiently and cheaply. Despite a clear preference for competition-driven self-regulation, few carrier managers object to the concept of a universal service funding (USF) mechanism, because they stand to benefit by receiving financial subsidies to support projects that they may have pursued even without government financial sponsorship. Critics of the USF regime object to a process that draws more than seven billion dollars annually from wireline, wireless, and some Voice over Internet Protocol telephone service subscribers and largely redistributes the money into the treasuries of incumbent carriers so that they can offer below-cost services to several constituencies. Apparently this type of marketplace distortion serves the public interest, even though the current subsidy mechanism cannot achieve complete success and taper down the amount of annual subsidies, because carriers identify what costs they need to recoup annually to provide subsidized services.

At the very time that a digital divide separates people with cheap and plentiful broadband access from those without, the FCC maintains a system largely designed to subsidize basic telephone service by applying a 10–11 percent surcharge on long-distance telephone service. Because the USF program mostly funds telephone companies that confer service discounts to qualified individuals, these carriers have every incentive to continue showing a subsidy need rather than employing new and cheaper technologies, such as VoIP and wireless telephone service, and adopting cost-cutting and efficiency-enhancing strategies. The carriers get to specify service areas with an eye toward extracting maximum subsidization, and no effective accounting and auditing mechanisms exist for corroborating carrier-disclosed costs.

Universal service funding, from its inception, has served political objectives first and the public interest second. Historically the universal service mission provided the rationale for preserving the national monopoly of Bell Telephone Companies,[2] transferring funds from urban to rural carriers and from long-distance callers to local service subscribers, subsidizing service even for consumers quite able to afford the full price, and making it possible for regulators to showcase extraordinarily cheap local calling rates.

THE UNIVERSAL SERVICE MISSION IN THE UNITED STATES

Most nations consider ubiquitous and low-cost access to basic telecommunication services a worthy public policy objective in the same vein as promoting access to electricity and water. "Telecommunications is not simply a connection between people, but a link in the chain of the development process itself," as one observer puts it.[3] A real, but not easily measured or quantified, correlation exists between access to telecommunications facilities and services and economic development.[4] This means that efficient, effective, and widely available telecommunications services can stimulate social and economic development by providing the vehicle for more and better commerce, political discourse, education, and delivery of government services, including job training, the issuance of permits, licenses, and other types of authorizations, and dissemination of information.[5]

A fundamental problem in achieving universal access to basic and advanced telecommunication services lies not in the goal itself but in developing cost-effective strategies for financing and achieving the goal, particularly if next-generation broadband access becomes a part of the mission. From the onset of universal service funding, lofty concepts of equity and equal opportunity have intertwined with other objectives. For example, in the early part of the twentieth century, the senior management of AT&T recognized that promoting universal service, using an internally generated financial subsidy, achieved the twin goals of promoting aspects of universal service and gaining support from unaffiliated rural telephone companies and politicians for allowing a "benevolent" Bell System to dominate the U.S. telecommunications industry.[6] Both elected government representatives and unelected government regulators recognize the benefits accruing from offering to citizen constituencies below-cost access to telephone services, particularly when the subsidizing parties—the citizen constituents—do not know how much the subsidies cost.

Until enactment of the Telecommunications Act in 1996, consumers of telecommunications services bore a universal service subsidy obligation without knowing the cost, because the FCC and state regulatory agencies could hide the expense primarily through high per-minute long-distance telephone charges. Using an implicit subsidy mechanism obscured the cost of the universal service mission as well as whether subsidy burdens blunted demand and caused other market distortions. Consumers could not readily determine the scope of their subsidy contribution, because carriers did not subdivide their single per-minute rates into specific line items on bills; there was no listed surcharge for universal service.

The universal service mission in the United States requires carriers to ensure that the largest possible number of residents have access to basic telephone service regardless of income and geographical location. Unlike in other nations, carriers and not the federal government have devised and managed the process of collecting and distributing universal service funds, as well as establishing the cost allocation and accounting rules used to determine the actual subsidy amounts flowing to telephone companies. This privately managed process put carriers in the position of charging rates that built in universal service subsidies. The carriers largely retained those surcharges in exchange for charging lower rates to preferred constituencies and for transferring part of the surcharge amount to carriers operating in high-cost, largely rural areas.

The Telecommunications Act of 1996 requires explicit subsidies,[7] codifies the universal service mission,[8] and establishes specific requirements for the FCC, including implementation of near parity of cost and access for rural subscribers. Carriers have responded to the explicit subsidy requirement by billing subscribers for the specific cost of universal service. For the second quarter of 2009, the "contribution factor" surcharge in subscribers' bills amounted to 11.3 percent of the interstate and international end-user service revenues of wireline, wireless, and interconnected VoIP carriers,[9] a rate that adds several dollars per month to the average consumer's bill.

The act also expanded the universal service mission to include discounted rates for basic (telephone service) and advanced (Internet access) telecommunications services by schools and libraries, commonly known as the E-Rate program, and subsidies for discounted access to services by rural nonprofit health-care providers.[10] After the Telecommunications Act of 1996 became law, the FCC delegated authority for collecting and distributing universal service funding to a nonprofit corporation known as the Universal Service Administrative Company (USAC).[11]

Universal service funding supports four programs:

1. The Low Income Program reimburses local wireline and some wireless telephone companies for providing service discounts to qualifying low-income consumers.[12] The LinkUp America program offsets half of the initial hook-up fee, up to thirty dollars. The program also encourages carriers to offer a deferred payment schedule for the initial installation fee. The Lifeline Assistance Program provides a discount of up to ten dollars per month for basic telephone service. Residents of American Indian and Alaska Native communities may qualify for up to an additional twenty-five dollars in support beyond current Lifeline support levels and expanded LinkUp support of up to seventy dollars in additional support beyond current levels. In 2008 this program provided $817.46 million in support.[13]
2. The High-Cost Program provides financial support to local wireline and some wireless telephone companies that offer telecommunications services in areas where the cost of providing service exceeds a national or state average by at least 115 percent to 135 percent, depending on the type of cost elements supported. High-cost areas are divided into rural and non-rural locales and have six different cost areas: (a) the first and last mile connection, known as the local loop; (b) the facilities used to switch traffic for companies lacking optimal scale economies, because they serve fewer than fifty thousand telephone lines; (c) long-term support for small carriers, subject to rate-of-return regulation, that do not fully recover, through the access charge fees imposed on long-distance carriers, the costs incurred in originating and terminating long-distance traffic; (d) interstate access support, a similar access charge as a financial offset for larger carriers subject to a cap on the rates they can charge; (e) financial support for non-rural carriers operating in areas with costs exceeding 135 percent of the statewide average; and (f) interstate common-line support for carriers with a small rate of return that do not fully recover their per-line costs from telephone subscribers who now pay a monthly $6.50 subscriber-line charge. In 2008 this program provided $4.47 billion in support.[14]
3. The E-Rate program for schools and libraries[15] provides discounts of between 10 percent and 90 percent, based on the percentage of students eligible for subsidized lunches, for access to basic, local, and long-distance telecommunications services, including voice, data,

video, and wireless services, Internet access, and the cost of installing and maintaining internal connections, including switches, hubs, routers, and wiring. A maximum of $2.25 billion is available annually; $1.769 billion was awarded in 2008.[16]

4. The Rural Health Care Program ensures that health-care providers located in rural areas pay no more than their urban counterparts for telecommunications services, including those "telemedicine" services needed to access advanced diagnostic and other medical services available at urban medical centers. In 2008 this program awarded $49.474 million.[17]

MACRO-LEVEL PROBLEMS WITH THE CURRENT SYSTEM

Marketplace Distortion

At the macro level, the current system for universal service funding distorts the marketplace for local and long-distance telephone services by creating artificial pricing signals.[18] Now that by law the FCC must establish a transparent subsidy process, experts and even ordinary consumers have a better sense of how much the USF regime costs. A line item on telecommunications service bills keeps growing higher over time, as does consumer resentment at what many perceive to be a tax, despite FCC-mandated language in bills disputing this perception.[19] Just about every carrier recovers its USF burden as a separate billing line item passed on to subscribers, which makes this charge look like other billing line charges that collect an actual tax.

The number of taxes, fees, and surcharges on telephone bills now matches the number imposed by car rental companies and airlines. Some entrepreneurial companies have recognized that they can accrue a substantial cost-of-business discount by configuring telephone services to avoid triggering USF and other regulatory burdens. Savvy consumers have adopted similar self-help strategies. Carrier and consumer tactics to save money by avoiding USF burdens primarily rely on the inconsistent, asymmetrical regulatory treatment of functionally equivalent services. The FCC exempts information services from USF contribution requirements, even though some of these services, including intra-corporate VoIP networks, offer consumers an alternative to basic telecommunications services whose providers have to make USF contributions.[20] Some telecommunications service providers and users have found ways to get voice communications, like those offered via VoIP, delivered via the conventional public switched telephone network (PSTN) without making USF contributions.

The Potential for Substantial Future Deficits

Technological innovations, conflicting FCC regulatory objectives, and a recent Supreme Court case jeopardize the financial viability of the current USF regime. The migration from analog to digital networks makes it possible for voice services to become a possibly free software application that rides on the link provided by Internet access services such as DSL and cable modems.[21] Currently, VoIP and other services provide a relatively small volume of voice telephony traffic in comparison to the traditional dial-up circuit-switched telephone services offered by wireline telephone companies. However, the very real potential exists for packet-switched Internet Protocol networks to become the primary medium for most voice and data services. Should this occur, information services will constitute the primary retail end-user service provided by those networks.

Although carriers providing information services need not make a USF contribution, the FCC has several motivations to classify as many services as possible as information services. It has wisely decided to refrain from automatically applying legacy regulations to services that might operate in a competitive marketplace and that might incubate and develop more robustly without substantial government intrusion. But instincts and incentives for deregulation or limited regulation have emboldened the Commission to extend the information service classification to include telecommunications services, among them ones, such as DSL, that it previously declined to classify as information services.

Poor Calibration of Benefits and Burdens

Since the principal goal of USF is to improve telephone subscriptions and line penetration, commonly referred to as teledensity, the current regime must get low points. USF provides financial benefits to some consumers fully capable of paying the full cost of the telecommunication services they use. These telephone subscribers do not need financial support, but their telephone company can qualify for USF support based on the costs it identifies for geographical areas it specifies in order to maximize the need for subsidies. Wealthy landowners, residing in rural enclaves in, say, Vail and Aspen, Colorado, pay a fraction of what they could and should pay were it not for a USF system that rewards them for residing within a high-cost telephone service area that includes less well-off residents in nearby rural locales. Other beneficiaries of the USF regime can acquire basic telephone services for a price well below what they might willingly pay. Nor does the USF system exclude from subsidization the costs incurred by a carrier located in a high-cost area that provides service to more than one telephone at a single residence, or incurred by two or more carriers serving the same high-cost area. Until reform initiatives in 2008, a second carrier serving the same high-cost area used the cost calculations of the first serving company, typically the incumbent wireline carrier, even if the newly eligible carrier had lower costs because it used more efficient technologies, such as wireless services.

The USF regime also imposes contribution obligations on consumers, including the working poor and others not well equipped to absorb an increased financial burden. The current surcharge paid by all dial-up long-distance telephone users places a comparatively higher burden on heavy users, who might include individuals with incomes just above the subsidy-qualifying level. For some telephone subscribers in suburban areas, many short-distance telephone calls trigger a toll charge and a USF contribution. Ironically, for these subscribers a cellular telephone might offer cheaper service, with VoIP offering an even greater discount if reasonably priced Internet access exists.

Inflexibility

Quite generous subsidies for basic service leave no funds available for targeting non-subscribers who would qualify for subsidized service but who do not currently subscribe. Little empirical research has been done to examine why people do not subscribe to basic telephone services and what strategies might create new and effective incentives for them to subscribe. Perhaps qualifying but nonparticipating individuals might prefer a telecommunications option other than basic dial-up voice service. With greater flexibility a USF system might offer these non-users the option of applying the amount of the wireline voice service discount to a wireless or high-speed connection.

Promotion of Avoidance Strategies

Telephone subscribers paying heavy monthly USF support may grow weary of this subsidy obligation and explore self-help options that reduce or eliminate their contributions. Through clever but not always lawful strategies, carriers, too, can eliminate their USF-support burdens by devising services that offer long-distance calling but that qualify for a regulatory classification other than telecommunications service. AT&T attempted to characterize long-distance calling-card service as an information service based on its insertion of recorded information during call setup. The FCC rejected this interpretation,[22] but instead of declaring all calling-card operators subject to USF liability, it initiated a rulemaking to examine the matter more broadly.

The price of basic dial-up telephone service in the United States has retarded the rollout of and subscription to advanced services. With rates typically not exceeding thirty-six dollars a month for unlimited local calling,[23] consumers may balk at adding broadband services that can cost double that amount. Consumers may stick with dial-up access to the Internet using modems attached to their telephone lines because they incur no additional charge for expanding usage of the local loop paid for on an unmetered, fixed monthly (all you can eat) rate. Users in other nations have migrated more readily to broadband service because many can reduce their out-of-pocket Internet access costs by doing so. For nations where carriers charge for local calling on a metered basis, consumers can reduce their Internet access costs by acquiring unmetered, usage-insensitive DSL or cable modem access.

Support of Narrowband Dial-Up Service

The emphasis on promoting basic service line penetration has a perversely negative effect on broadband market penetration. Except for schools, libraries, and rural medical facilities, current USF funding does not support access to broadband services. The combination of low dial-up telephone rates, comparatively high broadband rates, and no USF program outside three select constituencies helps explain why the United States currently does not rank in the top tier of industrialized nations in terms of broadband penetration. Not all U.S. carriers offer Internet access that is inexpensive in global comparisons or in terms of the best practices of carriers operating in robustly competitive markets. Growing competition, particularly in urban areas, may promote significant downward pressure on broadband rates, but rural localities may lack broadband options. Concerns about an urban-rural digital divide remain credible where robust facilities-based competition does not exist. For example, most DSL services cannot extend beyond fifteen thousand feet from a telephone company switching facility, which limits the DSL option in many suburban, exurban, and rural locales.

MICRO-LEVEL PROBLEMS WITH THE CURRENT SYSTEM

Preservation of the Status Quo

At the micro level the current USF system has created several constituencies keen on maintaining the status quo regardless of its efficacy and efficiency. Elected officials perceive a benefit in helping to maintain below-cost telephone service for some constituents. The Universal Service Administrative Company[24] has every incentive to make itself indispensable, even though its primary duty lies in the seemingly straightforward task of collecting and dispensing USF funds.[25] A cottage industry of USF consultants has developed to help school districts and libraries maneuver the USAC labyrinth of technology plans, forms, and reports for securing and retaining E-Rate funding.[26] Perhaps all too predictably, criminals have devised ways to defraud the USAC,[27] causing the FCC belatedly to increase audits and explore additional types of scrutiny.[28]

Individually and collectively, a large constituency has evolved for maintaining the status quo. Because the current USF regime involves discounted retail services and subsidies based on carrier-calculated costs, the universal service mission cannot be achieved. The USF process does not have a targeted goal, a point at which the FCC can declare partial or complete victory and establish a glide path for reducing subsidies.[29] The USF mechanism will apparently operate in perpetuity using monthly inbound contributions from interstate telecommunications subscribers, paid primarily to wireline and wireless local exchange carriers, which in turn discount their retail rates for select groups. Similarly, the system compensates carriers year in and year out based on the assumption that once a carrier operates in a high-cost area, it probably always will, even though demographic change might render a portion of an otherwise high-cost area more densely populated, cheaper to serve, or occupied primarily by wealthy individuals.

Few Auditing Safeguards

In the USF system, whatever costs carriers report are largely accepted, with no regard for whether carriers could operate more efficiently or whether new technologies might offer lower costs, particularly recurring operating costs—that is, costs regularly incurred in providing service. This means that neither the USAC nor the FCC does much by way of examining whether a carrier might more cheaply serve USF beneficiaries or, more broadly, whether USF goals are being reached.[30] Even though new technological options, such as fixed and mobile wireless services, might offer better value, the USF regime does not require competitive bidding among prospective service providers for the opportunity to receive subsidies to serve a high-cost area. The FCC now allows for multiple eligible telecommunications carriers (ETCs)[31] to serve the same rural and high-cost regions, but the carriers do not compete for the privilege. Instead, one ETC can tap into the USF funds otherwise allocated to another ETC, because universal service funding is "portable"[32] and can be reassigned on a per-line basis to another ETC without a net reduction in the total amount of the subsidy flowing to all carriers serving a specific high-cost area.[33]

An Abuse-Prone System

The current USF regime creates opportunities for fraud[34] and provides incentives for carriers and E-Rate beneficiaries to ignore technological innovations that would reduce their dependency on or qualification for subsidies. Arguably, a rural, high-cost telephone company could replace its expensive, high-maintenance analog copper-wire network with a possibly cheaper and more accessible wireless or VoIP alternative. Despite high initial sunk costs for the new network, much lower annual recurring costs might provide a cheaper way to provide service in the long term. However, carriers accrue no upside financial reward for taking the risk and making the investment in new technologies. The USF status quo assures a regular and predictable revenue flow with no risk and ample reward. As well, the current USF system expects carriers to have stable or increasing operating costs, even though new technologies offer the prospect of lower costs.

The USF also creates disincentives for beneficiaries to develop innovative alternatives to paying incumbent carriers for existing retail services. In specifying the types of services that qualify for subsidies, the USF regime emphasizes voice services to the detriment of data and Internet services and ensures that most money stays with or flows exclusively to incumbent carriers. Even the E-Rate system, which permits subsidies for Internet access, prevents schools and libraries from erecting wireless networks that could extend into a community, from aggregating requirements to qualify for higher-capacity services from carriers at lower per-unit costs, and from developing alternative Internet networks, such as the Internet-2 network used by a consortium of universities.[35]

Emphasis on Service Subscriptions

Instead of promoting pure and applied research and development aiming to solve access challenges, USF flows primarily to a small set of stakeholders who provide basic services and to constituencies receiving "tied aid," that is, funds tied to purchasing a narrow set of existing retail, commercial services primarily from incumbents.[36] Rather than promote a fair and transparent business environment, the USF rewards administrative skills, such as mastering the E-Rate application process and reliance on an incumbent carrier's voice network. With all the rhetoric about contestable if not competitive markets in telecommunications, the USF system appears somewhat anachronistic in supporting the perception that only "one carrier of last resort" can operate with limited technological options in rural and high-cost areas.

By emphasizing incumbent carriers' existing basic services, the USF regime does nothing to stimulate efforts to achieve digital literacy—to improve citizens' understanding of how best to use telecommunications technologies as tools for enhancing learning, medical care, access to electronic government (e-government) resources, and the quality of life. A school district or library finds it all too easy to follow a tried and true strategy to extract the most funding available from the E-Rate program rather than to think strategically on how best to achieve goals for which technology constitutes one part of the solution. In light of the growing complexity in telecommunications and information-processing technologies, USF beneficiaries might find it advantageous to develop at least some in-house expertise on using these technologies. Curiously, the USF does not readily support training in the design, installation, and maintenance of networks. Without such expertise USF beneficiaries have every incentive to outsource projects and to take generic services with little, if any, customization that might better meet special requirements.[37]

BEST PRACTICES IN PROMOTING ACCESS TO SERVICES

Nations other than the United States have consistently proven that more progress in promoting literacy in information and communication technologies (ICT), greater market penetration, and innovative uses can occur with less money, a smaller bureaucracy, and reduced marketplace distortion than are in place in the United States. Their best practices share the following characteristics:

- true technology neutrality coupled with a willingness to fund well-articulated and community-supported projects, whereas the United States tends to limit support to a fixed list of existing carrier services
- caps to government project funding set as a percentage of total cost, which requires project advocates to seek financial support from other grantors or from bank loans
- incentives for government and private users to aggregate demand, particularly for broadband and data services
- emphasis on onetime project funding rather than recurring discounts
- promotion of innovation and creativity in projects, including technologies that improve efficiency and reduce recurring costs
- encouragement of competition among universal service providers by auctioning off access to subsidies
- a blend of government stewardship and vision with incentives for private stakeholders to pursue infrastructure investments

Successful universal service programming requires governments to do more than throw money at the problem. If governments have no effective role in promoting universal service, then it might make sense simply to create a "phone stamps" program, with qualified beneficiaries receiving direct subsidies to treat as cash when paying for telephone and Internet access services. If governments have no function other than to order redistribution of telecommunication revenues, then they should limit their role to loan guarantor, as is the case in a parallel program administered by the U.S. Department of Agriculture.[38]

A government can provide constructive and desirable services as technology incubator, steward, partial underwriter, and anchor tenant user of ICT services without operating as central manager of the information economy. Some governments have successfully promoted universal service and infrastructure development by developing a vision of what market forces can achieve and augmenting it with limited and targeted support.[39] Best practices in the broader goal of ICT development show a promotional role for government through partial funding of specific projects while it primarily emphasizes private enterprise and facilities-based competition.

To support USF, governments in some nations blend efforts to develop digital literacy with financial support for procurement of equipment and services. Rather than limit USF funding to a closed and specific group of constituencies, as in the United States, some nations offer several types of financial support—loan guarantees, grants, and tax credits—to applicants that propose effective, efficient, and innovative ways to stimulate digital literacy and the provision of desirable services. Successful grant seekers know that they cannot buy equipment and lease services without giving thought to which equipment and services can satisfy specific community requirements, including health care, education, access to information, and government licensing.

Governments have a key role in developing safeguards to promote trust, security, privacy, and consumer protection in the access and use of ICE services, especially electronic commerce. Government stewardship is required, not heavy-handed, command-and-control, centralized management. Achieving improvements in ICE services requires both an articulated, cohesive, government-designed, top-down vision and user-proposed bottom-up projects in a community that can aggregate supply of services and demand for equipment and services. Best practices in ICE development do not rely exclusively or primarily on incumbent carriers to come up with innovative ways to serve a specific community's needs. Rather than rely on one-size-fits-all USF services, best practices typically come from innovative uses of technology proposed by and for users.

Best practices do not occur when incumbents have little incentive to innovate or to deviate from the status quo, nor do they occur when incumbents promote future investment in infrastructure by following a deregulatory or political agenda having little, if anything, to do with achieving the universal service mission. Governments can coordinate many possible funding strategies, including direct underwriting, loans, favorable tax treatment, and financial support for research, development, and technology-demonstration projects. Best practices also provide opportunities for residents to become suppliers and consumers of ICE services.

RESHAPING THE FCC'S MISSION

In view of changing technologies and consumer expectations, the concepts of universal access and universal service remain in flux. The FCC should reexamine the concept of universal access, including how it will accomplish the universal service mission articulated in the Telecommunications Act of 1996. It must propose an alternative to the current funding mechanism for universal service, because carriers can currently offer subscription-based, unlimited interstate voice traffic and avoid any USF burden.[40]

To begin with, the FCC should consider its universal service mandate in terms of four interrelated components:

1. Infrastructure—the scope and nature of networks that provide users with access to basic and advanced telecommunications and information services
2. Services—a revised determination of which services constitute basic lifeline services and which other services, including broadband, the FCC should include in its expanded universal service goals
3. Subsidizers—who should support universal service objectives and who could qualify for universal service subsidies for basic and advanced services
4. Maintenance and upgrades—what incentives regulators must create to ensure that universal service providers maintain and upgrade their networks but do not object to innovations, including user-operated telecommunications networks, that achieve scale, efficiency, and cost savings

With these four components in mind, Congress, the FCC, the USAC, subsidy contributors, and subsidy recipients must confront an acute, short-term problem: the potential for Internet-mediated telephone services and the expanding classification of USF-exempt information services to trigger a severe decline in revenues from interstate telecommunications services subject to the USF burden. As more and more long-distance traffic migrates to a USF-exempt safe harbor, consumers of conventional services will incur an increasing USF burden, most notably the USF contribution that carriers pass on to their customers as a billing line item. Consumers of conventional long-distance telephone service will quickly reach a state of compassion fatigue when they realize that their USF contribution grows while consumers of some VoIP services pay nothing. Strategies to avoid USF contributions will become the latest regulatory gaming opportunity, although the FCC should recognize the competitive harm and marketplace distortion caused by such strategies.

In the near term, the FCC will have to confront the likelihood that a minutes-of-use USF contribution scheme will become unsustainable. In reforming the policies and rules applicable to access charges paid by one carrier for interconnection with another carrier, it has readily acknowledged the inequity and poor calibration with actual cost recovery that results from use of time-based charging.[41] The FCC has launched a multiyear campaign to replace metered carrier-to-carrier access charges, particularly for recovering plant investment, whose cost does not vary with usage.[42] The Commission acknowledged the economic inefficiency in using a metered cost-recovery mechanism for non-traffic-sensitive plant investment, which constitutes a large portion of a telephone company's sunk costs. In other words, much of a carrier's investment does not vary with how much traffic traverses the network. This becomes clear when we note that installing the first and last few feet of copper wire linking a residence with the telephone network has a significant cost, but one that does not vary as a function of how many minutes the lines are used to originate and terminate calls.

Much of the cost incurred by carriers to achieve improved subscribership does not vary with usage, either; the number and density of subscribers taking the service and the average distance of the local loop linking a subscriber with telephone company facilities are among the variables that impact a carrier's cost of service. Accordingly, a minutes-of-use recovery system will overburden heavy users of interstate telecommunications services while recovering an insufficient contribution from light users whose local loop and network access still require the same carrier investment regardless of usage.[43]

The FCC should replace the current minutes-of-use USF contribution regime with either general taxpayer underwriting or a connection-based system that applies to the physical links used for telephone calls employing the current numbering system, regardless of whether calls traverse the Internet and combine with unregulated information services. Adding billions of dollars annually to the national budget would probably be politically unpopular, so a reformed user-financed USF system appears more feasible. In a connection-based regime the USF cost would be divided pro rata by the number of lines that a retail customer can use to receive or deliver voice-based telephone calls. Any subscriber to a service that can originate or terminate a call from or to a telephone handset would contribute to USF funding. This burden should be extended to ventures that require only call terminations, such as wireless to wireline network calls and vice versa. The USF burden should also apply to any VoIP service that may travel via a corporate or carrier network, including the Internet, but that eventually reaches a conventional telephone number.

This proposal may come across as controversial and unlawfully extending telecommunications service regulatory burdens on information services. However, the FCC retains jurisdiction, under Title I of the Communications Act of 1934, to subject information service providers to limited regulatory responsibilities that serve the public interest.[44] The court affirming the FCC's decision to require USF contributions from VoIP carriers determined that shoring up the USF regime constitutes an objective that reasonably serves the public interest.[45]

Another short-term strategy to achieve greater efficiency and cost saving in USF involves auctioning access to universal service subsidies.[46] Rather than accept the given costs of an incumbent carrier operating in a high-cost area, the FCC could auction access to USF to a carrier willing to provide service to a specific location with the least amount of subsidization. Currently, a telecommunications carrier can become eligible to receive USF funding regardless of whether it can operate more efficiently through, for example, the use of a cheaper and more efficient wireless network instead of a conventional copper-wireline network. The FCC[47] and many economists[48] tout the benefits of auctions for radio spectrum licenses and even satellite orbital slots.[49] The privilege of tapping into USF constitutes a franchise of sorts that, arguably, more than one venture might have an interest in securing, especially for exurban areas that may eventually become more densely populated and more profitably served than they now are.

FUTURE CHALLENGES AND REMEDIES

At some not-too-distant date ICE technologies and markets will converge, with the Internet serving as a central medium for access and delivery. In such an Internet-centric environment, most voice services will become available with the launch of software. The concept of dedicated, identifiable voice network links will become an artifact of the past as efficient bit transport bundles a variety of voice, audio, data, and video services. An Internet-centric ICE environment will make it impossible to fund universal service programs based on interstate telecommunications minutes of use.

The FCC's conceptualization of telephone service and voice telephony also will have to change. Obviously, people will continue to make telephone calls, but the calls will constitute but one feature of a rich and diverse array of services available via broadband networks. Because carriers may not have the technical capability to identify and meter their telephone customers' long-distance minutes of use, the FCC will need to devise a new and viable USF regime. Similarly, because broadband networks will have become the predominant medium for access and delivery of all ICE services, the FCC must consider universal service to include broadband delivery beyond schools, libraries, and rural clinics.

The expansion of the USF mission to include broadband even as the core funding source evaporates will surely present challenges, but it will also present opportunities for a more effective and versatile universal service mission. To facilitate this broader and more diversified sense of the universal service mission, the FCC should allow constituencies the opportunity to apply for and receive financial grants to pursue stand-alone telecommunications and information-processing projects in addition to, or in lieu of, discounted carrier services. Grants like those offered in Canada to stimulate rural access to telecommunications and information-processing services[50] would allow constituencies to aggregate demand, to link with geographically separate users, and to provide services otherwise unavailable from commercial ventures.

Canada and other nations have offered grants to community-based groups that deliver a variety of telecommunications and information-processing services to many different users, making it possible to create "smart communities" in quite remote areas; they have access to advanced services we would expect to be available exclusively in cities. Canada favors a bottom-up "community aggregator model," where government funding of programs and the delivery of electronic government services help stimulate the generation of sufficient demand to use existing network capacity and the construction of new facilities.

Incumbent carriers, as historically guaranteed beneficiaries of USF, predictably will oppose any expanded opportunities for universal service end-user beneficiaries to secure funding to construct networks and possibly provide some telecommunications services for themselves. In several states and municipalities, carriers have objected to community-based efforts to install and operate Wi-Fi data networks. Some state governments have enacted laws that prohibit such community initiatives or at least offer carriers the right of first refusal before allowing taxpayer financing of community initiatives.[51]

Carriers' oppose letting taxpayers underwrite telecommunications and information-processing networks because doing so shuts down private enterprise and risks substantial funds on ventures that may prove unsustainable. Community groups and governments may also lack expertise in managing such networks. However, USF operates in an environment where marketplace forces will not achieve the kind of service availability, subscribership, and prices that elected government officials believe would be optimal. If a rural town or a coalition of users seeks to operate a telecommunications or information-processing network, it is quite possible that no incumbent carrier offers, or is willing to provide, what the community wants.[52] Surely the universal service objectives contemplated by Congress are served when groups of schools, libraries, government agencies, or rural clinics propose to aggregate demand for facilities and services and achieve operational efficiencies by accessing their own quasi-public network rather than individually lease lower-capacity lines at a higher per-unit cost.

DEVELOPING NEW BROADBAND INFRASTRUCTURE

A substantial downturn in the global economy has renewed interest in using government funding to bolster the nation's infrastructure, including telecommunications networks. Both the Obama administration and a majority in Congress consider broadband development, especially in rural areas, an important element in a national strategy to spur economic development. The American Recovery and Reinvestment Act of 2009[53] allocated $4.7 billion to the National Telecommunications and Information Administration and $2.5 billion to the Agriculture Department's Rural Utilities Service program to encourage investment in and use of broadband services by awarding grants, loans, and loan guarantees.

NTIA, in consultation with the FCC, will administer the Broadband Technology Opportunities Program (BTOP). Its mandate is to facilitate access to broadband service by consumers residing in unserved areas of the United States. Other goals include improving access to, and use of, broadband service by public safety agencies; stimulating economic growth and job creation as well as demand for broadband; and providing broadband education, awareness, training, access, equipment, and support to schools, libraries, medical and health-care providers, community colleges and other institutions of higher education, and other community support organizations. While most of the allocated funds do not have specific earmarks, the law authorizes no less than $200 million for competitive grants to expand the capacity of public computer centers, primarily at community colleges and public libraries. A further sum of not less than $250 million is allocated for competitive grants proposing innovative programs to encourage sustainable adoption of broadband service. The law also includes funds for auditing and oversight of the funds allocated, plus up to $350 million for the purposes of developing and maintaining a inventory map of national broadband penetration.

The Agriculture Department's $2.5 billion will support a Distance Learning, Telemedicine and Broadband Program with financial grants, loans, and loan guarantees. The law requires that 75 percent of the area to be served by a project receiving financial support shall be in a rural area without sufficient access to high-speed broadband service to facilitate rural economic development, as determined by the secretary of agriculture. The law establishes a priority for projects that provide service to the highest proportion of rural residents who do not have access to broadband service and that offer end users a choice of more than one service provider. This program also establishes priority access for the telephone and cable television companies that currently have telecommunications loans or have previously borrowed money under the Rural Utilities Service program. Funds from the Agriculture Department's allocation cannot support any project already receiving funding under the NTIA program.

The law requires the FCC to provide a report to Congress containing a national broadband plan. The plan should seek to ensure that all Americans have access to broadband service, and it should specify benchmarks for meeting that goal. The plan must include an analysis of the most effective and efficient ways to ensure broadband access, with a detailed strategy to ensure affordability, including evaluation of ongoing projects and grants. The law requires NTIA to develop and maintain a comprehensive, nationwide, web-based inventory map of existing broadband service capability and availability in the United States, with specific information about the geographic reach of specific commercial and public network providers in each state.

The final version of the law lacks definitions for such key words as "unserved," "underserved," "broadband," and "high-speed broadband." This means that the involved government agencies, in consultation with the states and grant seekers, will have to establish baseline criteria. These criteria could easily include underserved urban areas in addition to remote locales. The law does not establish a preference for any type of broadband technology, nor does it favor public-sector over commercial ventures, except for the preference for existing or previous Rural Utilities Service borrowers.

The FCC launched a notice of inquiry to seek advice from all stakeholders on ways to facilitate and expedite the "build-out and utilization of high-speed broadband infrastructure"[54] with particular attention to such issues as:

- the most effective and efficient ways to ensure broadband access for all Americans
- strategies for achieving affordability and maximum utilization of broadband infrastructure and services
- evaluation of the status of broadband deployment, including the progress of related grant programs
- ways to use broadband to advance consumer welfare, civic participation, public safety and homeland security, community development, health-care delivery, energy independence and efficiency, education, worker training, private-sector investment, entrepreneurial activity, job creation, economic growth, and other national purposes

Because $7.2 billion allocated for broadband infrastructure development will not achieve the congressional goal of nationwide broadband deployment, the FCC must develop a plan that aims for ubiquitous broadband access with benchmarking to measure progress toward achieving that goal. It recognizes that increased infrastructure diffusion may require government-created incentives, similar to universal service funding for access to basic telephone services, in addition to marketplace competition. Government incentives will need to promote efficient and effective use of private and public funds for networks that may include wireless options, including open networks, such as Wi-Fi hot spots.

Despite having accepted broadband carriers' claims that where they do and do not provide service constitutes a trade secret, the FCC has recognized its statutory duty to compile market penetration data and to map progress geographically. The Commission has agreed to examine market penetration by census tract, instead of the much larger zip code areas, and to report service bitrates in several categories of speed. In addition, the Broadband Data Improvement Act of 2008[55] requires the FCC to include an international comparison in its annual broadband report and to conduct a consumer survey of broadband service capability.[56]

Technological innovations, declining sources of USF revenues, compassion fatigue on the part of telephone consumers, and changes in what a universal service mission should support make the current USF regime unsustainable. Internet telephony, such as VoIP, threatens the status quo by eliminating the distinction between local and long-distance telephony and between voice and data services. Declining revenues from conventional dial-up long-distance telephone service reduce the primary source of USF subsidies, thereby requiring ever-increasing contributions from consumers. An increasing number of consumers have noticed and become irritated by the USF contribution line item on their telephone bill. Intra-corporate and computer-mediated VoIP provide consumers with the opportunity to avoid making USF contributions and to reduce their expenses for long-distance telephone calls.

The universal service funding mechanism must change, and in changing it the FCC has an opportunity to ensure the financial viability of USF, improve operational efficiencies, and recalibrate the subsidy process while also expanding the universal service mission to include promoting broadband access in rural and high-cost areas. Renewed interest in universal service funding mechanisms should combine additional financial investment with effective financial oversight, not to mention critical thinking about how best to apply the $7.2 billion government stimulus. Technological innovations increase the scope and diversity of what the telecommunications infrastructure can provide. When not everyone has the same opportunities to access basic and enhanced services, the digital divide exacerbates the gap in opportunities available to digitally literate and illiterate people.

CHAPTER SIX

Understanding the Dotcom Implosion

DESPITE AMPLE BENEFITS accruing from ICE technologies, the Internet will not change everything, nor can it escape the impact of business cycles and other economic forces. With breathtaking speed, attitudes about the ICE marketplace have careened from irrational exuberance to extraordinary pessimism. Share prices, investors' enthusiasm, and prospects for an information revolution have waned since the gold rush mentality of the late 1990s. With growing demand for full-motion video services accessed by both computers and wireless handsets, the cycle has begun to swing upward. Increasing demand for fiber-optic-cable and satellite capacity has begun to reduce the overhang of excess capacity created during the dotcom boom.

Until the dotcom bust, many ICE makers and providers, consumers, and academics thought that the Internet had unlimited potential to change forever many of the ways we engage in social and commercial transactions. Forecasters confidently projected triple-digit annual increases in demand and healthy growth in revenues.[1] These forecasts promoted the view that the fundamental rules about business and markets did not apply to information-age industries. Belief that a "rising tide raises all ships" prevailed, so much so that companies could aim to gain market share and pay little regard to the short-term prospect for breaking even, much less generating a profit.

Through painful experience, we have come to realize that fundamental rules about business and markets do apply to ICE industries. The Internet does not change the human condition; fear, greed, wishful thinking, trust, and other traits affect consumer and business behavior. If greed previously drove short-term thinking, then fear now creates heightened concern for short-term profitability. Investors have moved from an expectation that share prices would rise indefinitely to finding reasons not to invest. A review of recent technological, marketplace, legislative, and regulatory history could help us usefully examine the real costs and benefits of ICE innovation, regardless of the current business cycle status.

TECHNOLOGICAL EXPLANATIONS

Many industry insiders would have us believe that a perfect storm overtook ICE industries, a view that absolves individuals of responsibility for having made overly optimistic blue-sky forecasts and frees them of legal and ethical responsibility for actions that collectively primed the pump for increased venture capital. The real truth about the recession in ICE markets lies in unimpeachable but ignored technological imperatives.

Moore's Law

The primary disruption to both information and telecommunications technologies came from the tremendous deflationary pressure caused by innovations. Gordon Moore, one of the founders of the chip-manufacturing firm Intel, predicted in 1965 that the processing power available from a computer microprocessor would double every eighteen to twenty-four months.[2] Moore's Law graphically and quantitatively captures how technological innovations can destroy business plans even as it adds value for consumers. When confronted with declining costs in some aspects of their business, ICE ventures must enhance the value of their products and services to justify existing prices.

Moore's Law identifies how technological innovations in computing enhance user productivity and computer power even as it destroys the status quo in terms of what consumers expect computer manufacturers to offer by way of price and features. To maintain the same sales price for a computer in the face of substantial downward pressure on the cost of providing the device, manufacturers must improve value by increasing processor speed, memory, and disk drive capacity and by offering additional peripheral devices, such as DVD read-write units. Otherwise, consumers will consider computers merely a commodity and base their buying decisions primarily on price, with an expectation of ever-declining rates.

Moore's Law also applies to telecommunications equipment and services, but service providers in particular do not have many opportunities to maintain prices by adding features, stimulating brand loyalty, and differentiating offerings.[3] The simultaneous increase in capacity and reduction in per-unit costs has helped make voice and data transport like a commodity business with vastly declining margins. Worse yet for operators, investment in telecommunications facilities involves sinking large amounts in facilities that have substantial capacity but that cannot generate revenues until the entire investment has been made and the facilities set up. Once sunk, the investments quickly lose value because subsequent generations of facilities offer the same voice and data transport at half the cost and with more than double the capacity.

Failure to Sustain Growth in Demand

The tremendous increases in capacity, even coupled with vastly declining margins, would not harm service providers if demand increased commensurately. For a time it appeared that steep increases in market penetration for personal computers, modems, and subscriptions for Internet access would offset the impact of Moore's Law. However, even substantial increases in demand proved insufficient to help service providers make up in volume what Moore's Law forced them to lose in margin.

Worse, the short-term increases in demand have the potential to cause congestion, particularly in the first and last miles of lines provided by local exchange carriers and in some routes managed by Internet service providers. Even with Moore's Law in effect, the failure of some ISPs to upgrade or replace existing and outdated plant created bottlenecks and burdens on companies that upgraded facilities. ISPs now face increasing demand for network capacity to support higher bit transmission speeds delivering ever-expanding amounts of traffic. Some ISPs have begun to deviate from an unmetered all-you-can-eat provision of services despite opposition from some customers. Heavy Internet users increasingly face the likelihood of having to pay more than low-volume users.

The Difficulty of Exploiting Convergence

Both technological and marketplace convergence have failed to occur as speedily and easily as forecasted. Technological convergence refers to the blending of previously separate functions, which possibly results in faster, better, smarter, cheaper, and more convenient functions. For example, technological innovations have made it possible for previously discrete voice and data networks to combine and to travel over the same telecommunications line. However, the combination of networks does not necessarily translate into benefits that business and residential users will readily seek when ventures offer bundles of services.

Integrating and exploiting raw technological innovations often generate delay, confusion, and frustration. These can be amplified by consumers' reluctance to vest with any single vendor the responsibility and pricing power to install, operate, and manage a single, one-size-fits-all network, notwithstanding the much-touted benefits of one-stop shopping for bundled services. Only recently have the telephone and cable television companies begun successfully to package a triple-play bundle of voice, Internet, and video services.

High Sunk Costs

The telecommunications technologies that drive the Internet, bringing large chunks of new capacity into the marketplace, have high sunk costs and generate no revenues until fully installed. Despite these unfavorable characteristics, many new ventures anticipated offering fiber-optic and other cutting-edge (or bleeding-edge) technologies that would help market entrants leapfrog existing technologies and develop a competitive advantage over the combination of retrofitted old and newly installed technologies offered by incumbents. But new technologies have only a fleeting competitive advantage because what destroyed the business plans and revenue expectations of incumbents soon will do the same to the market entrants.

Innovations in ICE technologies compress life cycles of products and services, largely because a big gap has developed between technologically feasible usable lives and commercially viable usable lives. A fiber-optic cable with a technological usable life of twenty or more years may, for example, become commercially obsolete in significantly less time because new generations of cables offer substantially more bandwidth. The introduction of dense wavelength division multiplexing[4] makes it possible to send several different laser-beam frequencies over the same strand of fiber-optic cable, thereby increasing capacity by more than 100 percent compared to previous cable vintages.

Costly Retrofits

During the dotcom ascendancy the conventional wisdom condemned incumbent telecommunications carriers to financial stagnation or worse. It was assumed that market entrants had insurmountable technological, entrepreneurial, and regulatory advantages. Moore's Law favored latest-generation technologies, and incumbents experienced great difficulty in developing a strategy that combined retrofitting of existing networks with installing new networks. Newcomers, lacking the incumbents' Bellhead culture and philosophy, thought they had better market development and entrepreneurial skills. In addition, the Telecommunications Act of 1996 provided newcomers with a leg up by mandating their access to incumbent network facilities at favorable rates, below what the incumbents would have preferred to charge.

For a time it appeared that incumbent telephone companies could not, or would not, learn from the recent market-entry upstarts. Even other incumbents, such as cable television operators, appeared more nimble. The telephone companies did not seem to want to compete; their planning and their deployment of broadband technologies were desultory. DSL services often lacked reliability, which caused the telephone companies to allocate more personnel and more visits to customers' premises. Broadband appeared to be an unproven market even as customers experienced frustration and prospective customers balked at the cost and perceived hassle. Now the combination of streamlined regulation, competitive necessity, and declining core revenues has motivated incumbent telephone and cable operators to embrace convergence.

MARKETPLACE EXPLANATIONS

During the dotcom boom just about every ICE venture bought the view that they must vertically and horizontally integrate to provide consumers —particularly large multinational corporations—with single integrated solutions to any and all requirements. ICE ventures integrated vertically by developing or acquiring new competencies up and down the complete array of services. For example, telephone companies like AT&T and Verizon perceived the need to provide both conduit and content. They invested heavily in video production only to realize that thcy could not easily replicate the success achieved by their cable television competitors, which bundled video, telephone, and Internet access.

Absence of Compelling and Legal Content

Just as technological innovations do not necessarily push consumers to buy ICE products and services, content does not always stimulate demand for costly broadband service upgrades. A significant portion of the demand for Internet-mediated content has come because of peer-to-peer networking[5] of files, shared in a violation of intellectual property rights (e.g., pirated music and video); commercial pornography sites; and unsolicited content such as spam. More rigorous enforcement of intellectual property laws, reluctance on the part of some content providers to use the Internet to distribute goods and services, and the maturation (loss of novelty) of the Internet market have moderated growth in Internet traffic. Furthermore, not all consumers have jumped at the opportunity to pay an additional thirty to eighty dollars monthly for broadband Internet access, nor will they until they perceive the value in faster downloads and streaming video content, including online access to content also available on broadcast and cable television.

Widespread expansion of the scope and nature of Internet content will require effective digital rights management so that providers of the most compelling content will feel comfortable making premium content available via the Internet. Until such time as consumers have options to access compelling content, many will refrain from upgrading the access devices and services needed to handle full-motion video files and to deliver music quickly. In the video marketplace, one of the most successful innovators, Netflix, couples Internet access and a menu of some downloadable content with conventional postal delivery of its entire inventory of movies on DVDs.[6] Content providers of music and movies embraced the Internet unenthusiastically until recently. That, together with consumers' reluctance to increase their ICE technology burden, contributed to the general doldrums that only recently has abated.

No Regard for Near-Term Revenue

In light of today's corporate and consumer pessimism, it seems foolish for venture capitalists and individual investors alike to have accepted the view that a splashy World Wide Web presence mattered even more than the prospect for generating sufficient revenues. Nevertheless, many different types of stakeholders bought the notion that the Internet provided nearly unprecedented opportunities to get in on the ground floor of a hugely profitable venture. Many of the investment pitches created the impression that someone could invest in new ventures with the same upside promise as the first shares of IBM and Microsoft stock, yet not all of the thousands of investment options could achieve best-in-class status. Still, the unbridled enthusiasm about future profits and opportunities made it possible to think that even market laggards could excel.

The quest for Internet shelf space meant that ventures had to acquire customers across the broadest-possible geographical footprint and to offer a diversified and comprehensive set of products and services. Presumably, the first to establish a wide Internet marketing presence could capture customers and secure such high brand loyalty that consumers would refrain from trying any of the numerous, readily available alternatives. Internet marketers talked about creating communities linked via telecommunications instead of by geographical proximity. Certainly, some Internet users fit the model in the sense that they have opted to stay within a walled garden with limited content options, such as that provided by or linked via Yahoo. However, many more users consider the Internet a platform for access to any store site or content source. These users employ search engines and electronic agents to seek out low prices or to match specific requirements.

The high costs of customer acquisition and expansion for expansion's sake bankrupted most Internet ventures that failed to establish best-in-class status. Establishing a national or international presence did not contribute to establishing positive economies of scale, nor did quick diversification of product and service lines. Even now, best-in-class Internet ventures such as Amazon.com struggle to blend profitable sales of hard-copy books with music and book downloads, which are the offspring of recent diversification efforts.

Low Interest Rates

We must not underestimate the market stimulation available from historically low interest rates, especially when coupled with readily available cash from eager investors and equipment vendors. During the information revolution, technology stocks so excelled that few investors—professional or individual—could resist the incentive to join the bandwagon. The herd mentality appeared safe: even if a venture's founder skipped Business Fundamentals 101, the "greater fool" theory suggested that optimistic investors would gladly buy stocks from other investors keen on cashing out.[7]

The vast amount of capital flowing into the ICE technology sector has resulted in a glut of transmission and switching capacity, particularly for domestic and international long-haul routes. Technological innovations, the product of Moore's Law, exacerbate the glut, making it possible for new generations of transmission capacity to duplicate or even exceed all of the previous operational capacity. Now, however, the growing demand for full-motion video and peer-to-peer file transfers has begun to draw down the surplus transmission capacity.

The Universality of Business Fundamentals

Stakeholders in ICE industries have learned the hard way that business cycles and other business fundamentals apply to their sector. A general downturn in the domestic and global economy has also exacerbated the negative industry-specific factors, such as a glut in transmission capacity, making the recession in ICE industries even more pronounced and with a possibly longer period of recovery than the general economy. Share prices and other indications of a golden future had created expectations of perpetual double-digit growth in demand. But economies tend to grow and contract cyclically, in part because technological innovations can enhance productivity and lead to accrued efficiency gains.

Few would dispute that electronic commerce and other Internet-mediated transactions offer the potential for faster, better, smarter, cheaper, and more convenient personal and commercial experiences. Likewise, ICE technologies have contributed to streamlined and improved transactions that can bring operational and cost savings. For example, real-time monitoring of inventories can support just-in-time production and delivery of products with a commensurate reduction in inventory holding times. However, these enhancements may not continue in perpetuity, nor should share prices and market forecasts be based on assumptions that they will.

False Claims for Stock Prices

The information revolution provided an unprecedented opportunity for new ventures to receive funding and for individuals to get rich quick. Stock options became the preferred currency for compensation based on the view that rising stock prices would appropriately reward innovation and entrepreneurism. Eventually stock prices failed to maintain their upward trajectory. For many stakeholders, the temptation to bolster stocks with false claims became irresistible. Stock analysts and chief executive officers alike "goosed" stock prices with overly optimistic forecasts about the future, based on assumptions even they did not believe.

The Misleading Y2K Stimulus

Anxiety about the operational impact that the arrival of the new millennium would have on equipment and networks provided a short-term boost in facilities investment and systems integration even as fundamental business conditions started to deteriorate. Despite evidence of a downturn, many stakeholders chose to consider preparations for the Y2K problem—the switch from 1999 to the year 2000—as proof that the information revolution remained healthy. On the contrary, preparations proved to provide a onetime boost in investment and expenditures.

LEGAL AND REGULATORY EXPLANATIONS

Legal, regulatory, and judicial actions regularly have a significant impact on ICE industries, and the extent of the impacts may have reached above-average levels in the past few years. Since 1996, with enactment of legislation comprehensively revamping basic telecommunications law in the United States, the FCC, reviewing courts, and stakeholders have struggled to interpret legislative intent. A more robustly competitive telecommunications marketplace, particularly for local services, was apparently the goal. With the act, Congress ordered the FCC to make regulatory changes to achieve it.

The Telecommunications Act of 1996, in its broadest sense, provided the major incumbent local exchange carriers (ILECs) an opportunity to generate new revenues from long-distance telephone service in exchange for the likely loss of market share and revenues resulting from having to open their local exchange networks for more extensive access by new competitors, typically referred to as competitive local exchange carriers (CLECs).[8] Both incumbents and newcomers achieved this quid pro quo by actively lobbying Congress. When the law was enacted, it appeared that most stakeholders could live with the bargain they had helped to shape, but over time ILECs came to feel that their costs well exceeded the benefits. The ILECs litigated and delayed their implementation of the act, perhaps with an eye to achieving opportunities in the long-distance market without having to comply fully with a fourteen-point checklist to ensure a level playing field in their core local-service markets. As it turned out, delays in implementing the act coincided with delays in the ILECs receiving FCC authorization to provide long-distance services. In time, technological and marketplace forces reduced the profitability of long-distance voice telephone services, so much so that ILECs saw their financial sacrifices, in terms of local access, as unfair and unlawful.

Litigation Instead of Competition

ILECs have come to consider the bargain they helped to negotiate as unlawfully obligating them to subsidize competition. With their considerable regulatory and legislative affairs budgets, the ILECs have reshaped the debate in new terms: as confiscation of their facilities investment by regulatory fiat. They claim that the FCC has ordered them to offer facilities access to CLECs at below cost. In retaliation, and in response to the overall downturn in the economy, ILECs drastically cut their investment in new facilities and concentrated on seeking judicial relief. The courts have not always accepted the ILEC position, but ILECs started to win in court more than they lost. Over time, litigation has required the FCC to scale back its pro-competitive initiatives.

The Telecommunications Act of 1996 has not triggered much local telecommunications competition beyond the telephone services provided by cable television companies. Increasingly, the local competition initiatives mandated by the act do not matter, because the law has been reinterpreted to foreclose compulsory sharing of broadband facilities and information services.

It comes as no surprise that incumbents seek to thwart competition and the loss of market share. Competition policy in many nations requires incumbent operators of essential and bottleneck facilities to provide access to competitors, including ventures unable or unwilling to invest in fully duplicative networks. Having every incentive to deny access but compelled to provide it, incumbents then resort to delay and to litigation and confiscation arguments to raise competitors' cost of doing business. Regulators and courts have to guard against stalling tactics and other strategies designed to thwart competition, particularly if they have determined that stimulating competition will serve the public interest. Congress made such a decision in mandating affirmative regulatory steps to expedite competition rather than waiting for newcomers to duplicate incumbents' facilities.

Litigation over access to ILEC facilities parallels a strategy executed by the Bell System when confronted with the onset of competition over long-distance service in the 1970s.[9] When AT&T operated as a near monopoly as the Bell System provider of both local and long-distance telephone service, it was in a position to offer superior technical access to its long-distance service through its local exchange facilities and to raise the cost of competitors' access to those facilities. Both the FCC and reviewing courts identified anticompetitive practices, required favorable terms and conditions for access by market entrants, and rejected the notion that consumers should not have competitive options unless and until new carriers could duplicate rather than access the facilities of incumbents.[10] Even the most facilities-rich long-distance competitors of AT&T, such as MCI and Sprint, started business with limited backbone networks. As long-distance market entrants concentrated on the long haul, they needed to access the local exchange facilities of incumbents to originate and terminate long-distance calls. That is, market entrants who had not yet installed facilities resold the services of incumbents.

The FCC made a determination that pro-competitive initiatives served the public interest.[11] In time, many market entrants weaned themselves from leased facilities and built their own networks. ILECs claimed that CLECs had no intention of building their own networks and that the FCC-prescribed access rates created financial incentives for entrants to continue reselling the services of incumbents. However, CLECs have invested and lost billions of dollars in facilities, which demonstrates that few consider resale margins sufficiently generous to foreclose the need to make sunk investments.

In at least one case, Congress determined that it was in the public interest to mandate competitor access to incumbent facilities even when there was no prospect that the competitor would duplicate the incumbent's facilities. Because incumbent telephone and electric utilities had already invested in poles and conduits and because ample space existed to accommodate an additional line, Congress ordered the incumbent utilities to provide cable television operators with shared pole and conduit access.[12] While the parties have debated and litigated the cost and scope of access,[13] no one has disputed the rationale for mandating access. It made no sense to hold up the availability of cable television service until such time as an operator installed its own conduits or poles to reach each and every household. Similarly, Congress made the determination that the local exchange telecommunications marketplace deserved regulator-induced competition and that such competition would serve the national interest.[14]

Pro-competitive Trade Initiatives

Even as technological and market forces stimulated investment in ICE industries, pro-competitive and trade initiatives provided additional incentives to invest. One of the first major market-restructuring initiatives in the United States involved the divestiture of AT&T in 1982 and the elimination of a captive market for telecommunications equipment by the spun-off local exchange carriers. After the divestiture, the RBOCs no longer had to commit nearly all of their equipment purchases to a corporate affiliate known as Western Electric. Companies such as Northern Telecom, Alcatel, Siemens, and Ericsson took advantage of new opportunities to sell to the RBOCs. These manufacturers achieved greater market access with the successive rounds of trade negotiations that culminated in the formation of the World Trade Organization[15] and an Agreement on Basic Telecommunications Services.[16]

One of the expanded opportunities for access to U.S. markets came with the relaxation of restrictions on foreign ownership of carriers operating in the United States.[17] The opportunity for greater foreign investment in the United States provided additional capital at the same time as venture capital and stock purchases flooded ICE industries.

Spectrum Auctions and New Carrier Licensing

Even as venture capitalists and individual investors were banking on a continuing upward trajectory in share prices, consumer demand, and company revenues, governments attempted to cash in as well. As ventures sought maximum financial leverage to acquire market share through investments and acquisitions, national governments sought to extract revenue from spectrum auctions and new license tenders. The FCC accrued billions of dollars from its spectrum auctions, particularly for additional spectrum and licenses to provide mobile radiotelephone services.[18] Tenders for third-generation cellular radiotelephone licenses also fetched billions in the United Kingdom, Germany, France, and other European nations.

As the ICE industry downturn began, winning bidders either could not meet their payment schedules or had second thoughts about the wisdom of making such substantial payments. Some bidders filed for bankruptcy protection, but even blue-chip incumbent carriers such as British Telecom, Deutsche Telekom, KPN, and France Telecom experienced significant financial distress.

NEAR-TERM OUTCOMES

The macroeconomic downturn, coupled with the severe ICE industry implosion, has triggered widespread pessimism, revived the importance of generating earnings instead of just market share, and caused stakeholders to exercise extreme caution in making capital expenditures. If businesses overinvested in the dotcom boom, many now underinvest to conserve capital despite historically low interest rates. Current conditions appear to favor incumbents, particularly ones with a proven customer base and the ability to generate positive cash flow.

Incumbents currently exploit the dire economic conditions in ICE industries to pursue aggressively a campaign for further deregulation and relaxed enforcement of antitrust laws. As the only stakeholders with the wherewithal to invest in new facilities, incumbents condition investment on legislative and regulatory relief. Their legislative and regulatory campaigns seek freedom from regulation, including the duty to provide competitors with access to facilities and services and to offer such access at favorable terms and conditions. Through relentless repetition, incumbents have gained traction in their argument that they should not have to subsidize competition, that resale of facilities and services does not provide any consumer benefit, and that having to share access creates severe disincentives to invest in facilities needed to make broadband access ubiquitous. It appears both ironic and unfortunate that just as the Telecommunications Act of 1996 belatedly caused some pro-competitive benefits to accrue, the FCC dismantled most of the requirements that could create viable competition in local exchange telecommunications services. Ostensibly to reduce regulatory uncertainty, the FCC has abandoned most pre-competitive initiatives, including ones arguably still required by the act.

Regardless of what Congress and the FCC do to stimulate facilities investment, the ICE sector has lost its traditional public-utility, low-risk characteristics. And it may not regain its high-growth nature until most consumers see the value in paying over one hundred dollars or more per month for a triple-play bundle of broadband, video, and telephone services. Incumbent carriers stand to benefit the most, or at least to tolerate conditions of low growth and suppressed facilities investment. Competition, if it exists at all, will result from incumbent carrier competition (e.g., cable television and fixed wireless service operators) and, less significantly, from market entrants. However, all competitors have the same incentives to conserve capital. On balance, it appears that ILECs are in the best position to survive the current downturn and to consolidate market control in the near term through mergers and acquisitions.

The dotcom implosion has shaken regulators and operators alike, increasing incentives for caution, even though prudent risk takers typically win in the marketplace. Congress and the FCC need to refrain from adopting a risk-adverse strategy that shifts from pro-competitive policies to incumbent-insulating ones. The way forward integrates incentive creation with strict enforcement of regulatory responsibilities and carrier commitments, including commitments made to secure regulatory approval for mergers and acquisitions.[19]

Reinvigorating the ICE sectors of a nation's economy constitutes an important and desirable public policy goal. Legislatures and regulators must take the initiative rather than rely on the conditional promises of incumbents that once free of unfair and burdensome regulations, they will conscientiously and robustly invest in new technology and make broadband service ubiquitous regardless of competitive necessity. Legislatures and national regulatory authorities can create more effective incentives for investment and universal service through well-crafted tax policy and loan guarantees than by abandoning regulation.

Jurisdiction over telecommunications in the United States is shared between federal and state agencies. The FCC regularly tries to preempt states' regulations based on the view that a single, consistent regulatory regime must apply nationwide. States reject this fear of balkanization because political, social, and economic circumstances widely vary among states, depending on such factors as size, wealth, and number of rural residents. State government agencies also provide consumer safeguards that the FCC may not consider necessary, such as assessing the fairness of wireless carrier two-year service contracts and financial penalties for early termination of service.

Bureaucrats in Washington, D.C., perennially offer an easy target for advocates of deregulation who claim that immediate progress would result from simply eliminating the regulator. But eliminating regulation at the same time that market forces stimulate industry consolidation establishes a recipe for re-monopolization or perhaps an oligopolization by a very few local and long-haul carriers.

Advocates for deregulation or unregulation point to the proliferation of wireless options as proof that a competitive marketplace exists, but mobile services remain metered and significantly more costly than wireline options. That some wireless users have abandoned their wireline services demonstrates only that some people, whether by wealth or preference, choose to pay more for the convenience of wireless services. The potential for telephony and other lower-cost wireless options to be delivered by cable television offers the promise, not the certainty, of future competition.

In the transition to competition, regulation becomes perhaps even more essential. Without a regulated transition period, conditions might revert to what prevailed before the dotcom bust. Re-regulation might be required to control a vastly reduced but even more powerful set of service providers. The declaration that ICE industries have already become so robustly competitive that governments should step aside and allow the marketplace to self-regulate is not valid, and the American people should not accept it.

CHAPTER SEVEN

The Fundamentals of Digital Literacy

EVEN IF EVERY nation had a conscientious and effective government that safeguarded consumers and promoted the public interest, individuals still would need to acquire and maintain digital literacy. They would need to have a general understanding of how ICE equipment and services work and what services enhance their personal well-being.[1] Technological mastery requires more than hand-eye coordination, the flexibility to type on wireless handsets with small keyboards, the ability to use such graphical user interfaces as the computer mouse, and the skill to maneuver in the World Wide Web. Mastery involves knowing how to exploit ICE technologies for individually beneficial uses and how to take advantage of new services that promise even greater value propositions. In addition, users of ICE equipment and services need to understand what the government can and cannot do for them: what regulatory safeguards the government can establish and what limited judicial remedies may exist when ICE actors misbehave.

Not all governments have abandoned regulatory oversight, but many have accepted the conventional wisdom that the ICE marketplace increasingly can self-regulate. Digitally literate citizens must evaluate this basic premise critically because political and other factors may skew decision makers' perception of actual market conditions. With analysis of the ICE marketplace citizens may find instances in which terms, conditions, price, availability, and features do not match what they want and need. Digital literacy enables ICE consumers to understand their rights, responsibilities, and limitations in seeking remedies to market and regulatory failures.[2]

Literate users understand that some forms of self-help constitute reasonable and lawful strategies to counteract and evade limitations on the use of equipment, services, and content imposed by manufacturers, carriers, and content distributors. Other forms of self-help violate the law or enforceable contracts. ICE law recognizes that in some instances service providers can enforce unilaterally created, take-it-or-leave-it contract language. But in other instances, consumers can devise clever and lawful ways to circumvent unreasonable limitations, including attempts by content creators and telecommunications carriers to limit consumers' fair-use rights to access copyrighted content.

BEING DIGITAL

Human beings use analog techniques for speaking, listening, and viewing content. Our eyes and ears create electrical waveforms that our brains can process. A shift in waveform translates into changes in the intensity of the signal, which our brains perceive as changes in frequency and volume. One way to conceptualize analog signal processing is to consider the vibrations created by the larynx when we speak or hum. The larynx contains a membrane that creates vibrations (waveforms), and the eardrum has a membrane that duplicates them. We talk by modulating—changing the frequencies of—the vibrations created as air moves across the larynx. We hear sound when vibrations make our eardrums vibrate, with the signal transmitted to our brain.

Even in an environment where digital devices and networks operate, human speaking, listening, and viewing will continue to occur in an analog mode. The devices that we use to listen to and view content must convert digital signals back into the analog format that humans naturally use. One way to understand this concept is to examine how speakers and microphones work. The speakers that we use to reproduce music receive electronic signals and convert them into physical vibrations that correspond to specific sounds. If you were to remove the grill of a speaker, especially the subwoofer in a high-end system, while playing music at a moderate volume, you would see speaker membranes physically moving and vibrating to the beat of the music. The larger the speaker, the more easily viewed the vibrations. Similarly, telephone handsets contain a small speaker that vibrates, albeit with less visibility.

The microphone function in telephones and other electronic devices operates in the reverse. Instead of translating electronic signals into sounds, microphones take vibrations created by the larynx and convert them into extremely low-powered electronic signals. Vibrations passing though a special membrane, one combined with a receptive electronic field created by wrapping copper wire around an iron core, create an electronic signal that can be amplified and subsequently converted into a digital signal. Digital signals can replicate a modulating waveform, corresponding to a conversation or music. Through the assignment of a sequence of binary numbers to the signals, on and off pulses come to represent ones and zeros, which combine to create a digital bitstream.

Music, still largely created in analog mode, can be converted into binary bits and stored on a compact disk (CD) or other medium. The bits, the ones and zeros, can translate into microscopic pockmarks created and also decoded by laser beams. When a copy of music contained on a computer hard drive is "burned" onto a compact disk, a low-powered laser beam etches small depressions on the disk that correspond to the ones and zeros that make up the sequence of bits representing the music. The bit sequence replicates the analog continuous waveform, but does so by frequent sampling of the waveform, not by completing duplicating it. Our brains cannot detect the sampling gaps or the difference between sampling and 100 percent duplication.

Converting analog signals into a digital format has several advantages. Digital signals do not degrade when duplicated, nor do they accumulate noise and other interfering signals when amplified. Devices such as computer hard drives can store and retrieve digital files, facilitating quick, cheap, and high-quality duplication of content. The current rampant piracy of music could not have occurred with analog formats, because duplication typically could not occur much faster than the length of the time it took to play the music. Analog storage media were not inexpensive, and the duplication was inferior in quality to the original. Analog duplicates display significant noise that appears as hisses, cracks, and signal distortions in audio formats and as snow, blurring, and color deviations in video displays. Digitally made duplicates more accurately replicate the desired signal and can more readily ignore and filter out noise. Basically, digital content reproduction offers superior signal regeneration.

Digital signals also lend themselves to easy processing to achieve a number of desired results. Because digital signals do not readily spill over into adjacent frequencies, many different signals can ride together, piggy-back style, on a broadband carrier. Substantial operating efficiencies accrue when a network can collect lots of traffic headed in the same direction and inject all the individual communications links onto a single link. A consumer application of this process, known as multiplexing, occurs when an FM radio receives a stereo signal and de-multiplexes it into two discrete and separate left and right channels.

Digital signals also make it possible to reduce the size (bandwidth) of the pipe needed to send multiple or high-complexity signals, such as a high-definition television channel. Because digital signal processing uses signal-sampling techniques, the number and type of sampling can be adjusted. The process known as compression uses techniques to predict the characteristics of the next sound or frame of video content. Using predictive techniques and reducing the frequency of waveform sampling can result in the processing of an inferior, but adequate, audio and video signal while using much less signal transmission capacity than otherwise. Such compression techniques are used for improved but not full-capacity high-definition television, the downloading or viewing of video content in real time via a personal computer, and the delivery of on-the-scene news via portable satellite transmitters.

Other advantages to digital signal processing include ease in coding and decoding signals to preserve privacy, commonly referred to as encryption and de-encryption. Digital technologies also lend themselves to the constant reduction in price per processing function examined previously in the discussion on Moore's Law. We see the application of Moore's Law on digital technologies in the regular decline in the price for digital processing devices such as compact disk and DVD players, digital televisions, and computers. Technologies that process digital signals interface well with innovative switching and transmission technologies, too, as we shall see.

Digital technologies have made exponential improvements in quality and speed possible, fostering consumers' desires for equipment and services that operate with ever-faster bitrates and ever-greater output. In other words, digital technologies contribute to the growing demand for broadband networks. The purchaser of a new digital television set expects to receive high-definition or enhanced-definition television signals. Most people with high-speed Internet access at work grow accustomed to quick file downloading and real-time streaming of full-motion video. Digital devices and services typically cost more than analog services because the combination of offered features exceeds in cost the savings that accrue from Moore's Law efficiency gains. And digital technologies need to convert to analog formats so that humans can understand the content, and at the same time they need to provide backward compatibility with existing networks and devices. Because of the cost of making the conversion to digital technologies, ventures typically convert incrementally. They often begin the transition by retrofitting existing analog networks to provide some digital services, such as telephone company DSL service, or they replace analog technologies but not the last few yards that link individual offices and houses from and to digital networks, by, for example, using hybrid fiber to the curb for cable television service.

DATA REPLACES VOICE

Until about the mid-1990s, carriers designed and operated the telecommunications infrastructure primarily with voice communications in mind. From the introduction of the telephone until the Internet's ascendancy, voice communications generated most company revenues and constituted the primary mode of communication. Over time, corporations developed internal and external data processing requirements, in addition to their voice telephone service needs. For example, firms providing financial services needed to support the transfer of electronic funds and the processing of credit card payments. Until the Internet-driven convergence of services, carriers engineered separate voice and data networks.

Voice communications and data communications have different technical characteristics, and until convergent technologies could accommodate both sets of requirements, it made sense to operate parallel, but separate, networks. Voice communications typically require a dedicated narrowband channel because the information delivery rate is small but constant. A conversation takes place generally throughout the duration of the link. Even before digital technologies became dominant, innovators came up with strategies for sharing voice channels, but the sharing had to occur unobtrusively, for voice communicators have little tolerance for delays, echoes, noise, and sound distortions. The two-way nature of voice communications also favored the use of two links, known as duplexing, so that both parties can talk at the same time. In other words, the technology for voice communications must support symmetrical traffic between two parties. Internet users typically have asymmetrical traffic requirements, as people typically download more content than they upload.

Data communications generate different traffic requirements and network designs than voice communications do. Data traffic patterns typically have "bursty" characteristics: a user needs to receive or send a lot of information in the shortest possible time. Bursty traffic generates short-term peak use followed perhaps by no transmission for some period of time. The peak demand–no demand requirements of individual users are met though shared access to a high-speed broadband data network. This type of network should have the capability of handling large but temporary demand while also having the capability of handling less time-sensitive traffic, such as electronic mail.

Data communicators have diverse network requirements and accordingly need a versatile network that can handle both time-sensitive and delay-tolerant traffic. Their networks must handle peak traffic bursts in an asymmetrical mode, either heavily downstream to or heavily upstream from users. They may also have to support widely dispersed users and transmit the same message to all network users simultaneously, that is, to multicast.

PACKET SWITCHING REPLACES CIRCUIT SWITCHING

Networks configured primarily for voice communications typically use a technology called circuit switching to set up and break down links between caller and call recipient. Circuit switching provides a dedicated narrowband link available for use only by the caller and the call recipient. This architecture provides a highly reliable, good-quality link appropriate for short-duration calls for near-continuous two-way traffic. The design does not work well for data communications, such as Internet traffic, because it cannot handle bursts in demand, nor can the lines provide switching and routing for other users when the initial parties have a temporary pause in communications. Configuring a voice line for Internet access ties up a line for the duration of the call even though the data communications may take up a relatively small portion of the total time that the line was engaged. When no traffic requirements exist, the line remains dedicated to the initial calling and called parties.

Packet-switched networks provide more-efficient data traffic management. The network architecture breaks down traffic into small units of bits that can be routed via any available network link. This means that networks become available to handle a portion of a communications link on a space-available, best-efforts basis; a network not needed by one set of communicators can become available for others. The digital nature of packet switching means that a single network can handle a variety of packet-based services, including voice, data, text, images, sound, and video traffic. The availability of nearly universally agreed-upon operating standards and protocols makes it possible for networks throughout the world to communicate freely and openly, despite differences in equipment vintage and manufacturer.

The downside of packet switching lies in the potential for delayed transmission and processing of data packets. When traffic routes via multiple networks across long distances the potential exists for higher latency —for a delay in the delivery of packets—as well as delivery of packets out of order. Packet-switched networks can process traffic on a immediate, real-time basis, including some ability to reassemble and reorder packets. However, lost packets or ones arriving too late for processing will result in outages in the flow of bits—lost words in a conversation or lost sound and picture in a videoconference or a television transmission.

BROADBAND REPLACES NARROWBAND

The circuit-switched telephone network worked fine when consumers used it infrequently to make telephone calls of limited duration. The bandwidth available for such calls measured 3,000–4,000 cycles per second, also stated as 3,000–4,000 hertz or 3–4 kilohertz (khz). A bandwidth of 3–4 kilohertz provides a very narrow channel within which to carry information. A channel of this size can carry a voice conversation adequately because most callers generate an audio signal in a relatively narrow band of frequencies. By comparison, an AM radio signal operates on a channel with 10 kilohertz in bandwidth. This slightly wider channel enables the transmission of both voice and low-fidelity music.

The more bandwidth that is available in a channel of communications, the greater the sound fidelity and the greater the amount of information available for reception. An FM radio signal operates with 200-kilohertz channels, making it possible to send a high-fidelity two-channel (stereo) signal. Broadcast television channels operate using 6 megahertz (6,000 kilohertz), which corresponds to 6,000,000 wave cycles per second. With this bandwidth available, a broadcaster can send a signal containing a video program with sound and associated picture-management functions.

Another way to think about bandwidth is to translate the size of the link into the measurement of output commonly known in ICE industries as throughput. The 3–4 kilohertz available from a dial-up voice telephone line translates into a data-handling capacity, or throughput, of 52,000 bits per second (bps) using a modem theoretically capable of handling up to 56,000 bits per second. Since eight bits correspond to one letter or number, another throughput measure, the byte, represents one number or letter processed. Cable modems, accessing broadband networks, can process several million bits per second, making it possible for users to download multi-megabyte files in a matter of seconds.

We can conceptualize bandwidth by thinking in terms of pipes used to transport water and natural gas to homes and offices. Pipes are measured in inches in diameter, but in use the key measurement lies in how much water or natural gas the pipe can deliver per unit of time. If we think of bandwidth in terms of the size of the pipe measured in number of cycles per second (hertz), output (gallons of water or cubic feet of gas per minute) is the measure of throughput. The bigger the pipe, the more water can flow through it per unit of time; the larger the available bandwidth, the more throughput can flow through the transmission line per second.

THE IMPORTANCE OF LOW LATENCY

Latency, the time it takes for content to travel from sender to receiver, is a key aspect of telecommunications. High latency—big delays in content delivery—can ruin the user experience and constitute an unacceptable degradation in service quality. Consumers expect telephone conversations to have pin-drop sound clarity without echoes, delays, and other types of distortion. Fiber-optic networks provide this quality of service, but wireless options, such as microwave and satellite links, typically offer inferior service.

Satellite delivery provides the primary means of communication for reaching many island nations not served by an underseas cable and for nations far removed from either underseas or major terrestrial cables. Satellite telephone communications have high latency, because of the half-second it takes to send a signal up to the satellite, located as high as twenty-two thousand miles overhead, and the additional half-second to receive the downlinked signal. Because telephone conversations often have interruptions and because both parties may talk at the same time, satellite latency can readily generate user frustration with echoes and signal distortion. Satellites rarely handle voice telephone traffic unless no alternative exists.

Operators of broadband networks currently work to reduce network latency and improve quality of service primarily because of competitive necessity and consumer expectations. Many ICE services require real-time, instantaneous delivery of packets so that a "live" conversation can take place. Real-time streaming of packets also provides the basis for making the Internet a medium for services that parallel radio, television, music players, and on-demand delivery of video programming.

THE MIGRATION OF INTELLIGENCE FROM CORE TO EDGE

Most legacy networks, such as the circuit-switched telephone networks, have an operating structure where simple and cheap devices, such as a telephone handset, access a network made intelligent by high-cost equipment centrally located on telephone company premises. The telephone network can switch and route calls to anywhere in the world thanks to a hierarchy of switches that can process a telephone number, identify where to route a call and which carrier to handle a long-haul transmission, and generate an accurate bill.

Centralized intelligence achieves operating efficiencies when a network offers few services—that is, when most consumers have similar requirements. Telephone carriers can scale up their networks to accommodate increasing demand, but diversification of services may prove difficult. For example, telephone companies can use centralized intelligence to provide enhanced calling features that inform users of another caller, provide answering-machine-type functions, and forward calls to another telephone number. However, centralized intelligence offers subscribers limited opportunities to customize features and to optimize the network for particular requirements.

The Internet architecture moves tools and systems from the core to the edges, where users operate. This migration makes it possible for users to treat the network like a generic bit-transport service. Users can apply information-processing technology on-site to configure their own services and to inject capabilities onto the basic building block of bit transport through software and other customized applications.

WIRELESS RULES

Consumers have readily and quickly embraced wireless telecommunications, particularly the provision of mobile access for personal and professional purposes. Consumer adoption of wireless services evidences the value of tetherlessness, of being free of limitations imposed by having a corded link to the rest of the world. Wireless options also provide enhanced access to those parties remaining on wireline networks. Overall, wireless telecommunications improve efficiency and convenience.

The migration from wireline to wireless services underscores the need for flexibility in how we use radio spectrum. Because nations typically allocate spectrum and specify the uses for each portion of spectrum, legacy decisions may adversely affect flexibility, cost, and accessibility for future ICE services. Mobile wireless ventures offering next-generation features, such as broadband Internet access, need more spectrum than was previously allocated for voice services. The slow accommodation of wireless demand in the United States has raised the price of wireless services and hindered deployment of new services, particularly compared to prices and available options in Asia and Europe.

NETWORKS OF THE FUTURE

Networks of the future will support the transmission, processing, and access of content via user-friendly platforms. Through the use of common, open, and widely used standards, ICE ventures can combine networks, making the Internet a central vehicle for any and all applications. The essence of ICE convergence lies in the combination of multiple kinds of content—voice, data, image, video, multimedia—all accessible from a single platform and available anywhere that Internet access exists.

Considering network access as a platform requires users of existing technologies to rethink how they access content. Legacy technologies delivered specific types of content, typically on a specified channel at a specific time. For example, broadcast and cable television content reaches consumers on particular numbered channels. Future networks will eliminate both the concept of a channel and any limitation on time of reception.

Networks of the future will help satisfy consumers' expectation that they can receive desired content anytime, anywhere, with any device. On-demand access eliminates "appointment television," whose consumers watch shows on specific channels at a specified time. "Anywhere access" requires network interoperability so that content initially transmitted via broadcast or cable networks can become available via other wireline and wireless networks providing Internet access. "Any-device access" removes many of the differences between television sets, computer terminals, and cell phone handsets. Next-generation networks will easily deliver content previously designed for delivery to only one of the three screens.

CLOUD COMPUTING AND REMOTE ACCESS

The digitally literate ICE consumer has to tolerate significant risk to accrue fully the benefits of cyberspace. In a developing trend, content, files, and information about individual consumers will reside not on the user's computer hard drive but somewhere inside the Internet cloud; the data will be stored on the site of a service provider. Even as consumers have concerns about the insertion and manipulation of files resident on their computers, "cloud computing" moves file creation, manipulation, and storage from their computers to off-site locations.

Cloud computing provides users with access to many services that previously required the installation of software onto individual computers, a process that takes time, effort, and possible expense. For example, most current users of word-processing software install it on their computer's hard drive or have it pre-installed there. A cheaper and possibly better alternative for word processing and many other applications replaces software installation with access to a World Wide Web Internet site that provides a user-friendly interface to the same sort of functions previously available only with software installed on a personal computer.

Cloud-computing users need to understand the risks and rewards of remote access to content, including content created by the user, such as a word-processing file. The evolving conceptualization of the next-generation Internet, Internet 2.0, includes widespread adoption of cloud computing; most popular social-networking sites already house the photographs and other content that make up an individual's page.

FASTER, BETTER, SMARTER, CHEAPER, AND MORE CONVENIENT

Another way to conceptualize digital literacy involves an examination of how individuals can gain benefits from ICE equipment and services that in general offer faster, better, smarter, cheaper, and more convenient options. By now, most Americans have found ways to use ICE technology to improve the value and utility of many personal and commercial transactions. But the likelihood exists that not every attempt at achieving progress has yielded a net benefit.

Improvements in data transmission technologies make it possible for networks to send packets at ever-increasing speeds. In a digital environment, we measure speed in terms of how many bits can traverse a network in one second. The faster the bitrate available from telecommunications transmission facilities, the sooner content can arrive. With the onset of full-motion video services, broadband networks must offer users the ability to receive multimedia (rich) content instantaneously (in a real-time stream) as content files containing millions of bits.

High-speed broadband networks offer Internet access even to residential users at speeds in the millions of bits per second. They require high-capacity telecommunications networks to transport bits that collectively make up content files that have become increasingly large and diverse. Consumers now expect broadband networks to handle full-motion video content without blurring, dropouts, or other forms of signal degradation. For networks to have the ability to deliver multimedia content, the bit-delivery capability must exceed 1,000,000 bits per second, so one baseline conceptualization of speed for ICE technology refers to the underlying network capability of speedily transporting large numbers of bits and the packets containing them. Digitally literate consumers of Internet services know about the need for accessible and affordable broadband networks. They also recognize the stakes in terms of lost productivity and connectedness when the market fails to generate facilities-based broadband competition, as still occurs in many rural locales. Without competition, costs remain high, and access remains low.

Digitally literate consumers understand the strengths and weaknesses of the two major broadband networks available to them, digital subscriber lines (DSL) and cable modem service. DSL uses the existing local copper-wire loops provided by telephone companies that upgrade the wire with a larger bandwidth of 15,000 hertz, more than is needed to provide voice service. With this larger bandwidth, telephone companies can offer bit transmission speeds in the range of 768 kilobits per second or more downstream, from the Internet to a subscriber, and 512 kilobits per second or more upstream, from a subscriber to the Internet. The telephone company upgrade constitutes a transitional retrofit; the copper-wire electronic technology cannot readily expand the bitrate to the multiple millions of bits per second that cable modem service provides, which users increasingly expect. On the other hand, telephone companies can offer DSL service at significantly lower prices than cable television companies can offer cable modem service, and the link they offer provides a dedicated, unshared line for the few miles that separate subscribers from the nearest telephone company switching facility. Unamplified DSL services cannot reach deep into the rural hinterland, because signals weaken after traveling three miles (4,500 meters) from a telephone company facility.

Cable modems offer subscribers service at multi-megabits per second, albeit at significantly higher prices than DSL prices. Cable television companies can easily upgrade their network to provide Internet access because the physical plant that the companies use already operates as a broadband link providing simultaneous access to hundreds of television channels, each occupying up to 6-megahertz (6,000,000 hertz). By pulling out only one 6-megahertz channel for Internet access, cable television companies can offer broadband data services at speeds in excess of 1.5 megabits per second downstream and 768 kilobits per second upstream. A process known as cable bonding combines three former television channels into a super broadband service capable of offering up to 50 megabits per second downstream and 5 megabits per second upstream. Consumers with an interest in downloading large media files and watching video streams on their computer monitors will find cable modem service better suited to their requirements. However, cable modem service typically costs three to four times the price of DSL.

The concept of speed has other meanings that a digitally literate consumer needs to know. Speed also refers to the ability of computer processors to deliver images quickly to computer screens and wireless handset screens and to quickly perform functions far from the end user. The speed of an upstream function is calculated by the time it takes an Internet-based venture to respond to and perform a requested service. Speed in this context refers to the speed in responding to a search query, delivering or receiving content, and consummating a transaction. The network can often respond with breathtaking rapidity, but we humans may need much more time to consider the output of what the network has delivered. For example, many Internet ventures offer prospective air travelers the opportunity to search for the lowest airfares. In an ideal scenario, the Internet combines fast telecommunications and information processing to deliver search results in a matter of milliseconds. Consumers can consummate the transaction in minutes, because airlines and travel companies have developed speedy order-processing, billing, and payment systems. But in many instances, consumers may not conclude their search after just one attempt for any of a number of reasons, including doubt about whether the initial search delivered the best or cheapest results and a desire to search for rates and travel options using many different departure dates, times, and other variables. A speedy network does not guarantee a speedy conclusion to an Internet-based transaction.

Whether or not new ICE networks offer consumers a better outcome than a transaction in the physical world depends on the individual. They do not guarantee better outcomes in and of themselves. Internet-mediated searches might deliver lower airfares. But what if the search process took hours before the researcher belatedly came to the conclusion that he or she had found the lowest fare?

In other words, "better" constitutes a subjective variable. Individual air travelers now have access to the same information-processing and telecommunications networks previously available only to travel agents and airline employees. Air travelers now can exploit complex information-processing networks to slice and dice fares and prospective itineraries, but in doing so they can just as easily waste hours in the search process and have nothing to show for their effort beyond what a ten-minute session probably would have produced.

Information-processing networks exploit speed rather than innate intelligence. For example, the Google search process provides a way to scan millions of Web pages in milliseconds to deliver results based on user-specified search terms. Software provides the instructions for generating search results and prioritizing them, a process not yet matching in intelligence, much less exceeding, how human brains consider the relevance of a possible content source. Information-processing networks appear smart because of the intelligence injected by programmers.

Networks can offer only the insights that programmers have built in. When Amazon.com appears to know a user's taste in books, when Hotwire remembers that a consumer has an interest in a particular travel destination, and when Google provides sponsored links to sites offering products and services of particular interest, they are simply executing computer programming codes. Software can be used to detect trends, to store information about a consumer's Web maneuvering, and to correlate searches with the results of similar searches by consumers.

Consumers increasingly believe that the Internet can help them save money through searches. They can find the lowest-cost options and eliminate intermediaries who would mark up prices. Networking can augment cost savings because users no longer have to accept the prices available from nearby brick-and-mortar stores, nor do they have to incur all the costs that they previously would have had to incur when determining price options from nonlocal vendors. However, for the consumer to save money in the end, the total cost savings from an Internet-mediated transaction have to exceed both the cost of the locally available option and the cost of searching for the lower-priced option.

The Internet can and frequently does provide cheaper options because consumers are no longer captive to local vendors and, in some instances, can find lower-priced goods previously available only to qualified wholesalers. Digital literacy includes the ability to launch effective Internet-based searches and the wisdom to know when to stop searching for possibly lower rates.

Internet access provides consumers access to the rest of the world from a desktop or portable computing devices, including wireless handsets. The option of not having to travel physically to the vendor or content source surely can save time, money, and effort, but there are trade-offs that can reduce the gain in utility and convenience. By not physically traveling to the source, consumers may increase the risk that the transaction will not achieve mutually beneficial results. Internet-mediated transactions place a premium on trust. In most instances, such trust is reasonable, as evidenced by the millions of transactions that involve unknown parties trading financial compensation in exchange for goods and services. But in a relatively small number of transactions, the convenience of trading within the Internet cloud triggers a net loss when the transaction involves fraud or unsatisfied expectations.

When Internet observers tout the benefits of using the Internet, digitally literate users also appreciate the risks. On balance, the Internet offers a compelling value proposition, but consumers need to operate with vigilance, sophistication, and skill, the acquisition of which takes both monetary and nonmonetary investments, including time and effort.

A STEEP LEARNING CURVE

Acquiring digital literacy may require substantial work, but anyone who has ascended the steep learning curve can avoid many of the penalties that victimize less-prepared consumers. By now, most people have come to understand that when someone offers something too good to be true over the Internet, the reward not will arrive as promised. Similarly, we have learned not to provide proprietary information about our financial accounts simply because someone has generated a warning of imminent shutdown. But if many of us have learned about spamming, "phishing" for financial account information, and other forms of deception and fraud, others have taken the bait. Spammers would presumably not expend the time and money to send e-mails if no one responded.

The Internet mirrors society with all of its flaws and criminality. It can enhance our well-being even as it can rob us of our identity, creditworthiness, and wealth. The Internet provides substantial rewards but also significant risks. Digital literacy enables users of the Internet to exploit the upside benefits while minimizing the downside risks. But to maximize the upside benefits, individuals need to understand how to protect their Internet-mediated transactions from harm. Doing so requires expertise in such esoteric subjects as data encryption, software filtering, and avoidance of contamination from worms, spyware, malware, and other invading forces that rob us of money, privacy, and even identity. Digital literacy requires that Web users install spam and antivirus filters, launch disk-drive scans, and remain vigilant. A digitally literate user will not click thoughtlessly on an icon purporting to represent an attachment sent even from a trusted source.

FLEXIBILITY AND OPPORTUNITIES AT A PRICE

Innovations in ICE technology enhance our opportunities to access content on our terms rather than those dictated by content creators and distributors. Not too long ago, with appointment television, we had to plan to watch a particular television show. Broadcasters and cable television networks could count on a sizeable audience making a conscious decision to watch a specific program at a specified time on a particular channel. With the introduction of the videotape recorder, viewers could "time-shift" content to another, more convenient time, provided they had ascended the learning curve for programming videocassette recorders (VCRs). Technological developments in content recording and playback now make it possible to use a number of devices to listen to and watch content ("device shifting"). With "format shifting," consumers can change the manner in which content is recorded and played back. Content on a hard plastic disk or computer or television set can be converted to a stored file on a media player's disk drive or internal flash memory. Alternatively, users can store content on a portable memory card and insert the card into a stand-alone media player or one of the multifaceted devices, such as a wireless handset, that accepts memory cards for music playback.

The digitally literate consumer of content fully understands the available options for using content at any time, with any device, using any compatible format. Some consumers take lawful, fair use opportunities to consume content, but the new technologies offer many ways to pirate and unlawfully copy content. The lawful-unlawful dichotomy is not sharply defined, particularly given the conflicting motivations of content creators and distributors, on one hand, and consumers, on the other. The former may want to lock down content and prevent consumers from "slinging" content from one device to another and making copies. Many consumers want to exploit any opportunity to shift devices and format even if doing so constitutes rampant piracy.

The digitally literate consumer expects to switch content to and from three screens, those on the television set, the computer monitor, and the wireless handset. Apprehensive that untethering content renders it vulnerable to unlawful duplication and distribution, carriers and content providers generally oppose the consumers' flexibility to switch. In many instances, detaching content from a single, tethered display device does increase the chances for piracy, but in other instances, consumers simply want to shift lawfully purchased content. Most conceptualizations of fair use, the lawful consumption of copyrighted content, include the right of purchasers of content to make personal copies for use via multiple playback devices. Only digitally literate consumers know their fair use rights as well as their technological options for fully exploiting anytime, anywhere, and with-any-device access to content. These informed and sophisticated users know how to exploit the increasing values and options afforded by Internet access and technological innovations.

CHAPTER EIGHT

Challenges and Choices

THE ICE ENVIRONMENT combines, and will combine in the future, many of the characteristics of the past with newly developed characteristics. The Internet does not change everything, as we have seen, but we should not ignore how analog technologies and markets have evolved into digital ones. Change seems to have picked up in velocity, and the stakes have increased, particularly as ICE technologies and markets converge and it looks as though a single Internet medium will provide access to nearly all ICE services. The failure to understand the opportunities and threats presented by a changing ICE environment has the potential to separate further the digitally literate from the digitally illiterate and to create a dichotomy between people able to exploit innovations and opportunities and those less equipped or inclined to do so.

Some key words constitute a shorthand list of descriptors for the current and future ICE environment with its legacy components. Many of these key words suggest both a preferred and a potentially harmful outcome. Outcomes that are polar opposites may occur, depending, as we shall see, on digital literacy. If sufficient numbers of people are digitally literate, we may expect better outcomes.

CONVERGENCE

Convergence refers to the combination of both technologies and markets as innovations convert analog ICE delivery into a digital format. Other factors may abet convergence, too. Convergence potentially offers consumers the opportunity to choose from an increasingly diverse group of technological options and providers. However, it also may increase risk as ventures strive to operate as one-stop shops for many services previously offered only on a separate, stand-alone basis.[1]

Convergence potentially also offers consumers the opportunity to use technologies for an increasingly broad set of applications. Software and technology features for personal computers have proliferated. Microsoft Windows and other operating systems have diversified the types of bundled applications and features available, making the computer an ever more versatile device. For example, a media player converts a personal computer into the functional equivalent of a radio, television, and music player. Improved sound and video cards inserted into expansion slots inside a personal computer enable it to serve as a gaming platform, telephone, and teleconferencing device.

Market convergence means that technological innovations can erode or eliminate barriers and boundaries that used to require separate commercial service arrangements. For example, digitization can convert all kinds of ICE content into bits, all of which a personal computer and the Internet can process. Both residential and business consumers no longer need to consider separate service providers for voice services and data services. Indeed the vision of the Internet as a centralized medium for accessing ICE content means that virtually all services can converge into a single bitstream with applications and bit processing reconverting the bits into separate telephone, video, music, text messaging, gaming, and other services.

IP-Centric Environment

As the Internet grows and diversifies, the potential exists for an Internet Protocol–based collection of networks to become the primary—if not the exclusive—medium for ICE services. With digitization, all content can be reduced to a least common denominator of packets capable of carriage through the same telecommunications network.[2] Previously both carriers and self-provisioning network operators established separate voice and data networks. Similarly, they treated wireline and wireless networks as separate conduits. Digital networks can packetize voice, data, video, and any form of content.

With the consolidation of networks, a convenient addressing system like that provided by the Internet Protocol makes it possible to commingle many different types of content and transmit and deliver them via a single array of networks. Because the Internet supports seamless connectivity between networks—regardless of who owns them and whether they use wires or wireless spectrum—efficiency gains may accrue from consolidating content and injecting it into a single IP network of networks.

Notwithstanding the potential for cost savings, network consolidation also has the potential to support a commensurate concentration of ownership and control over packet transmission networks. In the absence of facilities-based competition, an oligopoly or even a monopoly could develop. Such consolidation within a single industry can trigger anticompetitive conduct, because the remaining few operators now may have the capability to raise prices, thwart market entry by prospective competitors, drive existing competitors out of business, limit investment in innovation, scrimp on customer service, and favor corporate affiliates. The potential ability to corner the market for all types of ICE services creates ample incentive to pursue anticompetitive strategies. The few remaining players, with their need to grow in order to finance network expansion and exploit efficiency gains from operating at such a large scale, are able to affect the supply and price of ICE services and, in turn, the ease of access to, and reach and affordability of, essential services.

Conflict

ICE convergence creates many kinds of conflicts, primarily ones driven by clashes in culture, philosophies, and worldviews as incumbents butt heads with insurgents and as people in the telecommunications, information-processing, and content-creation worlds discover one another's differing mindsets. The telecommunications Bellheads, the information-processing Netheads, and the entertainment Contentheads will have to battle it out.

Competition

Despite the possibility of network consolidation and industry concentration, technological innovations also create the potential for consumers to access multiple platforms, offered by competing ventures, for switching, routing, and delivering ICE traffic.[3] Open and accessible networks like the Internet have stimulated much creativity and entrepreneurship as innovators think of ways to exploit broadband access and the increasingly ubiquitous Internet.

Facilities-based competition refers to the development of alternatives among ventures providing different ways to deliver ICE traffic to consumers. For example, incumbent telephone companies currently have upgraded their copper-wire local loops to provide subscribers with medium-speed Internet access in competition with cable television ventures that use a portion of their bandwidth carried over coaxial cables to provide the same service at a higher speed. Additional facilities-based competition can occur when wireless carriers offer cost-competitive Internet access services, when private users and commercial ventures offer access to high-speed wireless services such as Wi-Fi and WiMAX networks, when the electric utility company configures its wires to carry data as well as power (with the broadband-over-power-line [BPL] technology), and when the cable television, telephone, and other companies install high-capacity fiber-optic wires capable of replacing legacy copper lines.

Consumers typically benefit when they have a choice of two or more ventures using the same or similar technologies to provide similar services. If a second cable television venture has overbuilt a network to compete with the incumbent operator or if several networks in the same locality provide mobile telephone service or if several provide long-distance telephone service, consumers can choose among competitors.

Competition also occurs when facilities-based carriers have an incentive to lease bulk capacity for resale by other ventures, or when regulatory policy requires them to do so. When ventures sink money in facilities used to provide competitive services, they typically have a long-term commitment to serve their markets and offer a competitive alternative. On the other hand, resale competition can usually occur sooner and with less upfront capital expenditure. Generally, the sooner competition arrives, the sooner consumers benefit. However, resellers rely on access to competitors' networks, which can lead to disputes over the appropriate price for access and over the likelihood that the reseller will eventually install its own facilities.

Several wireless resellers operate in the United States and in other nations, often without extensive regulatory oversight. Although these ventures have to acquire capacity from facilities-based carriers at wholesale rates, their resale of that capacity can provide some degree of price competition and also diversify services. Many wireless resellers offer pay-as-you-go, per-minute service that does not require a multiyear service commitment. Others target specific demographic users and, in doing so, may achieve greater market penetration than do facilities-based carriers with their more general marketing pitches.

Consolidation

Even as the potential for competition grows, so, too, does the potential for mergers, acquisitions, and a move toward a concentrated market structure. How can the developing ICE marketplace support both competition and consolidation? Convergence partially explains this apparent contradiction. While technological and market convergence make it possible for single companies to provide more services and to enter more markets than before, it also raises the financial stakes and the scale necessary to compete. To exploit fully the new opportunities of ICE convergence, companies need to make major investments in technology upgrades.

Convergence forces incumbents with comfortable and previously impenetrable market shares to realize that competition could fragment markets, reduce revenues, and force innovation and improved customer service. When wireless voice technology became a partially competitive alternative to conventional wireline services, incumbent local exchange carriers such as Verizon and AT&T got serious about the need to upgrade their networks to diversify into new markets, including one offering great potential profits. Additional competition from a wireline alternative, cable television, underscored the sense of urgency, despite years spent experimenting and speculating about whether to diversify. Cable television companies, too, have experienced significant competitive incursions into their core video-delivery market from direct broadcast satellite operators, forcing them to upgrade their networks to provide an expanded inventory of television channels and telephone services, plus Internet access.

Empowerment

Consumers stand to benefit from convergence and the new ICE marketplace, provided they have the inclination and capability to pursue faster, better, smarter, cheaper, and more convenient options. In other words, consumer empowerment can occur, but at the expense of spending time searching, and search costs are often coupled with the need to ascend a new learning curve to make a new device, software, or Web site work. Some consumers will take the path of least resistance and not accrue many of the touted benefits of convergence—or of the vastly improved opportunities to access ICE services.

Since a variety of travel-related search engines offer the prospect of finding the best possible price for airfares, hotels, and car rentals, a consumer stands to benefit financially by learning how to use one of the many sites available. Typically no one Web site offers the best rate all the time, meaning that consumers can improve the odds of finding the lowest-cost alternative if and only if they use many search engines. As they increase the number of sites used, they expand their search time and effort. So much for empowerment. It can become more like enslavement if a consumer is determined to beat the airlines at their own game by finding that elusive rock-bottom fare even if it takes hours to do so.

Many consumers do not consider it fun to find the lowest airfare or the next best Web site. Some Internet researchers have determined that on average, consumers reduce their interactions with the World Wide Web to a handful of sites. Narrowing options despite so many other options might make sense in terms of efficient use of time. However, it increases the odds that a consumer will make decisions with less than full information. It might not make sense to waste hours to save fifty dollars in airfare, but a bigger ticket item, such as a new or used car, may stimulate more extensive and intensive information searches.

Compromise, Coordination, and Integration

The dotcom boom and the subsequent bust showed no small degree of irrational exuberance and pessimism in the ICE economy. Clearly, no one can chart growth in the ICE economy as a straight line.

The means by which the ICE economy grows require compromise and coordination among stakeholders. Success does not result simply from building the better mousetrap, the next best thing, or the killer application. It results from enhancing the users' experience, creating a community of users, adding value, and generating positive word of mouth. Achieving these kinds of enhancements typically takes time. Accordingly, the market penetration of new ICE technologies, while impressive, will not immediately destroy incumbent business plans and reshape the global economy. Legacy technologies will continue to greatly affect our private and business lives, with new options gathering momentum and increasing their impact as they become integrated with existing technologies and business methods.

Perhaps the best way to explain this compromise, coordination, and integration process lies in examining how one of the world's largest corporations embraces ICE technologies. Rather than view these technologies as a threat to their big-box commercial presence, Wal-Mart has devised ways to use ICE technologies to complement rather than cannibalize brick-and-mortar store sales. Wal-Mart uses its World Wide Web presence to sell goods and services, but also to provide linkages between Web commerce and in-store sales. For example, a consumer can upload digital photographs to a Wal-Mart Web site and direct the company to print pictures and have them available for pickup at a specified store. Wal-Mart probably increases the total volume of photo processing rather than redirecting customer traffic from stores to the Web. Indeed, Wal-Mart probably increases the number of store visits, because customers can avoid shipping charges by picking up photos themselves. Many customers, now in a Wal-Mart store to pick up processed pictures, might end up buying other products. Very successfully, Wal-Mart has integrated its store bricks with Internet-based clicks.

Privacy

ICE technologies, particularly the Internet, attempt to provide convenient, private, and confidential access to content, but they also provide many opportunities for surveillance that violate individuals' reasonable expectation of privacy. Access via computer can promote anonymity and eliminate the possible embarrassment that possibly would have resulted in the physical world. For example, someone concerned about a health problem can acquire helpful information that could preempt a trip to the doctor. But anonymity can also encourage risky behavior and the satisfaction of curiosity in ways that might not be attempted in the physical world. People who use ICE technologies may lack privacy and may inadvertently subject themselves to surveillance.

The lack of direct, person-to-person interaction may reduce trust and confidence in a commercial or private transaction. One of the major challenges to electronic commerce via the World Wide Web lies in creating safeguards that promote secure, risk-free transactions. This means that vendors must take affirmative steps to protect customers' credit and identities, as well as provide the same consumer safeguards available in physical transactions, including opportunities to return unsuitable merchandise.

In the private arena, we all should appreciate the consequences of how the Internet facilitates access to content, transactions, and interactions that violate the law or the widely accepted moral code. Electronic mail and listserves that process postings on a specific topic facilitate communications of all sorts, including predatory and harmful interactions. While we might not object to a sexual liaison between consenting adults, the Internet also provides a way to stalk people, exploit children, and harm the state of public health. Privacy advocates rightly champion confidential access to Internet-mediated resources. However, we need to appreciate the unseemly, dangerous, and potentially deadly risks generated by confidentiality in a variety of situations.

CONTRADICTIONS

ICE technologies have made life easier and more convenient in many ways, but the Internet also presents challenges to privacy as well as public and private safety. But heralding the Internet as either salvation or devastation is wrongheaded. Every user needs to assess the strengths and weaknesses of ICE technologies, estimate their worth, and make informed choices.

Advocates of electronic commerce regularly triumph the ability of the Internet to eliminate intermediaries whose involvement would add costs to a transaction without necessarily adding value. When the Internet eliminates one or more intermediaries, it provides consumers with opportunities to reduce costs and to manage a transaction to suit themselves. If a consumer cannot find a travel agent who will work hard to find the lowest possible airfare, the consumer now can deal directly with an airline at its Web site. Better yet, the consumer can select flights based on available seats. But on the negative and paradoxical side, the consumer can end up devoting a great deal of time to using assorted ICE technologies, often with little gain. The Internet provides ample challenges and distractions.

Platforms Instead of Channels

ICE technologies will eventually eliminate the current method by which we consume entertainment, news, and information. Instead of viewing content at a designated time and place and on a designated channel, we will have an access platform from which we can select and receive desired content anytime, anywhere, and via many different devices. For broadcast and cable television this means that viewers will not surf channels but will instead activate a platform that can scan multiple program sources for specific types of content or else offer content previously downloaded and stored based on consumer-specified preferences. To some extent, this future is already here with digital video recorders providing the content-recording function, but not yet intelligent search for preferred content. For wireless telephones with video screens, a similar search function can occur. The search and predictive downloading of content operates somewhat like a Web browser pointed to a search engine such as Google. The platform for accessing content operates smoothly and delivers the desired content.

The conversion from channels to platforms will have substantial commercial and social consequences. For example, advertisers will no longer have frequent opportunities to pitch messages to a mass audience. The television market has already become fragmented with the proliferation of channels; most cable television systems offer one hundred–plus options. Audience fragmentation increases when like-minded consumers can access the narrowest of niched programming. Social scientists have yet to assess fully the consequences when large parts of a population no longer have a shared video experience or when news consumers can screen out content that might challenge their viewpoints. On the other hand, since an Internet platform offers users the opportunity to search and to receive preferred, even idiosyncratic content, what advertisers lose by having less access to mass audiences, they can gain by targeting consumers with customized pitches.

In radio, national governments strive to reach a global or regional consensus on spectrum allocations for specific uses. Typically, once nations reach a consensus, they allocate national spectrum uses consistent with that consensus. Individual licensees receive authorization to use but not own radio frequencies and bandwidths in the spectrum for broadcasting, wireless telephone service, or other uses. When regulators make decisions about what types of bandwidth can provide which services, they can create scarcity; but technological innovations have now improved the capability for simultaneous use of identical spectrum by two or more users without interference. This means that nations need not carve out discrete slivers of spectrum for single types of use. It also means that regulators need not even require licenses to use some frequencies.

Content Rules

Digital technologies offer easy ways to make perfect copies of valuable content. Merging a technology that allows digital recording and playback with a technology that allows digital transmission and processing provides an ideal way to disseminate content. The problem lies in the ability of network users to avoid having to pay for content and, more basically, to accept the constraints on access and retransmission imposed by copyright holders.

Because of ease of use, readily available access to content, and, until recently, the nearly absolute freedom from civil or criminal liability for piracy, the Internet has become a forum for content piracy. Most providers of content available via the Internet offer at least some inventory free of charge, so perhaps users initially assumed that anything available via the Internet was free. Content owners and their trade associations have tried to educate and litigate away that assumption.

Many music lovers object to what they consider heavy-handed treatment by advocates of copyright ownership rights such as the Recording Industry Association of America (RIAA). Advocates of free access to copyrighted content rationalize their piracy involving access to content from anonymous sources as nothing more than the cyberspace equivalent to sharing a compact disk with a friend. Alternatively, some claim that because they have no intention of buying the music, they have not taken a sale from the copyright holder. Others argue that they have resorted to self-help because the record companies have refused to make music available via the Internet without restrictions on format and device shifting; the companies do not want the music to be converted into a format that facilitates copying and playback via many different devices. But few infringers of music copyrights equate music or video piracy with physical stealing.

Although many people think nothing of accessing content illegally, most accept the basic business premise that the Internet cannot become a major distribution medium for content unless and until a secure, uncrackable mechanism exists to protect content from piracy. Many current music pirates claim that they would pay for content if the copyright holders offered a fair deal. Some corroboration of that claim lies in the fact that Apple's iTunes and other online music sales and subscription services have achieved significant marketplace success.

The copyright stakes will grow as consumers upgrade their links to the Internet with high-speed options. Broadband Internet-access provides connectivity that can facilitate the downloading of large files containing complete movies. While some of us might consider it a waste of time and effort to devote several hours to downloading illegal content, high-speed Internet links and improvements in data compression and file delivery have reduced the time and hassle. However, the movie industry may not face the same degree of piracy, because consumers consider DVD prices reasonable, and the next-generation of Blu-ray DVDs will have sufficient capacity to hold a complete movie in high-definition video formats, along with additional special features than can make it worthwhile for prospective pirates to pay for the DVD. Remarkably, the movie industry has established a price point for a film and its associated music that is often below the price charged for the music alone.

Increased Risks

ICE convergence makes it ever more difficult for governments to determine the degree to which they must interfere with market forces in determining what users should pay for access to ICE services. In the telecommunications sector, governments apply regulations designed to protect consumers from disadvantages caused by the lack of competition and other market failures. Confident that competition has increased and that the market can therefore operate unfettered, governments have streamlined and eliminated regulations.[4] However, they have not completely abandoned their regulatory duties, because they still need to maintain consumer safeguards. The nature of telecommunications regulation has shifted from extensive government oversight, based on the governmental assumption that monopolies can exploit market power, to limited oversight, based on the assumption that the transition to full and fair competition has begun.

ICE convergence pits the view that telecommunications must be regulated to safeguard the public against the general view that information-processing industries already operate in such a robustly competitive marketplace that government has no major regulatory role to play. In other words, although the telecommunications industry is moving toward deregulation, the information-processing industry already has reached that point. When ICE technologies converge, disputes arise as to whether the service offered qualifies for the deregulated status of information processing or the regulated status of telecommunications. In the worst-case scenario, which exists today, competing services that are functionally the same qualify for different regulatory classifications, which artificially impacts a company's viability. When one venture offers a service classified as information processing but competitive with another venture's regulated telecommunications service, the information-service venture enjoys fewer regulatory burdens, which can translate into reduced operating costs. Conversely, the provider of a regulated telecommunications service incurs higher regulator-imposed costs, which it may attempt to pass on to consumers if it can do so and remain competitive.

Even outside the realm of convergence, consumers of ICE services regularly incur fees, surcharges, and other expenses resulting from legislative requirements and regulator-imposed duties. Consumers should examine their wireline and wireless telephone bills closely to see how extensive these fees have become. Current billing line items for cell phone service include contributions to universal access to basic telecommunications services, basic and enhanced emergency-911 access, access by deaf users, a general offset of regulatory costs, and reimbursement of telephone company expenses in providing consumers the ability to shift carriers while retaining the same telephone number.

Cannibalization and Disintermediation

Innovations in ICE technologies have a direct and potentially profound impact on ICE markets. Faster, better, smarter, cheaper, and more convenient innovations can improve the value proposition available from existing equipment and services. Predictably, consumers migrate to new options, possibly expediting the shift, because the new options may offer more features at or below the cost of the equipment or service they replace. When a new replacement option improves the value proposition, the price of existing equipment and services typically must drop significantly to meet competitors' prices.

Even if vendors substantially lower prices in response to ICE innovation, many consumers will migrate to new options. The term "cannibalization" refers to the overall loss in revenues and margins resulting when consumers migrate from one product or service of a company to another product or service of the same company having lower prices and commensurately lower profit margins. Cannibalization can destroy business models and profit expectations, but it need not trigger bankruptcy. Incumbents having to cannibalize existing product lines can respond by embracing new technologies and business methods.

If a market entrant has the potential to cut an incumbent's profit margin, the incumbent typically minimizes the financial harm by reducing margins and prices of existing services. At the same time, the incumbent must expedite the introduction of new equipment and services that use ICE innovations. For example, a long-distance telephone company that has offered conventional dial-up, circuit-switched service has to embrace Internet-delivered telephone service technologies to compete with newcomers with new technologies. Rather than charge for service on a per-minute basis, the incumbent may have to match or undercut the market entrant's monthly all-you-can-eat rate for service. An unmetered flat rate probably will result in lower margins and less profit for the incumbent, but the alternative—losing customers entirely—makes cannibalization the lesser of two evils.

Incumbents can survive and perhaps thrive upon the onset of new technologies and competitors. Their success depends on their agility, their responsiveness to the changed circumstances, and their attention to new market opportunities. Microsoft provides a textbook case study in successful adaptation. Microsoft faced the risk that Internet browsers might replace the Windows disk-operating system as the customer interface for both Internet access and software applications. Critics of Microsoft claim that the company courted and embraced competitors, such as the Internet-browser company Netscape, even as it planned to add in the software and services of potential partners. In short order, Microsoft succeeded in extinguishing a technological competitive threat.

A less pejorative view of Microsoft considers its strategy an effective way to co-opt and neutralize competition while also enhancing the value proposition of Microsoft's flagship product. For roughly the same price, subsequent generations of Windows software offer an increasingly diverse array of features, including a World Wide Web browser, a media player, and numerous utility applications, such as virus protection. With rare exceptions, a decision by Microsoft to incorporate a new feature results in lost market share and financial distress for companies marketing alternative software, particularly software offered at a price instead of free. By offering new features, Microsoft co-opts new technologies and stifles competition even as it distracts consumers from major defects that it is often remedying in the new version of a particular piece of software.

"Disintermediation" is an academic-sounding word for the simple concept of saving money by eliminating an intermediary. In a product or service distribution chain, intermediaries typically mark up the price, ostensibly because they offer some value-enhancing features. For example, travel agents have received commissions from airlines, hotels, and cruise lines because their intermediary function supposedly helped out both vendors and consumers. When airlines and other vendors stopped giving commissions, travel agents resorted to charging fees for their services. Prospective travelers not satisfied with the services of travel agents effectively cut them out by dealing directly with the airlines on their Web sites. In some instances, the lack of an intermediary may lower consumers' travel costs, but with the burden of doing what travel agents used to do, the possibility exists that travelers now have to incur the costs of searching for airfares and options without saving a commensurate amount of money.

Social Networking

ICE innovation provides enhanced opportunities for like-minded people to communicate and share content. Ironically, narrow interest groups and communities can evolve precisely because ICE technologies make global reach and scale possible. The near ubiquity of the Internet provides opportunities for both broadcasting and narrowcasting. Not only the most glitzy, glamorous, and timely content sources can expand their market penetration; millions of small groups can use the same ICE technologies to develop worldwide communities sharing the same narrow interests.

The Internet can provide an individual with opportunities to join a variety of cyberspace communities where participants share information, insights, and suggestions on chosen topics, such as bargain travel, telecommunications policy, copyright law, and podcasting (using the Internet to send audio and video programming). With regular interactions, members of a special-interest Internet community develop comradeship, despite the likelihood of having never met face-to-face.

SURVEILLANCE

Many consumers have a limited appreciation for the amount of data that can be gleaned from their Web activities. Worst-case scenarios involve identity and financial theft, which can mean countless hours reclaiming one's identity and reestablishing one's creditworthiness. Day in and day out, consumers consent to surveillance that few understand in terms of its pervasiveness and its potential for diminishing consumer advantages in Web-based transactions.

There are plenty of benign modes of surveillance that, with informed consent, may benefit consumers by selecting possibly desirable and customized advertisements based on buying and browsing behavior. But other types of surveillance provide the means for vendors to tilt a commercial transaction in their favor by acquiring data about individuals that vendors do not normally know in the brick-and-mortar world. For example, some vendors have deviated from a one-price-for-all strategy at their Web sites when their electronic surveillance detected that a prospective consumer had previously accessed Web sites that provided information on the asking prices of certain products at various outlets. When Internet-based vendors acquire information about what sites prospective customers have visited, they can size up the customers much the way that a car salesman in the physical world might assess the intentions and sophistication of a customer visiting an automobile showroom. Not all Web browsers offer informed consent to the tracking of their Internet navigation.

A grocery store owner might have hidden cameras capable of tracking a customer's every move to determine how many products were examined and how much time was spent at various locations within the store. If the grocery store management could extend the camera surveillance to all of a customer's grocery store visits and measure the customer's examination of competing store advertisements, the type, nature, and level of scrutiny would parallel what Web technologies can provide for Internet vendors.

Many grocery-store consumers have willingly consented to some degree of tracking in exchange for discounts available only to frequent buyers and club members. When a checkout clerk scans a club card, all purchases become part of a database compiled about that customer's purchasing behavior. The customer might benefit from this surveillance by receiving customized discount coupons based on purchases to date; for example, a paper-towel vendor might offer a special price or discount to induce the customer to shift brands. The grocery store management might even share the data in ways that might benefit the customer—for example, by offering discounts to health-food purchasers or by punishing with higher health insurance premiums those with a record of junk-food purchases.

A Web-based vendor may also raise prices for customers who apparently do not shop around and research product prices. Those who are offered inflated prices surely can take their business elsewhere. But how might customers learn of such price discrimination? For some consumers, factors such as convenience and speed in completing a transaction trump price. But when consumers pay a higher price in the physical world, most of the time they make a conscious decision to do so. Someone may pay more to buy ice at a convenience store than at a grocery store, but when shopping on the Internet, thanks to hidden surveillance and data mining, a buyer might not know that the detected lack of sophistication and diligence translated into a higher price.

POSITIVE NETWORK EFFECTS

ICE technological innovations have enhanced both the quality and the geographical scope of connections. Enhanced connectivity improves the quality of ICE access by speeding up downloading and uploading. Broadened geographical coverage increases the number of accessible content sites and the number of potential consumers—and the greater the number of potential users, the greater the value of the network. Economists term this improved-value proposition "positive network effects" because improved access typically translates into greater use of a network, more accessible points in the network, and greater benefits accruing to consumers in their use of the network.[5]

Positive network effects offer increasing value for content suppliers, service providers, and consumers. The story of the facsimile machine shows how this can work. As the number of offices and individuals having access to facsimile machines increased, the value of the machine increased as well. And with more facsimile machines accessible, their owners had greater occasion to use them. The Internet accrues the same sort of enhanced value as the number of communications points, users, and content sources increases. With simple and freely available software, just about every Internet user can create and receive the functional equivalent of a facsimile as an e-mail attachment. This nearly ubiquitous access to facsimile-like services—to text delivery—adds possibly significant value to users, particularly since they often incur no additional direct cost for sending and receiving text messages. E-mail attachments have significantly reduced the marketplace attractiveness of facsimile machines, which use the conventional wireline network to transmit bits at painfully slow speeds.

Companies able to ride the rising wave of network effects stand to benefit greatly, particularly if they provide the technology, software, or operating system used by most consumers. The more people who use Microsoft's word-processing software and operating system, the greater the value of the software and the greater the profits that the company generates. This example is somewhat misleading, however. It is not consumers enjoying all the wonderful and free content available via the World Wide Web that drive the Internet. Commercial transactions drive the Internet. Indeed, the vast majority of commercial transactions take place between businesses.

Business-to-business transactions are commonly referred to as B2B. The more visible commercial aspects of the Internet occur with B2C, business-to-consumer transactions. Businesses of all sizes can use the Internet to manage inventory, purchasing, sales, and deliveries, thereby enhancing productivity and efficiency. For example, the Internet makes it possible for retailers to reduce the cost of holding inventory through use of a just-in-time method for ordering replacement stock. Dell maintains virtually no inventory of computers; instead, it builds computers to meet a buyer's individual requirements and delivers them often within a week.

B2C commerce has captured most of the electronic-commerce headlines even though there are many more B2B transactions in terms of number and increasing value. Using the faster, better, smarter, cheaper, and more convenient template, many of the B2B transactions involve clothing, music, travel, software, gaming, gambling, financial services, books, and research on health and big-ticket purchases such as automobiles. Electronic commerce offers consumers access to many purchasing options and the power to search for the best prices. However, consumers have to become comfortable with transactions occurring at a distance; physical interaction with many products cannot occur, nor is a sales representative available as a reassuring physical presence. For many transactions, customers resort to a B2C Internet-mediated option for products that can be easily shipped or even delivered electronically. These products are typically subject to a low return rate and do not vary in quality or composition.

As more consumers become comfortable with B2C transactions, the monetary value and scope of the transactions will increase. The improved comfort levels will require improvements in transaction security, consumer confidence, trust in vendors, and adequate safeguards against fraud, identity theft, and deception.

MORE OR LESS: OPTIONS, REGULATION, AND VALUE

The potential impact of convergent ICE technologies elicits both optimism and skepticism. Although technologies favor anytime, anywhere access to content instead of access on a vendor-established schedule, content creators and distributors have many incentives to restrict access, sometimes by creating walled gardens, which limit consumer options. Fearful of losing control over subscribers if they have unconditional opportunities to access any content, wireless carriers have opted for the walled-garden approach. They have restricted subscribers' freedoms in many instances. AT&T, for example, has placed restrictions on the use of Apple iPhones for accessing Voice over Internet Protocol telephone services. Users of iPhones can access Skype's Internet telephone services when Wi-Fi access is available, but AT&T has embedded iPhones with software that blocks the use of the phones for accessing Skype via the AT&T network.

We can understand why AT&T would want to block access to Internet-based telephone services: AT&T stands to lose toll revenues, especially for international calls, if iPhone users can avoid expensive AT&T rates and opt for Skype's substantially lower rates. Arguably, AT&T has a lawful right to set conditions for the use of its network, especially when the company subsidizes handsets and needs to recoup the cost of that subsidy through monthly service fees. But even after a subscriber has paid subsidy-recovering rates for two years and even when a subscriber uses an unsubsidized phone, AT&T persists in blocking Skype access. In these instances, AT&T has deliberately reduced the value and utility of its service by forcing subscribers to stay within the company's walled garden of limited and more-expensive outbound long-distance calling options.

The FCC and other government agencies have not aggressively responded to this and other network closure strategies, which comes across as a type of regulatory failure. Absent evidence that AT&T risks catastrophic harm to its network by providing access to Skype services, a refusal to provide such access simply preserves a revenue stream by making subscribers captive to a single long-distance telephone service option. Wireline telephone subscribers would never tolerate such a company-imposed restriction, nor would personal computer users accept any limitation on the sites and services that they can access via links supplied by Internet service providers. When a rural North Carolina telephone company tried to block Skype access by DSL subscribers, the FCC swiftly intervened and imposed sanctions on the company leading to a small monetary forfeiture. Yet when a cell phone manufacturer or carrier employs the same tactic, the FCC so far has failed to act.

As we have seen, many governments and their ICE industry regulators seem to view market self-regulation as a future replacement for government oversight. We have seen plenty of evidence supporting this scenario, but an equal or greater volume of evidence indicates the onset of less-than-perfect competition. Digital literacy provides the greatest guard against stakeholders that pursue a deregulatory agenda and a government that, without empirical proof of competition, has shucked off its few remaining public interest responsibilities.

CHAPTER NINE

The Impact of Technological and Market Convergence

THE CONVERGENCE OF ICE technologies and markets substantially raises the stakes for haves and have-nots: for individuals and nations that have access to digital technologies and services, along with the skills needed for their effective use, and individuals and nations that do not. Those lacking access—whether because of financial limitations or reluctance to invest in digital literacy—risk falling further behind in the ability to exploit ICE technologies for personal, societal, and national gain. The stakes constantly rise. The issue is not just how best to access entertainment and communication links. More important is the question of whether and how a nation can use ICE technologies and services to exploit comparative advantages in the production and distribution of goods and services.

Access to leading-edge technologies and the knowledge of how to use them enhance what individuals and nations can achieve. So-called knowledge workers, who need to access, process, and distribute data, can exploit information-processing technologies to increase efficiency regardless of industry. Even knowledge workers involved in the production of raw materials, such as mining and agriculture, can help their firms operate more efficiently. While visions of a "frictionless economy" surely overstate the contribution of telecommunications and information processing, we should not dismiss their impact, particularly on information-intensive industries such as banking.

Digital divides in the past largely separated individuals with access to telephones and the ability to pay for calls from those with neither. In developed countries, the divide also separated individuals who owned and could program equipment, such as videocassette recorders, from those lacking the equipment or the skill to use all of its features. Now the digital divide separates individuals and nations with cheap, effective, and widely available access to the Internet at high bitrates from those with inferior and more costly access. Digital literacy richly rewards people and nations with access to ICE technologies and the skills needed to exploit fully the services that such technologies can provide.

DIGITAL LIBERTY

With digital liberty, users of ICE technologies have increasing control over the terms, conditions, and manner in which they communicate, access content, and activate services. Indeed, technological convergence eliminates a concrete sense of distance, place, and time. It offers users freedom of movement, choice, and access. Before ICE technologies converged and created a seamless web of functionality, users had far fewer and more constraining options. For example, telephone users had to remain tethered to networks via wires. Now an increasing number of wireline telephone subscribers consider cutting the cord permanently instead of augmenting wireline phone service with a wireless option, such as cell phones. Users of VoIP services can even "port into" the Internet cloud and access most telephone networks wherever a high-speed Internet link exists. The cost of most Internet services does not vary whether a link crosses the street, a nation, or the globe. Internet-mediated electronic commerce can occur twenty-four hours a day, every day.

Being able to sever the cord and access just about anything, anywhere, with many different devices and without regard to time or distance is a powerful tool for users. It is an equally powerful tool for destroying existing business models and the assumptions that drive them. Telecommunications and information-processing ventures can no longer establish a business plan and price services based on distance, location, time of access, and possibly even minutes of use. This loss of pricing control shifts the balance of power to consumers, but the wise business manager accepts this reality and strives to generate revenues through services and features for which consumers will gladly pay.

Technological convergence can add value to an ICE transaction. It can enhance efficiency and productivity while also lowering the underlying cost of a transaction or at least the cost of processing it. When consumers perceive an enhanced value proposition in an ICE technology, manufacturers and service providers need not suffer financially, because increased and diversified use may compensate for lower profit margins. Here are two examples of enhanced productivity and cost savings.

Insurance adjusters investigating claims make frequent use of cell phones equipped with cameras. The online delivery of from-the-scene photographs expedites processing of claims to the mutual benefit of insured parties, the insurer, the cell phone manufacturer, and the mobile telephone service provider. The insurer can make better use of adjusters' time and effort. The cell phone manufacturer can refute allegations that adding another feature to what used to be a telephone offers little value. The mobile telephone company can generate additional revenues either through the increased minutes of use or through per-photograph transmission charges. The insured party gets faster processing of a claim by the insurance company.

VoIP presents a similar win-win proposition even though at first blush it appears to harm incumbent telephone companies. VoIP lets consumers make telephone calls via the Internet and incur only a fraction of the charges currently imposed for conventional circuit-switched calls. By routing calls via the Internet carriers can reduce transmission and interconnection charges that come into play with conventional telephone services. With VoIP, a consumer can select a virtual location as the origination point for calls; that is, a VoIP subscriber can select any area code, regardless of which area code is associated with the geographical location where the person actually lives. All calls to and from the selected area code appear as local calls even though the VoIP provider might route the call to a distant location. A caller to a VoIP subscriber based thousands of miles away would likely incur no toll charges if the VoIP subscriber secured a telephone number assignment with the same area code as the caller's.

It may appear that incumbent local and long-distance telephone companies financially suffer when VoIP transforms long-distance toll calls into free local calls. But technological convergence is already forcing carriers to abandon the expectation that most of their revenues will accrue from voice telephone services. New competitors are providing phone service, and users are migrating from wireline to wireless service, so incumbents have to identify and serve new profit centers. A key new opportunity for incumbent local and long-distance carriers lies in providing high-speed Internet access to end users, as well as managing the high-capacity, high-speed telecommunications links that make up the networks used to route Internet traffic. The mutually beneficial outcome achieved by technological convergence and zero-charge VoIP international calls occurs when consumers save money, new VoIP providers acquire market share, and incumbent telephone companies adjust business plans to concentrate on providing new services (Internet access and data networking) to compensate for declining local and long-distance telephone revenues.

CARRIER FREEDOM

Carriers benefit from technological convergence by ridding themselves of service limitations. Telephone companies no longer provide only telephone service, just as cable television companies provide far more than cable television. Technological convergence removes the linkage between a specific service and a specific technology. As the rush to become one-stop shops for telephone, video, and Internet service grows, a carrier's wireline or wireless architecture can provide the medium for access to all three types of services. Telephone companies have retrofitted their narrowband copper-wire local lines to handle broadband Internet services. Cable television operators have adjusted their coaxial cable networks to handle increased bandwidth, which can be subdivided into channels for video programming, telephony, and Internet access.

Such ICE innovations and proliferating options have reduced somewhat the amount of time that consumers spend watching broadcast and cable television, especially those with broadband Internet connections.[1] However, the reduction in viewership marks neither a decline in total consumer demand for video content nor a reduction in the total amount of time spent by consumers in accessing ICE content and services. Early adopters of new ICE services allocate more time to such activities as video gaming, gambling, accessing Internet content via wireless devices (such as cell phones), surfing the Internet, and text messaging. Because many people consume multiple ICE services simultaneously, multitasking also increases the aggregate amount of consumption.

Content creators and distributors, as well as the advertisers that financially support access to content, face an increasingly daunting question: Where can they attract the most viewers and viewers with certain demographic characteristics? The answer to this question requires, among other things, data on where and with what devices consumers access content. For video content in a pre-convergent ICE environment, the vast majority of consumers watched televised shows from simple, inexpensive devices located primarily in family rooms. Consumption of entertainment and some information took place via television sets, while computers, located outside the family room, provided increasingly robust access mainly to information-processing and communications services.

With ICE convergence, the functions of television sets, computer monitors, and cellular telephone screens have merged. Many consumers no longer segregate content access as a function of a device, location within a residence, or the mobility of a device. The television set has become more complex, with greater picture resolution and the ability to provide access to far more than news and entertainment. ICE convergence also means that access via computer monitors will continue to expand; the computer monitor may grow in size and move from the desktop to the living room, where it might function as both a television screen and a computer monitor. In addition, ICE convergence will reduce gaps in the type, nature, and variety of content available via screens used in such mobile telecommunications devices as cell phones.

As options for content display proliferate, so do the options for content access. With consumers able to access a wealth of content anytime and anyplace, the mode of delivery typically involves digitized content either delivered in real time or previously downloaded to disk drives and flash memory chips, like those installed in computers and cell phones. These devices can collect and store digitized content. With improvements in screen resolution, options for temporary and permanent storage of content, and miniaturization of components, mobile telephones have also become a platform for access to video content.

As the functions of televisions and computer monitors merge, consumers will shift their perception of what constitutes a computer. Currently, most residential personal computers perform a variety of self-contained, software-managed functions. A user loads his or her computer with software designed to provide a particular function: word processing, say, or preparation of income-tax returns, e-mail, or photograph editing.

An internal or external hard drive provides ample storage for both software applications and work products. Individual personal computers may connect with the Internet for access to more software, content, and ICE applications.

The relationship between a personal computer and an external source of content involves a client, the computer, accessing content from a host computer located elsewhere. The concept of a home-based media server anticipates a massive upturn in demand for capacity to store content in both residential computers and the Internet cloud, and a networking technology able to deliver different content to different family members simultaneously. A media server operates as a highly functional computer. Not only can it store a very large amount of content, but it is capable of linking the stored content with a variety of devices that display content, including legacy devices such as personal computers, television sets, high-fidelity stereo amplifiers and receivers, and media players. A wireless networking technology such as Wi-Fi can deliver content to multiple playback devices located throughout a home. With the demand for content growing substantially, consumers will come to rely on a combination of on-site storage within their computers and other devices and cloud-computing options, which rely on off-site storage.

THE END OF APPOINTMENT TELEVISION

Access to content outside a particular device by media servers and via the Internet provides the basis for on-demand access to content from televisions and other ICE devices. Rather than having to arrange one's personal schedule around a onetime broadcast of a particular program, access to content becomes a matter of programming devices to search stored or quickly accessible content to satisfy specified tastes. Currently, devices such as digital video recorders enable consumers to copy specific television programming for later viewing. Smart televisions, video recorders, and other devices will continue to expand the search for content beyond a specific channel or inventory of channels to the broader content platform that makes up a portion of the Internet.

The end of appointment television will present major challenges to advertisers and the primary means by which they subsidize consumers' access to video and other Internet content. In most instances, financial support from advertisers reduces or eliminates the need to secure direct payment from consumers. With mass media, advertisers can secure access to an extremely large audience, thereby achieving the lowest cost per thousand or million exposures to an advertisement. Audiences have already fragmented into smaller and smaller segments as cable television networks proliferate and as consumers migrate from broadcast and cable television to other media and content sources. The major broadcast networks, which used to share 90-plus percent of the viewing public among them now typically share less than 32 percent.[2] Advertisers can attract huge audiences only for such major events as sporting championships.

Advertisers have already had to adapt to market segmentation. Some specialty advertisers gladly trade off large, undifferentiated audiences for smaller but better-targeted ones. Advertisers of soap and other mass-market products prefer to reach the largest possible audience, while smaller niche marketers, of, for example, medication used primarily by senior citizens, welcome the opportunity to reach a targeted audience.

Advertisers can easily calibrate and target their sales pitches over the World Wide Web. Because of the self-selected content available via the Internet, specialty advertisers have a readily available target audience. Travel advertisers, for example, can reach consumers who have pointed their browsers to Web sites devoted to travel or who have entered travel-related searches at sites such as Google. Web sites are so specific that advertisers can focus on small groups of consumers who are likely to buy, so a Caribbean resort might advertise on a Web site devoted to Caribbean resort travel.

For more general Web sites, advertisers can employ a variety of tactics to determine which advertisement to pitch to which consumer. Using both lawful and questionable techniques, advertisers can acquire information about an individual's Web-browsing habits and supply advertisements in which that particular person might have an interest. Lawful techniques include securing consent to track a user's Web viewership, downloads, and purchases; surveillance software inserted in consumers' computers is typically used for such tracking. Questionable and contentious tracking typically involves more pervasive and intrusive software used without informed consent on the part of consumers.

Currently, legitimate Web advertisers and Web site operators face a quandary caused by widespread abuse of advertising tactics and surveillance of consumers. Because of intrusive and annoying pop-up banners and other advertisements, consumers attempt to block any and all advertisements from reaching their computer screens, even though advertising provides the financial support for free access to desirable content.

Try as consumers may, however, they cannot prevent the proliferation of advertisements. Internet-blocking technologies only partially prevent unsolicited commercial spam—electronic junk mail—from clogging e-mail networks and the Web. But if consumers succeed in blocking advertisements more effectively, they risk losing opportunities for freely accessing content. When television viewers used digital video recorders to speed through conventional thirty- and sixty-second ads, advertisers threatened manufacturers with litigation and integrated advertisements into program story lines. With the potential demise of appointment television, then, consumers face a trade-off: the chance to access more and customized content but possibly at a higher cost.

On-demand television largely eliminates the opportunity for consumers to get a free ride—that is, to use an ICE product, subsidized by advertisers, without having to buy the advertised products and services. Although the time may come when youthful viewers may have to buy the medications and other products advertised during broadcasts of the network evening news, for now, anyway, they can lend their eyes and ears to advertisements in exchange for the opportunity to consume freely. With pay-per-view, consumers may have access to lots of premium material, albeit available for a price. ICE convergence and technological innovations may increasingly facilitate access to a "long tail" of content—to a great diversity of options associated with particular content—offered by advertisers eager to secure sales.[3] An alternative perspective on the future of advertising emphasizes the ongoing prominence of blockbuster mass-market content.[4]

The concept of appointment television assumes a static time, place, and distribution medium for delivering programs. As we have seen, technological convergence eliminates each constraint. Recording devices make it possible to shift viewing to more convenient times. The Internet makes it possible to deliver content to different places and viewing devices, making it accessible at different times, and making it accessible in different formats, including ones that make it possible to store the content for multiple viewings and possibly for network distribution to others. When consumers can access video programming via many devices, providers, and technologies, they gain freedom and flexibility.

Video consumers appear to be interested in accessing content via different devices, including cell phones and computer monitors, in lieu of or in addition to the conventional television set. Only recently have companies tested whether consumers will pay for such flexibility, but it is clear that access to video content can be achieved via different platforms, not just from incumbent broadcasters' antennas or cable television operators' wire networks. Providing flexibility can diminish control over consumption, but content creators and licensors have responded to consumers' nonconventional viewing with new techniques to manage and protect their intellectual property. Digitization of content contributes to the ease of copying programs, and the Internet facilitates rapid, low-cost distribution of program content with or without authorization. However, improvements in technologies to manage digital rights offer ways to limit time, format, and device shifting of content.

The Slingbox device and similar software options exemplify the new opportunities available for consumers to use content on their own terms and according to their own schedules. The Slingbox company provides consumers with a two-hundred-dollar device that can route cable, satellite, and recorded video programming to the Internet via a high-speed link for remote access with a computer or wireless handset—anywhere a similar high-speed Internet connection exists. In a way, the Slingbox is a virtual remote control for a home set-top box, satellite receiver, and digital video recorder. With a Slingbox, a traveler can tap into recorded television content in a home-based device or into television content being delivered to a home-based device. The Slingbox eliminates the exclusive right to distribute certain intellectual property, a right for which broadcasters and cable networks have paid handsomely. For content providers, remote access to content means that they cannot expect to segment all audiences by the physical location of the members.

Incumbents have begun to realize that place-shifting devices, such as the Slingbox, and piracy largely eliminate programming exclusivity. Rather than fight this technological imperative, the broadcast television networks have opted to make available via the Internet some of their most popular, prime-time programming. The networks stream the content—

download the programming for continuous display—rather than allow viewers to download the entire program as a single file. By streaming video content they make it more difficult for viewers to speed through advertisements and to redistribute the content as a file. Internet-mediated video programming displayed on televisions, computer monitors, and cell phones constitutes a major time-, place-, device-, and format-shifting option increasingly available to consumers.

BROADBAND FLAVORS

One of the key drivers of ICE innovation and consumer support lies in the migration from narrowband analog networks to digital broadband networks capable of providing high-speed data transmissions. Because of the expense in developing a ubiquitous broadband infrastructure and uncertainty about whether adequate subscribership will develop to make service profitable, incumbent operators in the United States initially balked at upgrading existing physical plant to provide higher data-transmission bitrates and ruled out the installation of new fiber-optic cables, except for some "greenfield" new construction. Many other nations, industrialized or not, with various degrees of population density and other demographic characteristics, have developed and executed strategies to expedite broadband development primarily by reducing risk for carriers, achieved through subsidies, tax credits, demand stimulation, and digital literacy campaigns and by service as an early supplier of broadband-delivered e-government services.[5] Notwithstanding a slow start, U.S. telephone and cable television companies recently have begun to accept the competitive necessity and upside potential in deploying broadband services.

Upgrading Legacy Networks

Most residences have two wires that enter the premises to provide essential ICE services. Copper is the metallic medium used to conduct and deliver these services based on quite old technologies. The telephone company uses a thin pair of twisted copper wires to deliver to and receive from telephones a narrowband analog signal designed to handle a voice telephone call. The two copper wires carry a direct current of low voltage onto which a weak audio signal travels much like an ocean surfer riding a wave. The cable television company uses a higher-capacity copper wire to deliver video programming. But a third wire also enters the residence, provided by an electric utility company to deliver power, and this wire has some potential to deliver ICE content riding piggyback on the electric current.

Without significant upgrades and refinement, none of the wires can provide a broadband medium. The bandwidth of the telephone line corresponds to less than 40 percent of the channel used to provide an AM radio signal. With only 4 kilohertz in bandwidth, a basic telephone line must be retrofitted to offer 1,500 kilohertz in bandwidth so that the maximum data transmission rate can increase from about 52,000 bits per second to 768,000 bits per second or higher. The conventional telephone line using traditional analog transmission technology requires a modem to simulate the binary ones and zeros used in data communications.

Both traditional and upgraded telephone networks require installation of an additional piece of equipment on subscribers' premises. For a traditional network a modem modulates audio signals to mimic a digital bitstream for transmission into the digital Internet and demodulates incoming data signals for conversion and delivery back through the analog telephone network. The narrow 4-kilohertz channel severely limits the throughput available from the telephone line; the type of line restricts the amount of data measured in bytes that the network can deliver on a timely basis. But because the telephone line has two wires, users can send and receive traffic simultaneously. The upgraded telephone network also requires a modem for accessing the digital subscriber line (DSL) bandwidth portion of the copper wire now configured to supply both telephony and Internet access.

The cable telephone line provides much greater throughput because the size of the carrier available for transmission of traffic is typically 750 megahertz, which means that the bandwidth available is vastly greater than a telephone line's. However, unless and until the cable operator chooses to allocate a portion of the bandwidth for Internet access and to add an upstream link, all 750 megahertz provide one-way video delivery. Cable operators need only one 6-megahertz channel to supply high-speed Internet access at bitrates three or four times faster than DSL rates.

The electric utility line provides a high-voltage alternating current that until recently created an inhospitable environment for the carriage of anything but electricity. Innovations in digital signal processing now make it possible to ferret out separate data-communications traffic amid the noise and interference caused by the torrent of electrons and by the powerful low-frequency signal transmitted by the electricity.

Digital Subscriber Lines

Telephone companies provide DSL service by upgrading the local copper-wire loop that connects subscribers with a company switching facility known as a central office or end office. To make the local loop capable of handling high-speed data services, telephone companies expand the bandwidth of the carrier signal that it generates at the central office. Lines with expanded carrier bandwidth continue to provide a narrowband medium for voice communications, along with the associated dial tones and call ringing, but they can also provide a two-way channel for Internet access.

The laws of physics and electronics create significant impediments to the utility of DSL largely because telephone companies designed their networks solely to provide narrowband, two-way voice services. To provide reliable service, a telephone company limits the distance between subscribers and the central office. At short distances, typically less than three miles, the company can use direct current (DC) electricity to power the links with each subscriber instead of having to rely on alternating current (AC) throughout the network to power the amplifiers needed to strengthen signals. A DC-powered network offers greater reliability because the network can use batteries located at each central office to maintain the low power needed to operate the network even when the electricity grid temporarily shuts down. The telephone company's DC-powered networks typically remain operational even when the AC-powered cable television networks fail.

Because the design of a telephone network requires short physical links between subscribers and the central office to sustain the amplifier-free configuration, not all prospective consumers qualify for access to DSL service. The physical distance between a prospective DSL subscriber and the nearest central office must not exceed three miles, and the line itself must not have certain equipment that blocks or impedes use of the additional, higher frequencies that the telephone company will activate for Internet access. When confronted with additional telephone subscribers located increasingly farther from a central office, telephone companies have used techniques that extend the permissible distance of local loops in lieu of building additional central offices. Loading coils extend the reach of the twisted copper wire for narrowband telephone service at low frequencies but block any use of the higher frequencies needed to provide DSL service. Another device, known as a bridge tap, cuts into an existing link in order to serve new subscribers. The new spliced wire configuration may increase the length of the copper wire used to link subscribers to the central office; in the worst-case scenario, it disqualifies prospective DSL subscribers now located beyond the three-mile range.

The operating limitations of DSL technology make it a short-term, transitional service. Most telephone companies have recognized the market attractiveness of higher-speed data services but cautiously chose to conserve capital by upgrading the copper local loops instead of replacing the wire with more expensive fiber-optic strands. As demand grows for ever-increasing bandwidth and throughput, telephone companies will eventually replace their copper wires with fiber-optic cables that use laser beams to transmit extremely wideband carriers capable of delivering extraordinary amounts of data.

Cable Modems

Cable television companies have an easier and less expensive way to upgrade their networks for high-speed data access largely because the coaxial cable they use already provides a wideband carrier. However, if they have not already done so, cable television companies need to add an upstream link to the large downstream carrier. Companies typically upgrade their networks with between 860 and 1,000 megahertz of bandwidth so that ample capacity exists for conventional analog cable television channels, advanced digital channels, downstream bandwidth (initially only 6 megahertz) for delivering Internet content, and some upstream bandwidth for Internet access, as well as pay-per-view and other customer links with the company.

Cable modem access to the Internet typically does not have the bandwidth limitations besetting DSL. However, other challenges exist. Unlike DSL, which extends the bandwidth of the local loop dedicated to a particular subscriber, cable modem service involves a shared medium. The coaxial cable serving a neighborhood carries all of the neighborhood's video traffic and all of the neighborhood's upstream and downstream Internet traffic, too, so the traffic requirements of neighbors affect network delivery speeds and performance.

Cable modem service operates much like a local area network (LAN), which companies and universities install within an office or throughout an office park or campus. Most LANs use Ethernet software, which manages traffic by creating addresses for each computer, ensures proper traffic delivery, and mostly prevents collisions between bitstreams heading to different destinations. LANs can simultaneously receive and deliver traffic to multiple destinations, or multicast. Cable modem networks offer similar multicasting capabilities, but during peak usage times, demand for the shared, high-speed network may lower bitrate transmission speeds to accommodate the requirements of each household. Nevertheless, the bit delivery speeds by cable modem exceed the bit delivery speeds by DSL, albeit at a higher price.

Like telephone service, cable modem service also uses a transitional technology; cable television companies are also increasingly replacing copper coaxial cables with fiber-optic links. Many cable systems already use fiber-optic links from the central facility that collects programming and processes Internet traffic. The central facility, commonly known as the headend, routes broadband traffic to nodes situated within a neighborhood. Eventually the copper wire linking nodes with individual homes will be replaced.

Broadband over Power Line

Broadband over power line (BPL) may provide a third wireline option into homes and businesses. Because electric companies directly link with home wiring, consumers can have residence-wide network access with the BPL technology. Since the 1940s, electric companies have had limited ability to piggyback slow-speed data, for meter reading and load management, onto of the powerful low-frequency carrier created by the flow of electrons delivered as electrical power. Innovations in digital signal processing enable electric companies to transmit data at rates up to 3,000,000 bits per second. Integrated circuit chips can process low-power data transmissions riding on top of the electrical current.

The key to effective BPL lies in its ability to transmit and receive signals despite a harsh, noisy, and high-voltage atmosphere. Technological innovations make this possible, but operators still face challenges, particularly where the electricity flow changes power levels, as occurs when a transformer steps down the power for home usage. At transformer locations, companies providing BPL may resort to a wireless option to avoid having the traffic route though the transformer. At any location where BPL traffic uses open-air radio spectrum the potential exists for interference with other spectrum users. Both BPL and expanded wireless options offer the potential for reducing the market dominance in Internet access shared by the local cable television company and its telephone company counterpart.

Decoupling Access and Content

The high-speed networks offered by telephone companies (DSL), cable television companies (cable modem), and utility companies (BPL) provide access to the Internet, but little, if any, content. The separation of conduit and content has made sense for public utilities, such as electric, gas, and water companies. Ventures that concentrate on the carriage of an essential commodity or service have no incentive to favor one source versus others. Such ventures have qualified for special privileges and incurred public responsibilities as common carriers. Common carriers agree to treat all consumers fairly and to provide service to any and all qualified users. Such nondiscrimination favors widespread access.

Internet service providers do not want to operate as common carriers even if they do not generate much of their own content. The Internet, to which ISPs provide access, seamlessly blends content and the network conduits used to link content source and content consumer. ISP subscribers pay a flat monthly rate that covers compensation to the ISP for its telecommunications link and any in-house content, as well as for links to and from content created by other ventures. Similarly, technological and marketplace convergence make it increasingly impractical to carve out the telecommunications, bit-delivery portion of a service that integrates transmission with content. For example, when a cable television company provides access to the Internet and ISPs offer telephone services, the companies qualify for limited regulation as providers of information services because the FCC has chosen to subordinate or ignore the telecommunications aspect of the consolidated services while emphasizing the information-processing features.

Separating conduit from content provides a convenient means to limit government regulation to the telecommunications functions involved in delivering content bits.[6] However, most ICE companies blend, or will blend, communications and information-processing services in ways that make it impossible for regulators to disaggregate or decouple the telecommunications element. Combining content and conduit presents severe regulatory challenges, as we have seen.

Absent a common-carrier requirement, specifically the requirement that a carrier provide services to the general public without discrimination, incentives may exist for bit transporters to favor a corporate affiliate or to discriminate among similar content providers. In a robustly competitive marketplace, consumers can punish ventures that engage in discrimination that reduces the flexibility and utility of their service. But in markets without robust facilities-based competition, the lack of a common-carrier-type requirement can result in preferential treatment for one content source over others. The ongoing debate about network neutrality sets the need for government imposition of a nondiscrimination requirement against total reliance on marketplace forces to ensure fairness.

ONE-STOP SHOPPING AND THE TRIPLE PLAY

ICE convergence creates opportunities for individual ventures to provide ever more equipment and services to consumers, who in turn receive financial inducements to become one-stop shoppers. In triple-play deals, consumers benefit from the convenience of having one bill for three ICE services—telephone, video, and Internet access—and can accrue significant savings.

Although consumers readily see the benefits in one-stop shopping, significant, less obvious disadvantages also may exist. Consumers do not typically consider the risk of relying on one venture for three major services. With triple the financial stakes in providing the services, ventures may perhaps have an incentive to engage in anticompetitive practices. Perhaps no single company will succeed in reacquiring a monopoly, but the playing field might easily tilt if one or more ventures perceive a competitive advantage in not cooperating with others on facilities interconnection, equipment standards, and other interoperability issues.

Advocates for regulator-imposed nondiscrimination responsibilities, posed for common carriers, claim that anticompetitive practices can occur in each of three major service sectors. Local telephone companies might favor long-distance corporate affiliates by blocking, delaying, degrading, or charging extra to deliver calls from non-affiliates. Cable television companies that provide telephone services might engage in similar disruptions. In the video programming marketplace, cable television ventures that have made investments in both programming and program distribution might refuse to make programming available to telephone companies and other entrants in the business of retailing access to such content. In the Internet access market, consumer advocates complain that cable television ventures can exploit their largely unregulated status even when providing new services.

Triple-play customers may also encounter unexpected technological limitations and hassles. Most probably do not understand that buying the triple-play package may limit their ability to make and receive calls during power outages. VoIP customers may not have access to all emergency-911 features or the option of making and receiving calls from numerous phones unless there is a wireless home network that links all phones to a router that accesses the DSL or cable modem line. Use of cordless phones may present new operational challenges and possibly the need for replacement phones.

THE CONTENT CREATORS' DILEMMA

ICE convergence has both positive and negative impacts on content creators, but the potential is often underestimated, and fears of piracy and lost control often predominate. Convergence forces change, usually including a significant modification in how an ICE venture does business. Content creators favor the status quo because it has led to ample profits, growth opportunities, and the ability to manage access to products. Convergence generates higher risks but, possibly, greater rewards.

Historically, content creators and other incumbents have perceived financial threats from new technologies, even though in most instances incumbents have retained control over innovations. New technologies often augment markets and provide new opportunities to display content. Usually the new technology becomes a profitable alternative distribution channel for content rather than completely disrupting a market, forcing incumbents to offer lower service rates or risk losing market share. Where a new technology replaces an old technology, incumbent operators have managed to make the transition to the new technology without losing customers.

ICE innovations can stimulate piracy by making it easier to copy content without detection and punishment. But vilifying innovation makes little sense; the underlying technology can facilitate lawful uses as well as criminal behavior. Ironically, too, disparaged innovations can in time offer financial salvation. For example, spokespersons for the movie industry at first considered videocassette recorders, with their ability to duplicate video content, as likely to impose severe economic harm. Jack Valenti, then president of the Motion Picture Association of America, testified before a congressional panel in 1982 "that the VCR is to the American film producer and the American public as the Boston strangler is to the woman home alone."[7] As it turned out, except for a few blockbuster films, most movies generate far greater revenues from videotape and now DVD sales and rentals than from theater receipts. Technologies promoting home viewing of commercial movies have generated far more revenues and profits than losses, even though video-recording devices may preempt a visit to a theater and provide a pirated and lower-cost alternative.

But innovations in ICE technology do appear to shift the ratio of lawful to unlawful copying. In a digital environment, anyone can make a nearly identical copy quickly. Analog copies evidenced a significant degradation in quality and typically took as long to make as it would take to view the original, with few ways to accelerate the copying process. Making a tape recording of a vinyl record or another tape with a videocassette recorder involved a tedious process. With software and computer hard drives, the duplication process has become simple and convenient. Adding the Internet to the mix even makes it possible for strangers to share content anonymously.

Content creators have every reason to worry about piracy and, in particular, the heightened ease and frequency of piracy made possible by ICE innovations. However, they need to create impediments to illegal copying, but do it in a manner that does not prevent the use of ICE technologies for legal copying or in the promotion of new business models. For what seemed an eternity, the music industry thought the best tactics for fighting piracy involved aggressive litigation, public "education," and a refusal to embrace Internet-mediated content delivery. But it learned that attempting to block technological innovation does not significantly impede its use. Industry leaders also belatedly understood that consumers will resort to legal and illegal self-help to circumvent an undesirable and unsustainable business strategy—for example, requiring consumers to buy content in multitrack albums.

The recording industry used to sell content in the form of inexpensive singles, with a hit song on one side of a vinyl record and a B-side supplemental song on the other. The long-playing multitrack album—a record with multiple or very long pieces of music—largely replaced singles in the 1970s and 1980s. When compact disks replaced vinyl records, the music industry chose to raise album prices, even though companies saved money after the initial migration. Music consumers resented the profit-maximizing tactics so much that many considered digital piracy reasonable retaliation for price gouging and the refusal to sell single songs.

Today the music industry has begun to realize that Internet delivery of individual songs can provide supplemental revenues rather than always cannibalizing 100 percent of CD sales. Even for sales that might otherwise have taken place at a retail store, content owners (not necessarily the creators) financially benefit from Internet delivery capturing a larger share of the sale price. When a music company creates its own e-commerce Web site to sell music or when it collaborates with an intermediary that sells music, fewer companies operate in the channel of distribution. The fewer the intermediaries, the greater the financial share available to the remaining ventures. The Internet provides many opportunities to eliminate the intermediary—to disintermediate.

Coupling digital technologies, which provide quick and near-perfect duplication of content, with the Internet, which provides a cheap and widespread distribution medium for digitally formatted content, creates an incredibly powerful engine for both commerce and piracy. Digital literacy requires an appreciation for the ownership rights of content creators. Rampant piracy shows a fundamental disregard for ownership and a dismissal of the basic premise that creators of desirable content deserve financial compensation in addition to popularity and other nonmonetary rewards. The users of the digital technologies make the decision—informed or otherwise—to violate intellectual property rights or not, to be pirates or good citizens.

The fact that Apple and other online vendors can sell millions of dollars in music downloads annually despite illegal but free options attests to the ability of technologies to facilitate development of new markets, not just black markets. In any case, not every technological innovation facilitates piracy even as it provides consumers with new and better options for using content fairly. Governments should not deem unlawful the use of any technological innovation just because it might facilitate piracy.[8] In the coming years, legislatures and the courts will have to find ways to balance the rights of content creators and content consumers. Content creators may want to control their digital rights and manage the licensing of rights to others, but they cannot invoke intellectual property rights to justify the use of new technologies to lock down content in ways that prevent lawful uses. On the other hand, fair, noncommercial uses of content do not extend to each and every Internet and wireless option that technological innovations can provide.

FINDING A BALANCE IN DIGITAL RIGHTS MANAGEMENT

Currently a war rages between individuals and groups using technological innovations to achieve effective copyright protection and those looking to circumvent or crack these safeguards. The U.S. Congress has enacted legislation that makes it a crime to circumvent copyright protection techniques,[9] but the law possibly also makes it a crime to use legitimate and lawful innovations to consume content. Using technology to improve digital rights management (DRM) should not go so far as to foreclose what has been deemed fair use; it should not prevent the lawful consumption of copyrighted material in ways that do not materially and financially harm the content creator while quite possibly contributing to overall social welfare.

Fair use makes it possible for teachers to copy portions of copyrighted material for research and educational purposes. The concept also applies to critics and commentators who quote from copyrighted works. Fair use extends the flexible use of content by consumers interested in recording broadcast television programming for later viewing and in converting purchased music from one format to another so that it can be replayed over a different device—for example, converting music on a purchased CD into MP3 files that can generate the music on portable playback devices such as the iPod.

Many types of content shifting from one time, device, or format to another constitute fair use.[10] At some point, however, technology-facilitated fair use might so extend consumer flexibility as to foreclose sales or make it too easy for piracy to occur.[11] Legislatures and courts need to allow new fair-use opportunities—for example, use of a device that provides remote access to purchased content from a different location—while also legitimizing new DRM techniques that foreclose or block some forms of time, place, format, and device shifting.

The Interface for High-Definition Multimedia

The current DRM/fair-use debate includes a dispute over what copying and device-shifting opportunities consumers of high-definition video content should have. High-definition televisions display the best video resolution only when a High-Definition Multimedia Interface (HDMI) cable is used to connect a video source, such as a DVD player, to the television set. Content creators can insert DRM instructions (flags) for a television set that specify the extent to which those who access that television set can use content in ways beyond simple, one-time-only passive display. The HDMI connection makes it possible to record onto and display high-definition content on and from digital video disks and other content storage devices, but only if the DRM flag allows such use, not on the basis of what a court might consider fair use. In its most restrictive form, a DRM flag on a high-definition television interface could attempt to resurrect the concept of appointment television by allowing once-only viewing at a time specified by the broadcaster and the cable television network operator without the options for playback, recording, and subsequent use. A DRM flag sends a signal to television receivers, cable television set-top boxes, digital video recorders, and computers specifying what kinds of subsequent recording, playback, and distribution options the consumer of specific content shall have. DRM flags can operate quite effectively, but they can also foreclose lawful options previously available to consumers. In the worst-case scenario, DRM flags could vest in copyright holders and licensors the power to specify unilaterally what uses they deem permissible.

Content creators, particularly ones contemplating the distribution of high-quality programming to high-definition television sets, need assurance that unscrupulous consumers will lack readily available options for distributing such programming either via the Internet or to other home-based display terminals. Holders of intellectual property rights may not want to foreclose uses, but they may believe that desperate times require desperate, self-help measures to prevent rampant piracy of high-definition televised content. In their zeal to protect content from widespread, unlicensed distribution still in the high-definition format, video programmers appear to welcome opportunities to foreclose time, place, format, and device shifting even if the shifting might not violate the copyright laws—that is, when a consumer simply wants to shift viewing from a television set to a computer monitor, or vice versa.

Analog Holes

With or without reasonable justification, many consumers have considered their own self-help options when content creators foreclose or condition flexibility in usage and recording. Even at the risk of engaging in a practice that might constitute unlawful circumvention of a copyright protection process, consumers might proceed with such an option. They do not welcome what they consider unreasonable and unlawful restrictions on the use of content, particularly content that they have already purchased, or content distributed by conventional broadcast or cable television systems. The latest in a number of self-help strategies involves using "analog holes" in devices that primary operate in digital modes.

Analog holes exist in digital devices because equipment manufacturers, broadcasters, and other stakeholders have recognized that consumers would revolt if a "flash cut"—immediate changeover—to digital technologies occurred. Even now, more people watch standard-definition analog television than higher-definition digital television. Likewise, high-definition DVD players have only begun to achieve marketplace success. Until most people watch digital television, the devices that make digital viewing possible must still provide consumers with the option of accessing even digital content via inferior, lower-resolution analog devices. While these analog interfaces make it possible to still use old television sets, they also provide a self-help opportunity to avoid DRM restrictions on access and distribution of content. Many DRM safeguards do not apply to analog interfaces, thereby making it possible for consumers to route content to recorders and wireless home-networking devices. The resolution of video content transmitted via an analog hole remains at the standard, non-high-definition level, but consumers have a readily available means to evade DRM restrictions that might otherwise foreclose time, place, format, or device shifting.

HOW NEW TECHNOLOGIES HELP MAKE NEW MARKETS

We can appreciate the threat presented by ICE innovations. However, the potential exists for new ICE technologies to follow in the track of previous innovations that created new market opportunities rather than cannibalize them and reduce revenues. Radio did not eliminate the demand for newspapers, nor did cable television squelch consumers' interest in seeing films in theaters. Incumbents made necessary adjustments and moved forward. For example, the owners of AM radio stations changed their programming formats to talk and news and created ethnic niches when FM radio technology offered a better medium for delivery of high-fidelity music. AM radio stations may never again achieve the kind of audience share that they had before the proliferation of stations using the FM frequency band, but most station owners did not shut down.

Even as markets converge and new technologies evolve, several tautologies—bordering on rules—have passed the test of time. For several generations of new technologies, incumbents have integrated and controlled the new technologies when they appeared; they thought the technologies had the potential to be disruptive, to change everything. Although incumbents and insurgents typically find it expedient to battle in the courtroom, then in the marketplace, rough-justice accommodations typically result, whether regulator sponsored or marketplace imposed. Accordingly, we should view with skepticism any claim that a new ICE technology or a convergence of technologies and markets will destroy the status quo and eliminate incumbents or any claim that the new technology or convergence offers few benefits.

Rethinking Subscription Television

DRM challenges and innovations in content delivery have stimulated consideration of new pricing strategies. Generally, both old (broadcast, cable) and new (Internet) media rely heavily on an advertiser-supported one-way distribution strategy or a subscription-based all-you-can-eat (AYCE) model. Operators in both old and new media now consider whether a pay-per-view or a per-download alternative makes greater financial sense. If a supportive billing and collection infrastructure exists, coupled with timely content-delivery options, a pay-per-view pricing strategy can generate higher revenues, paid by large-volume users who have benefited the most from a "one size fits all," flat-rate subscription. AYCE pricing typically works best when metering is costly or when operators need to stimulate interest in a service.

Pay-per-view lets content creators collect revenues for each download, thereby foreclosing most free-rider opportunities. New DRM techniques improve the security of downloads, thereby reducing the risk that content, once downloaded, would end up being freely available via the Internet. On the other hand, pay-per-view may mean that consumers will limit their consumption to manage their entertainment budget. In the market for recorded music, the opportunity to download individual songs means that consumers need not pay the album rate for ten or more tracks but instead can download only the most popular and more desired tunes. Cable television operators have rejected a per-channel, à la carte pricing model, fearing that they would accrue lower revenues, particularly for programming that blends advertiser revenues with consumer subscription payments. Nevertheless, pay-per-view appears to have gained traction as a pricing option.

Prospects for Today's Cutting-Edge Devices and Services

Market forecasters generally expect digital technologies to replace analog incumbents, wireless services to replace wireline options, and complex and elegant broadband services to replace the simple existing narrowband services, all with great marketplace success. The forecasts seem uncontroversial, particularly if replacement costs take a steep downward path as has occurred for CD and DVD players, high-definition televisions, and cellular telephones. CDs have largely replaced vinyl records and analog cassette tapes, just as DVDs have replaced videocassettes. As of June 2009, all television sets must operate in a digital mode; older units can receive such content via cable and satellite without modification, and off air with installation of a digital-to-analog converter.

Other forecasts are less certain. We would have a harder time concluding that wireless telephone services will eliminate wireline services, that pay-satellite and digital radio services will eliminate advertiser-supported broadcasting, and that all telecommunications users will require high-speed, broadband links. Wireless services predominate in some nations, and we might infer that it is just a matter of time before all nations, or at least all industrialized nations, make the migration. Mobile radiotelephones have achieved amazing success for a technology launched in 1984. But now that operators have plucked all the low-lying fruit, how might they reach more? That would mean increasing market penetration with a technology that competes with services offered on a very low, flat-rate subscription basis. Most users of wireline telephone services pay less than thirty dollars a month for unlimited local calls. While cellular telephone companies tout "unlimited nights and weekends," they offer a largely metered service as opposed to an unlimited subscription model. Cellular telephone subscribers typically pay two to three times as much for far fewer minutes of use than do wireline telephone subscribers. The value proposition of mobility and "free" long-distance calling may not appeal to everyone.

A similar value challenge lies in the trade-off between advertiser-supported access to video and audio content and premium access that requires direct payment from subscribers. Surely a market exists for paid access to premium content ranging from blockbuster movies to special-format digital radio services via satellite to pay-per-view sporting events. Perhaps at some future date, we may reach a limit on the amount of time and budget that consumers have available for ICE equipment and services. Recent statistics, however, show a general increase in both television and Internet viewing in the United States, and consumers have begun to add minutes to mobile devices such as cell phones.[12]

For the time being, most ICE consumers appear willing to invest more and more time, money, and effort in accessing ICE services. The total pie has increased even as each ICE equipment and service vendor appears to have honed marketing pitches to capture a larger percentage of the pie. Telephone, cable television, Internet access, and other vendors would like nothing more than to provide every consumer with an array of services that collectively costs more than one hundred dollars monthly. But once the cost reaches triple digits, consumer satiation or fatigue can occur, as we have seen. After paying for, and using, wireline and wireless telephone service for local and long-distance calls, Internet access, and access to video programming, how much time remains for additional fee-based services such as video gaming, gambling, music downloading, shopping, text messaging, and sending digital photographs? Individual consumers will make specific purchasing decisions from the ever-increasing set of options, but the future may not offer a financial gain to every venture.

The Internet as All Things to All People

Relying on the Internet as a centralized medium for delivering all forms of ICE content will achieve operating efficiencies and cost savings primarily because users can partially or completely consolidate previously separate networks. Multinational corporations no longer need to have separate voice telephone and data networks, for both types of services can ride along Internet transmission links. Networks using radio spectrum for radio and television broadcasts will not abandon their frequencies, but we can anticipate that the Internet will provide a supplemental medium for these services.

We have only begun to consider the implications of an Internet-centric environment. Operational reliance on a single medium instead of two or more does not necessarily result in greater risk, at least for the network cloud, which has numerous redundant networks available. The Internet's design builds in multiple routing options because network access occurs on a space-available, best-efforts basis. Initially designed to route essential military traffic around outages on a real-time, immediate basis, the Internet now, for commercial utility, depends on similar on-the-fly detour-taking routes. So the Internet as a bit transport network does not appear to present a reliability problem, despite the potential for sabotage, including efforts to disrupt access by launching a barrage of service requests at a single source, resulting in crashes and an inability to provide service to anyone.

However, problems can occur in how we access the Internet at the first and last miles that link individual residences and businesses with the Internet cloud. While a handful of competitive options exist—consumers can link to the Internet with DSL, cable modems, and wireless (cellular and satellite) connections—few consumers respond to the potential for blockage by leasing two access options. When the cable or DSL line becomes inoperative, the Internet remains fully operational, but an individual can no longer access it. First and last mile access remains the weakest link.

Even if we assume that an Internet-centric operating environment functions adequately, new challenges await consumers and providers largely because legacy networks have operated independently under different commercial and regulatory assumptions. For example, the cost of doing business and, in turn, the rates that consumers pay have varied as a function of time of day, minutes of use, distance between parties, and other factors. Regulators have imposed rules that affect cost and consumer rates based on, among other things, whether content travels across state or national borders, what type of network provides the service, and what financial contributions the service should make to support public policy objectives, such as subsidized service access by rural and poor residents. But the assumptions do not apply, at least in the same way, to the Internet.

The Death of Distance and Other Service Distinctions

Technological developments in telecommunications and information processing increasingly make it unsustainable for operators to charge different rates for service based on distance between parties,[13] the time of day, and even the duration of the linkup. Many of the installed plant costs in telecommunications networks do not vary with usage;[14] from the outset most Internet service providers have charged flat monthly subscription rates. However, regulatory agencies in the United States and elsewhere have encouraged carriers to recover non-traffic-sensitive costs on a metered basis[15] and to recover many types of both non-traffic-sensitive and traffic-sensitive costs by averaging the different costs incurred by high-volume and low-volume users.[16] Cost averaging provides a simple, rough-justice solution to complex cost-allocation problems,[17] but it blunts cost differences among carriers, routes, and users. Inefficient and inequitable investment recovery would occur if carriers charged by usage or mileage to recoup such sunk and embedded costs. High-volume users would overcompensate the carrier, and low-volume users would underpay.

ISPs quickly reached the conclusion that they should not bother measuring the distance between call originator and call recipient because the cost of such metering appeared to exceed the cost differences in handling traffic of different distances. Telephone companies, particularly long-distance carriers, typically average long-haul and short-haul traffic costs so that they can offer a flat rate for all calls.

Insensitivity to distance and traffic volume means that telecommunications and Internet service providers can offer a single per-minute or monthly rate for all calls within a wide geographical area—perhaps the entire United States for long-distance telephone companies and the entire world for ISPs. Such a "postalized" rate averages out whatever cost differentials still exist.[18] Acknowledging the largely sunk investment in telecommunications plant, some carriers now offer a flat monthly rate for unlimited local and long-distance calls. AYCE pricing[19] has become standard for Internet access in the United States, and ISPs have never priced access based on the distance separating users and the sources of content or separating senders and recipients of electronic mail.

The "death of distance" largely erodes the rationale for using geography or political boundaries as the basis for differences in how carriers allocate costs and price services. Indeed, many of the reasons for such differences never had a justification on the basis of cost; rather, other political, social, or public policy factors came into play, as an FCC proposal makes clear: "[E]fficiency has not been the only goal of intercarrier compensation rules. For example, in order to encourage universal services . . . [the Federal Communications] Commission and state regulators historically set access charges [paid to local exchange carriers] above cost. By doing so, they hoped to be able to keep local telephone rates low, and thus telephone penetration rates high."[20]

Federal and state telecommunications regulators and telephone companies have saddled long-distance callers, especially ones making intrastate calls, with higher margin rates and surcharges to fund universal service programs. Revenues from over-priced long-distance calls made it possible for local exchange telephone companies (LECs) to offer possibly below-cost local services and to tap into subsidies for achieving universal service objectives, including intentionally below-cost service to rural residents, poor residents, and residents of tribal and insular locales.

Distance insensitivity in telecommunications also eliminates the rationale for having different charges for accessing the same local-exchange facilities; variables like whether the call crosses domestic or international borders, originates from a wireless or wireline carrier, or traverses the Internet need not affect price. Yet LECs continue charging different rates largely because regulatory policies force them to do so or because political factors favor their decision to overprice or underprice a particular service.

Set out below is a continuum of LEC access costs from lowest to highest.

1. The exchange of traffic between LECs occurs on a reciprocal basis using zero cost (bill and keep) rates, negotiated rates, or rates prescribed by a regulatory agency. The last two rates are typically several decimal places below one cent.[21]

2. The exchange of traffic between long-distance interexchange carriers (IXCs) and LECs occurs on a uniformly tariffed basis with rates that have declined substantially but still significantly exceed the reciprocal interconnection rates paid by LECs.
3. The exchange of traffic between a wireless carrier and a wireline LEC depends on whether the call appears to involve a local exchange of traffic (even if it originated a long distance away) or a conventional long-distance exchange, which would make the range variable.
4. The exchange of international long-distance traffic on routes lacking significant competition occurs at a per-minute accounting rate,[22] ranging from a few cents to more than one dollar, which covers long-haul and local carriage.[23]
5. For routes where an accounting rate settlement does not occur, the rates for call delivery vary widely. The highest LEC access cost applies to the exchange of international long-distance traffic with a foreign wireless operator. The termination charge may exceed fifty cents per minute just for using the wireless carrier's network.[24]

Arguably, the costs incurred by LECs do not vary significantly when traffic originates or terminates on their networks and uses the same facilities regardless of origination location and type of carrier involved. Yet even if the traffic types listed above travel the same facilities—and they typically do—the imposed access charges vary substantially. Such cost differentials have little, if any, basis in rational cost allocation and recoupment; rather, they occur as a result of cost attribution: the purposeful loading or unloading of costs onto traffic-switching and traffic-routing functions that are in effect the same and basing the costs on political, social, and public policy rationales.[25]

The FCC has acknowledged inconsistency in the rates that LECs charge: "Interconnection arrangements between carriers are currently governed by a complex system of intercarrier compensation regulations. These regulations treat different types of carriers and different types of services disparately, even though there may be no significant differences in the costs among carriers of services. The [existing] interconnection regime that applies in a particular case depends on such factors as: whether the interconnecting party is a local carrier, an interexchange carrier, a [wireless] . . . carrier or an enhanced service provider; and whether the service is classified as local or long distance, interstate or intrastate, or basic or enhanced."[26] It may have made sense, on political or social-equity grounds, to load costs onto wealthy long-distance and wireless callers when such services were luxuries enjoyed mostly by elites. But now a far larger set of users incur higher charges or qualify for subsidized rates.

Cost attribution provides a quasi-scientific basis for targeting subsidies, but its calibration has limits, resulting in overinclusive and underinclusive groups of subsidy payers and recipients.[27] Subsidies flow unnecessarily to some beneficiaries with ample financial resources to pay the full costs and burden some individuals who should not have to subsidize the unwarranted beneficiaries. The FCC, to its credit, has expressed reservations about whether its cost allocation policies can jointly serve economic efficiency goals and public policy objectives.[28]

Cost attribution also creates beneficiaries and payers among carriers: some are subsidized, and some pay subsidies.[29] If the subsidy obligation is substantial, the paying carrier becomes saddled with a financial burden that can adversely affect its ability to offer competitive rates, upgrade facilities, secure debt financing, and attract investors. Beneficiaries of subsidies may have bolstered opportunities to lower their rates, but they might just as easily capture the benefits without passing them on to consumers and without making necessary plant investments. Unless there are compelling reasons, regulatory agencies should not create policies that support or handicap carrier competition.

ARBITRAGE AND GAMING OPPORTUNITIES

When the Internet becomes the medium of choice for a variety of services but legacy regulations impose different requirements and costs on the services, the playing field tilts to some ventures' advantage or disadvantage. Rather than acquire market share and profits based on superior performance, some Internet-based operators can secure a competitive advantage simply by qualifying for lower-cost access to other ventures' networks even as competitors offering functionally the same service have to pay more. The cost of access as shaped by regulatory policy becomes a vehicle for arbitrage, the ability to extract profits by exploiting a regulation-conferred lower cost of doing business. When a regulatory agency confers an arbitrage opportunity on some operators, it distorts the competitive marketplace, and disadvantaged stakeholders try to remedy the situation in court or by lobbying the legislature to provide relief. Regulatory gridlock and endless litigation result when stakeholders with ample financial resources object to real or perceived handicaps.[30] Worse yet, these burdened stakeholders begin to think they should not continue complying with long-standing, fundamental responsibilities established by law because according to their perception, the regulatory process has confiscated resources by forcing them to make facilities available to competitors at rates below cost. When opportunities exist for regulatory arbitrage, stakeholders see advantages accruing from efforts to game the system, litigate, and delay initiatives that might eventually lead to reduced regulation and near parity of regulatory status among competitors. Stakeholders' concerns about short-term profitability may obscure the long-term prospects for a level playing field.

Regulatory arbitrage in telecommunications has created readily identifiable gaming strategies among stakeholders hoping to qualify their services as interstate instead of intrastate;[31] obscure the origin of traffic so that international traffic appears domestic and long-distance traffic appears local; characterize traffic as local instead of long-haul if doing so would change the classification of the traffic so that it would generate a reciprocal payment obligation instead of an access charge payment; distort or obscure the origin of traffic and method of transmission to reduce or avoid charges imposed by another carrier to deliver the traffic to the intended recipient;[32] route traffic via the Internet; and offer telecommunications services as ancillary to, or a minor transport element for, an enhanced information service.[33]

Regardless of whether arbitrage strategies legally or illegally exploit regulatory loopholes, they cause marketplace distortions and reduce the effectiveness of regulatory policies justified by public interest concerns. If it were not for the failure of legislatures and regulatory agencies to make necessary adjustments on a timely basis, we might consider the unjust enrichment that such tactics accrue to particular carriers as perhaps a necessary short-term by-product of regulatory reform. But when regulatory adjustments do not quickly occur, stakeholders can accrue substantial financial gains simply by exploiting regulatory loopholes while others unfairly suffer.[34]

Gray Market Strategies

Not all regulatory arbitrage strategies violate laws and regulations even if they deviate from regulatory intent or exploit loopholes. Arguably, when a customer or a carrier exploits an arbitrage opportunity, other carriers have an incentive to close the loophole and correct inconsistent charges and policies. The sticky resilience of some loopholes means that carriers might also gain even as they claim that others are unjustly enriched. When carriers create arbitrage opportunities, absent a regulatory obligation, we should examine why the loophole persists. Carriers might tolerate lost traffic and revenues if the losses are more than offset by such benefits as regulatory relief, insulation from competition, and opportunities to price-discriminate profitably. Most carriers and consumers cannot avoid paying rates ostensibly raised to offset costs of regulatory arbitrage.

Gray-market regulatory arbitrage refers primarily to self-help strategies available to consumers that can let them share in the cost savings or capture greater revenues. Consumers can execute some tactics unilaterally, but most tactics require the involvement of a business venture. Most gray-market regulatory arbitrage strategies allow consumers to save money by avoiding or reducing a transaction with an associated charge. For example, telecommunications users can change the apparent origination point of a call to make it appear local, thereby avoiding long-distance toll charges. Masking the true origination point of a call can lower costs by converting long-distance calls into local calls, with their lower interconnection rates.

Leaky Private Branch Exchanges

A long-standing regulatory arbitrage opportunity for business customers involves the use of an on-premises switchboard, commonly referred to as a private branch exchange (PBX), that can link long-distance lines with outbound local telephone lines. Even businesses with only a few telephone lines can use a PBX to "leak" traffic into the local exchange, including calls originating a long distance away, by hooking up with an intercity private line.[35] For example, a law firm with offices in Washington, D.C., and New York City might lease a private line to provide a direct link between telephones situated in either office. Carriers typically offer private lines on the assumption that users need a link between their offices and nowhere else. With the proliferation of PBXs, businesses can easily engineer local exchange access at both ends of the private line without having to make additional payments to either the long-distance or the local carriers handling the traffic. The PBX links regular local business lines in both cities with the private intercity line. While such leaky PBXs might technically violate carrier service terms and conditions, few carriers enforce them, even when the terms are filed as a public tariff[36] with the FCC or a state utility commission.[37]

Resale of Private and WATS Lines

Back in the 1970s and 1980s, new telecommunications ventures, often operating with limited seed money, could market themselves as national long-distance telephone companies through the resale of private lines and Wide Area Telecommunication Service (WATS) calling—that is, making outbound long-distance telephone calls via an 800 or other number that allows billing at a bulk rate. Resale provided the first major competitive domestic service options in the United States.[38] The FCC supported linkage of private lines with local exchanges in part because doing so forced long-distance carriers to reduce rates and to narrow or eliminate the opportunities for financial arbitrage created by the big gap between retail long-distance rates and the far lower per-minute costs borne by large-volume users: "We find that elimination of the restrictions on unlimited resale and sharing of private line service will bring about public benefits which include: (a) the provision of communications service at rates more closely related to costs; (b) better management of communications networks and the provision of management expertise by users and intermediaries to the carriers; (c) the avoidance of waste of communications capacity; and (d) the creation of additional incentives for research and development of ancillary devices to be used with transmission lines."[39]

Private line resale also has provided the first significant downward pressure on costs and the first significant competitive option for international calls in many nations.[40] Consumers with private lines need not await the onset of facilities-based competition to save money, but incumbents may experience competition from poorly capitalized ventures with little incentive or ability to invest in facilities of their own.

International Call Reorigination

Before the introduction of VoIP, international call-back services provided regulatory arbitrage opportunities resulting from the vastly different charges that exist for international long-distance calls from country to country.[41] Call reorigination enabled callers in high-cost nations to secure international long-distance service at much lower rates. Callers in high-cost areas used a service that triggered a request for a dial tone in a low-cost nation, making it appear as though the call originated in the low-cost area and was made to the high-cost area. While some nations deemed call-back illegal, little could be done to block the importation of outbound calling access from lower-cost areas to higher-cost areas.

The FCC initially agreed to enforce a foreign country's law prohibiting call-back services out of respect for the sovereignty of the nation imposing restrictions.[42] However, in early 2003[43] the Commission abandoned its enforcement of other nations' call-back prohibitions, saying that international call reorigination benefits consumers by forcing carriers throughout the world to reduce rates to cost plus a reasonable profit.[44] Call-back also helped dismantle the accounting rate system used by telephone companies providing international long-distance service for dividing the revenues generated from international toll charges. The accounting rate ostensibly covers the cost of using local and national facilities to originate and terminate an international call, plus cross-border network usage, but the figure used vastly overstates actual costs.[45] Call-back and other routing strategies disrupt the accounting rate system by using arbitrage strategies that offer retail international calling rates well below what incumbent carriers charge using the accounting rate as a pricing floor. However, in disrupting the accounting rate system, entrepreneurs substantially have reduced hard currency payments from industrialized to industrializing countries, because the call-back strategy made it impossible for any nation to enforce an inordinately high accounting rate as a proxy for the actual cost of service. When ventures settled accounts using a lower figure, or paid an access charge for using national and local network services, carriers in industrializing nations accrued much lower revenues than when the official accounting rate applied to all traffic.

VoIP

Opportunities for regulatory arbitrage that existed with international call reorigination have largely evaporated because a greater arbitrage opportunity is provided by using the Internet to route long-distance telephone calls. Making the conversion from dial-up circuit-switched telephony[46] to the packet-switched Internet[47] qualifies the traffic for favorable regulatory treatment, possibly including fee exemptions. When providing conventional long-distance telephone service, a long-distance telephone service carrier must pay access charges to LECs for using their networks to originate and terminate traffic—that is, for using the local loop facilities of LECs from the call originators to a facility where the long-distance carrier receives calls for the long-haul carriage and for LEC delivery of calls received from long-distance carriers and delivered to call recipients. Instead of paying per-minute access charges, some VoIP carriers need only acquire inbound business telephone lines that their customers can use to access their services. Alternatively, consumers of VoIP telephony can use DSL and cable modem links to originate and receive calls without incurring any LEC access charges.

The Internet provides a medium for real-time processing and delivery of packets corresponding to voice conversations. Although the quality of the initial VoIP services was inferior to conventional dial-up long-distance telephone service, the gap has narrowed, and VoIP offers consumers ample cost savings, partly because they can reduce or avoid the obligation to pay LEC access charges.[48] The FCC, consistent with its attempt to keep the Internet regulation-free, considers at least some forms of VoIP a largely unregulated information service,[49] even though it has subjected retail VoIP carriers to many types of regulations previously applied only to telephone companies.

Technological innovations in VoIP work to make the service closer to a functional equivalent of dial-up long-distance telephone service. In particular, a user now can access VoIP services via an ordinary telephone handset, a far more convenient option than was previously available via specially configured personal computers. In a report to Congress on universal service,[50] the FCC tentatively concluded that phone-to-phone VoIP appears to constitute a "telecommunications service" under the Telecommunications Act of 1996 and acknowledged that such a classification would mean liability for access charges. However, the FCC refrained from using a congressional report as the means of issuing a definitive ruling, even though it subsequently required VoIP operators to contribute to universal service funding[51] and to comply with numerous requirements applied to telephone companies.

Call Terminations

Another type of arbitrage opportunity occurs when one carrier can leverage access to its subscriber base to extract higher access payments than other carriers charge for functionally the same sort of network access. Some competitive local exchange carriers (CLECs) and cellular radio carriers have charged higher rates for call terminations than their incumbent counterparts (ILECS) have, without having to prove that the CLEC or wireless call delivery costs substantially more than when ILECs perform the same service. The differential in charges has grown to such an acute level that the FCC has investigated CLEC access charges[52] and also the surcharges that U.S. IXCs impose to recoup payments made to foreign wireless carriers for terminating international calls to their subscribers.[53]

THE BUSINESS OF BIT TRANSMISSION

The Internet increasingly serves as a medium for transmitting, switching, and routing all kinds of packets corresponding to just about any type of content. An IP-centric medium can enable a few carriers providing bit transportation to dominate if the market becomes increasingly concentrated through mergers and acquisitions. On the other hand, carriers providing the underlying telecommunications transmission capacity that makes up the Internet do not want to be foreclosed by law or policy from diversifying into value-adding services. Facilities-based telecommunications carriers worry about government-imposed limitations on their ability to operate intelligent networks rather than "dumb pipes."

The Internet favors the migration of some intelligence and network control from carrier switches at the core to users' computers at the edge. Accordingly, incumbent carriers have a keen interest in technologies that enable them to reassert network control, including the ability to monitor the nature and type of traffic that runs through their networks. Rather than allow their networks to operate as low-margin utility pipelines, incumbent carriers want to add value by customizing networks to meet particular user requirements.

Moreover, incumbent carriers want to differentiate quality of service especially under congested conditions, the terms and conditions for interconnection, and bit delivery speeds. In the chapter on the government's role, we will examine whether carriers should be forced to operate in a standard, network-neutral manner that would limit the ways they price, brand, tier, and differentiate services. Here we will consider the more basic issue of whether and how underlying telecommunications networks have become generic pipelines.

Ventures operating the telecommunications networks that deliver Internet traffic have experienced a loss of control over what kinds of traffic enter their networks. The increasingly distance-insensitive nature of telecommunications and information means that carriers providing both the local and long-haul portions of a complete end-to-end routing may not know the exact origination point of traffic. Worse yet, they may not know whether a particular traffic stream should trigger an interconnection charge, nor do they know what kind of access charges should apply.

As noted earlier, the cost differences of Internet traffic are typically limited, regardless of whether a link crosses a town or an ocean. Conversely, telecommunications toll traffic historically has triggered metered charges based on both time and distance. Commingling conventional and Internet traffic on a single network can reduce a carrier's ability to single out and meter particular types of traffic. This inability to differentiate traffic means that incumbent facilities-based carriers may end up partially transporting toll voice traffic without participating in the division of toll revenues. For example, some VoIP operators have found ways to inject traffic into a carrier's circuit-switched telephone network without paying for the privilege. Without effective "bit sniffing" or "packet sniffing" technology,[54] a facilities-based carrier may not be able to differentiate between truly local traffic, which would not necessarily trigger a metered toll charge, and long-distance traffic, which would. If a VoIP operator can mask the point of origin of voice telephony traffic, the incumbent carrier may not know that some of the traffic that it routes for free should have triggered a metered toll charge.

VoIP software, which can provide companies with a way to evade otherwise appropriate toll and interconnection charges, also can change the complexion and appearance of a bitstream. VoIP traffic that traverses public-switched telephone networks for free can do so because the software riding on the telecommunications pipeline may obscure the nature and origin of the traffic. What triggers a split in toll charges, or generates fees for accessing a facilities-based carrier's local exchange network, may appear to be Internet traffic for which no call-specific charges apply. With VoIP software, users can complete telephone calls for next to nothing because interconnection and other fees applicable to voice telephony may not kick in. Carriers entitled to a share of the toll or access charges cannot determine whether and when chargeable traffic traverses their networks.

Software innovations make it possible for VoIP carriers to evade toll sharing and interconnection payments, but also may help incumbent carriers identify particular types of traffic and impose different traffic-specific fees. Just as software can provide a means to obscure and mask traffic streams, it also can examine packet "headers" and determine the kind of traffic contained in the payload portion of the packet. With packet-sniffing technology, network operators can inspect traffic streams to identify characteristics of the traffic for both routing and billing purposes. Carriers may claim that they have no technical means to enforce DRM techniques against piracy, but this technology also makes such enforcement possible.

Since carriers can identify traffic payloads with packet sniffers, they can price-discriminate, even though one type of traffic may not cost more or less to switch, route, and deliver. Whether differentiating bits and charging different prices is lawful and prudent depends on whether the prices, quality of service, interconnections, and other factors are fairly applied or whether they are designed to disadvantage a competitor and favor a corporate affiliate. In any event, bit and packet sniffing may provide carriers with better tools for determining the origin and composition of traffic generated by other carriers.

Replacing best-efforts traffic routing with variable quality of service, and rough-justice cost sharing with metered service and packet inspection, imposes traditional telephony interconnection, cost-recovery, and consumer-marketing strategies onto Internet traffic routing. The value proposition currently enjoyed by Internet consumers, who have the option of unlimited, unmetered, all-you-can-eat service subscriptions, will change and may decline should incumbent carriers succeed in imposing pricing arrangements and service plans that incorporate the traditional telephony strategies. Advocates for flexibility in pricing, interconnection, and quality of service consider that flexibility—a gain in its own right—will bring about lawful price discrimination that can possibly lower bills for low-volume users. Opponents and advocates for network neutrality see the initiative as an attempt to legitimize network bias, bit discrimination, and fragmentation of the Internet into networks with different service levels and brands.

THE RISKS OF PREEMPTED TECHNOLOGY AND SERVICE OPTIONS

With the onset, or even the prospect, of competition, incumbent operators generally redouble their efforts to secure abandonment of government regulation. In principle, regulatory streamlining in the direction of deregulation surely makes sense. Marketplace forces, such as consumer choices on how to spend their dollars, will work better to trigger operator efficiency, lower prices, improve customer service, and increase diversification of options than any centralized government decision making. But when monopolies or oligopolies provide an essential good or service, prices will exceed competitive prices, and the monopolist can establish terms and conditions designed to thwart competitive incursions. Unless one operator or a small group operating collusively has control over Internet access, competitors will not be able to individually or collectively establish take-it-or-leave-it terms.

Notwithstanding the logic of theoretical economics and the reasonableness of built-in assumptions, the real world does not work so smoothly. Markets typically do not operate with perfect competition, nor do they become completely dominated by a monopoly. This means that ICE technological innovations can promote competition but not necessarily eliminate the power of a single firm, or group of firms, to suppress innovations that incumbents do not want consumers to use. Technological innovations can destroy existing business models by expediting market entry and by empowering consumers will self-help opportunities to evade vendor-imposed limitations on, for example, network usage. But other innovations can help firms thwart consumer freedom and foreclose new and cheaper options.

Even in a market served by multiple vendors, the robustness of competition and the scope of consumer options may decline if vendors can limit consumer access to specific technologies and features. Antitrust laws designed to ensure a level playing field may point out and sanction such tactics, but using the law this way requires forensic skills and litigation expertise and can achieve a remedy only after competitive harms have occurred. The history of telecommunications regulation and litigation provides plenty of cases where consumers lacked specific technological options because incumbent vendors could secure a government prohibition on access or provision their equipment and services in ways that denied consumers opportunities to maximize use of the technology.

An example of government-sanctioned denial of access to a competing technology includes the prohibition on consumer purchase or rental of telephone handsets not offered by the carrier providing telephone service. Until the 1970s and 1980s, telephone companies throughout the world managed to convince legislators and regulators of the technological impossibility in separating telephone service from the devices used to make and receive calls. Telephone companies claimed that telephones that they did not manufacture, resell, or lease might harm the network or even telephone company personnel, but they never could substantiate such claims. With hindsight, we now realize that no credible technological reason supported the bundling of handset with service, yet to this day wireless companies in the United States and elsewhere can readily steer subscribers to a handset-plus-service package, nor do subscribers have the right to modify or circumvent handset use restrictions imposed by carriers. The compulsory combination of wireline handset and telephone service promoted corporate objectives—for example, creating a mechanism for subsidizing telephone services with overpriced handset rental rates without most consumers even knowing such overcharging was taking place. In the wireless sector, bundling handsets with service locks subscribers into multiyear service commitments and reduces churn, the migration from one carrier to a competitor.

Some nations prohibit use of the Internet for telephone services. Few, if any, government officials or even incumbent telephone company managers would attempt to claim the technological infeasibility or the potential for network harm that might result from using the Internet for telephony. Nevertheless, a prohibition on a technologically feasible option exists because incumbent telephone carriers have convinced decision makers that VoIP competition would be unfair and would hamper their ability to offer subsidized service to rural and poor users and to achieve other public policy objectives.

More subtle but possibly more harmful prohibitions on consumer access to technological innovations occur when incumbent ventures thwart the use of new equipment, fail to develop services that use readily available technological innovations, or refuse to cooperate with equipment manufacturers keen on offering new technological features. In the data-processing arena, Microsoft's domination of the user interface for personal computers helped the company catch up with and foil competition from unaffiliated ventures offering arguably better technological options for accessing the Internet and for using personal computers to play various types of media files. Currently Apple Computer tries to block creative consumer self-help strategies to download and store on the iPod music player and iPhone music files other than those using an Apple proprietary recording standard and to access software from sources other than an Apple-approved collection.

Cellular Telephones

Cellular telephone companies limit the options available to subscribers and the flexibility of their use largely because subscribers might find faster, better, smarter, and cheaper options than what the carrier provides. The prominent *Wall Street Journal* technology writer Walter S. Mossberg characterizes cell phone companies as akin to anti-free-market communist bureaucracies in Russia because the companies "restrict what technologies can actually reach users."[55] Cellular telephone companies are unlikely to encourage manufacturers to install universal serial bus plug access to handsets, which is readily available on handheld computers, because the companies want to manage how subscribers access content and services. The argument that unauthorized services might harm a cellular company's network has the same lack of credibility as prior arguments that telephone handsets and services not provided by the wireline telephone company would result in physical or financial harm to the network. Worse yet, anecdotal information exists about decisions by cellular carriers to disable existing technical functions—for example, Wi-Fi access and Bluetooth short-range wireless connections to synchronize handsets with other sources of content, such as personal computers.

The lack of an interface to and from a cellular telephone forces the subscriber to rely exclusively on the carrier to provide that link. If a subscriber wants to add a ringtone to a cell phone—a distinctive musical tone that announces an incoming call—the subscriber's easiest option lies in downloading a selection from the carrier. People who regularly download music without payment via the Internet have generally accepted the obligation to pay for ringtones because most have not found a way to install the content outside of prescribed distribution channels. This constitutes a victory for DRM but a loss in consumer flexibility. Cell phone carriers and manufacturers reduce consumers' freedom and the benefits of a cell phone subscription when they allow only prescribed and limited distribution channels for access to ringtones and access to other ICE content, including music, news, software applications, and video games.

Narrowcasting and Broadcasting

Technological innovations enhance the opportunities for consumers to access content that is custom-tailored to their specific interests, as well as content targeted at the traditional, largely undifferentiated mass audiences. Consumers used to have to choose a medium based on whether it could serve one or the other group. Typically the broadcast medium offered the "least objectionable" programming to large audiences whose access was underwritten by advertisers of mass-market items—laundry detergent and such. Books and specialty magazines came closest to providing customized, narrowly tailored content. The proliferation of cable television choices has provided programming for narrower but still large audiences; some networks provide just sports, news, women-oriented content, or weather information.

The Internet provides a medium for both mass-market and narrow-market content. In so doing, it has generated new challenges and opportunities for content owners to accrue revenues and for advertisers to attract target audiences with subsidized content. Curiously, even though the Internet provides unprecedented access to diverse content, after an initial infatuation with the boundless variety and potential of the medium, most consumers typically rely on a handful of sites that they regularly visit, one that covers a specialized subject or one that offers content of broader interest. To become a preferred site and to attract large audiences, site operators can collect diverse but still mass-market-oriented content.

Web ventures such as Yahoo have become a portal to this kind of content. Subscribers can customize portal sites by selecting particular types of content for presentation on a personalized home page.

Portals like Yahoo's present consumers and advertisers with what is possibly the best of both their worlds. Subscribers interested in a quick and convenient place to access content can click on their personalized home page. Their ICE interests and requirements are satisfied, and Yahoo benefits from having a walled garden within which subscribers spend much of their Web-viewing time. Because it has such a willingly captive audience, Yahoo can offer advertisers a large audience for the mass-market content provided and a smaller but somewhat specific audience for more narrowly targeted and better-calibrated commercial pitches.

The Internet provides other opportunities to cater to consumer interests and target advertising. Through special interest Web sites, consumers can access preferred content, and advertisers can promote goods and services about which such consumers might have an interest. Podcasting provides another opportunity to provide and link with specialized ICE content. With podcasting, content creators can use the Internet to distribute audio and video content packaged as a downloadable file, and Internet users can access professional and amateur sources of audio and video content by downloading software that can regularly scan subscribed Web sites for new content, which the users can then view or listen to.

Podcasting is like radio and television but without limitations imposed by spectrum scarcity and licensing and other regulations. It provides the medium for delivery of sound and video files at little cost because a podcaster need only acquire a small amount of storage capacity from a hosting venture on the Web. Rather than stream content at the same time to hundreds or thousands of listeners and viewers, podcasters provide sequential downloading of the same file. Interested consumers can download at their convenience. A software feature called RSS—which can refer to any of several ways to syndicate Web content—allows users to subscribe to a podcast and automatically download new content. With broadcasting, consumers must listen to and view content as it is broadcast or streamed via the Internet, or they must otherwise make provisions for a real-time recording of the transmission. With podcasting, in contrast, subscribers do not have to tune in at a specific time or even to visit and revisit a Web site to acquire new content. Instead, an RSS content aggregator automatically visits each subscribed site and determines whether new content is available for downloading. The reference to Apple's iPod in the term "podcasting" highlights the ability of subscribers to shift content of a podcast from a computer onto a portable device at any time.

Podcasting has the potential to promote sales of portable content players like iPods, but it might further fragment radio and television audiences. Some consumers of broadcast content might reduce their consumption, even during the primetime hours (commuting times for radio and eight to ten in the evening for television). Many ICE content producers have embraced podcasting as a source of programming without necessarily expecting to generate new revenues from the service. Established media ventures, including the major broadcast networks, newspapers, and even radio stations, have created podcasts. Like other traditional ICE content producers, they perceive the need to retain consumers who now have the power to shift the time, place, and device they use to access content.

Cutting-Edge Versus Bleeding-Edge Technologies

Countless new ICE devices and services have flooded the marketplace. Technophiles and early adopters readily embrace many of them, but the true indication of successful adoption of a new technology occurs when mainstream consumers buy in. The proliferation of handheld and stationary devices shows that a large percentage of consumers see the value in, and will pay for, new music storage and playback options, mobile telephone calling, wireless home networking, high-speed Internet access, and digital video recorders.

But plenty of new technologies and services fail to generate a critical mass. Few readers under the age of twenty have probably ever heard of quadraphonic stereo, particularly now that digital signal processing technology makes it possible to simulate a music-listening experience with six or seven channels plus an enhanced low-frequency subwoofer channel. AM stereo came and went in a matter of a year or so, as have numerous false starts in the evolution of third-generation mobile telephone services.

Much evidence supports the view that less elegant but much cheaper technology trumps superior, more complicated, and more expensive technology. We see this repeatedly. Thirty years ago a cheaper videotape recording and playback technology known as Video Home System quickly replaced the technologically superior but more expensive Betamax system developed by Sony. To record and play back video content in the days of videotape recorders, most consumers appeared willing to forgo quality in exchange for longer playback times and lower prices. Earlier still, a committee working on the standard for broadcasting color television signals agreed to a picture with lower resolution but one that was more easily and cheaply produced than the alternatives.

Today consumers appear to favor lower-priced digital television sets over more expensive sets that display pictures with the highest resolution. Perhaps some consumers of the cheaper sets do not know the limitations of their devices, but an explanation that is just as plausible supports the view that consumers will trade off quality for price, provided the new technology offers a perceivable enhancement in quality and value. In addition to a price-quality trade-off, many consumers seem to favor simpler options, particularly if simplicity comes with a lower price tag. For example, although some cell phone customers regularly replace handsets well before the device's anticipated end of life, about eighteen months, many subscribers have no immediate interest in cameras and other new bells and whistles that quickly deplete batteries and add complexity to the handset. In China, simple-to-use and cheap Personal Handy Phones compete with more complex, feature-rich, and expensive wireless handsets.

Complexity, cost, and global aspirations frustrate the development of new technologies. For example, in the 1990s Motorola formed a six-billion-dollar consortium that launched a constellation of sixty-six satellites capable of providing telephone service to anyone, anywhere, anytime. The Iridium low-orbiting satellite network offered unprecedented telecommunications access using elegant technologies. Motorola revolutionalized satellite manufacturing by creating an assembly line instead of building one-of-a-kind "designer" satellites. Although the Iridium satellite network proved the viability of launching multiple satellites at once, and although the system worked mostly as planned, the venture failed miserably because consumers expected Iridium handsets to work like cell phones. Iridium handsets communicate with fast-moving satellites more than four hundred miles overhead. Satellite signals do not usually penetrate into buildings, and users had to learn how to operate a bulky handset that required a line-of-sight link to a satellite. This elegant solution to a perennial problem of remote access failed because terrestrial-based cell phones offered access most of the time in most of the places where people had the desire and financial capability to pay for calls.

The Power of Time, Device, and Format Shifting

Just as consumers like the freedom of having no wires attached to ICE devices, they also seek the added flexibility that innovations offer in terms of when, where, how, with what device, and in which format they access content. We have previously examined the potential for the demise of appointment television. Already consumers have access to recording technologies that make it easy and inexpensive to record content for later playback. Consumers have enjoyed time shifting for many generations of technologies, starting with home video-recording devices. New technologies have made significant improvements in how to record and maneuver through content, as well as in the capacity to store content.

Although device shifting offers consumers additional convenient options for accessing content, this type of flexibility enhances the risk of piracy. As we have seen, one of the major challenges in DRM lies in establishing a fair balance between flexibility in device usage and copy protection. Consumers should have the options that technological innovations provide to move paid-for content from and to computer hard drives, portable hard drives, music/video players, television sets, home entertainment centers, and mobile devices such as cell phones instead of having content tethered to a single device. If piracy becomes too rampant, however, content providers will not authorize even lawful device shifting.

The proliferation of formats and the incompatibility between formats forces consumers to devise clever ways to circumvent limitations on format conversion and device usage. Apple Computer used to have a music recording and playback format that limited the number of places and devices that could use even paid-for content. These limitations frustrated the goal of interoperability and interchangeability of content that consumers expected. Before the proliferation of music storage and playback formats, consumers could take a compact disk and play it on any number of CD players. Both compact disks and the devices that play them back operated on one format. Now, with more music formats available, consumers no longer have 100 percent interchangeability of music files; not every playback device supports all formats. Consumers understandably resent limitations on their ability to reformat music to make the content playable on another device.

CHALLENGES TO INCUMBENTS

Innovations in ICE technologies have had a profound and largely negative impact on such incumbents as newspaper and book publishers, movie studios, music companies, advertising agencies, and television networks. As the *Wall Street Journal* summarized their situation a few years ago, "Their old way of doing business isn't as profitable as it used to be, but they haven't found a new way that's as profitable either."[56] Simply put, technological innovations have threatened the business models and plans of incumbent equipment and service providers largely because they offer consumers more and better options. Consumers have greater latitude in managing how and what ICE products and services they will consume. For content producers, this presents both challenges and opportunities: a challenge to the status quo, particularly when market shares decline, but also new opportunities for repackaging content and making it available in the time, place, and manner that consumers want. Newspaper publishers, who have experienced declining circulation for many years, have recognized that not as many people as before prefer to satisfy their curiosity about the news at the breakfast table. Many publishers now see the Internet as a necessary and possibly profitable forum. It may replace the hard copy, yet few have found an Internet-based business model that generates additional revenue, much less profit.

The general population has not lost its interest in news and the other products contained in a newspaper. But people have found faster, better, smarter, cheaper, and more convenient ways to get subsets of what a newspaper historically has offered. For example, instead of selling and buying cars through classified ads in a newspaper, people now use specialized Web sites, many of which offer greater geographical reach and viewership than a general metropolitan newspaper. The Web can provide price information and car options that make it more likely that car buyers can get a fair deal and pay a price close to what they would pay a competitive high-volume dealer, even if they have to drive to another locality to purchase the vehicle. In previous purchases, car buyers had no knowledge of options available outside their local market. In response to the changing approach to buying, local newspapers, striving to remain the primary car search medium, provide portals to car purchase options and information.

Book publishers face a similar dilemma now that information and even books are available in "soft copy" formats: on portable screens and as sound files on music players, among other options. People have not stopped reading books, but the Web has provided unprecedented opportunities to access idiosyncratic and specialized content. For the most part, book publishers have responded by offering more titles in hopes of increasing their chances to come up with an unexpected blockbuster. Although the surprise best-seller can and does appear, book publishers have generated millions of unsold books that retailers return for massive discounting or recycling. Few book publishers have fully embraced the Web to distribute content even though Amazon has proven that the Web can serve as a robust portal for buying books and that portable display devices, such as the Kindle, can provide an acceptable alternative to hard-copy books.

CONSUMER EMPOWERMENT

It has become almost trite to consider the information age and the ascendancy of the Internet as a boon to consumers. Words like "empowerment" herald their ability to choose among vendors and find deals. Consumers are no longer tied to local merchants and merchandise and compelled to use intermediaries but can access Web sites that scan other Web sites to find the best offer for a product or service. They can have a great deal of control over transactions—for example, by viewing airline seating charts to avoid the dreaded middle seat on a long trip.

But empowerment occurs if and only if consumers possess the skills needed to maneuver through Web sites. They often have to ascend steep learning curves to find out how to record, transfer, and reformat content. And Web-based searches can require more time and effort than using a sales representative or other agent, just as the self-checkout option at a grocery store may actually take longer than having an employee ring up the purchases, assuming no queue. Far too many times, a potential buyer can spend countless extra hours in Web-mediated research for a trip, say, pursuing the prospect of a rock-bottom price, a nonstop flight, or an aisle seat. Being able to do Internet searches empowers us to waste time looking for the perfect deal.

Empowerment costs money as well as time. Early adopters pay a premium for first-generation access to new technologies. But later adopters may have to pay more for access to equipment and services using these new technologies than they paid previously. For most consumers, the willingness to pay a high price occurs if and only if it offers a greater value proposition than the old technology did. Consumers by the millions have embraced digital photography even though the new cameras cost significantly more than preceding generations of film cameras. Being able to take countless photographs and edit or jettison them prior to printing saves money in the long run. Accordingly, incumbent companies like Kodak must reshape business plans and camera production lines.

Of course, not every new technology has been adopted as widely as digital cameras, DVD players, and microwave ovens have. The leading edge of technology may well couple expense with unproven or proprietary standards and inconvenience. Many prudent technology consumers avoid first-generation software and devices to avoid the bleeding edge. Less elegant but cheaper technologies often suffice, particularly when a device comes with different formats.

WINNERS AND LOSERS IN MARKET CONVERGENCE

Because new services and devices merge functions, previously separate markets will also converge. As we have seen, this means that we can no longer think in terms of discrete markets (telephone and cable television service, for example) or brick-and-mortar companies separate from their wireless and Internet ventures. This also means that devices that used to provide one function can facilitate many services. The cell phone is a prime example; it can provide a platform for text messaging, photography, music downloading, electronic funds transfer, Internet access, and video program viewing, as well as voice telephony.

These converging markets present challenges to regulators, policymakers, and consumers, primarily because each has considered companies in terms of their core services and the primary technology used to provide these services. AT&T used to stand for American Telephone and Telegraph Company. The name identified what services the company provided, now vastly expanded beyond what a company founder would recognize.

Television is another example of a service that has greatly changed. For dozens of years, broadcasters have reached viewers primarily through a closed-circuit coaxial cable. Yet regulators still treat broadcasters as though they continue to reach most audiences wirelessly. Broadcasters benefit from prolonged regulatory inertia by qualifying for special treatment based on the fact that a declining number of viewers still watch via the airwaves, and a smaller percentage still cannot readily migrate to pay-television services. Regulators fail to recognize that broadcasters face many new competitors, many of which have no regulatory burden at all.

With the convergence of video programming markets, television broadcasters now compete with video programming options available from many different wireline and wireless media. The market does not include just broadcast, cable, and satellite television but also downloads of video programming via wireless and wireline Internet media, such as cell phones and computers, as well as real-time streaming delivery of content via the same media. Market convergence is having a profound impact on the price, variety, accessibility, exclusivity, and scope of government regulation, however laggard it is.

Impact on Consumers

It would be easy and quite wrong to predict that market convergence will always enhance the value proposition for consumers, increase competition, empower consumers to the detriment of suppliers, and reduce production costs. Consumers will possibly benefit by having more options at possibly cheaper prices, particularly because market convergence reduces the ability of any single content distributor to keep content creators from pursuing multiple distribution outlets. But market convergence also has the potential to affect consumers in seriously negative ways. Market convergence may result in concentration: consolidated markets with fewer suppliers and greater market shares. Concentrated markets may not have robust competition, because potential competitors may act in "consciously parallel" ways by implicitly agreeing not to compete as vigorously as they could and as they would have to if the market had more competitors. On the other hand, the prospect of new competition, particularly in a volatile and changing marketplace, might keep even a tight oligopoly of operators honest.

Market convergence does not necessarily improve or expand the volume and quality of available services. In broadcast radio, concentration of ownership and control of stations has prompted many industry observers and general listeners to regret the lack of innovation and diversity. When ventures streamline operations, perhaps to achieve efficiency gains to offset the cost of an acquisition, they have every incentive to centralize management and operations. Cookie-cutter programming, delivered via satellite without regard to local events and conditions, including weather emergencies, offers a qualitatively inferior product that many consumers reject. Consumers stand to gain the most when converging markets offer an increase both in the number and type of distribution options and in the diversity of available content.

Customer Surveillance. Converging markets provide consumers with greater options for accessing ICE content and various services and for processing, manipulating, reformatting, storing, replaying, editing, and redistributing the content. The products, services, and content that consumers have available keep increasing in value and utility thanks to new technologies and the heightened interest on the part of equipment manufacturers and service providers to offer more consumption options. With the greater options and flexibility, consumers are empowered—and so are manufacturers, service providers, content creators, and content distributors. Market convergence means that consumers buy more expensive devices, services, and programs or simply more of everything, which generates revenues for those who successfully target buyers. With the stakes of customer acquisition rising, ventures want to learn as much as they can about consumers' needs and desires, and technological innovations and market convergence make it easier for them to acquire such intelligence; more information can be acquired by tracking the behavior and buying patterns of consumers generally. Accordingly, consumers have greater opportunities to get what they want when they want it, but ventures can find out what they might want in ways that violate their privacy. An individual might appreciate receiving music suggestions based on prior listening and purchasing decisions, but the predictive nature of such marketing may come across as intrusive.

The Digital Home. Commercial opportunities increase as the functions embedded in devices proliferate. Heretofore the cable television set-top box has facilitated transactions pertaining to video programming, such as pay-per-view. But as cable television ventures diversify into new markets, the set-top box will become a platform for many different commercial transactions, including payment for access to content, telephony, and Internet-mediated purchases. Couch potatoes will be ordering pizzas via their television sets.

Wireless networking, particularly for residences, adds value by providing consumers with access to ICE content and services from multiple locations and from different devices. Perhaps the expansion of content playback options will increase consumers' willingness to pay for wireless networking, which provides opportunities for Internet access to be shared across multiple computers and for peripherals and content to be shared as well: printers, music, games, and video. In a digital home, with seamless communications and enhanced location tracking, ICE devices will interoperate smoothly.

A digital home offers consumers many opportunities for accessing ICE. Television programs, movies, podcasts, and other visual and audio content can stream in to multiple display devices. Telephony, Internet messaging, and e-mail can route through multiple devices to find the intended recipients. Information access and storage will promote effective personal and household management, including health and home security.

Although content creators and content distributors have legitimate concerns about the potential for piracy that interconnection provides, ventures involved in electronic commerce should welcome the opportunity to access consumers and to be accessible to consumers in many new and potentially user-friendly ways. Currently, however, the interconnection of devices requires more expertise, patience, and luck than many consumers have. Perhaps as efforts to ensure intellectual property protection succeed, so, too, will efforts to simplify the process for interconnecting devices within a wireless network.

Impact on Suppliers

Suppliers, particularly ones creating and distributing content, must have ambivalent feelings about market convergence. On one hand, the successful venture can become a one-stop shop for an increasing percentage of consumers' content and device requirements. On the other hand, consumers will have far more ways to allocate their time and money: they can choose not only what to consume but where, when, and how they listen to and view content. Whether manufacturers and content producers benefit from market convergence depends largely on whether and how they can exploit new opportunities to expand consumption or at least continue to supply desirable products. Otherwise they will lose customers or suffer lower profit margins.

The Costs and Benefits of One-Stop Shopping. If suppliers and consumers can sufficiently expand the services available in an existing or prospective commercial relationship, one-stop shopping is the result. We can see how it comes about with broadcast television. Television networks used to distribute the content created by others. Later, benefiting from relaxed regulations, the networks had the option of creating and distributing their own programming. Now the broadcast networks have to consider the risks and rewards of using the Internet and other distribution networks to distribute programming.

As consumers become comfortable with Internet-delivered and wireless-delivered content, even viewed on tiny screens, broadcast networks have to consider new distribution options. Yet in serving consumers by allowing time, device, and format shifting, television networks risk financial harm to themselves and their broadcaster affiliates. Without technological safeguards that prevent consumers from copying programs and eliminating or fast-forwarding through advertisements, broadcast networks risk harming the financial prospects for DVD sales of compiled episodes and for advertising revenues. In other words, broadcast networks and other content creators and distributors cannot ignore consumers' desire for Internet and wireless access to content, particularly since they resort to self-help regardless of the legality of their tactics. However, in accommodating consumers, they have to ensure that the wireless and Internet options help them accrue additional revenues and audiences rather than shift or reduce profits.

Cannibalization occurs when access to a new market diverts audiences and revenues from an existing option. Currently, for example, instead of watching some episodes of popular television programs at the appointed times on the designated channels or later via a recording option, consumers can download files containing the programs for a small price or stream the content, complete with advertising, at no charge. If the payments from consumers or advertisers effectively offset the commensurate reduction in ratings and advertiser payments for the broadcast option, then no cannibalization will occur. Otherwise, accommodating consumers' aversion to appointment television ends up costing the content provider money.

Strange Bedfellows. Market convergence creates many new opportunities for growth and diversification, often achieved by new alliances between content creators and ventures providing wireless and Internet access. Convergence-driven joint ventures may lead to strange bedfellows as telecommunications ventures, such as wireline and wireless telephone companies, team up with Hollywood content creators like Disney, Time Warner, and Viacom. As we saw earlier, collaboration between Netheads, Bellheads, and Contentheads can lead to culture clashes. But collaboration will have to become more frequent and productive as content and conduit merge and as consumers become indifferent and technologically agnostic about the medium used to deliver content and about the devices receiving it.

CHAPTER TEN

Capturing the Benefits of Convergence

DESPITE THE IRRATIONAL exuberance and pessimism displayed in the ICE marketplace over the past decade, few would disagree that on balance, technological innovations have generated ample dividends. As we have seen throughout this book, whether the benefits flow to the public requires limited but effective government oversight and digitally literate consumers. ICE technologies and markets have begun to converge in ways that potentially increase both the rewards and the risks for the public and for ICE ventures. Most people stand to benefit from the cost savings and efficiency gains resulting from digitization, packet switching, and the proliferation of broadband access. But all too frequently, various individuals and groups exploit opportunities to capture a disproportionate share of the benefits by gaming the regulatory process.

Stakeholders have learned how to extract unnecessary incentives to invest, to capture financial gains from comparatively less regulation than competitors face, and to overstate the nature and scope of competition in the often-successful campaign to secure premature deregulation and unwarranted abdication of government oversight. If more consumers had worked diligently to understand the rewards and risks of digitization, convergence,[1] and the developing information age, then ICE ventures might not have so easily manipulated both the regulatory process and the commercial marketplace. But perhaps the public has not fully appreciated that even in a converging ICE marketplace, having an effective government referee remains essential.

THE REWARDS OF CONVERGENCE

The benefits accruing from technological and marketplace convergence seem straightforward and enticing. They are worth repeating. With digitization, a single technology, such as that used to operate and manage the Internet, can provide a medium for delivering several services that previously required different technologies, formats, and media. As technologies become more versatile and able to deliver more ICE services, previously stand-alone markets also converge. Consumers see the end product of convergence when incumbent companies have to stop relying on their long-standing core service offering for the bulk of revenues and profits and instead begin to find and serve new markets.[2] Telephone companies seek to position themselves in the marketplace as providers of a bundle of communications services: video programming, Internet access, wireless telecommunications, and voice communications. Cable television companies offer a similar bundle, with less emphasis on television, their core service, and more on the their ability to offer telephony and broadband Internet access. Wireless companies seek to convert the telephone handset into a third screen for accessing a variety of ICE contents and services, including video programming, Internet access, and telecommunications.

The bundling of previously discrete services carried by separate networks adds scale, scope, and operational efficiencies for the provider and some financial savings for consumers. Scale efficiency refers to the ability of a service provider to provide service at reduced per-unit costs because of an improved ability to spread costs over a growing group of users and service categories. Scope efficiency refers to the ability of a service provider to leverage the skill and efficiency it acquired in one core market onto adjacent and related ones. Operational efficiency refers to a carrier's ability to exploit digital technologies to provide services that enhance its delivery of desirable services.

The Internet will serve as the focal point for delivering convergent services. With IP-centric networking, carriers offering interconnected networks to exploit common technical standards can make the Internet a universally accessible medium for most ICE services. In other words, any ICE venture able to provide or access an Internet connection can typically offer a large variety of ICE services via that connection. No longer does an enterprise have to invest in a costly infrastructure capable of delivering just one type of ICE service, as has been the case heretofore. An IP-centric network allows any network operator to become a broadcaster, multichannel video program distributor, and telephone company. Being able to bundle previously separate services provides companies with new marketing opportunities even as it creates a regulatory quandary over what degree of government oversight such companies should have. In addition, regulators have developed different oversight models for different media. These models apply to a single medium (print, broadcast, cable, telephone, Internet) as though each were self-contained. However, in a convergent environment, mutual exclusivity does not exist, either because a single medium, such as the Internet, offers all previously discrete services or because competitive necessity and declining core-service revenues force ventures to diversify into two or more media services.

Aside from the possibility of becoming more regulated as they enter new markets, ICE ventures exploiting convergent technologies and markets have great opportunities to generate more revenues per customer. The ability to bundle services lets ICE ventures look forward to triple-digit monthly revenues per subscriber. When consumers pay more than one hundred dollars per month to a single venture, they expect to share in the venture's gains in operational efficiency, scale, and scope. Digitization and convergence should provide consumers with out-of-pocket cost savings.

THE OPPORTUNITY FOR BETTER-CALIBRATED REGULATION

Historically, telecommunications laws[3] and regulations[4] in the United States and in other nations[5] have established policies based on fixed service definitions and relatively static assumptions about the industrial organization of telecommunications and information processing. Vertical top-down regulatory policies typically apply regulated or unregulated status to a service based on definitions contained in laws whose authors made assumptions about market share,[6] essentialness,[7] pervasiveness,[8] and the use of public resources. The makers of these laws, policies, and regulations contemplated mutual exclusivity between services; that is, they imagined that broadcasters, cable television operators, and telephone companies could not use their content delivery technologies to provide anything but their core services. Vertical silo-based regulations apply different degrees of government oversight based on the method for delivering possibly the same content.[9] These regulations create incentives for regulatory arbitrage and opportunism by ventures hoping to exploit loopholes to qualify for a reduced regulatory burden, or one smaller than competitors', and increased profit margins.[10]

Under long-standing regulatory regimes, providers of basic telecommunication services fit under the common carrier classification,[11] while providers of enhanced services and information services, which add value to basic telecommunications,[12] fit under a private carrier classification. Being a private carrier means less regulation and no requirement for just and reasonable rates. These basic-enhanced and telecommunications–information service dichotomies worked when markets aligned in a neat, vertical array with limited horizontal market integration. In such a nonconvergent "old world order," markets and regulatory policies could fit into broad categories having different degrees of government oversight based on different assumptions about how a single service functioned.[13] The lack of integration made it feasible and possibly justifiable for the application of single different regulatory requirements to various ICE ventures.

Differences in regulatory classifications for functionally equivalent services have created incentives for stakeholders to find and qualify for designations that require the least regulation[14] or, alternatively, the most benefits conferred by law or regulation, such as subsidies, exemption from financial obligations, or qualified immunity from competition. Stakeholders can game the vertical regulatory structure and qualify for a preferred product or service classification even as other ventures, offering functional equivalents, incur more burdensome requirements based on static assumptions about their market share, on their past actions, or on their comparatively less effective advocacy in legislative, judicial, or regulatory forums.

The combination of convergence and exploitation of existing regulatory classifications for financial and competitive benefit has destabilized the basis on which the U.S. government calibrates the scope of marketplace oversight and intervention. When ICE ventures exploit technological and convergence opportunities, they enter new markets that often have a different degree of regulation than applies to the ventures' core services. The FCC has evidenced a near-complete inability to apply two or more regulatory classifications to a company serving multiple markets. The Commission seeks to continue applying a single regulatory model, often by ignoring the simple fact that when an ICE venture enters markets, various regulatory issues arise.

For example, wireless carriers, classified as common carrier telecommunications service providers, have diversified into information and video services. The FCC properly refrains from extending the preexisting common carrier model to mobile telephone carriers' new market forays. However, the fact that these carriers now also provide largely unregulated services provides a faulty and unlawful basis for the Commission to neglect its still necessary duty to regulate telecommunications services. The Commission appears to assume that it can apply two parallel but different regulatory models over (1) common carrier telecommunications services and (2) non-common-carrier information services. Because the FCC does not require mobile telephone carriers to separate the two functions between two stand-alone business ventures, the single integrated firm largely qualifies for limited regulation. The FCC acts as though service diversification somehow fundamentally changes the composition of wireless companies so that it can largely abandon oversight of the core telecommunications services that the companies continue to offer.

The FCC applies either/or regulatory models based on its use of vertical regulatory models that treat a venture as providing one and only one type of regulated service. These vertical models are quite static and inflexible. They were created when legislators and regulators could assume that once a venture opted to provide a specific service, it would continue doing so without any diversification that, as we have seen, triggered the applicability of another separate and different regulatory classification. Under this regulatory regime, common carrier telecommunications service providers appear condemned to significant regulatory oversight, based on long-standing assumptions about the need to impose economic safeguards on ventures providing essential and typically noncompetitive services.

When new competitive or nonessential services evolved, such as information and video services, the existing vertically oriented regulatory regime created new classification silos based on the view that the new services were not like the existing ones, but also that new and old services had nothing in common. Of course, new and old media services do have much in common; for example, a single company can provide both types of services. Regulatory arbitrage can occur when market entrants qualify for a new, less-regulated classification while incumbents remain burdened by legacy regulations that are no longer fully appropriate to retain. The type of regulatory arbitrage opportunities that have occurred are typically the opposite of those described in the above scenario: incumbents successfully convince the FCC that the new services they offer qualify for less regulation, and the Commission seems to lose track of, and interest in, the incumbents' old services, even if the carriers retain market dominance. This scenario appears to be playing out in the wireless marketplace as incumbents diversify and qualify for limited oversight when they offer video services and Internet access, even as the wireless carriers acquire market share and dominance in basic cellular telephony through mergers and acquisitions.

A BETTER EUROPEAN ALTERNATIVE

The European Union (EU) has implemented a better regulatory alternative by shifting from stand-alone vertical models, based on non-converging services, to a horizontal model that takes into account all ICE services collectively and subdivides them into separate layers of functions that grow in complexity and sophistication.[15] EU regulators first consider how ICE ventures provide the basic transport medium for delivering services and whether any company, or group of companies, dominates that market. At this level of analysis, the regulator does not consider what type of service rides along the conduit, but instead whether the conduit marketplace, composed of wireline and wireless options, operates competitively. Only if a venture has significant market power, by dominating the means for originating and terminating traffic, do regulatory safeguards apply.

Layered regulation brings about government oversight only when specific types of services lack sufficient competition, regardless of the current or prospective technologies capable of providing the services. The meshing of content and conduit in a convergent environment notwithstanding, horizontal regulators concentrate on the hierarchy of identifiable layers involved in the provision of information and telecommunications, including the network/physical layer (the wireline, wireless, or optical medium), the services carried over the network (one-way, two-way, narrowband, or broadband), and the applications/content (voice, data, video, software, and content) riding on top of the layered stack.[16]

In the United States a horizontal orientation would trigger a substantial revamping of regulatory treatment because it might free some ventures that have historically operated under extensive regulation and impose new regulatory burdens on ventures historically exempt from regulation. A horizontal orientation also would establish a regulatory regime based on how technologies function, ending the need to make semantic distinctions between such converging concepts as telecommunications used in the provision of information services, and telecommunications services provided directly to users.

The EU has acknowledged a simple premise that other nations, including the United States, have failed to appreciate fully: "The convergence of the telecommunications, media and information technology sectors means all transmission networks and services should be covered by a single regulatory framework."[17] The EU approach establishes definitions for an electronic communications network, an electronic communications service, and information society services, which are a specified set of information services whose telecommunications carriage component can be recognized as subordinate to the information service provided; an example is home banking. The EU's harmonized, horizontal regulatory model subjects ICE industries to government oversight geared to remedy specific instances of ineffective competition, but solely "in markets where there are one or more undertakings with significant market power, and where national or Community competition law remedies are not sufficient to address the problem."[18]

The EU approach separates content from conduit and subjects any single horizontal layer to regulation only where market distortions have occurred or where they potentially may occur in view of the market power exercised by one or more participating ventures. The EU uses antitrust and competition policy analysis as its primary regulatory oversight model rather than making assumptions about how competitive a specific ICE industry or service has been historically. Regulation occurs if and only if competition does not exist in a particular geographic or specific market; existing regulatory obligations may be withdrawn on the basis of subsequent market analysis showing newly robust competition.

The horizontal regulatory approach championed by the EU offers a rational and consistent alternative to the vertical regulatory model used in the United States. In the horizontal model, content and conduit fit into separate regulatory classifications, with content providers generally exempt from regulation. Conduit providers, regardless of the medium, are subject to economic regulation, but the scope of government oversight is finely calibrated as a function of the particular carrier's market share and the level of competition in the various conduit submarkets. Regardless of whether telecommunications provide bit transport for an information service or offer stand-alone content delivery, the EU specifies that the conduit function be regulated to the extent that any operator has market power, a condition still requiring government oversight to promote sustainable competition and consumer protection.

Rather than make empirical assessments of current ICE market competition, the FCC has decided to abandon carrier regulation simply by reassessing classifications in the vertical regulatory model in order to eliminate services like DSL that previously triggered regulation as telecommunications services. Telecommunications law permits the Commission to eliminate most regulations if an empirical record proves that competition and other safeguards provide adequate consumer protection. Rather than use the deregulatory flexibility available to it, however, the FCC appears intent on eliminating all telecommunications service regulations if it can come up with plausible rationales for subsuming or subordinating telecommunications functionalities within cable or information services. This semantic tinkering satisfies the FCC's assumption that services must fit entirely within one vertical model, but only by creating two ambiguous and not necessarily mutually exclusive categories: telecommunications as a capability or building block for another service and telecommunications as a stand-alone retail service.

To sustain several parallel vertical models (telecommunications, cable, and information services) the FCC has erected a mechanism for ignoring, subordinating, or dismissing telecommunications functionalities that previously constituted regulated telecommunication services. Identifiable telecommunications service functions do not evaporate, however, particularly since carriers can take a telecommunications functionality used as a building block for an information service and configure it for a stand-alone conventional wireline or wireless telecommunications services. To achieve preferred deregulatory status, formerly regulated carriers have succeeded in masking telecommunications functionalities used conventionally by emphasizing their supporting or subordinate role in the provision of information services. In either instance, the telecommunications functionality exists, as do the common carrier regulatory responsibilities, unless and until the FCC undertakes a specific deregulatory initiative, under section 10 of the Telecommunications Act of 1996,[19] to determine whether the public interest supports selective deregulation.

The EU has devised a more straightforward and viable regulatory model, but we should not expect Congress or the FCC to embrace it. No regulatory model that possibly increases the scope of governmental oversight has any likelihood of adoption, no matter how rational and necessary oversight may be. The FCC may express a reluctance to extend legacy regulations, but it emphasizes legacy legal and regulatory status, except when its grand regulatory mission to offer something new requires otherwise. So the FCC maintains the status quo—regulated status for telecommunications services providers—but makes every effort to reduce the number and type of ventures that quality for this classification.

The FCC has commensurately expanded the number and type of firms qualifying for the information services classification, a deregulatory safe harbor,[20] even though it has found it necessary to reimpose some regulatory burdens, such as the obligation to pay universal service subsidies. The FCC makes do with inconsistent regulatory models. It extends private carrier status to cable television operators even when these ventures offer what appear to be telecommunications services, and it eliminates regulatory burdens for any venture providing any information service. The common carrier model can easily be avoided and ignored.

THE RISKS OF CONVERGENCE

ICE convergence raises the stakes when governments rightly perceive the need to recalibrate the scope and reach of regulatory oversight. With convergence, single companies can offer an array of ICE services, presumably contributing to the overall degree of marketplace competition. But if the marketplace becomes more concentrated, the potential exists for less competition across more ICE sectors. Accordingly, government legislators, policymakers, and regulators have to consider the implications of convergence for the near-term level of competition in ICE market segments, because ventures with market power probably have the technological means to diversify easily and efficiently. Such diversification may make it possible for formidable new competition to arise from among incumbents or newcomers. However, diversification can also make it possible for a powerful incumbent to extend its dominance across segments of the ICE marketplace.

The easiest way for nations to fail to exploit the benefits of convergence lies in premature deregulation based on faulty calculations or biased estimates of actual competition. The presumption that competition exists, or soon will appear, may motivate legislators and regulators to conclude that ICE convergence will contribute to the trend toward competition or at least have no negative impact on competition. Yet convergence favors ventures that can exploit economies of scale and scope by increasing the array of ICE services that they offer, but to do so a venture must have the financial wherewithal to invest and maintain expensive facilities that typically have large initial sunk costs.

Because most ICE ventures have substantial fixed costs, which they must incur before generating revenues, the ICE market has substantial barriers to market entry and to robust facilities-based competition. Technological convergence does not reduce these barriers to market entry by any significant extent. It increases the prospects that market incumbents will have to generate more revenues and achieve higher average revenues per user by adding new services and by exploiting their ownership of essential and not readily duplicated facilities, such as the first and last miles of a network used to originate and terminate subscriber services.

Ventures must have very deep financial pockets to operate in a convergent environment. Those unable to invest in network upgrades and retrofits to exploit convergence opportunities have become takeover targets for ventures that have ample funds. But rather than acknowledge the potential for less competition and greater concentration as convergence proceeds and as incumbents expand into new ICE industry segments, the FCC perpetuates the myth that robust competition already exists and that more industry consolidation will not adversely affect competition.

WRONGHEADED CLASSIFICATIONS: VOIP AND DSL

We could readily conclude that VoIP constitutes an unregulated information service, based on its use of software to configure lines already regarded as providing information services. Similarly we could conclude that in light of the inertia in regulatory classification, a service deemed common-carriage telecommunications would remain so classified. In both cases our assumptions would be wrong. The FCC increasingly treats VoIP as a regulated service, and it reclassified DSL to free it of any telecommunications service regulatory burdens.

VoIP

Some VoIP services offer a functional equivalent of and competitive alternative to local and long-distance telephone service, while others provide a communications link for activities that typically do not include a telephone call—for example, video games. All VoIP services use software and other applications typically accessed by consumers via cable modem and DSL links already classified as information services. If the Commission classified VoIP as a telecommunications service, the decision would cast doubt on the rationality and lawfulness of imposing regulatory burdens on packagers of software-enabled services that ride along a bitstream generated by Internet service providers. If the FCC classified VoIP as an information service, the decision would exempt VoIP from conventional telecommunications service regulation under the Communications Act of 1934 and would force the FCC to stretch its ancillary jurisdiction to apply regulatory safeguards and requirements, previously applicable only to telecommunications service providers, based on a general public interest mandate contained in Title I of the Communications Act.

Even as the FCC avoids deciding which regulatory classification applies to VoIP services, it has received rulemaking and declaratory ruling petitions that have obligated it to make several decisions resulting in the imposition of regulatory burdens on VoIP and the partial re-regulation of information services, even including DSL and cable modem services. Faced with the need to shore up a subsidy mechanism for supporting universal access to basic telephone services, which is done by way of a surcharge on voice telephony minutes of use, the Commission now requires VoIP service providers to make mandatory contributions to the universal service fund.[21] In response to public safety concerns about VoIP customer access to emergency telephone services, the FCC now requires VoIP service providers to retrofit their networks to support emergency-911 calling[22] and access by disabled users[23] and to enable new subscribers to use previously assigned and used telephone numbers.[24] In response to national security concerns expressed by government agencies such as the Department of Justice, the FCC has found a way to interpret the Communications Assistance for Law Enforcement Act (CALEA) as requiring that VoIP service providers and all providers of broadband access to the Internet enable wiretapping, despite an express exemption on applying CALEA to providers of "information services."[25]

The FCC, in not classifying VoIP while nevertheless applying some of the regulatory burdens traditionally borne exclusively by telecommunications service providers, is invoking its broad public interest regulatory authority under Title I of the Communications Act, as amended, and combining it with a focus on the telecommunications transmission link in VoIP. In short, when the FCC wants to subject VoIP services to regulatory requirements, it finds a way to emphasize the telecommunications component, but when it wants to avoid regulation, it considers the very same telecommunications component a subordinate, unseverable, and integrated component of a cable modem, DSL, power line,[26] or wireless[27] information service.

DSL

In the case of DSL, the FCC, following up on the Supreme Court's endorsement of its decision to deem cable modem Internet access an information service, the FCC reclassified DSL, making it an information service as well.[28] This reclassification did not trigger a court appeal or much scrutiny because the Supreme Court had already expansively deferred to the Commission's expertise in differentiating telecommunications from information services. The Court also agreed with the FCC on the need for regulatory parity between cable modem and DSL services. Notwithstanding the Court's unwillingness to second-guess the FCC's interpretation of its legislative mandate, including the classification of services by using the definitions contained in the Communications Act, the FCC faced a challenging task.

Cable television ventures can offer cable modem service by retrofitting their video programming distribution network, which the FCC never deemed a telecommunications service. For DSL, the FCC had to rationalize a reclassification of a service that telephone companies can offer only by retrofitting their existing copper-wire network, initially used exclusively to deliver regulated telecommunications services. By reclassifying DSL, the FCC exempted telephone companies and their DSL subscribers from having to contribute to universal service funding, even though the FCC soon concluded that the sustainability of its universal service funding program required the expansion of compulsory contributors to include VoIP services accessed via DSL.

The FCC justified its reclassification of DSL on several grounds: (1) deregulation will promote wider access to broadband access;[29] (2) benefits to consumers will accrue from subjecting both cable modem and DSL service to minimal regulation;[30] (3) deregulation will create incentives for investment in next-generation networks;[31] (4) several facilities-based broadband providers will be offering competition;[32] and (5) the legislative mandate to promote the availability of "advanced telecommunications capabilities"[33] includes deregulatory initiatives to promote access to information services.[34]

The FCC never directly addressed how the telecommunications transmission component of DSL service had changed from a stand-alone, common carrier service to an integrated and unseverable component of a telecommunications service. Instead, it simply reiterated its rationale for finding the integrated and unseverable aspects of telecommunications in cable modem service. The FCC deems DSL services functionally equivalent to cable modem services because "wireline broadband Internet access"[35] has the same integration of basic telecommunications and enhanced information-processing functions[36] and because it apparently cannot decouple or sever the telecommunications component: "Because wireline broadband Internet access service inextricably combines the offering of powerful computer capabilities with telecommunications, we conclude that it falls within the class of services identified in the Act as 'information services.'"[37]

Having effectuated the reclassification of DSL as an information service, the FCC removed all previous regulatory safeguards designed to promote a level playing field among competing providers of enhanced services that apply information processing to basic transmission links. In its Second Computer Inquiry the FCC established several interconnection and fair-dealing requirements for telephone companies offering basic telecommunications services, as well as a requirement that these companies separate basic services from enhanced services and offer the former on a common carrier basis. The FCC subsequently concluded that technological innovations and the possibility of gains in operational efficiencies supported the elimination of a regulatory barrier against integrating basic and enhanced services. The elimination of the regulations freed telephone companies to offer intelligent networks and not dumb pipes that other ventures could enhance with software and other applications. To ensure that telephone companies have every incentive to build basic and enhanced networks, the FCC promoted full exploitation of technological and market convergence. In doing so, it risked relinquishing the most effective lawful regulatory tool to remedy abuses and to protect the public interest when self-regulation does not suffice to promote competition and fairness in the information services marketplace.

The Commission has no doubts that a competitively level marketplace has already evolved, ensuring widespread availability of retail broadband access for consumers, even for ventures that want to operate a broadband business using capacity acquired from an incumbent telephone company for resale.[38] The Commission has such confidence in the evolution of competition that it ignores current evidence of a duopoly: that broadband Internet access is controlled by cable and telephone companies. Curiously, the Commission does not consider it necessary even to assess whether any venture has dominant market power in the broadband or wireline broadband marketplace.[39] It has concluded that such a market assessment was appropriate only for the previous market environment dominated by telephone companies with separate telecommunications and information service markets.[40] For specific problems not remedied by a competitive marketplace, the FCC reserves the option of using its Title I authority[41] in such areas as consumer protection, network reliability, and national security.[42]

On balance, the FCC has contributed to regulatory uncertainty rather than maintaining a clear line between regulated telecommunications services and unregulated information services. Technological convergence and technological innovations challenge whether Congress can fashion long-standing definitions that the FCC will use to determine the scope of government oversight. But the FCC has exacerbated the difficulties of using the old rules in a changed environment by aggressively pursuing a deregulatory mission even as it backtracks and reimposes regulatory burdens on information services. As we have also seen, the FCC has overstated the current and prospective degree of facilities-based and resale competition in next-generation services by using unrealistic definitions of what constitutes high-speed broadband service and by generating faulty statistics of market penetration. By concluding that robust competition exists when it does not, the FCC rationalizes the appropriateness of a campaign to eliminate conventional telecommunications service regulation even for services that retrofit plant used to provide voice telephone service. Fuzzy math, creative economics, and compilations of deceptively optimistic market penetration statistics are some of the tactics that the FCC has used to rationalize its chosen inconsistent regulatory, re-regulatory, and deregulatory decisions.

Judicial review has not provided a reliable bulwark against decisions that are "arbitrary, capricious, an abuse of discretion, or otherwise not in accordance with law."[43] With far too few exceptions, courts do not scrutinize the FCC's statistical compilations, empirical evidence gathering, or conclusions about marketplace conditions. Most courts willingly defer to the FCC's projections about the impact of a policy shift, including policies designed to promote competition but permitting media consolidation and mergers, as well as the abandonment of conventional common-carrier regulatory safeguards.

Lax judicial and legislative oversight combined with the FCC's pursuit of political, philosophical, and economic policy objectives without regard to the factual record have adverse effects. Poor market penetration by next-generation networks and even the failure to install and operate such networks can no longer be attributed to "confiscatory" regulatory policies, to cite standard objection of incumbent telephone companies.[44] The safe harbor of limited regulation for information services has largely removed government oversight, including its requirement that certain traditional common-carrier interconnection responsibilities be met.[45] Instead of promoting investment and competition in next-generation networks, the safe harbor has helped create a broadband duopoly with a record of mediocre performance.

The growing regulation of VoIP and the convenient flip-flop deregulation of DSL provide two current examples of flaws in the FCC's vertical regulatory models. The FCC professes to favor light-handed regulation, yet it accepts any invitation to impose conventional telephone company regulations on VoIP and to shoehorn into the telecommunication service category what could easily be classified as an information service. Without significant consideration of the marketplace impact of regulating and then deregulating DSL service, the Commission emphasizes regulatory parity as it attempts to shoehorn another service into a questionable category. We should bear in mind that DSL constitutes a retrofit of existing telephone lines, paid for all these years by telephone service subscribers. In a sleight of hand the FCC ignores this fact and shuffles DSL into the information service category, which allows providers to capture the value of benefits conferred on the assumption that the carrier provides public-utility common carrier services, including free rights of way over public and private property.

CHAPTER ELEVEN

What Government Should Do

IN THE UNITED STATES, extraordinary politicization, wishful thinking, and research sponsored by stakeholders have all but guaranteed that ICE policies will fail to promote best practices, competition, and enhanced consumer welfare. Policymakers operate from the assumption that competition exists, or soon will exist, if only the legislators and the regulators would remove disincentives to investment. The United States used to provide a model for what nations should do to stimulate the ICE economy: remove barriers to market entry, promote competition between private ventures, and have an independent regulator with the resources to ensure a level playing field and sustainable competition.

Now the United States offers little leadership, offering a model in which the regulator largely disengages from close regulatory scrutiny, based on the misguided notion that it need not do more. This model encourages stakeholders to consider regulation a key means by which to secure an artificial competitive edge: by qualifying to receive monetary benefits, such as subsidies and tax credits and by avoiding costly regulatory burdens that competitors still must bear. ICE ventures have come to understand that substantial monetary benefits ("rents" in the economists' terminology) accrue when they invest in lobbying legislatures and regulators, litigating disputes to increase an artificial competitive advantage, and framing policy, academic, and political debates in terms of how government regulation "harms" competition.

Regulators may need to create incentives for incumbents to make investments in next-generation networks, and they may need to stimulate market entry. However, incentives should augment a preexisting motivation to invest for long-term gains and be coupled with a commitment by the FCC to enforce rules designed to promote fair and sustainable competition. Regulators need to change the nature and scope of regulation, not abandon it.

To ensure a level playing field, regulation should impose rules that promote full and fair competition without favoring any specific technology, service, or company. Few competitors want to compete in the marketplace when they can resort to less expensive and exhausting strategies to achieve higher revenues and profits. If the playing field is level, both incumbents and market entrants have to capture market share based on superior business acumen, better products and services, and lower prices, not by suppressing or hampering competitors or by convincing regulators through superior tactics to regulate it less while subjecting competitors to greater regulatory burdens. To achieve and maintain sustainable competition, regulators have to anticipate ways that both incumbents and newcomers will try to game the system to secure an artificial competitive advantage.

Legislators and regulators need to consider whether and how to enhance competition. This objective does not automatically translate into deregulation and the relaxation of regulatory burdens imposed on incumbents any more than it guarantees market entrants regulation-free opportunities to compete. Incumbents may qualify for streamlined or abandoned regulations, and market entrants may require some degree of regulation. Neither the passage of time under a regulatory regime nor technological and marketplace convergence entitle incumbents to regulatory relief without regard to current marketplace conditions. Nor should market entrants qualify for special incubation and insulation from competition or from industry regulations simply because of their newness.

THE SHIFT TO LIGHT-HANDED REGULATION

Throughout the world, the nature and scope of regulation has changed over the past twenty years. Nations show a clear preference for less regulation and more reliance on competition. They do not need heavy-handed, command-and-control regulation when structural and market conditions favor competition. Structurally, nations have supported a less intrusive regulatory posture by eliminating government-sanctioned monopolies. Most nations, including many industrializing countries, have privatized the state-owned Post, Telegraph, and Telephone monopoly and have allowed market entry in other previously monopolized ICE sectors. Most of them have also separated ICE services into two regulatory categories: (1) services that remain essential, for which the government has an obligation to promote universal access at fair prices, and (2) optional services, for which the government can defer to marketplace competition where it exists.

Even for essential services, such as basic voice telephone service, regulators should fine-tune the scope of government oversight. This recalibration responds to circumstances that favor less stringent regulation. While nations previously considered it essential to require carriers to file public service contracts (tariffs) and secure authorization before offering or discontinuing service, many countries have relaxed the rules now that service alternatives exist. The FCC does not need to regulate wireline telephone service as aggressively as it once did because facilities-based and software-generated alternatives exist. Telephone companies remain common carriers, obligated to provide a public utility service on a nondiscriminatory basis and without unreasonable terms and conditions. However, the FCC can remove many, but not all, of the traditional common-carrier regulations, such as the duty to file tariffs and to secure authorization to introduce or abandon services.

When only one venture provided a particular service, command-and-control regulation imposed comprehensive financial scrutiny over the terms, conditions, and prices for the service. Regardless of whether the enterprise secured its monopoly by franchise or achieved a natural monopoly on economic grounds, the regulator needed to scrutinize the carrier's behavior. The heavily regulated companies could rail against the costly regulatory burdens foisted on them, but they also qualified for ample statutory and regulatory benefits as public service companies and public utilities. The benefits included the opportunity to install facilities over public and private property, often with little or no financial compensation owed to the property owner, plus some degree of insulation from competition, tax credits, and a rate of return all but guaranteed by the government.

Under light-handed regulation, in contrast, the government acts more like a referee than a handicapper. Referees enforce rules that promote fairness without impeding the ability of players to compete fully. Some of the most competitive sports have regulators on the field to enforce the rules. Few would dispute the view that without on-site referees a sporting event might break down. Similarly, ICE regulation by a referee ensures full and fair competition without collusion among competitors and without opportunities for competitors to secure an unfair and artificial advantage.

FORESTALLING VERSUS REMEDYING COMPETITIVE HARM

In recalibrating the nature and scope of light-handed regulation a key question is whether the government should anticipate the likelihood of marketplace abuses and have in place a mechanism to remedy a situation quickly. Nations less enamored of market self-regulation typically maintain the presence of a regulatory authority to establish and enforce rules instead of relying on judicial relief after anticompetitive practices have harmed consumers and competitors. These nations typically have agencies with expertise specific to industry sectors, rather than relying on a generalist court or regulatory agency to enforce antitrust and competition laws.

Ex ante rules are set forth in case ICE ventures push the deregulatory envelope to acquire a competitive advantage; the rules anticipate and offer remedies for anticompetitive and discriminatory conduct. Ex post facto rules establish remedies only after possibly unanticipated anticompetitive practices have occurred. In nations applying ex ante rules, the opportunity exists to establish a regulatory framework with the government establishing baseline expectations and intervening when it identifies violations or receives a complaint. In nations applying ex post facto rules, remedies are generally limited to financial compensation for the harm that has occurred; there may also be orders to reform. Financial remedies may provide compensation only after an industry segment and consumers in that segment have suffered from a loss of service options and a reduction in the benefits accruing from competition, such as lower prices and the innovations generated by entrepreneurs. Even the most innovative and creative market entrant may not survive in a market where the absence of regulatory oversight emboldens an incumbent venture to engage in below-cost pricing to customers, refusals to interconnect with competitors, agreements to interconnect but only at unreasonably high rates, and other such anticompetitive practices.

Anticompetitive Practices in ICE Markets

ICE markets have perhaps greater vulnerability to anticompetitive practices than other sectors of the economy. In many instances, two or more competing ventures must cooperate in the delivery of a service. Such cooperation occurs through the voluntary interconnection of separate networks that make up the Internet and also through the government-mandated interconnection of separate telecommunications networks, which occurs when unaffiliated long-distance and local telephone networks cooperate in routing calls and when unaffiliated wireless and wireline networks handle traffic that originates and terminates on different networks.

ICE ventures often have substantial incentives to cooperate in the routing of traffic because they may not have installed facilities throughout a nation or the world. Internet peering agreements, which set out the terms and conditions for accepting traffic generated by subscribers of another carrier, help make both content and subscriber mailboxes globally accessible. Both wireline and wireless carriers realize that their subscribers expect to have the ability to make calls to, and receive calls from, subscribers of unaffiliated networks, even ones that use different technologies.

But in plenty of instances one carrier sees an opportunity to handicap a competitor by refusing to interconnect or by interconnecting on terms and conditions that adversely affect the competitor, perhaps making the competitor unable to offer a cost-competitive service or a service of comparable quality. When AT&T attempted to maintain its monopoly over long-distance telephone service after market entrants offered competitive technologies, such as microwave radio transmission, its primary strategy to repel competition involved unlawful refusals to interconnect its local telephone networks; without interconnection, competitors could not accept long-distance traffic from AT&T (Bell System) local service subscribers, nor could they deliver calls to AT&T subscribers. Even after the FCC ordered AT&T to provide access, the company made sure that interconnection generated inferior service compared to straight AT&T service: poorer sound quality and more digits to dial manually. To compound the misery of a firm bold enough to challenge AT&T, the company deliberately underpriced services to stave off customer migration and attempted to charge extortionately high interconnection charges when compelled to provide access to its network.

Setting below-cost prices to drive out competitors is called predatory pricing; after successfully suppressing the competitors, the surviving venture can raise prices back to monopoly levels. A price squeeze occurs when an incumbent venture raises the cost of an essential element of service needed by a market entrant to provide a complete service—for example, access to the Bell System local loop used to originate and terminate long-distance telephone calls. Ex ante regulation provided by a government agency with expertise in telecommunications can identify and presumably remedy instances of predatory pricing, refusals to deal, price squeezes, and other types of interconnection discrimination. Relying on ex post facto remedies because an expert telecommunications regulatory agency does not exist or is ineffectual may provide a remedy, but only after one or more competitors have gone out of business. Even the FCC during its command-and-control, heavy-handed regulatory days could not or would not discipline AT&T and prevent it from engaging in anticompetitive practices. A federal district court, with jurisdiction to enforce antitrust law, had to step in, resulting in a delayed remedy and claims that a judge had become a telecommunications law and policy czar.

Ex ante regulators can react to anticompetitive practices on a timely basis and can establish structural safeguards against harmful vertical and horizontal integration. Vertical integration helps create or maintain a monopoly by enabling a single venture to operate in each of the production elements and service segments that make up an industry. In telecommunications, lawful vertical integration resulted when AT&T manufactured equipment used to provide telephone service, operated the telephone companies that provided telephone service, and both manufactured and leased the telephone equipment that subscribers used to make telephone calls. AT&T's vertical integration violated the antitrust laws when the company made sure that no competitor could sell equipment to Bell System telephone companies and guaranteed a monopoly for its corporate affiliate Western Electric.

In telecommunications, horizontal integration results when companies own affiliates, or acquire competitors that provide competitive alternatives. For example, AT&T provides wireline local and long-distance telephone service, wireless local and long-distance telephone service, and Internet-mediated services, including VoIP. A broader definition of complementary and competitive services would include AT&T's entry into video program delivery and its joint venture with a direct broadcast satellite firm. Unlawful horizontal integration occurs when a firm with significant market power in one or more competing markets merges or acquires the assets of a competitor, resulting in such concentration of ownership and power as to thwart competition.

Expert regulatory agencies should have lawful authority to investigate and remedy anticompetitive practices before they substantially harm markets and competitors. This mandate does not have to result in heavy-handed or intrusive regulation. The European Union horizontal regulatory model allows ventures to operate largely free of government intervention unless and until one venture or a group reaches a level of market power where anticompetitive outcomes can occur. A small group of ventures, uninterested in competing, can achieve the same sorts of anticompetitive outcomes. When a market has only a handful of competitors, the operators may conclude that they have more to gain by fixing prices, rigging bids, and acting collusively than by competing. Conscious parallelism is collusive behavior that occurs even without person-to-person meetings to fix prices and otherwise refrain from competing.

Open Access and Compulsory Interconnection

Common-carrier-type interconnection between operators of competing networks should continue to be required under light-handed regulation. One could argue that market forces would guarantee interconnection because network operators would recognize the mutual benefit for themselves and their customers. However, as we will see later, ample opportunities and motivations exist for subtle and not easily detected discrimination that can tilt the playing field.

To interconnect and to refrain from unreasonable, unfair, and anticompetitive practices are necessary commitments in a convergent marketplace where multiple ventures compete to provide an expanding bundle of services. Ventures with a sizeable market share and deep financial pockets may perceive an opportunity to acquire larger, possibly dominant market share in all ICE sectors by refusing to cooperate and interconnect facilities. Currently, for example, wireless carriers have a keen interest in creating walled-garden collections of video and audio content in lieu of providing access to everything the Internet has to offer. Consumers may be tempted to subscribe in order to gain access to a select collection of content, provided in a user-friendly environment and requiring little effort to locate, but the wireless carriers that create the walled gardens may be tempted to reduce the accessibility and connectivity of their networks for subscribers who want to leave the walled gardens and access content and software elsewhere within the Internet cloud. In some instances, walled gardens may not harm competition, and may even stimulate it; for example, wireless carriers may try to develop the best package of programming. But in other instances, the absence of a duty to interconnect networks may balkanize networks, resulting in an overall reduction of convenience, value, and utility. The possible outcome would be a World Wide Web with small portions of its content available to subscribers in convenient walled gardens with the rest of the content blocked off or made more expensive and difficult to access.

Risks in Extending Legacy Regulations

So far, we have examined instances where governments prematurely deregulated ICE sectors after making flawed assumptions about the current or prospective degree of competition. We have seen that exempting ICE services from regulation may provide an artificial competitive advantage to a class of ICE providers. Fairness requires that we also consider the harm to competition and consumers when governments blindly extend regulation to new technologies and services even though changed circumstances support reduced or eliminated regulation.

Sometimes governments decide to apply existing regulations to new technologies and services based on a possibly inflexible interpretation of statutory definitions and regulatory classifications. Applying legacy regulations may not impose substantial burdens, because the regulator may have the flexibility to streamline the scope of regulation. However, the decision to apply existing regulations means that specific types of technologies and services, which might have qualified for little or no regulation, nevertheless acquire possibly more burdensome obligations. Just as a legislature and regulator may underprotect the national interest by abdicating responsibilities based on unrealistic conclusions about competition-driven self-regulation, so might the government overprotect: it can apply unneeded and costly regulatory safeguards when competition could foster effective self-regulation.

When recalibrating regulation, governments need to ensure that a level playing field exists. Regulatory parity requires governments to subject incumbents to that degree of regulation necessary to guard against market manipulation through anticompetitive practices. If a market truly becomes robustly competitive with a multitude of facilities-based operators, then regulatory parity requires governments to deregulate incumbents, particularly where market entrants never had to bear the same regulatory responsibilities as the incumbents. Conversely, where markets have not become competitive, governments should not remove legacy regulatory burdens prematurely based on the expectation that future market entrants may arise and obviate the need for regulation.

The removal of legacy regulations should be calibrated to existing and near-term competition. It is not enough to say that certain statutory or regulatory changes would make it possible for competition to arise through liberalized market-entry rules. Incumbent operators will seek to convince governments to abandon legacy regulations, just as existing or prospective market entrants will seek exemption from ever having to comply with legacy regulations. Because both incumbents and market entrants may seek government-conferred competitive advantages, governments should remain wary of extending legacy regulations to either type of venture, but also of exempting either type of venture from legacy regulations.

When a government draws incorrect conclusions about the state of competition or the potential for either an incumbent or a market entrant to promote or harm competition, the error can enable a venture to exploit the inconsistent regulatory treatment of competitors. With regulatory arbitrage it may be able to take advantage of dissimilar regulatory classifications to secure an artificial competitive advantage. Many regulatory arbitrage opportunities occur when a market entrant, legally or otherwise, can operate free of regulatory burdens or with fewer regulatory responsibilities than incumbents have. But sometimes an incumbent, diversifying into another ICE industry sector, may exploit regulatory arbitrage opportunities as well.

VoIP ventures initially had a regulatory arbitrage opportunity vis-à-vis incumbent wireline and wireless networks. The FCC did not immediately decide to treat VoIP operators as carriers subject to costly regulatory requirements. Also some VoIP operators could configure their services in ways that obscured where calls originated, which let them reduce or eliminate the charges they would have had to pay conventional telephone companies to deliver VoIP traffic to the intended call recipients. In some extreme cases, VoIP traffic became commingled with conventional wireline and wireless local traffic, completely robbing conventional carriers of their ability to meter and charge for delivering VoIP traffic to call recipients.

Sometimes a national regulatory authority (NRA) deliberately confers a competitive opportunity on market entrants by exempting them from regulatory burdens because they enter an ICE industry sector without market share and possibly with significant handicaps compared to one or more incumbents. The view here is that the government should help jumpstart or facilitate competition even at the risk of unregulating market entrants and adding more financial burdens to incumbents. Regulatory arbitrage opportunities like this can help market entrants gain market share and generate the revenues needed to become long-term, possibly facilities-based competitors. However, governments risk the wrath of incumbents, well equipped with the political resources to redress such grievances and harboring concerns that an overzealous regulator has become a biased advocate for competition, regardless of whether competition is sustainable in the absence of regulatory arbitrage opportunities, and a handicapper of incumbents.

Incumbent ventures are not always disqualified from exploiting regulatory arbitrage opportunities. Well-funded ventures such as AT&T and Verizon have begun distributing video programming in competition with incumbent cable television companies. Regulatory parity typically would require that legacy cable television rules apply equally to incumbent cable television firms, such as Comcast, and to market entrants, such as AT&T and Verizon, or that both incumbents and market entrants equally qualify for the same degree of reduced regulation. Regulatory arbitrage may occur if cable operators remain subject to legacy regulations while new competitors qualify for less regulatory burden—for example, by being allowed to secure statewide service franchises in lieu of municipality-specific franchises and by being exempted from geographical service commitments. The market entrant might be allowed to redline—to serve only upscale neighborhoods—because cable operators already serve the entire locality.

A RECENT EXAMPLE OF REGULATORY ARBITRAGE

Creative entrepreneurs regularly devise new ways to exploit regulatory arbitrage opportunities. For example, a venture can profit by increasing the volume of inbound calls for which it receives compensation from other carriers. An egregious example of this type of arbitrage occurs when some rural, independent telephone companies advertise free international telephone calls or free conference calls. For wireless subscribers with rate plans offering "unlimited nights and weekends" a call into the rural telephone company's switch may trigger no additional charge. The subscriber can make an international call, and the rural telephone company can charge, on a per-minute basis, a sizeable access fee to the wireless carrier offering unlimited nights and weekend calling. In most instances, the wireless carriers would have to pay a per-minute rate in the hundredths or thousands of a cent. But for call terminations provided by some rural telephone companies, the rate may exceed five cents per minute. Subscribers of the rural telephone company typically make comparatively fewer outbound calls given the absence of free international or conference-calling opportunities offered by major carriers. Accordingly, the rural telephone company can generate a sizeable surplus of call terminations, entitling it to receive substantial access-charge payments from other carriers.

ACHIEVING BEST PRACTICES IN ICT DEVELOPMENT

Few would dispute that information and communication technologies (ICT) can effectively prime the pump of a nation's economy.[1] Efficient information-age infrastructures enhance productivity by providing networks that can handle converging voice, data, and electronic commerce applications. These infrastructures provide a comparative advantage in "knowledge-based"[2] industries, which include such diverse fields as data processing, banking, insurance, technical consulting, travel planning, customer relations, and business logistics. With reduced trade barriers, an increasingly global economy, and the companies' quests to find new growth opportunities, there are substantial incentives for public and private players to exploit their competency in information and communication markets both domestically and abroad.[3]

The track record for ICT implementation achieved by individual companies and nations does not always correlate with other indicators of success in trade, development, and quality of life. Nations must continually improve ICT innovation, incubation, and exploitation because an increasingly integrated global economy can quickly erode a nation's comparative advantages, particularly advantages prone to volatility as a result of technological innovation. For example, ICT provides industrializing nations with opportunities to accelerate their technology competency and use through technology transfer and foreign direct investment. Although ICT might at first generate threats to employment in industrialized nations through outsourcing, it might subsequently jeopardize wealth generation in knowledge industries as industrializing nations establish their own research and development prowess. When industrializing nations wean themselves of dependency on industrializing nations' patents and innovations, they gain revenue-generating opportunities.

China, for example, which at first provided cheap labor for assembling cellular telephones and other ICE devices, now challenges industrialized nations on the intellectual property and equipment standards used by next-generation devices. In the span of a few years, Chinese companies have increased the amount of value that they add to a product and, in turn, the financial returns accruing for the product. Chinese mobile telephone manufacturers initially assembled handsets for sale at home. Soon, these companies provided world-class quality assurance, in addition to cheap labor, so their assembled handsets rivaled anything offered in the global marketplace. Not content with low-margin assembly work, some Chinese manufacturers have collaborated with their government and local universities to develop patented innovations contained in next-generation mobile networks and wireless handsets. In short order, Chinese companies have moved from manufacturing original ICT equipment for other companies to paying royalties and marketing their own ICT equipment to coming up with ICT innovations for which they may soon require royalty payments from other manufacturers.[4]

ICT development presents both challenges and opportunities to all nations. Industrializing nations no longer have to organize their economies solely for the benefit of the industrialized countries that provide the market demand for cheaply produced products. Industrialized nations can no longer consider technology transfer as largely a one-sided transaction that expands market penetration without risk of lost markets in the future.

The Role of Government in ICT Incubation

Regardless of political and economic philosophy, national governments have significant roles in ICT development. Successful strategies have included an expansive governmental role in several areas. These include developing a vision and strategy; promoting digital literacy; investing in infrastructure; aggregating demand and serving as an early anchor tenant; fostering facilities-based competition; creating incentives for private investment and disincentives for litigation and other delaying tactics; offering electronic government services, including health care, education, access to information, and licensing; promoting universal service through subsidies and grants; and revising and reforming governmental safeguards to promote a high level of trust, security, privacy, and consumer protection for electronic commerce and other ICT uses.

Nations with successful ICT development strategies do not appear to quibble about whether the government should meddle in areas that the private sector possibly could manage exclusively. However, one person's view of government stewardship might come across to another as centralized, socialistic management by the public sector. Successful ICT incubation appears to require public-sector intervention, albeit with a light hand, to stimulate and reward investment, reduce unneeded regulatory scrutiny, and promote the global market without favoring one technology or company.

What Works?

Nations as diverse as Canada, Japan, and Korea provide insights on how to achieve maximum success in ICT development and what roles governments can effectively undertake. Government-led integration of technology incubation and development can generate ample dividends. But these governments, besides readily encouraging private enterprise and direct foreign investment in technology ventures, pursue an active and vital role. In vivid contrast to the U.S. model, where the government incubates technology, then quickly departs, best-practices ICT development in many nations demonstrates the benefits of long-term involvement by honest, technologically sophisticated government officials who understand the stakes involved and work conscientiously to establish a transparent, efficient, flexible, and positive business environment for the long run.

In many nations, governments sponsor science and technology parks where the government or a government-appointed manager integrates all necessary elements to produce and commercialize advanced technologies by "forging synergies among research centers, educational institutions and technology-based companies."[5] Governments can achieve these synergies primarily through investments, preferential policies, and focused leadership under the auspices of an economic development board that underwrites programs designed to finance research and development projects and to promote commercialization of applied research. More specifically, the nations have expedited ICT development by fostering an efficient and favorable business environment. This environment results in part from cooperation between scientific research institutes and laboratories in both pure and applied research and development; ease of access to venture capital; the availability of professional, technical, administrative, and legal assistance; state-of-the-art information and telecommunications services; and a fair and transparent business infrastructure.

Indigenous Comparative Advantages

Before considering what public and private actions can do to expedite ICT development, we should appreciate that a significant set of indigenous factors promote or thwart progress. Some localized characteristics favor ICT development independent of concerted actions. Geography and demographics, for example—nation size, population density, per capita income, percentage of high-rise housing, ownership of computers, education, and size of households—can make ICT development tasks easier or harder.

Nations and administrative regions such as Korea, Singapore, and Hong Kong should have good ICT development opportunities simply because telecommunications carriers can install lots of lines in densely populated localities. Geographically small nations, with little rugged terrain and a population with generally high incomes, can achieve ubiquitous digital network access in a timely and efficient manner, perhaps without having to create a sizeable fund to subsidize service to rural and low-income residents. Similarly, in countries whose population is skewed to youthful urban apartment dwellers, telecommunications carriers can readily introduce new services and achieve high penetration rates compared to what can be achieved in older, more rural nations. Korea, for one, enjoys a fairly high percentage of early adopters of technology who are keen on accessing services that provide faster, better, smarter, cheaper, and more convenient solutions to existing requirements and who are willing to use technologies to serve new wants, needs, and desires. Well-educated Korean youth with sufficient discretionary funds supported ICT development at first by frequenting personal computer gaming rooms, known as PC bangs, and later by embracing the Internet, streaming music, sending wireless messages, and sharing photos online.

We cannot underestimate the impact of attitudes toward ICT nor the extent to which entrepreneurs will take risks to provide services offering consumer benefits. A culture favoring education, speedy resolution of problems, and risk taking supplies fertile ground for ICT development. The push of new technologies meets an equally aggressive pull from demand.

Acquired Comparative Advantages

Indigenous comparative advantages cannot reliably propel a nation into ICT development, nor do the identified factors above explain why some nations excel while others falter. Acquired comparative advantages result from concerted efforts by the public and private sector to achieve ICT development with the goal of fostering improvements in the quality of life, individual wealth, and national economic development. The best advantages result when governments effectively match the scope of their intervention to the degree of market stimulation required and accurately estimate the extent to which ICT development would not occur but for government subsidization, demand aggregation, and sponsored pilot projects.

The acquisition of comparative advantages in ICT development requires some degree of government involvement. No matter how attractive technologies appear, governments may need to jumpstart their adoption and thereby accelerate the accrual of a critical mass to achieve scale economies and services at rates that a mass market will support. Before private enterprises can operate largely free of government meddling/support, a technology incubation phase typically must occur, as was the case for satellite and Internet development in the United States and elsewhere.

Governments willing to undertake an active role need to reach closure on a vision of what ICT development success would look like and what steps they should take to achieve it. Currently, ICT development includes promoting a widely available and affordable broadband infrastructure capable of delivering ICE services in full-motion video. In the United States, the public and private sectors are struggling to form a working partnership to improve broadband market penetration.

In the 1990s the Canadian government launched a series of ICT development projects to abate the negative impact of its large geographical size and low population density. The Ministry of Industry articulated a strategy to make Canada the most connected country in the world and to achieve ICT development primarily through the promotion of online access, ICT-intensive "smart communities," incentives for the creation of indigenous content for transmission via the Internet, electronic commerce, and electronic government services. In 2001 a National Broadband Taskforce specified a strategy for achieving ubiquitous access to broadband networks and services by 2005. Specifically, the task force established several priorities: all communities, including small businesses and residential users, should have Internet access at throughput speeds in excess of 1.5 megabits per second, rural access costs should not exceed urban rates, and the local broadband infrastructure should extend to schools, public libraries, and other public access points. The task force identified two funding vehicles for achieving these goals: (1) a government support model with top-down infrastructure that creates incentives for investment in broadband networks and services and (2) a bottom-up community-aggregator model with government-funded pilot programs and the delivery of electronic government services to help stimulate the generation of sufficient demand to use existing network capacity and the construction of new facilities.

The Korean government came up with an action plan in 1997, entitled *Cyber Korea 21*. In it the Ministry of Information and Communications laid out a vision of a "knowledge-based economy" in which every citizen would have access to a personal computer, the government would expedite development of an information infrastructure, and all ICT stakeholders would work together to increase productivity, employment, and exports. The Korean government recognized that a plan of such scale and ambitiousness would require several types of initiatives and financial inducements, including efforts by regulatory authorities to encourage infrastructure investment by incumbents and market entrants; regulatory parity among operators to promote facilities-based competition as well as market entry by operators who might need to access some of the incumbents' facilities at fair rates; direct underwriting, loans, favorable tax treatment, and other types of financial support for construction of new high-capacity digital broadband networks; financial support for research, development, and demonstration projects; subsidies for purchase of personal computers by low-income citizens; promotion of digital literacy, including the ability to use information technologies for interacting with the government and for acquiring information, communications, and entertainment services; and support for electronic government, education, e-commerce, health care, and ICT-mediated services.[6]

Japan developed a high-level "e-Japan" strategy in 2001 with ambitious goals for infrastructure, human resources, e-commerce, e-government, and network security.[7] Perhaps smarting from less robust development than nearby Korea and concerned about the consequences of an aging population, Japan expedited the development of the world's most advanced telecommunications and information networks, blending private-sector and public-sector initiatives. The e-Japan strategy triggered the development of 220 separate projects in its first year and achieved the goal of linking thirty million households to high-speed Internet access. Today Japanese residential consumers have the highest bitrate speeds and the lowest monthly rates per megabit delivered of any citizens in the world, even as a u-Japan strategy aims for ever-greater speeds and more ICT development.[8]

Perhaps the key regulatory initiative pursued in Canada, Korea, and Japan was changing the regulatory climate without setting off rounds of costly and protracted litigation, as has occurred in the United States. Nations can use regulatory change to promote facilities-based and resale competition through incremental deregulation of the sector, liberalization of rules affecting incumbent carriers, and mandates to incumbents to provide cost-based and compulsory access to an unbundled inventory of its switches and transmission capacity at fair and compensatory rates. Progressive tax policies, including investment tax credits, further stimulate incentives to build next-generation networks.

NRAs have to find ways to create incentives for incumbents and newcomers alike to invest in the infrastructure needed to provide high-speed broadband data services. The essential driver for such investment lies in the development of sustainable competition with a multiplicity of viable operators in each of the technologies providing broadband services now or prospectively. As a result of competition in conventional voice telephone services, incumbents typically face declining margins and a limited ability to differentiate their telephone services from those offered by other carriers. Faced with competitive necessities, incumbents have to diversify their services and pursue new profit centers, including value-added networks providing Internet-mediated services.

The need to respond to declining revenues in core business lines and to new deregulatory opportunities have begun to stimulate interest in expediting delivery of broadband services by United States carriers. Years earlier, carriers in Canada, Japan, and Korea made such investments as a result of governmental encouragement, real or perceived competitive necessity, and internal market forecasts. Meanwhile, in the United States, incumbent telephone companies complained about the unfairness in having to unbundle their networks and offer access to individual elements at below-market rates. Cable television ventures succeeded in thwarting efforts to force them to provide open access to any Internet service provider in lieu of dedicated access to corporate ISP affiliates or joint venture partners.

Carriers in best-practices nations accepted the regulatory mandate and turned their attention to capitalizing on new market opportunities. Carriers in the United States resorted to litigation and delay with an eye toward conserving capital until such time as the demand for broadband services became unassailable. The stalling tactics arose from heightened fear, uncertainty, and doubt, the products of an economic downturn largely caused by declining confidence in the Internet as an engine of perpetual growth in demand. Generally, carriers willing to embrace change and accept the onset of a new world order predominated by information services appear better equipped to capitalize on new market opportunities than carriers clinging to the old order. Wireline carriers keen on conserving capital and reducing risk appear less able to migrate from a business plan predominated by voice services, even though this once-core market has declined in profitability and will continue to decline as consumers migrate to wireless and Internet-based services.

Stimulation of Supply and Demand

Nations offering best practices in supply-side stimulation recognize the importance of triggering an expedited migration from narrowband to broadband services and promoting widespread availability of new services at attractive prices.[9] While preferring that private carriers make the transition to broadband on the basis of competitive necessity and declining margins in basic voice telephony markets, governments at the local, provincial, and federal levels volunteered to provide financial support under conditions of market uncertainty—that is, when private firms are unwilling to make the investment because they are not certain of earning adequate profit. In the end, government-supported programs brought broadband digital services to hinterland locations north of the arctic circle in Canada, primarily through assessment of the business plans of community groups, known as "community champions," and the grant of up to 50 percent of the eligible costs anticipated to develop a broadband program.

Nations offering best practices in demand-side stimulation spark and aggregate demand primarily by offering citizens improved ways to acquire government, education, and health services. Although youthful video gamers needed no inducement to appreciate the benefits on high-speed Internet access, others may require demonstrations of the time-saving and productivity-enhancing services available with broadband Internet access.[10] People are likely to sign up, for example, where high-speed data networks help remote communities secure medical consultations between local nurses and doctors based at urban teaching hospitals and make quick transmission of X-ray images possible. Another valuable use is in education: high-speed access to databases and multimedia learning tools and the ability to videoconference with teachers in a virtual classroom environment.

New Challenges to Industrialized Nations

Industrialized nations increasingly have to rely on ICT markets to accrue competitive advantages that generate wealth and support high existing standards of living. Since they can no longer simply assume that industrializing nations will serve as largely untapped markets or as low-cost assemblers and manufacturers of goods using intellectual property created in industrialized nations, ICT development generates new risks and insecurity. They face not only employment losses due to outsourcing but also challenges from industrializing nations that are becoming innovators as well as low-cost assemblers. ICT incubation provides opportunities for all nations, industrialized and industrializing alike.

ICT development, including investment in a robust broadband infrastructure, requires extensive coordination and cooperation among private-sector and public-sector players. Successful ICT development typically occurs if and only if both types of participants stick to roles proven to maximize benefits. For government, the empirically proven role involves neither a laissez-faire abdication of responsibility nor the intrusive, heavy-handed command-and-control regulation that predominated when private or government monopolies largely controlled the rollout of ICT. Governments can enhance ICT development by articulating at the top a broad vision of what ICT can do for a nation and its citizens but leaving to community champions the flexibility to propose specific bottom-up projects that aggregate the supply of services needed to support the building of a telecommunications infrastructure.

For the private sector, the proven role does not involve extensive litigation, delayed investment, or the leveraging of ICT investment for unwarranted deregulatory relief. The private sector needs to make the necessary investments in ICT incubation, but the government can create incentives for those investments.

Governments do not serve as a catalyst simply by throwing money at the problem of insufficient ICT development. Wasted investment in ICT development can occur if a government relies on one category of private-sector participant—incumbent wireline telephone companies, for example—to administer the major programs designed to promote universal access to basic telecommunication services. The incumbent develops a reliance on this funding source and has little incentive to achieve a universal service goal; rather, it will devote itself to justifying this ongoing source of subsidies for preferred beneficiaries, primarily itself. Developing a recurring subsidy and funding mechanism, as opposed to relying mostly on ad hoc project funding, typically requires an extensive bureaucracy similarly keen on maintaining the status quo.

Nations achieving comparatively greater success in ICT development demonstrate the value in having a specific mission and achievable, well-designed goals and policies. At the macro level, these nations have enacted laws that created incentives for risk taking and innovation and penalized litigation and strategies to delay making necessary investments in capital-intensive projects. At the micro level, these nations have linked public funding to private initiatives that aggregate demand, generate matching funds, and justify the installation of ICT even in comparatively unattractive locales.

The United States has largely failed to match its comparative advantage in private ICT incubation in Silicon Valley and elsewhere with similar world-class governmental incubation despite having achieved success in developing and then privatizing the Internet. The lack of success in recent governmental incubation efforts—for example, in broadband market penetration—stems largely from the failure to appreciate the need to blend and integrate private-sector entrepreneurialism and public-sector stewardship. Stewardship requires active governmental involvement: the government must act as cheerleader, referee, loan guarantor, grant funder, and anchor tenant in a sector that many in the United States believe warrants little, if any, government involvement. Nations exhibiting best practices in ICT development show the benefit of combining public and private initiatives.

FINDING THE RIGHT BALANCE IN NEXT-GENERATION NETWORK REGULATIONS

The Internet evolved quickly from a collection of specialized networks, primarily for electronic-mail correspondence among government and academic users, to a worldwide web of networks and services providing a widely available blend of ICE services.[11] Governments financially underwrote the construction and use of the first-generation Internet but withdrew funding and management as soon as commercial enterprises could assume the responsibility. In its second generation the Internet proliferated and diversified as a largely privatized World Wide Web offering user-friendly graphical interfaces and other enhancements. The Internet has begun to develop into its third-generation version, which will provide users with high-speed access to an ever more diverse array of ICE services.

In its third generation, the Internet may become more centralized as it provides the key medium for many services that heretofore operated separately. As it becomes the key medium for most ICE services, industry observers, academics, consumer representatives, and others have expressed concern over whether service providers will manage their networks fairly. Advocates for network neutrality seek carriers' assurance and possibly regulator-established rules to ensure that the Internet continues to operate in a nondiscriminatory manner, both in terms of how subscribers access and receive Internet-transmitted services and in terms of how content providers and other service providers reach subscribers.

Throughout the phases of its development, the Internet has benefited from prudent decisions by governments to use a light hand when regulating and safeguarding national interests. Governments correctly recognized that they could rely on the motivations of mostly private stakeholders to build the telecommunications links and to diversify the services available from the World Wide Web. On the other hand, as the Internet consolidates previously discrete ICE services, the stakes have risen: Do consumers have open access to the variety of services available via the Internet, and do service providers have open access to consumers?

The Internet continues to evolve as it incorporates technological innovations and becomes a conduit for many services that previously traversed dedicated telecommunications networks. As it begins to offer convergent services, such as VoIP telephone services and Internet protocol television (IPTV), some operators may see an opportunity to accrue a financial or competitive benefit by deviating from a plain-vanilla, one-size-fits-all Internet characterized by nondiscriminatory, best-efforts routing of traffic and unmetered subscriptions.

Some ISPs seek to diversify the Internet by prioritizing bitstreams and by offering different quality-of-service guarantees. To some observers, this strategy constitutes harmful discrimination that violates a tradition of network neutrality in the switching, routing, and transmission of Internet traffic. To others, offering different levels of service provides the means for consumers and carriers to secure and pay for premium, better-than-best-efforts service if so desired.

WHAT IS NETWORK NEUTRALITY?

The initial designers of the Internet and the technical protocols established for its management contemplated the operation of a seamless global network of networks. The original architecture had a built-in addressing system and a traffic management regime that treated all traffic equally. It had best-efforts routing, designed to establish nondiscrimination as standard operating procedure in the switching, routing, and transmission of digital bitstreams. Such a one-size-fits-all topology helped promote widespread proliferation of networks and emphasized timely, efficient, and low-cost delivery of traffic. Operators participating in the creation of the Internet optimized their networks to handle traffic as quickly as possible. To achieve this goal, network managers configured their routers to handle traffic as fast as possible without examining the type of traffic or metering it. Examining traffic might have provided the basis for prioritizing particular types or sources of traffic and to measure usage by specific sources of traffic with an eye to charging for network access. Telecommunications network operators typically prioritize and distinguish types of traffic so they can render accurate bills based on network usage, but Internet managers opted not to do so, figuring that the Internet could develop faster if carriers devoted all network resources to promoting connectivity and reach instead of dividing resources between connecting networks and metering usage.

Network neutrality advocates seek to require ISPs to continue adhering to the principle of nondiscrimination even though technological innovations in routers and other networking devices make it easier and less of a resource drain to prioritize, meter, and actively manage traffic. Network neutrality advocates want ISPs to continue operating their networks without favoring any category of content provider, bitstream, or consumer. In application, network neutrality would require ISPs to continue routing traffic on a best-efforts basis, ostensibly to foreclose the possibility that the Internet would balkanize, with operators offering various types of access arrangements, available at a premium, which would make the public Internet increasingly prone to real or induced congestion.

Opponents of compulsory network neutrality seek to differentiate services in terms of quality, price, and features to accommodate the increasingly diverse user requirements. For example, ISPs want to offer more expensive services to online game players, IPTV viewers, and VoIP subscribers who may need prioritization of their traffic streams so that their "mission critical" bits arrive on time, even during periods of network congestion. To provide this premium service, ISPs would need to identify and favor specific traffic streams.

There are efforts afoot to prevent ISPs from tiering consumers' access to the Internet and content providers' access to consumers. Opponents of network neutrality oppose these efforts. Consumer tiering could differentiate services by bitrate speed, amount of permissible traffic carried per month, and the way an ISP handles specific types of traffic, including content that might require special treatment, particularly when network congestion is likely to occur. While consumer tiering addresses quality-of-service and price discrimination at the first and last miles, access tiering could differentiate how ISPs handle content upstream and into the Internet cloud—the network of networks—that links content providers and end users.

Network neutrality advocates have expressed concern that the potential exists for ISPs to use diversifying service requirements as a pretext for a deliberate strategy of favoring their own content and extorting additional payments from users and content providers threatened with intentionally degraded service. The worst-case scenario envisioned by network neutrality advocates sees a reduction in innovation, efficiency, consumer benefits, and national productivity.

Many network neutrality advocates speak and write in apocalyptic terms. They say that allowing price and service discrimination will eviscerate the Internet and enable carriers to delay or shut out competitors and ventures unwilling or unable to pay surcharges. The head of a consumer group has claimed that incumbent telephone and cable companies can reshape the nation's digital destiny by name-branding the Internet and closing down many of its societal and cultural benefits. On the other hand, opponents of network neutrality reject as commercially infeasible scenarios in which ISPs unreasonably discriminate among users and services by degrading traffic even in the absence of a need to do so in light of network congestion.

Opponents of network neutrality see no actual or potential problems resulting if ISPs have the freedom to discriminate among and diversify services. The most caustic opponents of network neutrality scoff at the notion that an ISP would deliberately degrade service to some types of subscribers. Arguably, in a robustly competitive marketplace any unnecessary degradation of service would motivate subscribers to take their business elsewhere. But in most nations, such a competitive marketplace does not exist for first-mile wireline or wireless access. While content providers upstream from end users can readily shift from one Internet backbone provider to another, residential subscribers typically have few facilitates-based carrier options. Despite vehement claims by ISPs that they would never disserve a customer, the number of proven instances of service degradation has increased to the point where the threat is more than a matter of speculation and anecdote.[12]

Although the Internet started as a neutral, nondiscriminating medium, commercialization, technological development, increased diversity among users, and proliferating service options have collectively created the ability and the incentive for ISPs to pursue price and service discrimination. The migration from government ownership to government subsidization and finally to privatization and commercialization has motivated ISPs to find new ways to generate revenue. Technological innovations provide the means by which ISPs can differentiate the management of traffic, including the ability to prioritize specific bitstreams and to delay or even block delivery of standard traffic. As the nature and the type of Internet users diversify, ISPs seek to offer different service tiers with different prices based on users' requirements and intensity of need; they would offer premium rates for power users needing high bandwidth and timely delivery of packets.

Although no government or private forum comprehensively regulates the Internet, decisions by governments and private operators, primarily in North America and Europe, have had a substantial impact on the Internet's development and governance. The U.S. government helped create the Internet by supporting research and development and by serving as an anchor tenant. The decision to abandon public financing of the major U.S. backbone network in 1995 created the opportunity for former government contractors to become operators of the backbone networks providing transcontinental and transoceanic links. For the most part, largely unregulated private parties have the power to make sweeping decisions affecting the terms and conditions for network access. However, privatization is supposed to create an environment in which competition and consumer sovereignty predominate.

First Phase: Active Government Stewardship

As discussed above, we can see the Internet's evolution in terms of technological generations, first to third so far. Alternatively, we can see the Internet in terms of successive industrial stages: (1) administration by the U.S. government, first through the Defense Department and later through the National Science Foundation (NSF), as well as universities and research institutes throughout the world (1980s–1995); (2) privatization of the government-financed networks and the ascendancy of Internet contractors and other major local and interexchange carriers (1995–1998); (3) the dotcom boom, marked by irrational, excessive investment and overcapacity (1998–2000); and (4) the dotcom bust, market retrenchment, and resumed growth (2001–present).

Until 1995, the government, acting through the Defense Department and later the National Science Foundation, underwrote the development and maintenance of the core Internet network (NSFnet). National governments in other parts of the world pursued similar network projects. After incubating the Internet as a medium for traffic associated with research and education, the NSF concluded that it could abandon public financing of the network, and a commercial, privatized Internet could evolve.

The NSF's 1993 public solicitation document anticipated a privatized Internet with a structure much like what we have today: a hierarchy of many small ISPs serving localities and regions, fewer interregional, Tier 2 ISPs, and even fewer backbone, highest-capacity, Tier 1 ISPs serving entire nations. At the outset of Internet development, government contractors engineered national networks accessible primarily by government, academic, and research users. With few operators, generally having the same characteristics in user populations, bandwidth, traffic switching capabilities, network management staffing, and geographical reach, the parties could agree to simple interconnection and access arrangements. The Internet network routing was set up to achieve efficiency and to route around outages and congestion. Because all the ISPs in this phase had roughly the same characteristics and traffic volumes, their routing assignments generated approximately the same financial burdens.

The goal for Internet access was primarily to extend geographical reach and sign on users; little regard was given to what the cost of access was or what users caused an ISP to incur those costs. In this first promotional phase the emphasis was on the accrual of positive network externalities, so much so that the parties did not seek to monitor traffic flows. Because few ISPs existed and because each had the same characteristics and operated with government funding, the parties saw little benefit and significant cost in negotiating interconnection agreements and metering traffic.

In this phase, all participating ISPs agreed to network peering, meaning that they would provide reciprocal access to one another's subscribers in a free exchange of traffic that would take place at a few shared, "public" peering points or network access points (NAPs). The few ISPs operating at this time agreed to receive traffic from the other ISPs for onward delivery to the final intended destination or to another ISP in exchange for the same traffic acceptance and delivery commitment from the other ISPs. Because of the rough-justice expectation that an ISP would deliver roughly the same amount of traffic generated by other ISPs that it handed off for delivery by those ISPs, no funds were exchanged. In the lingo of telecommunications carriers this arrangement constituted a bill-and-keep or "sender keep all" arrangement, because each ISP retained all revenues it generated from traffic carriage regardless of whether it provided solely the transmission or whether it handed off the traffic for carriage by another ISP.

Second Phase: Privatization Creates a Hierarchy of Operators

The NSF's path to privatization largely succeeded. Former contractors achieved supremacy in both the ownership and operation of backbone networks and NAPs. MCI, now part of Verizon, won the solicitation to take over the very high-speed backbone network that previously had served NSF-sponsored research institutions, including Cornell University, supercomputer centers in Pittsburgh and San Diego, and several government facilities. MCI upgraded its Asynchronous Transfer Mode network from OC-3 (155 megabits per second) to OC-12 (622 megabits per second). The NSF privatization solicitation also created four private NAPs in Chicago, operated by the Ameritech Bell Operating Company (now part of AT&T), and Bellcore, the former research arm of AT&T, spun-off to the divested Bell Operating Companies; in metropolitan New York–Philadelphia, operated by Sprint and the San Diego Supercomputer Center; in San Francisco, operated by Pacific Telesis, now part of AT&T, and Bellcore; and in Washington, D.C., operated by Metropolitan Fiber Systems, a networking firm subsequently acquired by MCI.

With the privatization of the Internet, a hierarchical industrial structure developed. At the top of the pyramid stood a handful of Tier 1 ISPs whose network size, customer base, and operational success qualified them for direct and cost-free exchange of traffic. While peering used to predominate as the primary mode of the NSF network interconnection, the commercialization of the Internet created opportunities for market entry by more ISPs and new incentives for all ISPs to charge what the market would bear for network access. The composition of ISPs diversified in terms of available bandwidth, geographical reach, subscribership, and types of available content.

Given this diversification and proliferation of ISPs, universal peering became unsustainable. ISPs not having sufficient size and importance became customers of Tier 1 and other ISPs. The smaller ISPs had to pay the larger ISPs for the privilege of accessing their customers and their network connections. The term "transit"—borrowed from telecommunications lingo—refers to a negotiated business relationship whereby one ISP sells access to its customers, its network, and its NAP locations.

No ISP beneficiary of cost-free peering appreciated its demoted status: now it had to pay for access as a customer and as a reseller. Yet this demotion appeared to occur on the basis of sound business judgments made by individual Tier 1 ISPs and not on the basis of collusion or concerted refusals to deal. ISPs in Asia-Pacific and Africa have borne the greatest financial burden because they have to provide their own lines to and from NAPs in North America and Europe, as well as pay for transit. But smaller ISPs everywhere bear a similar, albeit less expensive burden. ISPs in North America incur less telecommunications expense in reaching a Tier 1 ISP's NAP because of the proliferation of network access points and their close proximity to most ISPs. An ISP located in a remote area has to secure and pay for a complete link to an Tier 1 ISP facility, even though once installed, such a two-way link provides the Tier 1 ISP with cost-free pathways downstream to the smaller, remotely located ISP and its subscribers.

ISPs in remote regions objected to having to provide the typically well-financed Tier 1 ISPs with free rides for their traffic. Certainly it appeared that the remote ISPs underwrote the full cost of return traffic instead of having to pay half the cost. However, in the context of Internet service the free-ride attribution breaks down. The Internet seamlessly combines telecommunications bit transport with access to content. Particularly during the second phase in the Internet's development, ISP subscribers could access most of the content available via the Internet for nothing more than the cost of their ISP subscription. When an ISP pays another, larger ISP for transit services, the smaller ISP acquires access to the larger ISP's subscribers and the content available from not only these customers but the customers of other ISPs with which the larger ISP peers or pays for transit. Although smaller ISPs had to pay for access to and from larger ISPs in North America and Europe, they could then deliver content that their subscribers sought. Much of the most desired content resided on servers located in North America and Europe, so remote ISPs had to secure access to them to be able to deliver the content that their subscribers expected to access.

Arrangements for access to Internet transit do not match in geographical scope the arrangements for telecommunications transit. In telecommunications service, a transit arrangement typically secures an indirect link to one carrier in one location, primarily because a small carrier might not have sufficient traffic volume to secure a direct link. In Internet service, in contrast, transit arrangements typically provide access to a vast array of networks, which are certainly not limited to one country. One Internet transit payment arrangement with one major Tier 1 ISP can, at its most expansive, provide a small, remote ISP with access to the rest of the world if the Tier 1 ISP has secured ubiquitous access and therefore can offer ("advertise") an extensive list of routing opportunities.

Third Phase: The Dotcom Boom Stimulates Buildup of Internet Infrastructure

During the dotcom phase of the Internet, investors had a gold rush mentality. Undocumented and belatedly refuted claims that the Internet doubled in size on a monthly basis encouraged risk taking. Investors assumed the rising tide would raise all ships: all investors would reap ample returns. With "irrational exuberance," investors sank several hundred billion dollars into incumbent and new telecommunications and ISP networks.

The resulting glut in local and long-haul transmission capacity created substantial downward pressure on Internet transport costs and precluded any pricing discipline by Tier 1 ISPs individually or even collectively had they attempted to collude. Even before the dotcom bubble burst, several Tier 1 ISPs experienced financial distress. Still, the continuing infusion of capital helped create aspiring Tier 1 and Tier 2 operators through acquisitions, and smaller ISPs and individual consumers could choose among even more hungry, possibly desperate competitors.

Fourth Phase: Retrenchment and a Proliferation of Interconnection Options

The vast investment in transmission capacity during the dotcom years still imposes a price ceiling, and it will until demand matches capacity. Meanwhile, the downward trajectory of the costs of Internet transmission capacity has leveled off; anecdotal information suggests that the burden of transit payment obligations is minor relative to the overall cost of doing business.[13]

Even as telecommunications costs drop as a percentage of the total cost of doing business, ISPs continue to explore ways to reduce this expense because new types of traffic are creating the need for more bandwidth. Peer-to-peer sharing of music and video files makes up a significant percentage of the growth in traffic volume despite efforts to reduce copyright piracy. The growth in broadband access from residences and small businesses also contributes to the upswing in bandwidth requirements, as does the growth in electronic commerce, streaming audio and video services, and wireless access to the Internet.

The ongoing need to upgrade infrastructure to handle applications that are increasingly bandwidth intensive creates a powerful financial incentive for ISPs to change the terms and conditions for service. Many ISPs initially offered an all-you-can-eat, unmetered service plan based on the correct perception that all but early adopters would need financial inducements to test-drive the Internet. Now that the Internet marketplace has evolved, many ISPs see unmetered service as conferring an unnecessary windfall on high-volume users to the detriment of the carrier and low-volume users. ISPs also perceive network neutrality initiatives as foreclosing pricing flexibility.

Wireless Network Neutrality

The network neutrality debate has focused almost exclusively on Internet access via wireline carriers. Recently the issue of wireless Internet access has surfaced. Wireless services are growing in importance, and consumers are frustrated with carrier tactics that disable handset functions and block access to competing services.[14] While wireless handsets generally can access Internet services, most carriers attempt to favor content they provide themselves or secure from third parties under a walled-garden strategy: they make deliberate efforts to lock consumers into accessing and paying for selected content and services.

Just about every nation in the world has established policies that mandate the right of consumers to own their own wireline telephone and to use any device to access any carrier, service, or function, provided that it does not cause technical harm to the telecommunications network. Once regulators unbundled telecommunications services from devices that access network services, a robustly competitive market developed for both devices and services. Remarkably, wireless carriers in many nations, including the United States, have managed to avoid having to comply with this open network concept. Even though consumers own their wireless handsets, the carriers providing services will operate only with specific types of handsets programmed to work only with a specific carrier's network. Carriers justify this lock-in and their high fees for early termination of service because they sell their handsets at subsidized rates—sometimes "free"—based on two-year subscriptions. The value of the two-year lock-in period offsets the handset subsidy because subscribers cannot easily shift to another carrier, the rates charged include a surcharge to offset the true cost of the handset, and increasingly carriers hope users of the newest and most expensive smartphones will pay additional charges for new services. In the United States, wireless carriers sell more than 60 percent of all wireless handsets; they typically make the sale when a subscriber commences service or renews a subscription. No market for used handsets has evolved, because wireless carriers do not offer lower service rates for subscribers who bring their own handsets.

Wireless network neutrality would require carriers to stop blocking the use of non-carrier-affiliated handsets and to stop locking handsets so that they work only with a particular carrier network. More broadly, wireless network neutrality would prohibit wireless carriers from preventing subscribers' access to the content, services, and software applications of their choosing. It also would require carriers to support an open interface so that handset manufacturers and content providers could develop equipment and services that do not have any potential for harming wireless carrier networks.

Opponents of wireless network neutrality consider the initiative unnecessary government intrusion in a robustly competitive marketplace. They claim that requiring nondiscrimination, including letting customers supply their own handsets, would risk causing technical harm to wireless networks and would generate such regulatory uncertainty that the carriers might refrain from investing in next-generation enhancements to their networks. Separating equipment from the service constituted an appropriate remedy when a single wireline carrier dominated, they say, but such compulsory unbundling should not occur when consumers have a variety of carrier options.

Opposition from ISPs

ISPs oppose network neutrality on a number of theoretical and practical grounds. Fundamentally, they oppose network neutrality because it would probably entail government regulation, or at least legitimize its making and enforcing rules. Most ISP managers favor hands-off, laissez-faire governance; they believe that ISPs operate in a competitive marketplace that can self-regulate. More practically, ISPs fear that actual or potential involvement and intervention by the government would foreclose or at least condition operational flexibility.

In most nations, ISPs operate largely free of conventional telecommunications service regulations; the lack of regulation is based on the premise that they provide value-added enhancements to telecommunications links. In the United States, ISPs qualify for an information services safe harbor—exemption from common carrier telephony regulations. In addition, U.S. ISPs qualify for a status that exempts them from liability for carrying tortious or harmful content, in light of the actual or perceived burden such content scrutiny would impose.

ISPs generally operate as private carriers and often bear no legal responsibility for the content they carry. Governments granted this freedom to promote robust development of the Internet and to remove concerns about liability if subscribers used their Internet access for nefarious and illegal purposes. At the time of such grants of immunity, ISPs lacked the technological wherewithal to examine the content that they transmitted. Now, ISPs have a far greater ability to meter and examine Internet traffic, and they want to exploit their technological opportunities to examine traffic packets and to prioritize them based on payments received, but they do not want to relinquish their exemption from regulation and liability.

As we have seen, ISPs want to expand their ability to diversify services and to engage in price discrimination based on the quality of service they provide. Network neutrality, whether imposed by law or by NRA rules, would probably impose restrictions on ISP pricing and diversification of services based on such factors as reliability, allocated bandwidth, performance during network congestion, ability to handle spikes in demand, and quality of service. Some service differentiation already exists; ISPs offer their customers different subscription rates based on bandwidth and bitrates. Additional differentiation could involve variable service quality, based on the ability to handle demand bursts, as occurs in peer-to-peer networking, video gaming, delivery of large files, and real-time streaming of video programming. The ability to inspect traffic streams makes it possible for ISPs to identify priority traffic and to provide superior and preferential processing for a premium price. They could tier services according to differentials that parallel tiering in commercial aviation (first class, business class, and economy class) and on some roadways (toll versus free lanes). Most network neutrality advocates oppose tiering.

ISPs also want to price-discriminate, charging different rates upstream from end users into the Internet cloud all the way to sources of content. Such access tiering would offer different options for service providers, a more controversial matter, because ISPs might use network management tools to degrade standard traffic delivery, even when conditions do not necessitate it, to facilitate timely delivery of premium traffic. It makes perfect sense for ISP executives to expect payment from all content providers every time their traffic traverses an ISP network.[15] However, unlike telephone companies, which typically meter traffic and secure payment based on usage, ISPs typically do not meter traffic, opting instead to negotiate peering agreements[16] that establish reciprocal traffic carriage without payment. ISPs benefit from the streamlined and uncomplicated aspects of peering agreements, but they also want to single out large-volume users of their networks—Google, for example—and extract additional direct payments from them, even though they agreed to carry such traffic as part of their peering agreements.

The Need for Network Neutrality Rules

Little middle ground exists between advocates and opponents of network neutrality, but the Internet will probably continue to deviate from providing one-size-fits-all service. Accordingly, the dichotomy will be, practically speaking, between types of discrimination that make economic sense and will not harm consumers and those that constitute unfair trade practices and other anticompetitive practices.

The Internet largely functions as a product of countless interconnection arrangements flexibly negotiated and executed free of government oversight, as opponents of network neutrality hasten to point out. ISPs correctly note that only in rare instances has an interconnection dispute triggered allegations of anticompetitive practices or resulted in consumers losing access to a content source or e-mail addressee as a result of network inaccessibility or balkanization.

On the other hand, network neutrality advocates have identified instances in which ISPs have unilaterally blocked traffic to reduce subscribers' network demand, handicap a competitor, punish ventures for not agreeing to pay a surcharge, and to stifle criticism about the ISP and its parent corporation. Even if we were to dismiss such evidence as anecdotal or exceptional, it appears that an ISP's ability to discriminate in the switching and routing of bits matches or exceeds the ease with which employees of electricity-generating companies have been able to create artificial congestion and run up costs, thereby accruing exorbitant profits. Employees of Enron and other electric utilities engaged in a number of anticompetitive practices that caused the spot market price for electricity to skyrocket; their tactics were designed to mimic a dramatic increase in demand that the electricity distribution grid could not handle. If Enron employees could manipulate the market for the switching and routing of electrons, then ISP employees might engage in similar tactics when switching and routing packets. Policymakers should consider seriously the potential for harm to consumers and content providers when ISPs deviate from network neutrality.

Permissible and Impermissible Discrimination

Many types of diversification in the pricing and provisioning of Internet-mediated services make economic sense and do not violate a reasonable expectation of network neutrality. ISPs should have the conditional option of providing both end users and content providers with better-than-best-efforts routing. Just as airline passengers can choose first-class, business-class, and economy-class seating and car drivers can choose free or toll highways, Internet consumers should have access to different Internet experiences based on bandwidth, monthly allocation of throughput, and traffic prioritization during periods of network congestion. ISPs should have the option of metering service instead of offering unlimited-use plans that force light users to subsidize heavy users. Likewise, ISPs should be allowed to partition network capacity so that priority users have access to links less likely to suffer from congestion than standard links.

On the other hand, both content providers and consumers have a legitimate expectation that they should not experience dropped packets and service degradation simply because they declined to pay for a superior service tier. ISPs should not have the option of triggering delays and losing packets in the absence of congestion. Regulators should devise network reporting requirements that require ISPs to identify the number and cause of instances when the public Internet so suffered congestion that an ISP had to drop packets and degrade service. An ISP should not partition its network in such a way as to all but guarantee that non-priority bitstreams experience lost packets and degradation of service when the ISP could avoid dropping any packets. Faked congestion on a network, to punish, discipline, or competitively outmaneuver competitors or to discipline customers refusing to pay newly imposed surcharges, looks the same as the faked congestion that energy traders employed by Enron were able to create.[17] Rather than threaten lawful or unlawful retaliation through delayed, degraded, and dropped packets, incumbent carriers should market a superior Internet experience for high-volume content generators and their customers. They should offer these premium options on a fully transparent basis by offering all service options to every subscriber.

As technological innovations and the convergence of services available via the Internet create the ability and incentive for ISPs to diversify services, regulators need to refrain from imposing public interest safeguards that restrict legitimate quality-of-service diversification. However, these very same regulators need to remain vigilant against tactics that create false congestion as the justification for degrading service to subscribers and content providers unwilling to pay for premium services. To facilitate oversight, ISPs should operate in a transparent environment; they should disclose all premium service options and report all instances in which congestion forced them to drop packets and degrade service.

The network neutrality debate comes at a particularly contentious time in ICE policymaking. Stakeholders appear to have little inclination to find a middle ground, and decision makers appear to have even less. Policymaking is shaped by sponsored research, politics, campaign contributions, and rhetoric. In light of the apparent disinterest in facts, it is no surprise that the network neutrality debate highlights opposing perceptions about the impact of changes being brought about as the next-generation Internet emerges. Regrettably, no unbiased fact finding is readily available; the issue has inspired too much intense lobbying and hyperbole.

Network neutrality opponents have overstated the case for competition, presenting it as the remedy for any and all instances of illegal network bias. A fully self-regulating Internet marketplace does not exist, nor can anyone confidently assert that Internet marketplace forces can remedy all attempts at unreasonable network bias. On the other hand, the Internet has not failed to function when network operators and content providers have cut exclusive and preferential deals or when network providers have offered premium routing.

For better or worse, the next-generation Internet will adopt many of the biased networking characteristics of vintage cable television and the current, third generation of cellular telephony. Cable and satellite television operators enjoy substantial freedom to cut deals offering special content delivery, but lawful must-carry obligations impose affirmative carriage duties, notwithstanding cable operators' non-common-carrier status. Wireless carriers retain the status of telecommunications service providers, subject to common carrier regulation, yet they can use new broadband carriage capabilities to deliver biased, walled-garden access to video and Internet content. To deal with all these contradictions and potentialities, regulators should agree to examine allegations of network bias and to evaluate the complaints from a public interest point of view. The question to be asked each time is whether the discriminatory practice constitutes an unfair trade practice or a reasonable attempt at diversifying and proliferating information services.

CHAPTER TWELVE

Unresolved Issues

THROUGHOUT THIS BOOK, we have examined instances in which action or inaction by governments, companies, and individuals prevent the full exploitation of ICE technological innovations. Many governments have become so enamored of the concept of competition that they ignore the need for regulations to curb market power, respond to anticompetitive conduct, and remedy market failures that occur when industry segments do not become as competitive as expected. Companies have come to understand that they can accrue valuable competitive advantages by exploiting governments' predilection to favor marketplace competition, hence companies' skillful participation in the political, regulatory, and lawmaking process. Compounding regulatory mistakes is the failure of most consumers to acquire digital literacy, which encompasses skills they need to become knowledgeable and demanding users of new technologies.

Despite major problems in the regulation and pricing of ICE technologies, innovations have generated ample dividends, and some governments have blended regulation and reliance on market forces to ensure fair, widespread, reasonably priced access to new technologies and services. ICE innovations do offer enhancements that are faster, better, smarter, cheaper, and more convenient. The Internet has become an integral part of how we acquire information, communicate, transact business, and enjoy our leisure time. Although we have observed woeful deficiencies, the current ICE marketplace has achieved many successes.

Still, the information revolution has not realized the substantial enhancement in the quality of life that forecasters promised. The less-than-optimal outcome is partially due to the ease with which stakeholders can game the legislative, regulatory, and judicial processes to their advantage. Major incumbent facilities-based operators and content providers have shaped the perceptions of decision makers on such fundamental issues as the extent of existing and prospective competition in ICE markets, the ongoing need for government oversight, and the value of mergers and acquisitions in helping or harming consumers. Time after time, incumbent operators have successfully framed public policy debates, emphasizing how competitive ICE markets are despite the empirical data that unequivocally shows many concentrated markets becoming increasingly concentrated. Worse yet, government decisions makers often do not collect and analyze data and statistics but instead rely on the filings of stakeholders, who have every incentive to submit flawed data and to interpret the data as justifying preferred policy outcomes.

Despite all the verbiage about a robustly competitive broadband marketplace, for example, the FCC's own statistics identify extreme domination by two technologies, DSL and cable modem, provided by incumbent telephone and cable companies.[1] The FCC's most recent statistics on broadband market penetration show continued improvement in the availability of high-speed access to the Internet,[2] although the improvement is overstated given its continued use of a low threshold (200 kilobits per second for download or upload) for defining high-speed lines. Many would dispute whether lines carrying bits at this rate qualify as broadband.

Using the FCC's current broadband definition—transmission at the rate of 200 kilobits per second—the Commission estimates that 83 percent of all households in the United States that have access to wireline telephone service also have access to high-speed DSL connections, and 96 percent of the households with access to cable television service also have access to high-speed cable modem service.[3] The FCC also reports that residents in 99 percent of all zip codes have access to high-speed wireless services, 93 percent have satellite broadband access, 87 percent have DSL access, and 67 percent have cable modem access.[4]

The terrestrial wireless marketplace offers mixed statistical results in the United States. On one hand, the FCC proudly reports that "U.S. consumers continue to reap significant benefits—including low prices, new technologies, improved service quality, and choice among providers—from competition in the Commercial Mobile Radio Services ('CMRS') marketplace, both terrestrial and satellite CMRS."[5] Cellular telephone subscribership is high, and minutes of use continue to increase. On the other hand, cost per minute has stopped dropping, and the market has become quite concentrated. According to the 2006 data used in the FCC's 2008 report, the wireless market is dominated by four firms: AT&T (formerly known as Cingular Wireless), Sprint Nextel Corporation, T-Mobile USA, and Verizon Wireless, and we can expect attempts by these companies to consolidate further.

The FCC dismisses the potential for collusion and anticompetitive conduct by the four firms, even though they offer generally the same prices and none offers discounted services to subscribers that do not require a subsidized handset. The FCC emphasizes the need for large economies of scale, the number of national operators that most nations have (four or fewer), and the availability of ample radio spectrum for competitive services. These factors offer little support for the conclusion that wireless carriers can self-regulate because they need to compete. Because of the costs of acquiring spectrum and installing facilities present high entry barriers, governments cannot expect robust facilities-based competition to occur in every market segment in every locality. On the contrary, the four or fewer national carriers in the United States have every incentive to match prices rather than set off a price war.

The FCC likewise offers little justification for concluding that access to additional spectrum will stimulate competition as opposed to allowing incumbent carriers to acquire and warehouse spectrum. When the FCC auctioned off choice spectrum, formerly used by UHF television stations but available after the digital conversion, incumbent carriers, not newcomers, acquired almost all of it. Most of the spectrum identified by the FCC as potentially offering a competitive alternative to cellular radiotelephone service does not have technological and propagational characteristics for commercially feasible voice and data service to mobile subscribers, and even if these allocations did, incumbent operators would no doubt strive mightily to lobby Congress and the FCC to preclude such direct competition. For the spectrum that does have favorable technical and propagational characteristics, history shows that incumbents typically acquire the bulk of newly available spectrum. The FCC rarely prevents incumbents from acquiring newly available spectrum so that market entrants might provide competition. Even when new firms qualify to bid for spectrum, incumbents acquire the potential competitors soon afterward.

LACK OF COMPETITION

The FCC's acquisition and interpretation of statistics call to mind the often-quoted reference to "lies, damn lies and statistics." The FCC purposely interprets its often-questionable statistics to corroborate its view that competition has arrived in all ICE sectors and will continue to thrive despite mergers and acquisitions that achieve further industry concentration. The statistics constitute an important element in results-driven decision making. The FCC seeks to justify deregulatory initiatives on the grounds that competition forecloses the need to regulate, but as we have seen, the competition that it finds is far less robust, ubiquitous, and sustainable than the Commission would have us believe.

THE IMPACT OF ACADEMIC RESEARCH

Given the ease with which we can identify flaws in the FCC's statistical compilations and its interpretations of the data, we would hope that academic analysts could help set the record straight. Alas, far too many academics and think tank affiliates accept direct or indirect financial support and offer in exchange sponsored research that supports the FCC's deregulatory predilections without disclosing obvious conflicts of interest. Worse yet, academics have come to realize that they have little to gain by offering independent and controversial assessments.

In an ideal world, uncontaminated by partisanship and political agendas, academic researchers have much-needed qualifications and skills that can contribute to rational decision making by regulatory authorities. In the United States, the FCC has to comply with laws requiring it to combine its in-house expertise with a transparent and complete collection of evidence when establishing rules, regulations, and policies. Sadly, the FCC's notice and comment proceedings rarely include filings from academic researchers lacking financial sponsorship from a stakeholder with the resources and incentives to steer the Commission to a preferred outcome. Without a financial incentive, both tenured and tenure-track professors eschew policy advocacy, largely because such efforts have little influence on the FCC and generate limited recognition as academic contributions.

Despite having been established as an independent and expert regulatory agency, the FCC cannot operate outside politics. The president appoints commissioners in part precisely because of their political party affiliations. Congress authorizes the FCC's budget and regularly holds oversight hearings where individual senators and representatives may "regulate by lifted eyebrow" in support of or opposition to an FCC initiative. However, the political sensitivity of the FCC appears to have increased in recent years because of two relatively new developments: (1) As the scope, reach, and influence of the Internet have grown, so too has the number of advocacy groups, particularly ones affiliated with or financially supported by stakeholders. (2) Faced with the need to generate a comprehensive evidentiary record, the FCC increasingly relies, not on independently acquired statistics and other data, but on sponsored research that is not subject to peer review.

Incumbents and market entrants alike seek limited regulation, and the majority of FCC commissioners from both parties agree. But at some point, government oversight might provide necessary safeguards against anticompetitive conduct or practices that harm consumers and the public interest. Deregulatory advocates predictably seek to dissuade the FCC from identifying market failures or other reasons for government regulation. Advocates for regulatory safeguards seek to persuade the Commission of the need for light-handed oversight.

To bolster advocacy and to contribute to a perception of public support, stakeholders have unprecedented options for securing additional filings in an FCC notice and comment rulemaking. Countless new advocacy groups purport to represent the public interest, although they typically do not fully disclose their affiliations and financial sponsorship. "AstroTurf" organizations,[6] which purport to operate as grassroots representatives of the public, are mainly funded by a company or companies with a major financial stake in the outcome of an FCC rulemaking. An ever-increasing number of not just advocacy groups but foundations, institutes, centers, and organizations offer assistance to the FCC in generating an evidentiary record. However, most of the work represented as empirical research and attached to advocacy filings suffers from the taint of financial support from organizations with obscure or undisclosed affiliations with specific stakeholders. Much of it would not pass a rigorous peer review, financial strings aside, because the research seeks to endorse a preordained outcome. The FCC receives reams of such "research" documents, but few, if any, reflect anything more than rationales for specific policy recommendations.

Most policy advocacy lacks independent, peer-reviewed contributions for several reasons. With infrequent exceptions the FCC lacks the finances or inclination to sponsor independent research. Apparently, it must first suffer an embarrassing judicial rebuke before seeking untainted research. After a stinging remand from the Third Circuit Court of Appeals in *Prometheus Radio Project v. FCC*, on the failure to generate a record supporting relaxed media-ownership restrictions, the FCC adopted a further notice of proposed rulemaking and specifically commissioned peer-reviewed studies. In this rare instance, the FCC implicitly recognized that stakeholder-sponsored research might not have provided sufficient analysis of such issues as how people get news and information, how much competition exists within and between types of media, what marketplace changes had taken place since FCC last reviewed its ownership rules, how the FCC promotes local ownership, to what degree minorities participate in today's media environment, how available independent and diverse programming is, and what impact ownership has on the production of children's and family-friendly programming.

Another reason for the lack of independent research as part of the policymaking process is that academics prefer traditional peer-reviewed forums for their work. To gain tenure, academics need to acquire a record of publications in peer-reviewed journals. Even tenured academics have concerns about whether policy-oriented research might generate controversy and adversely affect their prospects for securing research grants. The smoother path is to write about research for academic journals instead of seeking to influence regulatory agencies' policies.

A POLICY FOR ACHIEVING SUSTAINABLE COMPETITION

The rise in real or assumed competition in the ICE marketplace has emboldened stakeholders to argue for further deregulation, possibly including the elimination of national regulatory authorities like the FCC. Such a libertarian perspective assumes that having a sector-specific regulator, able to act with future developments in mind, imposes unnecessary costs on operators and consumers. Advocates for nonregulation—the end point of deregulation—argue that a court with general jurisdiction to adjudicate disputes can remedy problems after they allegedly have occurred.

Credible statistics do not support either the elimination of NRAs or the reliance on adjudication to remedy disputes. First, no one has produced data that support the twin conclusions that robust marketplace competition currently exists in all ICE sectors and that competitive ICE markets can self-regulate. Even if one or more ICE sectors did operate in a fully competitive environment, a regulator serving as a referee would still be needed to resolve disputes, especially ones relating to interconnection obligations. Even competitive markets may need light-handed regulation that provides quick resolution to disputes between competitors and between consumers and service providers. The need for timely resolution of disputes and the technological complexity of ICE markets do not favor problem solving by generalist courts.

In addition, the trend toward concentration of ownership and control of even competitive market segments indicates a need for government oversight. Technological and marketplace convergence supports one-stop shopping for ICE services, and companies recognize the financial benefits in providing bundles of ICE services. Those with ample financial resources recognize the competitive advantage accruing from timely packaging of service bundles, including the acquisition of companies providing services that the acquiring firm does not provide. The need to achieve economies of scale and the incentive to acquire market share on an expedited basis further embolden incumbents to acquire competitors. At the same time, they maintain that the marketplace remains robustly competitive.

NRAs and their legislator overseers should not buy the argument that sustainable competition can last in perpetuity without government oversight. NRAs must remain vigilant for any sign that an ICE market lacks self-regulating features, particularly in light of trends favoring concentration and barriers to market entry. The ICE marketplace has begun to demonstrate the same monopolistic features as occurred when AT&T dominated the U.S. telecommunications industry, and most nations had a single Post, Telegraph, and Telephone organization. Telecommunications companies—AT&T, Verizon, and Comcast in the United States; NTT in

Japan; Deutsche Telekom; and British Telecom, to name some—are among the world's largest and mostly highly capitalized firms. AT&T's anticompetitive conduct forced its divestiture into seven companies in 1984, only three of which remain.

Because of the potential for anticompetitive conduct within a firm that carriers traffic generated by its subscribers and subscribers of other carriers, an increasing number of nations have encouraged or required incumbents to split into two companies, one to offer fair and equal interconnection to first and last mile links with end users and one to compete in other ICE markets. Divestiture is a fail-safe way to remove incentives for a telecommunications carrier to favor corporate affiliates providing content and services. Opponents of divestiture claim that it thwarts the evolution of operational efficiencies, development synergies, and optimal scale. They also object to the alternative regulatory remedy of separating the telecommunications carrier from its corporate affiliates. If divestiture is eliminated as a way to control anticompetitive conduct, structural and regulatory safeguards are needed, along with effective government oversight. The general behavior of monopolists and the historical behavior of telecommunications monopolies in particular necessitate the government's ongoing regulatory presence.

THE RISK OF A CABLE-TELCO DUOPOLY

The quest to achieve economies of scale through mergers and acquisitions, exploitation of technological convergence, and bundling of ICE services has made it possible for incumbent firms like AT&T, Verizon, Comcast, and Time Warner to become larger and more powerful. These companies can offer consumers a combination of telecommunications and information services with limited government oversight and few restrictions on how they package, price, and deliver services. For consumers, their flexibility means attractively priced service bundles, although such bundles are available from only a small number of ventures in any particular locality.

Extraordinary vertical and horizontal integration in the ICE marketplace poses serious risks to consumers and the public interest generally when only a handful of companies have the resources and capabilities to offer a bundle of desirable services. AT&T and Verizon leveraged their telecommunications networking strengths into local and long-distance wireline telephone services, wireless telephone services, and broadband access. Both companies are expanding into content creation and content delivery though independent and joint ventures for example, with direct broadcast satellite companies. Cable companies have already vertically and horizontally integrated conduits and content creation. They lack wireless telecommunications corporate affiliates but may pursue joint ventures.

A cable television company–telephone company duopoly already exists for the physical network links to most residences and businesses. Advocates of competition emphasize that three or more links have already become available (DSL, cable modem, wireless) with more on the horizon, yet the technologies that might increase the number are either unproven (broadband over powerline, for example), expensive (satellite and terrestrial wireless), or metered. Broadband over powerline service remains in a test and demonstration mode. The power companies' third wire to homes and businesses solves the right-of-way problem and defrays the cost of completing the first and last mile of an ICE link. However, broadband over powerline has yet to mature as a cost-effective and workable technology that can deliver broadband content over long distances.

Both terrestrial and satellite wireless services could dislodge the cable-telco duopoly, but the prices for these services and the quality of their performance remain quite inferior to the prices and quality of the two wire-based options. Currently, cellular companies offer comparatively slow services at or above the cost charged by cable and telephone companies. Next-generation wireless services will reach true broadband speeds, but one of the two wire-based broadband options is provided by the major wireless carriers, and neither AT&T nor Verizon will risk cannibalizing revenues from either type of broadband service in their zeal to compete.

Satellite companies may offer somewhat faster bitrates at the same price as wireline broadband companies, but subscribers need to install equipment costing four hundred dollars or more. So, for the time being, most consumers will look to two companies in any one locale for most ICE services. Regrettably, most trend lines indicate that these companies will consolidate control instead of gradually or quickly losing market power. Under these marketplace conditions, eliminating or reducing regulatory oversight is an abdication of responsibility all but guaranteed to result in outcomes adverse to the national interest.

CHAPTER THIRTEEN

The Way Forward

ICE TECHNOLOGICAL and marketplace convergence has become a reality. Yet many ICE ventures, consumers, and governments appear remarkably ill equipped to respond to information-age changes. Given such poor preparation, some of the anticipated positive benefits may not arise, and some of the avoidable problems will. Consumers lacking digital literacy will find themselves increasingly on the have-not side of the digital divide, even though many can afford new ICE products and services. Governments that have bought into the "robust competition exists" argument may lack the inclination, resources, and perhaps even legislative authority to provide necessary and effective regulation. Since ICE technologies have enormous potential to enhance individual, national, and global well-being, incumbent ventures, citizens, and governments should consider what they can do to derive the most benefits from ICE convergence.

HOW INCUMBENTS CAN EXPLOIT ICE CONVERGENCE

Many incumbent ICE ventures have already found ways to exploit the ICE convergence, the changing nature of government oversight, and access to substantial retained earnings to secure real or artificial competitive advantages. Some incumbents, particularly ones able to secure access to non-competitive infrastructure, will continue to thrive. Incumbent cable television and telephone companies have successfully transitioned into an environment where vertical and horizontal integration can achieve expanded operational coverage and market penetration. They will continue to diversify and increase market share by acquiring competitors unless and until government regulators start to worry about market concentration. Other incumbent ventures have not made a successful transition, including ones that had acquired market niches. Newspaper owners and the music industry have suffered declining revenues and market share despite the opportunity to diversify presented by technological and market convergence. Convergence has generated mixed outcomes for various ICE ventures for several reasons.

Local Broadcasters and Broadcast Networks

Broadcasters have experienced perhaps more volatility for a longer time than most ICE ventures. The relatively recent conversion to digital technologies and the Internet's rise constitute additional challenges to an industry that has already experienced market fragmentation and new challenges to formerly all-but-certain revenue streams. Even before ICE convergence, the broadcast industry had to confront the reality that while content matters a lot, the proliferation of content sources and distribution options can dilute broadcasters' market share and their market dominance. Cable television, audio and video streaming over the Internet, the ease of copyright piracy, portable music and video players, and the transition to digital technologies all contributed to market fragmentation.

If the broadcast industry can find ways to use the proliferating options for content distribution to reach consumers who are willing to pay for access or whose consumption of content advertisers will underwrite, it has a chance to thrive in the new environment. Broadcasters continue to have a comparative advantage in news collection and distribution, as well as in the creation of mass-market content. A major weakness lies in their comparatively high operating costs, but expanded distribution options, coupled with merger and acquisition activity and cost cutting, could enable broadcasters to achieve the scale and reach necessary to operate efficiently and cost effectively. It helps that governments still consider broadcasters largely in the context of a pre-convergent world, where broadcasters helped elect candidates, identified what mattered in the political and public policy spheres, and operated as public trustees of the spectrum that they freely used.

Newspapers

Newspaper owners continue to face a harmful combination of declining circulation and reduced advertising revenues. Apparently, fewer and fewer people have the time or inclination to read a document whose composition, production, and delivery have not changed much for dozens of years. What has changed is the manner in which people acquire news and advertising. An alarming number of people rely on television or the Internet for both. People can acquire news from cable news networks, broadcasters, the Web sites of both, blogs, and even the typically free Web sites of newspapers. Many of the core sources of newspaper advertising revenues, from employment, real estate and automobile ads, are available in a free and user-friendly format on the Internet.

Newspaper owners have attempted to embrace change by setting up Web sites, blogs, twitters, podcasts, and all the rest. But the predominant current strategy appears to be cost cutting, offering a streamlined product, which reduces a newspaper's value proposition, and distress sales to acquiring firms that will cut costs further. Like broadcasters, newspaper ventures need to find ways to exploit their strength in content creation, because people have not lost their interest in the news product. Although the Internet has diverted revenues and subscribers away from newspapers, it may also offer a cost-effective medium for delivering news. Newspaper owners need to leverage their content through joint ventures with wireline and wireless carriers and operate through other portals, with gatekeepers, and with walled garden operators.

The Music Industry

People have not lost their interest in news, nor have they lost it in music. Now, however, they want their news, information, and entertainment customized to their tastes and available anytime, anywhere, and via any of a number of devices. The music industry, like newspaper ventures and broadcasters, has resisted the need to make accommodations to ICE convergence. When ICE ventures fail to accommodate changing consumer desires, they risk losing market share and revenues from both customer migration and customer self-help efforts.

The music industry's continued insistence that consumers buy products containing both desired and undesired content packaged in a multitrack album format met resistance and retaliation. When technological innovations made it possible for music consumers to acquire just the desired music tracks, often for nothing, the music industry reluctantly offered access to music by the track, making it accessible via the Internet and available in formats that promoted device shifting. Now music lovers can download their favorite songs to their iPods and listen away.

The music industry could have anticipated and prepared for changes in the customer interface and the perceived value proposition the industry has to offer. Remarkably, a lack of digital literacy on the part of industry executives appears to have contributed to the failure to recognize that music lovers will find ways to access music on their terms, regardless of whether the access is sanctioned by the music industry and lawful.

Advertisers

Early on, advertisers seem to have understood the strengths, weaknesses, opportunities, and threats presented by convergence and the Internet's rise. Yet some advertisers have suffered because they lack digital literacy as well: they failed to understand how digital video recorders can speed through or pass over advertising segments, and they underestimated the self-help tactics that people will undertake to avoid intrusive advertising. Now advertisers have learned to temper their messages, even to subliminal levels, by placing products in video content, and to offer consumers enough value so that they willingly access advertising that addresses specific interests.

On balance, the traditional ICE industries may have lacked an appreciation of the need to change, but they have learned the hard way that ICE convergence induces permanent change.

THE CHALLENGE TO CONSUMERS AND SOCIETY

One of the best ways for citizens to assess their level of digital literacy involves a stroll through a large electronics store such as Best Buy, with a dizzying array of choices in computers, DVD players, television sets, high-fidelity receivers, cameras, and cell phones. Sales staff are eager to introduce the highest-margin-generating items and to pitch accessories and extended warranties. The manner of presentation both within the store and in advertisements that might have induced a visit can make it difficult to make the best decisions, but anyone who easily navigates through the store and confidently knows how to use the devices and knows what limitations and options exist is well on the way to digital literacy.

Even before entering the store, prospective buyers should have done their homework. Many words and phrases used in marketing and technical specifications do not have a common, reasonable, and rational meaning. Consumers cannot readily distinguish between commercial puffery and references to features and performance statistics that do not pan out in the real word. For example, wireless component manufacturers tout geographical coverage. Granted, they avoid liability by stating "up to" such-and-such distance, but many Wi-Fi home wireless networks do not even come close to extending throughout a modest ranch home.

Makers of the latest generation of short-range transceivers for families claim a range of up to several miles for unlicensed operation and up to twelve miles for transceivers requiring an FCC license. The manufacturers must have tested these devices in optimal conditions to achieve this kind of coverage, because most real-world uses peter out after less than one mile for unlicensed handsets and a mile or two for the higher-powered radios. Cordless telephones suffer from the same dichotomy between touted and realized coverage distance.

Much ICE advertising borders on deceptive. Here are a few examples. Cable and satellite television companies have opted to subordinate cost differences and instead emphasize reliable service. Anyone listening to the cable ventures would think that satellite technology has yet to get the kinks out. Allegedly, the signal fades out on rainy or snowy days. One company quotes a former satellite customer who reports that the bolted satellite dish actually became full of snow and moved out of alignment. The sophisticated consumer knows that both satellites and satellite-receiving dishes stay in line-of-sight alignment and that signal attenuation due to rain or snow rarely occurs in nontropical locales. Of course, satellite ventures offer equally dubious claims about the unreliability of cable television. Although cable systems do need systemwide access to electricity, the power grid typically operates quite reliably.

A venture offering a wireless service to enhance automobile safety uses advertising that shows disabled and distressed car drivers getting help through a direct satellite connection. Viewers can easily infer that the service relies on continuous satellite access to provide real-time monitoring. However, the actual technologies used by the venture integrate conventional cellular telephone service with satellite-provided geolocation. In other words, drivers communicate with their safety-net provider via a conventional cellular telephone link. The venture tracks subscribers via the global positioning satellite service offered free of charge by the U.S. government.

Becoming Digitally Literate

As the number of electronic devices and available services for consumers grows, the digital vocabulary increases; so do the number of acronyms. Consumers need to know what the words and letters represent for several reasons. First, these words and letters constitute a kind of shorthand that identifies the features and characteristics of services and equipment. Second, if consumers know terms and features, they can distinguish standard features from nonstandard ones by recognizing special words or acronyms coined by a single manufacturer to showcase particular selling points. Third, brief descriptions and acronyms may identify what a service or device can and cannot offer.

Upselling, Lock-In, and Lock-Out

Consumer electronic stores have every incentive to sell devices that add features at an increased cost. So do service providers, such as cellular telephone companies, which want to sell each consumer a newer, more expensive headset with a lower subsidy or perhaps with an attractive profit margin based on all the additional services it can access. Upselling refers to strategies designed to increase the out-of-pocket purchase price for a device or service. Upselling requires sellers to convince consumers that products and services offer greater value if consumers agree to pay more for additional features and services. A plain-vanilla cell phone primarily provides voice telephone service. The average revenue per user is low for basic service subscribers. Upselling increases it when cellular telephone consumers upgrade their service to include additional services such as the ability to send and receive text messages and photographs, download ringtones, access the Internet, and download or receive real-time delivery of video content, including games. Upselling typically also includes the sale of the more expensive and complicated devices needed to access the enhanced features and services.

Offers of extended warranties can fit into the upselling category. The key factors for a digitally literate buyer to use in determining whether to buy an extended warranty involve knowledge of product life expectancies and product life cycles. If a device can probably function without failure for several years and still offer the basic expected functions, then a warranty offers no more than expensive peace of mind. Likewise, if technological change makes it unlikely that consumers would want to hold on to a device for more than a few years, then they might not care about a warranty that places a bet on extended life expectancy.

Consumers have unprecedented opportunities to acquire ICE anytime, anywhere, and on a plethora of devices. The expectation of ubiquitous access makes them largely indifferent to which technology and which company provides the access. Indifference contributes to a lack of product and brand loyalty. To prevent customer migration, ICE ventures need to add value to their products and services regularly. One successful strategy involves tapping into the rising benefits accrued from positive network externalities, that is, the value resulting in the ability to send and receive content to and from an ever-increasing number of network users. Wireless companies understand the power of network externalities when they offer "free" calling between existing subscribers—no debited minutes of use when a call stays on the wireless carrier's network.

In far too many instances, however, ICE ventures can limit subscriber migration, or churn. Subscribers can have few options and even fewer opportunities to improve the value proposition when, despite the appearance of competition, all ICE ventures offer roughly the same products and services, on generally the same terms and conditions. This also can occur when ICE ventures contractually lock consumers into one or more years of service by offering a free or below-cost ICE devices. Consumers cannot churn without significant financial penalties for early termination of their cell phone, cable television, or direct broadcast satellite service contracts.

Some consumers may not churn because they do not fully understand what options are available. Wireless companies in particular appear inclined to disable technical features in authorized handsets and to offer subscribers walled-garden access to content. A closed operating environment can raise the average revenue per user, reduce competition for service and handsets, and enable a wireless carrier to favor affiliates and preferred vendors of content, software, and other applications. Ironically, the arrival of the Apple iPhone, with its tight restrictions on subscriber access to content, has helped consumers identify the kinds of carrier-imposed restrictions that most did not know even existed. At the risk of voiding the warranty or, worse yet, breaking the phone, many iPhone users have resorted to self-help remedies upon discovering that they cannot use their handsets to access a carrier other than AT&T, music in formats other than iTunes, and unapproved software.

Digitally literate consumers can push back against unreasonable device restrictions and other tactics designed to increase ICE ventures' profits by locking in subscribers and locking out the competition. Digital literacy requires a significant effort by citizens to understand the potential for ICE ventures to offer faster, better, smarter, cheaper, and more convenient products and services. Rather than being thrilled that a service actually works, the digitally literate consumer wants to know why another ICE venture cannot or will not offer a particular service or allow subscribers to use all the features available from an ICE device. Digitally literate citizens let their government representatives know when ICE ventures fail to compete vigorously and when they act collusively and anticompetitively.

IMPROVING THE REGULATORY PROCESS

Digital literacy among the citizenry offers grassroots, bottom-up pressure on ICE ventures to innovate, compete, and deal fairly. But marketplace forces and consumer sovereignty have limits, particularly when many ICE sectors become concentrated and dominated by a few firms. Although courts do provide a forum for consumers and businesses to seek compensation for harmful and damaging practices, the regulatory process offers ongoing and possibly prospective consumer safeguards. Set out below are suggestions on how to make the regulatory process more effective without its becoming unnecessarily intrusive and costly.

Independence and Nonpartisanship

National regulatory agencies need to operate within their statutory authorization but independently of the legislative and executive branches. An independent agency can make decisions based on the merits of a case instead of considering what is politically expedient or consistent with a party line, economic assumptions, or a political philosophy. The FCC and other NRAs need to make decisions and establish policies based on the record as augmented by in-house research untainted by a political agenda and separate from the sponsored research filed by stakeholders in notice and comment proceedings. In-house research is the work product of staff experts who determine the lawfulness and viability of a proposed outcome: whether it complies with applicable statutory mandates and serves the public interest. In-house research can also determine technological truths, not theoretical interpretations of what technology can or cannot achieve. In-house researchers should apply long-standing economic principles, rather than newly hatched conceptualizations created to legitimize a stakeholder's point of view.

In this book we have examined many instances in which the FCC did not conduct an open, transparent, and independent assessment of the law, the technology, or the economic principles applicable to a case or policy analysis. For example, the Telecommunications Act of 1996 clearly and unconditionally ordered the FCC to promote local telephone service competition, even going so far as to order incumbent carriers to open their networks and price service elements on terms and conditions favorable to market entry. Even the Supreme Court acknowledged that the legislature can determine that the national interest is served by market entry and that the FCC can act on this mandate to order interconnection between incumbents and market entrants on terms and conditions that favor the entrants. Governments outside the United States have forced such reluctant cooperation, apparently without adversely harming incumbents, creating disincentives for investment in next-generation networks, or excessively benefiting market entrants. Their stewardship has accrued ample dividends in the form of sustainable competition, investment in next-generation networks, and market penetration even as the United States suffers from lackluster performance.

Remarkably, the FCC cannot seem to reach any verifiable conclusions on questions about technology and economics that have answers based on empirical evidence. It conveniently outsources such difficult assessments to stakeholders and their sponsored researchers. So when proponents and opponents speak with relatively equal force, the FCC does not act. We would think, for example, that an expert regulatory agency could calculate market penetration by cable television, broadband, and other service providers. As we have seen, it relies on stakeholder statistics. We would also expect it to determine whether low-powered transmissions can occur on unused television channels and to what extent. But rather than conduct the necessary internal, independent research, the FCC appears to accept claims by broadcasters and manufacturers of cordless microphones that sharing such "white spaces" may prove quite difficult. If spectrum sharing cannot occur, according to the views expressed by certain politically connected stakeholders, then it becomes easy for the Commission to decide against reallocating spectrum for most shared and unlicensed uses.

On matters of economics, the FCC similarly refrains from independent empirical research. Because the existence of competition is the foundation for so much of its deregulatory work, the FCC has to come up with best-case evidence that competition exists. Whether its specific findings and the sources of the data are publicly disclosed depends on whether the findings corroborate the conclusion that competition exists. The FCC has accepted questionable claims that market penetration data constitute a trade secret the disclosure of which would harm individually reporting companies

Narrowly Targeted Incentives

The FCC takes quite seriously any legislative mandate to remove disincentives for infrastructure investment and instead create incentives. But it tends to overshoot the mark, particularly given its persistent claim that just about all ICE markets are robustly competitive. The follow-up question has been asked many times: If an ICE market operates competitively, doesn't competitive necessity force an ICE venture to make the investments that consumers expect the venture to make?

Sponsored researchers have declared that incumbent ventures at first refrained from investing substantially in next-generation networks because of regulatory uncertainty and that they released a torrent of investment once they had confidence that the FCC would not highly regulate these networks and force incumbents to provide access to competitors. The story line makes sense, particularly since researchers can set a date and generate data that show pre-date investment as significantly less than post-date investment. The selection of the date matters because other major factors affecting investment by incumbent carriers could have arisen at a particular date and affected investment decisions far more than the FCC did. If the date selected marks the end of the post-dotcom market recession, then a general upturn in the business cycle undoubtedly had as much effect on incumbent carriers' investment decisions as whether the FCC had abandoned most requirements for facilities interconnection. In other words, incumbent carriers, like just about every ICE venture, had to reduce investments in the years after the dotcom recession because the equity and debt markets no longer favored high-technology ventures. Economy recovery in the telecommunications sector naturally made it easier for ICE ventures to secure funds to invest. The onset of competition in core markets and the resulting drop in market share and revenues must also have motivated incumbent carriers to embrace ICE convergence and to get serious about finding new products and services to offer.

If regulation has the potential to create investment disincentives and market distortions, it follows that regulator-created incentives to invest can also distort the market, particularly when ample motivation already exists for investment in next-generation networks. NRAs need to think carefully about whether they should create investment incentives, particularly if these very same regulators believe the ICE markets are robustly competitive. Arguably, the need for incentive creation results from a finding of market failure, something most sponsored researchers are paid to dispute.

Citizens and the FCC

The breadth of the current campaign to educate consumers on the migration to digital television shows that, in some instances at least, the FCC recognizes that the ICE marketplace has special characteristics. A typical market does not have devices that work one day and stop working forever the next day. As a result of legislative and regulatory decisions, analog television sets not connected to a satellite or cable network and lacking a digital converter failed to display a video signal after June 19, 2009. A former FCC chairman considered a television nothing more than a toaster with pictures, but most toasters do not stop working in homes because of a government decision.

The FCC-orchestrated digital-literacy campaign for digital television sought to inform everyone of the need to prepare for the change to digital signals. The Commission required every broadcaster, cable operator, cable network, and retailer of consumer electronic devices to spread the news. The information campaign targeted the ten to twenty million citizens who viewed television off air with antennas and offered them two coupons worth forty dollars each to defray the cost of buying the necessary digital converter.

Outside this campaign the FCC has undertaken limited efforts to educate citizens about innovations and convergence in ICE technologies and to solicit their views on ICE policy issues. Only on rare occasions does the FCC hold meetings outside Washington, D.C., or take special efforts to provide a forum for or pay special attention to citizens. The list of participants at any FCC notice and comment proceeding includes all the major ICE ventures affected, as well as their trade associations, but few individual citizens ever participate. The FCC has upgraded its Web page and offers a variety of informative fact sheets. However, few people outside Washington, D.C. know the procedure for filing complaints and comments at the FCC.

With consumers' increasing digital literacy, promoted by the digital television campaign, use of the iPhone, and access to myriad ICE devices, applications, and services, perhaps consumers will play a larger part in helping the FCC face the challenges brought by ICE convergence. Recent efforts by the FCC to organize workshops and enlist support from academic organizations about how to prepare a national broadband policy offer some hope.

THE WAY FORWARD

In the 1980s regulatory officials from throughout the world visited the FCC. At that time, the United States offered best-practices leadership in embracing competition by removing impediments to market entry and forcing cooperation between incumbents and newcomers. Officials from other nations came to Washington for insights on how to transition from franchises or government-owned monopolies to a competitive marketplace. In the ensuing thirty years, the United States has had very little to offer to anyone interested in promoting sustainable competition and the public interest. The best-practices leadership comes from other nations now, largely because the FCC seems preoccupied with its stock message about how robustly competitive the ICE marketplace has become and with constant reassessments of how well the United States ranks in terms of constructing and providing access to next-generation networks. It acts as if it has accomplished its statutory mission and has very little left to do beyond resolving disputes about broadcast decency and, recently, informing the public about digital television.

The FCC's statistics and preoccupations notwithstanding, the United States does not come close to global best practices in terms of access to affordable advanced telecommunications, nor has the FCC recalibrated the nature and scope of its regulatory mission in response to real marketplace conditions. There may come a time, perhaps sooner than we think, when our inferior ICE products and services hamper national productivity and our ability to compete in information-intensive industries. Some rural localities have already resorted to self-help in upgrading their telecommunications infrastructure when incumbent firms cannot seem to get around to the task. The localities that make such investments do so to compete effectively in the global marketplace, not to take opportunities away from private enterprises.

Some elected officials realize the comparative and competitive advantages accruing from access to affordable broadband networks, but the FCC and its counterparts in the executive branch seem intent on overemphasizing the positive with little regard for finding ways to improve what we have. The U.S. regulatory model seems to operate from self-satisfaction and complacency. But the transition to digital networking has only begun, and the ICE marketplace is volatile and requires constant vigilance. There is work for the FCC and the broader government to do.

When a nation gains competitive and comparative advantages in ICE industries, the accruing benefits multiply. When a nation lacks competitive and comparative advantages in ICE industries, its citizens lose the financial and quality-of-life advantages accruing from improvements in efficiency and productivity. The way forward is clear: promotion of digital literacy, marketplace competition, and light-handed regulation.

NOTES

CHAPTER ONE. THE LAW OF UNINTENDED RESULTS

1. Sponsored research is research performed by professors, think tank employees or affiliates, and others who receive outside financial support. Researchers should disclose such funding because it can influence their work product, and readers of their reports should know of this potential conflict of interest. Not all sponsored research results in a biased work product, but most sponsors of research typically seek to influence the legislative and policymaking processes.
2. In a civil society government operates transparently and fairly with an engaged and vigilant electorate.
3. "It's becoming increasingly evident that the wireless growth engine is data—text messaging, instant messaging (IM), video, games, social networking and more. Data applications are exciting and popular among highly coveted, younger subscribers, but rising data average revenue per user (ARPU) has not translated into rising total ARPU. Wireless ARPU in the U.S. currently averages $50 per month. Data's percentage of that has grown from zero to 20 percent (or $10 per month) but total wireless ARPU is remaining relatively flat. If voice revenues continue to decline, this presents a challenge for wireless companies in 2009: Are they bringing data services online that people value and will purchase at a fast-enough rate to offset any decline in voice revenue? Carriers need to push the technology envelope to translate data ARPU into increased total ARPU. But therein lies another challenge: Rapid technology evolution is costly and spectrum is scarce." Deloitte, *2009 Industry Outlook: Telecom,* http://www.deloitte.com.
4. *See* Thirteenth Report, *Implementation of Section 6002(b) of the Omnibus Bud-*

get Reconciliation Act of 1993, Annual Report and Analysis of Competitive Market Conditions with Respect to Commercial Mobile Services, DA 09-54 (rel. Jan. 16, 2009). Verizon's acquisition of Alltel's wireless assets added slightly over 1 percent to the market concentration total. *See* Memorandum Opinion and Order and Declaratory Ruling, *Applications of Cellco Partnership d/b/a Verizon Wireless and Atlantis Holdings LLC for Consent to Transfer Control of Licenses, Authorizations, and Spectrum Manager and De Facto Transfer Leasing Arrangements,* 23 F.C.C.R. 17,444 (2008).

5. "CNNfn.com asked the market data and research firm Birinyi Associates of Westport, Conn., to calculate the market value of the 280 stocks in the Bloomberg US Internet Index at their respective 52-week highs and their current market value. The combined market values of the 280 stocks had fallen to $1.193 trillion currently from $2.948 trillion at their peak, a loss of $1.755 trillion, most of which occurred between March and September of this year." David Kleinbard, CNN Money, *The $1.7 Trillion Dot.com Lesson,* Nov. 9, 2000.
6. The digital divide is the gap between people with the financial wherewithal and interest in acquiring the equipment, services, and skills needed to access digital ICE services and those lacking such resources. *See* Digital Divide.org, *Ushering in the Second Digital Revolution.* The digital divide separates "those [people] with access to new technologies and those without." United States Department of Commerce, National Telecommunications and Information Administration, FALLING THROUGH THE NET: DEFINING THE DIGITAL DIVIDE, Introduction, xii (July 1999); Lynne Holt & Mary Galligan, *State and Federal Policies to Accelerate Broadband Deployment: A Policy Checklist,* 17 COMMLAW CONSPECTUS 141 (2008); Jaime Klima, *The E-Government Act: Promoting E-Quality or Exaggerating the Digital Divide?* 2003 DUKE L. & TECH. REV. 9 (Apr. 15, 2003); James E. Prieger, *The Supply Side of the Digital Divide: Is There Equal Availability in the Broadband Internet Access Market?* 41 ECON. INQUIRY 346 (2003); Peter K. Yu, *Bridging the Digital Divide: Equality in the Information Age,* 20 CARDOZO ARTS & ENT. L.J. 1 (2002); Organisation for Economic Co-operation and Development, UNDERSTANDING THE DIGITAL DIVIDE (2001).
7. The purpose of universal service funding is to promote access to basic telephone service by offering financial subsidies to qualifying individuals and carriers. The subsidies defray the nonrecurring cost of initiating service and the recurring costs of dial-up telephone service. In addition, wireline and wireless telephone companies receive funding to offset costs incurred to provide service primarily in rural areas lacking sufficiently high population density for regular service. *See* Universal Service Administrative Co., 2008 ANNUAL REPORT, at 5 (2009), http://www.usac.org/about/governance/annualreports/.
8. A walled garden is an easily accessed source of content provided by a service provider with an eye to making it more costly or inconvenient for subscribers to access content elsewhere. For example, Yahoo offers subscribers readily

available access to content in lieu of access to similar content available through searches in the World Wide Web.

9. Despite technological superiority in many areas the United States lags in broadband market penetration. The Organisation for Economic Co-operation and Development (OECD) reports that it ranked fifteenth among OECD nations. OECD, *Broadband Statistics*, Table 1d, OECD Broadband subscribers per 100 inhabitants, by technology, December 2008 (2009), http://www.oecd.org/sti/ict/broadband. The Information Technology & Innovation Foundation's 2008 ITIF Broadband Rankings also place the United States in fifteenth position; *see* www.itif.org/files/2008BBRankings.pdf. *See also* S. Derek Turner, Free Press, *"Shooting the Messenger" Myth vs. Reality: U.S. Broadband Policy and International Broadband Rankings* (July 2007), http://www.freepress.net; Presentation of Dr Tim Kelly, Lead ICT Policy Specialist, infoDev/World Bank, FCC Workshop: *International Lessons* (Aug. 18, 2009), http://www.broadband.gov/docs/ws_int_lessons.html.
10. The International Telecommunication Union ranks the United States 10th in broadband prices per hundred kilobits per second. International Telecommunication Union, ITU INTERNET REPORT 2006: DIGITAL.LIFE, Broadband prices per 100 kbits top 75, 2006, at 174 (ITU, 2006) [hereinafter cited as ITU Internet Report].
11. And perhaps in the longer-term environment, too. *See* Robert Horwitz, THE IRONY OF REGULATORY REFORM: THE DEREGULATION OF AMERICAN TELECOMMUNICATIONS (Oxford University Press, 1989).
12. The International Telecommunication Union ranked the United States 61st in the world for mobile subscribers per hundred inhabitants. ITU Internet Report at 146. The United States ranked twenty-fourth in mobile broadband penetration per hundred inhabitants. ITU Internet Report at 157.
13. Jon Fine, *Mobile Broadcasting: Manana*, BUSINESSWEEK, Apr. 2, 2007, at 24.
14. The FCC justified classifying broadband access delivered via cable modem as an information service because a firm deregulatory decision would "remove regulatory uncertainty that in itself may discourage investment and innovation." Declaratory Ruling, *Inquiry Concerning High-Speed Access to the Internet over Cable and Other Facilities, Internet over Cable*, 17 F.C.C. R. 4798, 4802 (2002), *affirmed sub nom.*, Nat'l Cable & Telecomm. Ass'n v. Brand X Internet Servs., 545 U.S. 967, 125 S. Ct.. 2688, 162 L.Ed.2d 820 (2005); *see also* Jonathan E. Nuechterlein, *Incentives to Speak Honestly About Incentives: The Need for Structural Reform of the Local Competition Debate*, 2 J. TELECOMM. & HIGH TECH. L. 399 (2003); George Bittlingmayer, *Regulatory Uncertainty and Investment: Evidence from Antitrust Enforcement*, 20 CATO J., No. 3, 295 (Winter 2001).
15. "Unbundled network elements were mandated too widely, without regard for the disincentives such wholesale access would likely have in the construction of advanced systems and competitive networks." Thomas W. Hazlett, *Rivalrous Telecommunications Networks With and Without Mandatory Sharing,*

58 FED. COMM. L.J. 477 (June 2006); Michael A. Heller, *The UNE Anticommons: Why the 1996 Telecom Reforms Blocked Innovation and Investment,* 22 YALE J. ON REG. 275 (Summer 2005); Allan T. Ingraham & J. Gregory Sidak, *Mandatory Unbundling, UNE-P, and the Cost of Equity: Does TELRIC Pricing Increase Risk for Incumbent Local Exchange Carriers?* 20 YALE J. ON REG. 389 (2003).

16. Verizon's fiber-optic service provides downloads at thirty megabits per second and uploads at five megabits per second. *See* Verizon, *Who Wins—FiOS vs. Cable?* http://www22.verizon.com.
17. AT&T offers a mix of fiber-optic and copper cable. *See* AT&T, *U-verse, How AT&T U-verse TV Is Delivered,* http://www.att.com.
18. *See, e.g.,* Greg Sidak & Hal Singer, *Überregulation Without Economics: The World Trade Organization's Decision in the U.S.-Mexico Arbitration on Telecommunications Services,* 57 FED. COMM. L.J., No. 1, 1 (Dec. 2004). The piece contains a disclaimer that the American Enterprise Institute takes no position on specific legislative, regulatory, adjudicatory, or executive matters. But the reader gets no disclosure on whether or not TelMex provided AEI any funding before or after this legal scholarship made its way into print.
19. "An examination by Larstan Business Reports of publicly available documents indicates that certain 'independent groups' claiming to represent consumer interests are actually undercover stalking horses for the special interests of the large phone companies." Larstan Business Reports, *Records Indicate Bells Engaged in "Astroturf" Lobbying, Creation of Faux Consumer Groups Designed to Influence Pending Legislation* (Nov. 9, 2005), http://www.ip97.com. *See also* Source Watch, Center for Media and Democracy, http://www.sourcewatch.org.
20. David Kleinbard, CNN Money, *The $1.7 Trillion Dot.com Lesson,* Nov. 9, 2000.
21. Bill Gates, THE ROAD AHEAD (Penguin Books, 1995).
22. *See* Mike Dash, WHEN THE TULIP BUBBLE BURST (Crown Publishers, 2000).
23. *See* Shigenori Shiratsuka, Institute for Monetary and Economic Studies, Bank of Japan, *Asset Price Bubble in Japan in the 1980s: Lessons for Financial and Macroeconomic Stability,* Discussion Paper No. 2003-E-15.
24. *See* Rob Frieden, *Killing with Kindness: Fatal Flaws in the $6.5 Billion Universal Service Funding Mission and What Should Be Done to Narrow the Digital Divide,* 24 CARDOZO ARTS & ENT. L.J., No. 2, 447 (2006).
25. Sec. 254 of the Telecommunications Act of 1996, Pub. L. No. 104-104, 110 Stat. 56 (1996) (codified in scattered sections of 47 U.S.C.), establishes a national universal service policy. 47 U.S.C. § 254.
26. "The Federal Communications Commission (FCC) and Congress recognize that telephone service provides a vital link to emergency services, government services, and surrounding communities. To help promote telecommunications service nationwide, the FCC, as directed by Congress and with the help of the Universal Service Administrative Company (USAC), administers

the federal Universal Service Fund." Federal Communications Commission, *The FCC's Universal Support Mechanisms*, http://www.fcc.gov/cgb/consumerfacts/universalservice.html. *See also* Jonathan Weinberg, *The Internet and "Telecommunications Services": Universal Service Mechanisms, Access Charges, and Other Flotsam of the Regulatory System*, 16 YALE J. ON REG., 211 (1999).

27. "The notion that everyone should be provided the opportunity to receive basic telephone service at an affordable rate, regardless of geographic location or economic status, has been widely adopted as national policy. The goal of quality, widely available and reasonably priced telephone service has been achieved through a myriad of regulatory policies such as rate averaging, cost support funds and loan programs." Patricia M. Worthy, *Racial Minorities and the Quest to Narrow the Digital Divide: Redefining the Concept of "Universal Service,"* 26 HASTINGS COMM. & ENT. L.J. 1, 4 (2003).
28. Samuel L. Baker, *Economics Interactive Tutorial: Marginal Cost and the Output Rate Under Competition* (2000), http://hspm.sph.sc.edu/COURSES/ECON/MCost/MCost.html.
29. *See* Federal Communications Commission, *Contribution Factor & Quarterly Filings*, http://www.fcc.gov/omd/contribution-factor.html.
30. Cable modems provide Internet access by modulating a digital signal via a small portion of the bandwidth previously used by cable television companies to provide video service. *See* Cable-Modems.org, *The Cable Modem Reference Guide*, http://www.cable-modems.org/.
31. Wireline local-exchange telephone companies provide Internet access by extending the bandwidth of the copper-wire line that links local subscribers to the central switching facilities. *See* Curt Franklin, *How DSL Works*, http://electronics.howstuffworks.com/dsl.htm.
32. *See, e.g.*, HughesNet, *Service Plans*, http://www.nationwidesatellite.com.
33. *See, e.g.*, Verizon Wireless, *National Access Data Plan*, http://www.verizonwireless.com.
34. For technical background on how VoIP works *see* Intel White Papers, IP TELEPHONY BASICS, http://www.intel.com.
35. *See* Vonage Web site, http://www.vonage.com.
36. John Markoff, *Microsoft Trying to Dominate the Internet*, THE NEW YORK TIMES, July 16, 1996.
37. United State Government Accountability Office, *Broadband Deployment Is Extensive Throughout the United States, but It Is Difficult to Assess the Extent of Development Gaps in Rural Areas*, GAO 06–426 (May 2006), http://www.gao.gov/; *see also* WebSiteOptimization.com, *U.S. Falls to 25th in Broadband Penetration Worldwide—US Broadband Growth Below OECD Average*, APRIL 2007 BANDWIDTH REPORT, http://www.websiteop timization.com. Other assessments do place the United States at or near the top. *See, e.g.*, Economist.com, *E-Readiness Rankings* (2009), http://www.economist.com; LECG, *Connectivity Scorecard 2009*, http://www.lecg.com.

38. *See, e.g.*, Letter from Ambassador David A. Gross, United States Coordinator, International Communications and Information Policy, Department of State, to Mr. Angel Gurria, Secretary-General, Organisation for Economic Co-operation and Development, Apr. 24, 2007, http://www.ntia.doc.gov; United States Department of Commerce, National Telecommunications and Information Administration, *Fact Sheet: United States Maintains Information and Communication Technology (ICT) Leadership and Economic Strength*, http://www.ntia.doc.gov.
39. "Internet cloud" refers to the numerous telecommunications and information networks that transport Internet traffic seamlessly and, typically, without delay. Network managers cooperate so well that the Internet appears to be a user-friendly network of networks.
40. *See Imran's Everything Cellular*, http://www.mobileisgood.com.
41. Network neutrality refers to the view that the Internet and other telecommunications and information-processing networks should remain open, nondiscriminatory, and largely managed by users rather than carriers. The principle supports end-to-end connectivity and the kind of access equality provided by best-efforts routing of network traffic. Opponents claim that network neutrality would impose common-carrier nondiscrimination responsibilities on information service providers, create disincentives for investment in next-generation network infrastructure, and generate regulatory uncertainty. *See* Policy Statement, *Appropriate Framework for Broadband Access to the Internet over Wireline Facilities*, 20 F.C.C.R. 14,986 (2005) (articulating network neutrality policy objectives); Rob Frieden, *Internet 3.0: Identifying Problems and Solutions to the Network Neutrality Debate*, 1 INT'L J. OF COMM., 461 (2007); Rob Frieden, *Network Neutrality or Bias?—Handicapping the Odds for a Tiered and Branded Internet*, 29 HASTINGS COMM. & ENT. L.J., No. 2, 171 (2007).
42. Voice over Internet Protocol (VoIP), much like ordinary telephone service, offers voice communications capabilities, but it uses the packet-switched Internet for all or part of the link between call originator and call recipient. VoIP calls originating or terminating over the standard dial-up telephone network require conversion from or to the standard telephone network's architecture; the standard architecture creates a dedicated circuit-switched link, as opposed to the ad hoc best-efforts packet switching used in the Internet. *See* Melissa Winberg, *Calling All Angles: Perspectives on Regulating Internet Telephony*, 10 VAND. J. ENT. & TECH. L. 241 (Fall 2007); Mark C. Del Bianco, *Voices Past: The Present and Future of VoIP Regulation*, 14 COMMLAW CONSPECTUS 365 (2006); Jerry Ellig & Alastair Walling, *Regulatory Status of VoIP in the Post–Brand X World*, 23 SANTA CLARA COMPUTER & HIGH TECH. L.J. 89 (No. 2006); Amy L. Leisinger, *If It Looks Like a Duck: The Need for Regulatory Parity in VoIP Telephony*, 45 WASHBURN L.J. 585 (Spring 2006); R. Alex DuFour, *Voice over Internet Protocol: Ending Uncertainty and Promoting Innovation Through a Regulatory Framework*, 13 COMMLAW CON-

SPECTUS 471 (2005); Stephen E. Blythe, *The Regulation of Voice-over-Internet-Protocol in the United States, the European Union, and the United Kingdom,* 5 J. HIGH TECH. L. 161 (2005); Robert Cannon, *State Regulatory Approaches to VoIP: Policy, Implementation, and Outcome,* 57 FED. COMM. L.J. 479 (May 2005); Sunny Lu, Note, *Cellco Partnership v. FCC & Vonage Holdings Corp. v. Minnesota Public Utilities Commission: VoIP's Shifting Legal and Political Landscape,* 20 BERKELEY TECH. L.J. 859 (2005); Chérie R. Kiser & Angela F. Collins, *Regulation on the Horizon: Are Regulators Poised to Address the Status of IP Telephony?* 11 COMMLAW CONSPECTUS, 19 (2003); Robert M. Frieden, *Dialing for Dollars: Should the FCC Regulate Internet Telephony?* 23 RUTGERS COMPUTER & TECH. L.J. 47 (1997).

43. "Rather than 'broadcasting' a constant stream of all available programs, as cable does and Verizon plans to do, Internet Protocol television (IPTV) stores a potentially unlimited number of programs on a central server, which users then call up on demand. SBC will not replace the copper lines that currently run into customer premises. Instead, to make sure there is sufficient bandwidth between the neighborhood node where the optical fiber terminates and the household premises, it will upgrade the DSL equipment currently at those nodes and in households with very high speed DSL (VDSL) technology. At the household, the viewer will use the IP technology to send a signal to the SBC end-office to send a particular channel or video on demand selection. That signal will be sent over the same bandwidth used for data and VoIP service. In SBC's system, a single customer line will have enough bandwidth to support up to four active television sets per household at a time, or up to two high-definition television (HDTV) channels at a time." Charles B. Goldfarb, *Telecommunications Act: Competition, Innovation, and Reform,* Congressional Research Service 37 (Jan. 13, 2006), http://www.educause.edu; *see also* Micah Schwalb, *IPTV: Public Interest Pitfalls,* 5 J. TELECOMM. & HIGH TECH. L. 305 (Fall 2006).

44. "TCP/IP [Transmission Control Protocol/Internet Protocol] routes packets anonymously on a 'first come, first served' and 'best efforts' basis. Thus, it is poorly suited to applications that are less tolerant of variations in throughput rates, such as streaming media and VoIP, and is biased against network-based security features that protect e-commerce and ward off viruses and spam." Christopher S. Yoo, *Beyond Network Neutrality,* 19 HARV. J.L. & TECH. 1, 8 (Fall 2005).

45. *See, e.g.,* Associated Press, *Comcast Admits Delaying Some Traffic,* Oct. 23, 2007.

46. "[I]n Load Shift, Enron traders submitted false energy schedules and bids to the California market to create the appearance of congestion on a transmission line. This would trigger payments attached to easing congestion and let Enron profit from its own lies when it used its transmission rights to ease the sham congestion." Mary Flood & Tom Fowler, *The Fall of Enron: Ex-Trader Pleads Guilty to Schemes; Prison, Fines Likely in California Deals,* THE HOUSTON CHRONICLE, Feb. 5, 2003, at Business 1.

47. *Joint Statement of Chairman Kevin J. Martin and Commissioner Deborah Taylor Tate Re: AT&T Inc. and BellSouth Corporation Application for Transfer of Control*, WC Docket No. 06–74 (Dec. 29, 2006).
48. "The Commission has also used the term 'high-speed' to describe services and facilities with more than 200 kbps capability in at least one direction." Notice of Inquiry, *Inquiry Concerning the Deployment of Advanced Telecommunications Capability to All Americans in a Reasonable and Timely Fashion, and Possible Steps to Accelerate Such Deployment Pursuant to Section 706 of the Telecommunications Act of 1996*, 22 F.C.C. R. 7816, 7819 (2007), *citing* Fourth Report to Congress, *Availability of Advanced Telecommunications Capability in the United States*, 19 F.C.C.R. 20,540, 20,551 (2004). In 2008 the FCC belatedly sought to assess broadband market penetration with greater specificity by using more granular census tract data to identify service areas and by using several different bitrates. Notice of Proposed Rulemaking, *Development of Nationwide Broadband Data to Evaluate Reasonable and Timely Deployment of Advanced Services to All Americans, Improvement of Wireless Broadband Subscribership Data, and Development of Data on Interconnected Voice over Internet Protocol (VoIP) Subscribership*, 22 F.C.C.R. 7760 (2007), Report and Order and Further Notice of Proposed Rulemaking, 23 F.C.C.R. 9691 (2008); *on partial reconsideration*, 23 F.C.C.R. 9800 (2008) (requiring wireline, terrestrial fixed wireless, and satellite broadband service providers to report, for each census tract and each speed tier in which the provider offers service, the number of subscribers and the percentage of subscribers that are residential).
49. "In the 2008 Broadband Data Gathering Order, the Commission updated the broadband reporting speed tiers and created the term 'first generation data' to refer to those services with data rates greater than 200 kbps but less than 768 kbps in the faster direction, and the term 'basic broadband tier 1' to refer to services equal to or greater than 768 kbps but less than 1.5 megabits per second (mbps) in the faster direction. Subsequent tiers were labeled 'broadband tier 2' through 'broadband tier 7.'" Notice of Inquiry, *A National Broadband Plan for Our Future*, 24 F.C.C.R. 10,505 (2009). *See also* Broadband Data Improvement Act, Pub. L. No. 110-385, 122 Stat. 4096 (2008) (BDIA), *codified at* 47 U.S.C. § 1301 *et. seq.;* Report and Order and Further Notice of Proposed Rulemaking, *Development of Nationwide Broadband Data to Evaluate Reasonable and Timely Deployment of Advanced Services to All Americans, Improvement of Wireless Broadband Subscribership Data, and Development of Data on Interconnected Voice over Internet Protocol (VoIP) Subscribership*, 23 F.C.C.R. 9691 (2008), *on partial recon.* 23 F.C.C.R. 9800 (2008).
50. "No consideration is given to the price, speed or availability of connections across the ZIP code." S. Derek Turner, Free Press, *Broadband Reality Check—The FCC Ignores America's Digital Divide* (2005), http://www.freepress.net.
51. Mark Twain popularized this saying, which is attributed to British prime minister Benjamin Disraeli.

52. *See, e.g.*, J. Gregory Sidak, *A Consumer-Welfare Approach to Network Neutrality Regulation of the Internet,* 2 J. OF COMPETITION L. & ECON. 349 (2006).
53. Federal Communications Commission, *Number of Holding Companies Reporting High-Speed Subscribers by ZIP Code as of June 30, 2008,* http://www.fcc.gov/Bureaus/Common_Carrier/Reports/FCC-State_Link.
54. The *Wall Street Journal* columnist Walt Mossburg calculates that the cutting-edge 3G iPhone offered bitrates at 200–500 kilobits per second, not a blazing speed but still an improvement over the 70–150 kilobits per second previously available via AT&T's EDGE network. *See* Walter S. Mossberg, *All Things Digital: Newer, Faster, Cheaper iPhone 3G Software and Online Store Will Widen Its Versatility, But There Are Hidden Costs,* http://ptech.allthingsd.com. There are many claims that the United States has best-in-class wireless networks, but the *Economist* magazine offers a far less sanguine assessment: "Pity us poor mobile-phone users in America. While the rest of the world enjoys network speeds that let people watch television on the move, surf the mobile web in its living glory, download videos in a trice, or exchange video messages with one another, we celebrate Apple's launch of its iPhone 3G today as if were some great leap for mankind." Economist.com, Science and Technology, *The iPhone's Second Coming,* July 11, 2008, http://www.economist.com.
55. *See Section 257 Triennial Report to Congress Identifying and Eliminating Market Entry Barriers for Entrepreneurs and Other Small Businesses,* 22 F.C.C. R. 21,132 (2007).
56. *See* Organisation for Economic Co-operation and Development, *OECD Broadband Portal,* Table 1d, Broadband subscribers per 100 inhabitants (Dec. 2008), http://www.oecd.org.
57. *See* Richard A. Epstein, *Takings, Commons, and Associations: Why the Telecommunications Act of 1996 Misfired,* 22 YALE J. ON REG. 315 (2005); Michael A. Heller, *The UNE Anticommons: How the FCC Deters Broadband Innovation,* 22 YALE J. ON REG. 275 (2005); Daniel F. Spulber & Christopher S. Yoo, *Access to Networks: Economic and Constitutional Connections,* 88 CORNELL L. REV. 885 (2003); J. Gregory Sidak & Daniel F. Spulber, *Deregulatory Takings and Breach of the Regulatory Contract,* 71 N.Y.U. L. REV. 851 (1996).
58. *See* American Recovery and Reinvestment Act of 2009, Pub. L. 111–005 (signed into law, Feb. 17, 2009).
59. A CableCard is a small integrated circuit card that consumers can insert into a slot located on most new television sets and that will provide cable television subscribers with digital rights management and authorization for access to digital content, including premium channels.
60. Report and Order, *Implementation of Section 304 of the Telecommunications Act of 1996, Commercial Availability of Navigation Devices,* 20 F.C.C.R. 6794 (2005), *pet. for review denied,* Charter Communications Inc. v. FCC, 460 F.3d 31 (D.C. Cir. 2006).

CHAPTER TWO. FEAST AND FAMINE IN THE INFORMATION AGE

1. *See* John Cassidy, DOT.COM: HOW AMERICA LOST ITS MIND AND MONEY IN THE INTERNET ERA (Perennial, 2002); Rory Cellan, DOT.BOMB: THE RISE AND FALL OF DOT.COM (Aurum Press, 2001); J. David Kuo, DOTBOMB—INSIDE AN INTERNET GOLIATH; FROM LUNATIC OPTIMISM TO PANIC AND CRASH (Little, Brown, 2001); Manuel Castells, THE INTERNET GALAXY: REFLECTIONS ON THE INTERNET, BUSINESS AND SOCIETY (Oxford University Press, 2001).
2. *See* Rob Frieden, *Lessons from Broadband Development in Canada, Japan, Korea and the United States,* 29 TELECOMM. POL'Y, 595 (Sept. 2005).
3. *See* OECD, *OECD Broadband Statistics,* Table 4f, Average broadband monthly price per advertised Mbit/s, USD PPP, October 2008, http://www.oecd.org; Communications Workers of America, *2009 Report on Internet Speeds in All 50 States,* http://www.speedmatters.org/.
4. Chong-Moon Lee, William F. Miller, Marguerite Gong Hancock & Henry S. Rowen, *The Silicon Valley Habitat,* in Cohg-Moon Lee *et al.*, eds., THE SILICON VALLEY EDGE (Stanford University Press, 2000).
5. Telecommunications service is "the offering of telecommunications for a fee directly to the public, or to such classes of users as to be effectively available directly to the public, regardless of the facilities used." 47 U.S.C. § 153(46). The Communications Act of 1934 defines a telecommunications carrier as "any provider of telecommunications services, except that such term does not include aggregators of telecommunications services (as defined in section 226). A telecommunications carrier shall be treated as a common carrier under this chapter only to the extent that it is engaged in providing telecommunications services, except that the Commission shall determine whether the provision of fixed and mobile satellite service shall be treated as common carriage." 47 U.S.C. § 153(44).
6. Title II of the Communications Act of 1934, as amended, 47 U.S.C. §§ 201 *et seq.* (2008), requires providers of basic telecommunications services to operate on a nondiscriminatory basis and to provide services for just and reasonable charges; the services are also subject to numerous entry regulations, tariffing, interconnection, and operating requirements.
7. *See, e.g.,* J. Gregory Sidak & Daniel F. Spulber, *Deregulatory Takings and Breach of the Regulatory Contract,* 71 N.Y.U. L. REV. 851 (1996); J. Gregory Sidak & Daniel F. Spulber, *Givings, Takings, and the Fallacy of Forward-Looking Costs,* 72 N.Y.U. L. REV. 1068 (1997); J. Gregory Sidak & Daniel F. Spulber, *Deregulation and Managed Competition in Network Industries,* 15 YALE J. ON REG. 117 (1998). The regulatory takings argument is challenged in Jim Chen, *The Death of the Regulatory Compact: Adjusting Prices and Expectations in the Law of Regulated Industries,* 67 OHIO ST. L.J. 1265 (2006); Adam Candeub, *Network Interconnection and Takings,* 54 SYRACUSE L. REV. 369 (2004).
8. *See, e.g.,* George S. Ford, Thomas M. Koutsky & Lawrence J. Spiwak, *Competi-*

tion After Unbundling: Entry, Industry Structure, and Convergence, 59 FED. COMM. L.J. 331 (2007); Michael A. Heller, *The UNE Anticommons: Why the 1996 Telecom Reforms Blocked Innovation and Investment,* 22 YALE J. ON REG. 275 (2005).

9. "The U.S. experience suggests that specialized local carriers, long-distance companies, or unintegrated DSL providers will not generally be able to compete against integrated communications companies. The United States is very close to the end of a costly experiment in regulatory promotion of entry. At least 90 percent of the $60 billion or more in capital expenditures by CLECs has been written down, written off, or otherwise discarded." Robert W. Crandall & Leonard Waverman, *The Failure of Competitive Entry into Fixed-Line Telecommunications: Who Is at Fault?* 2 J. COMPT. L. & ECON. 113, 125 (2006).
10. Francis Cairncross, THE DEATH OF DISTANCE: HOW THE COMMUNICATIONS REVOLUTION WILL CHANGE OUR LIVES (Orion Publishing Group, 1997).
11. "Voice can be converted into data packets and sent over the packet-switched networks of the Internet just like any other form of data. There are currently two main types of IP telephony. 'Computer-to-computer' IP telephony requires both parties to the call to have compatible software with microphones on their PCs and to be connected to the Internet at the same time. 'Phone-to-phone' IP telephony, which connects to the public switched telephone network (PSTN), generally works through a 'gateway service.' The FCC has tentatively defined 'phone-to-phone' IP telephony as services in which the provider (1) 'holds itself out as providing voice telephony or facsimile transmission service'; (2) 'does not require the customer to use [customer premises equipment (CPE)] different from that CPE necessary to place an ordinary touch-tone call (or facsimile transmission) over the public switched telephone network'; (3) 'allows the customer to call telephone numbers assigned in accordance with the North American Numbering Plan, and associated international agreements'; and (4) 'transmits customer information without net change in form or content.' The gateway service performs the function of transforming the circuit-switched call to IP data packets, and routing the call to the destination gateway. The destination gateway connects the call to the user through a voice switch." Antonia M. Apps & Thomas M. Dailey, *Non-regulation of Advanced Internet Services,* 8 GEO. MASON L. REV., 681, 701–702 (2000).
12. *See* Report to Congress, *Federal-State Joint Board on Universal Service,* 13 F.C.C.R. 11,501, 11,538 (1998) (acknowledging that ISP-provided services might constitute the functional equivalent to telecommunications services, but declining to change regulatory classifications without a full notice and comment rulemaking and further scrutiny).
13. One of the first published references to Bellheads and Netheads occurred in 1996: Steve G. Steinberg, *Netheads vs. Bellheads,* WIRED 4.10 (Oct. 1996).

See also Dawn Bushaus, *Bellheads vs. Netheads,* TELE.COM MAGAZINE (May 1998).

14. *See* Rob Frieden, *Does a Hierarchical Internet Necessitate Multilateral Intervention?* 26 N.C. J. OF INT'L. L. & COM. REG., No. 2, 361 (Spring 2001) (examining the conversion from a sender-keep-all, zero-charge interconnection regime to a settlement-based system, except for the largest Tier 1 ISPs, which continue to use zero-charge "peering").
15. *See, e.g.,* Munn v. Illinois, 4 Otto 113, 125–132, 94 U.S. 113, 125–132, 24 L.Ed. 77 (1876) (regulation of warehouse operations not a violation of due process).
16. "The history of economic regulation shows that industry-specific regulatory agencies tend to lose sight of their public interest mission over time. That is, although an agency may be created to control a particular industry, experience reveals that most regulatory agencies eventually adopt the perspective of the regulated industry. This is referred to as regulatory capture. Thus, eventually, the regulated industry frequently benefits from the regulation." Terrence A. Rosenthal & Robert T. Alter, *Clear and Convincing to Whom? The False Claims Act and Its Burden of Proof Standard: Why the Government Needs a Big Stick,* 75 NOTRE DAME L. REV. 1409, 1464 (May 2000). *See also* Michael E. Levine & Jennifer L. Forrence, *Regulatory Capture, Public Interest, and the Public Agenda: Toward a Synthesis,* 6 J. L. ECON. & ORG. 167, 168 (1990); David R. Johnson & David G. Post, *And How Shall the Net Be Governed? A Meditation on the Relative Virtues of Decentralized, Emergent Law,* in Brian Kahin & James H. Keller, eds., COORDINATING THE INTERNET, at 62 (MIT Press, 1997) (arguing that the Internet poses problems of regulatory capture).
17. Some industry observers dispute that Internet stakeholders can sustain, much less benefit from, self-regulation. *See, e.g.,* Neil Weinstock Netanel, *Cyberspace Self-Governance: A Skeptical View from Liberal Democratic Theory,* 88 CAL. L. REV., 395 (Mar. 2000).
18. *See* United States v. Microsoft Corp., 97 F. Supp. 2d 59 (D.D.C. 2000) (order); United States v. Microsoft Corp., 87 F. Supp. 2d 30 (D.D.C. 2000) (conclusions of law); United States v. Microsoft Corp., 84 F. Supp. 2d 9 (D.D.C. 2000) (findings of fact).
19. For background on the Internet's history and evolution *see* National Research Council, Computer Science and Telecommunications Board, THE INTERNET'S COMING OF AGE (National Academy Press, 2001), http://www.nap.edu. *See also* Barry M. Leiner, Vinton G. Cerf, David D. Clark, Robert E. Kahn, Leonard Kleinrock, Daniel C. Lynch, Jon Postel, Larry G. Roberts & Stephen Wolff, A BRIEF HISTORY OF THE INTERNET (Internet Society, 2003), http://www.isoc.org/internet/history/brief.html.
20. Economists refer to positive network externalities when the cost incurred by a user of the Internet does not fully reflect the benefit derived with the addition of new users and points of communication. *See, e.g.,* Joseph Farrell & Garth Saloner, *Standardization, Compatibility and Innovation,* 16 RAND J. OF

ECON. 70 (1985); Michael L. Katz & Carl Shapiro, *Network Externalities, Competition and Compatibility*, 75 AM. ECON. REV. 424 (1985). Positive network externalities are an accrual in value, including increased access to information, increased ease of communication, and a decrease in a variety of transaction and overhead costs. *See* United States v. Microsoft Corp., 84 F. Supp. 2d 9, 20 (D.D.C. 1999) (findings of fact) ("A positive network effect is a phenomenon by which the attractiveness of a product increases with the number of people using it."). "Network effects, also known as positive network externalities, arise when the value of a network increases with the number of its users. A single firm, perhaps because it is the first mover, becomes or threatens to become the only supplier of certain products or services because of the value of compatibility or interoperability. Consumers are more likely to remain with the established network because of their sunk costs (sometimes referred to as 'lock-in') and suppliers of complementary products will tailor those products to the established network and resist preparing products for would-be challengers." Robert Pitofsky, *Challenges of the New Economy: Issues at the Intersection of Antitrust and Intellectual Property*, 68 ANTITRUST L.J., 913, 916 (2001).

21. "The [National Science] Foundation designated a series of Network Access Points ('NAPs')—on ramps—by which private commercial Internet providers could 'interconnect' to the backbone." Julian Epstein, *A Lite Touch on Broadband: Achieving the Optimal Regulatory Efficiency in the Internet Broadband Market*, 38 HARVARD J. ON LEGIS., 34, n.34 (Winter 2001).
22. "Bill and keep" and "sender keep all" predate their ISP usage. Telecommunications carriers use these terms to refer to a traffic interconnection and routing arrangement in which no monetary transfer takes place. For example, two local-exchange carriers may agree to accept each other's traffic to expand their local toll-free geographical service area. Local-exchange carriers typically agree to hand off and receive traffic at a "meet point."
23. "NSF had already begun funding cooperative private-sector Internet research and development in 1986 and continued to do so on an increasingly large scale until 1995." A. Michael Froomkin, *Wrong Turn in Cyberspace: Using ICANN To Route Around the APA and the Constitution*, 50 DUKE L.J., 17, 19 (2000).
24. Even in policy-setting and standard-setting areas dominated by Netheads, the stakes and the complexity of the issues have created a need for specificity, permanence, and formality. *See, e.g.*, Jonathan Weinberg, *ICANN and the Problem of Legitimacy*, 50 DUKE L.J. 187 (2000); David G. Post, *Governing Cyberspace*, 43 WAYNE L. REV. 155, 157 (1996); David R. Johnson & David Post, *Law and Borders—The Rise of Law in Cyberspace*, 48 STAN. L. REV. 1367, 1367 (1996).
25. A safe harbor in this context refers to the opportunity for ventures to qualify for a regulatory classification that confers exemption from most government oversight that would otherwise apply.

26. The Telecommunications Act of 1996 defined information services and directed the FCC to give this classification limited regulatory oversight. An information service is defined as "the offering of a capability for generating, acquiring, storing, transforming, processing, retrieving, utilizing, or making available information via telecommunications, and includes electronic publishing, but does not include any use of any such capability for the management, control, or operation of a telecommunications system or the management of a telecommunications service." 47 U.S.C. § 153(20). "[T]he language and legislative history of . . . [the Telecommunications Act of 1996] indicate that the drafters . . . regarded telecommunications services and information services as mutually exclusive categories." Report to Congress, *Federal-State Joint Board on Universal Service,* 13 F.C.C.R. 11,501, 11,522–23 (1998). *See also* Vonage Holdings Corp. v. Minnesota Pub. Utils. Comm'n, 290 F. Supp.2d at 994, 1000 (2003) (applying the FCC's dichotomy). Although information service providers use telecommunications to transmit bitstreams, the FCC has chosen not to separate this functionality from the information processing that also occurs. In other words, the FCC considers telecommunications to be subordinate to and fully integrated with the predominant information service.
27. *See* Rob Frieden, *What Do Pizza Delivery and Information Services Have in Common? Lessons from Recent Judicial and Regulatory Struggles with Convergence,* 32 RUTGERS COMPUTER & TECH. L.J. 247 (2006).
28. *See* Milton Mueller, *ICANN and Internet Governance: Sorting Through the Debris of "Self-Regulation,"* 1 INFO., 497 (Dec. 1999) (arguing that Internet self-regulation involves policy issues subject to government regulation).
29. Tier 1 ISPs operating in the United States include AT&T, Verizon, and Sprint. *See* Mark Winther, IDC, *Tier 1 ISPs: What They Are and Why They Are Important* (May 2006).
30. *See, e.g.,* Fifth Report, *Inquiry Concerning the Deployment of Advanced Telecommunications Capability to All Americans in a Reasonable and Timely Fashion, and Possible Steps to Accelerate Such Deployment Pursuant to Section 706 of the Telecommunications Act of 1996,* 23 F.C.C.R. 9615 (2008); United States Department of Commerce, National Telecommunications and Information Administration, *Networked Nation: Broadband in America 2007* (Jan. 2008), http://www.ntia.doc.gov; Scott Wallsten, The Progress and Freedom Foundation, *Everything You Hear About Broadband in the U.S. Is Wrong,* Progress on Point, Release 14.13 (June 2007), http://www.pff.org.
31. *See, e.g.,* The Information Technology and Innovation Foundation, *2008 ITIF Broadband Rankings,* http://www.itif.org/files/2008BBRankings.pdf; Robert D. Atkinson, Daniel K. Correa & Julie A. Hedlund, The Information Technology and Innovation Foundation, *Explaining International Broadband Leadership* (2008), http: www.itif.org.

CHAPTER THREE. HOW THE UNITED STATES LOST ITS DIGITAL ADVANTAGE

1. *See* Organisation for Economic Co-operation and Development, Directorate for Science, Technology and Industry, *Broadband Portal,* http://www.oecd.org/sti/ict/broadband; John Windhausen, Jr., Educause, *A Blueprint for Big Broadband,* 19–25 (2008), http://net.educause.edu; John Horrigan, Pew Internet and American Life Project, *Home Broadband Adoption 2009,* http://www.pewinternet.org.
2. *See, e.g.,* Government of Chile, *Digital Strategies—2007–2012,* http://www.agendadigital.cl/; Government of New Zealand, *Digital Strategy—Creating Our Digital Future,* http://www.digitalstrategy.govt.nz/; Library and Archives, Canada, *The Digital Strategy,* Appendix II—International strategies and resources, http://collectionscanada.ca/cdis/; Canadian Radio-Television and Telecommunications Commission, *Internet and Broadband Availability,* http://www.crtc.gc.ca; Industry Canada, Maps of Broadband Distribution in Canada, http://www.broadband.gc.ca; Industry Canada, Broadband for Rural and Northern Development Pilot Program, http://www.broadband.gc.ca; National Satellite Initiative, http://www.broadband.gc.ca; United Nations Conference on Trade and Development, *Information Economy Report, 2007–2008* (United Nations, 2008), http://www.unctad.org; Partnership on Measuring ICT for Development, *The Global Information Society: A Statistical View* (United Nations, Apr. 2008), http://www.unctad.org; Bridge the Digital Divide, *Bridging the Digital Divide,* http://www.bridgethedigitaldivide.com/.
3. *See* Rob Frieden, *Killing with Kindness: Fatal Flaws in the $6.5 Billion Universal Service Funding Mission and What Should Be Done to Narrow the Digital Divide,* 24 CARDOZO ARTS & ENT. L.J., No. 2, 447 (2006).
4. The National Telecommunications and Information Administration explained why the scope of broadband access in places such as government offices and coffee shops meant that the OECD ranking underestimated market penetration. *See* http://www.ntia.doc.gov.
5. "We note that opponents of net neutrality regulation have pointed to evidence on a national scale that (1) access speeds are increasing, (2) prices (particularly speed-adjusted or quality adjusted prices) are falling, and (3) new entrants, including wireless and other competitors, are poised to challenge the incumbent cable and telephone companies. We note, too, that statistical research conducted by the FCC has tended to confirm these general trends." Federal Trade Commission, *Broadband Connectivity Competition Policy,* FTC Staff Report, 8 (June 2007), http://www.ftc.gov; Cabletechtalk, Blog site, *The Trouble with Broadband Deployment Statistics,* http://www.cabletechtalk.com.
6. Stephen Levy, *True or False: U.S.'s Broadband Penetration Is Lower Than Even Estonia's; Answer: True,* NEWSWEEK, July 9, 2007, at 58.
7. *See* Federal Communications Commission, Industry Analysis and Technology Division, Wireline Competition Bureau, *High-Speed Services for Internet Access: Status as of June 30, 2008* (July 2009).

8. The Telecommunications Act of 1996 established a process for eliminating line-of-business restrictions on the Bell companies in exchange for Bell companies allowing local exchange competitors access to their networks at favorable below-market rates. 47 U.S.C. 271(c) (2) (B).
9. *See* Order on Reconsideration, *Review of Section 251 Unbundling Obligations of Incumbent Local Exchange Carriers; Implementation of the Local Competition Provisions of the Telecommunications Act of 1996; Deployment of Wireline Services Offering Advanced Telecommunications Capability*, 19 F.C.C. R. 20,293 (2004); Memorandum Opinion and Order, *Petition for Forbearance of the Verizon Telephone Companies Pursuant to 47 U.S.C. § 160(c); SBC Communications Inc.'s Petition for Forbearance Under 47 U.S.C. § 160(c); Qwest Communications International Inc. Petition for Forbearance Under 47 U.S.C. § 160(c), BellSouth Telecommunications Inc. Petition for Forbearance Under 47 U.S.C. § 160(c)*, 19 F.C.C.R. 21,496 (2004).
10. *See* Rob Frieden, *Lies, Damn Lies and Statistics: Developing a Clearer Assessment of Market Penetration and Broadband Competition in the United States* 14 VA. J.L. & TECH. 100 (Summer 2009), http://www.vjolt.net.
11. "Because an incumbent LEC [local exchange carrier] currently serves virtually all subscribers in its local serving area, an incumbent LEC has little economic incentive to assist new entrants in their efforts to secure a greater share of that market. An incumbent LEC also has the ability to act on its incentive to discourage entry and robust competition by not interconnecting its network with the new entrant's network or by insisting on supracompetitive prices or other unreasonable conditions for terminating calls from the entrant's customers to the incumbent LEC's subscribers. Congress addressed these problems in the 1996 Act by mandating that the most significant economic impediments to efficient entry into the monopolized local market must be removed. The incumbent LECs have economies of density, connectivity, and scale; traditionally, these have been viewed as creating a natural monopoly. As we pointed out in our NPRM, the local competition provisions of the Act require that these economies be shared with entrants." *In Re Implementation of the Local Competition Provisions in the Telecommunications Act of 1996*, 11 F.C.C.R. 15,499, 15,508–09 (1996), *vacated in part sub nom.;* California v. FCC, 124 F.3d 934 (8th Cir. 1997), *rev'd in part sub nom.;* AT&T Corp. v. Iowa Utils. Bd., 525 U.S. 366 (1999), *aff'd in part, rev'd in part sub nom.;* Verizon Commc'ns Inc. v. FCC, 535 U.S. 467 (2002).
12. "In implementing the Act's prescription that rates for UNEs be based on cost, the FCC determined that costs should not be the embedded or historical costs of the network, but instead the total, forward-looking, incremental costs of providing each element (the 'TELRIC' method; the acronym stands for total, element, long-run, incremental costs). Properly implemented, this approach requires calculating the forward-looking economic value of each part ('element') of a network, which might appear to resemble the fair-value approach with all of its attendant difficulties. The FCC, however, developed

models of a hypothetical, most-efficient network to generate rates for UNEs instead of using cost data based on networks actually in place. State commissions followed the FCC's lead and similarly applied a hypothetical 'most-efficient technology' standard to assessment of network costs." Howard A. Shelanski, *Adjusting Regulation to Competition: Toward a New Model for U.S. Telecommunications Policy*, 24 YALE J. ON REG. 55, 79 (2007).

13. See Title II of the Communications Act of 1934, as amended, 47 U.S.C. §§ 201 *et seq*.
14. Verizon Commc'ns Inc. v. FCC, 535 U.S. 467, 122 S. Ct. 1646 (2002).
15. "The ECPR requires that the price of the wholesale service (unbundled network element) be set equal to the direct incremental cost of providing the wholesale service plus the net contribution foregone (opportunity cost) in not providing the downstream retail service." Dennis L. Weisman, *Did the High Court Reach an Economic Low in Verizon v. FCC?* 1 REV. OF NETWORK ECON. 90, 99 (Sept. 2002). *See also* Daniel F. Spulber & Christopher S. Yoo, *Access to Networks: Economic and Constitutional Connections*, 88 CORNELL L. REV. 885 (2003); William J. Baumol & J. Gregory Sidak, TOWARD COMPETITION IN LOCAL TELEPHONY 95 (MIT Press, 1994); Alfred E. Kahn & William E. Taylor, *The Pricing of Inputs Sold to Competitors: A Comment*, 11 YALE J. ON REG. 225 (1994); Jean-Jacques LaFont & Jean Tirole, *Access Pricing and Competition*, 38 EUR. ECON. REV. 1673 (1994); Alexander C. Larson & Dale E. Lehman, *Essentiality, Efficiency, and the Efficient Component-Pricing Rule*, 12 J. REG. ECON. 71 (1997); Robert D. Willig, William J. Baumol & Janusz A. Ordover, *Parity Pricing and Its Critics: A Necessary Condition for Efficiency in Provision of Bottleneck Services to Competitors*, 14 YALE J. ON REG. 145 (1997); J. Gregory Sidak & Daniel F. Spulber, *Deregulation and Managed Competition in Network Industries*, 15 YALE J. ON REG. 117 (1998).
16. "The pricing method favored by regulators is to set the input price equal to the incumbent's incremental cost with only a small mark-up for covering common costs. The underlying theory is that entrants would have difficulty competing if input prices were set according to the ECPR because entrants would be denied the opportunity to take retail profits from the incumbent. Furthermore, the ECPR is efficient only under strict assumptions, which do not apply in telecommunications." Mark A. Jamison, *Competition in Networking: Research Results and Implications for Further Reform*, 2002 L. REV. MICH. ST. U. DET. C.L. 621, 627; *see also* Nicholas Economides & Lawrence J. White, *Access and Interconnection Pricing: How Efficient Is the Efficient Component Pricing Rule?* 40 ANTITRUST BULL. 557 (1995); Nicholas Economides & Lawrence J. White, *The Inefficiency of the ECPR Yet Again: A Reply to Larson*, 43 ANTITRUST BULL. 429 (1998).
17. For example, on October 21, 2004, the Securities and Exchange Commission charged Qwest Communications International, one of the largest telecommunications companies in the United States, with securities fraud and other violations of the federal securities laws. The Commission lodged a complaint

alleging that between 1999 and 2002, Qwest fraudulently realized more than $3.8 billion in revenue and excluded $231 million in expenses as part of a scheme to meet revenue and earnings projections. It alleged that Qwest fraudulently characterized nonrecurring revenue from indefeasible rights of use and equipment transactions as recurring "data and Internet service revenues," thereby masking its declining financial condition and artificially inflating its stock price. The CEOs of MCI-WorldCom and Qwest were convicted of various crimes. Carrie Johnson, *Ebbers Gets 25-Year Sentence for Role in WorldCom Fraud,* THE WASHINGTON POST, July 14, 2005, at A1, http://www.washingtonpost.com; Dan Frosch, *Qwest's Nacchio Convicted of Insider Trading,* THE NEW YORK TIMES, Apr. 18, 2007, http://www.nytimes.com.

18. "This Galaxy 11, together with its cost of launch and insurance, represents an investment on our part in excess of $300 million. This is a high-risk–high-return business. It's not often that a company chooses to invest $300 million and finds out within hours if this investment pays off." Douglas Kahn, president and CEO of PanAmSat, quoted in Frederic Castel, Space.com, *Galaxy 11, Largest Commercial Satellite Ever, to Launch Tuesday,* Dec. 21, 1999, http://www.space.com.
19. See Rob Frieden, *Privatization of Satellite Cooperatives: Smothering a Golden Goose?* 36 VA. J. INT'L L. 1001 (Summer 1996).
20. Background on INTELSAT's privatization is available at: Kenneth Katkin, *Communication Breakdown? The Future of Global Connectivity After the Privatization of Intelsat,* 38 VAND. J. TRANSNAT'L L. 1323 (Nov. 2005).
21. *See* S. G. Sreejith, *Whither International Law, Thither Space Law: A Discipline in Transition,* 38 CAL. W. INT'L L.J. 331 (2008).
22. "INTELSAT left in place a small residual International Telecommunications Satellite Organization (ITSO). ITSO's primary charge is to ensure that the new owners of INTELSAT's former satellite system preserve global connectivity and continue to serve those poor or underserved countries that remain highly dependent on INTELSAT for international telecommunications service. ITSO, however, has no role in operating the privatized satellite system, nor any satellites of its own. Thus, for the first time since 1971, the sole public international organization charged with ensuring that every country on earth receives international telecommunications service lacks the technological facilities to provide the service itself. Instead, ITSO must rely entirely on political and legal tools to accomplish its mandate." Katkin, 38 VAND. J. TRANSNAT'L L. at 1326–1327.
23. *See* Robert M. Frieden, *International Telecommunications and the Federal Communications Commission,* 21 COLUM. J. TRANSNAT'L L. 423 (1983).
24. "To 'fill the gap' between its actual and projected revenue, Qwest, at the direction of its senior management, began selling indefeasible rights of use (IRUs). An IRU is an irrevocable right to use a specific fiber strand or specific amount of fiber capacity for a specified time period. Thus, to meet revenue expectations that it created, Qwest sold what the company had previously

identified in Commission filings and press releases as its 'principal asset.' When the demand for IRUs declined, Qwest engaged in IRU 'swaps' whereby Qwest bought IRUs from other companies in exchange for agreements from those companies to buy IRUs from Qwest." United States Securities and Exchange Commission, Litigation Release No. 18936, Oct. 21, 2004. *See also* Accounting and Auditing Enforcement Release No. 2127, Oct. 21, 2004; SEC v. Qwest Communications International Inc., Civil Action No. 04-Z-2179 (OES) (D. Co.); *SEC Charges Qwest Communications International Inc. with Multi-Faceted Accounting and Financial Reporting Fraud; Qwest Agrees to Anti-Fraud Injunction, $250 Million Penalty, and Maintain Permanently Chief Compliance Officer Reporting to the Outside Directors of the Board,* http://www.sec.gov/litigation/litreleases.

25. Simon Romero & Riva D. Atlas, *Worldcom's Collapse: The Overview; Worldcom Files for Bankruptcy; Largest U.S. Case,* THE NEW YORK TIMES, July 22, 2002.
26. Brooke A. Masters, *WorldCom's Convicted Jury Finds Former CEO Guilty on All Nine Counts,* THE WASHINGTON POST, Mar. 16, 2005, at A1.
27. Dan Frosch, *Qwest's Nacchio Convicted of Insider Trading,* THE NEW YORK TIMES, Apr. 18, 2007.
28. *See* Administrative Procedure Act, 5 U.S.C. §§ 551–559, 701–706, and 801–808.
29. 5 U.S.C. § 706(2) (A).
30. The FCC ordered incumbent local exchange wireline carriers to "unbundle" their local loop facilities, making it possible for market entrants to acquire only those access elements needed to provide a competitive service. *See* First Report and Order, *Implementation of the Local Competition Provisions in the Telecommunications Act of 1996,* 11 F.C.C.R. 15,499 (1996), *aff'd in part and rev'd in part,* AT&T Corp. v. Iowa Utils. Bd., 525 U.S. 366 (1999); *on remand,* Iowa Utils. Bd., v. FCC. 219 F.3d 744 (8th Cir. 2000); *aff'd in part and rev'd in part,* Verizon Commc'ns Inc. v. FCC, 535 U.S. 467 (2002); *see also* Third Report and Order and Fourth Further Notice of Proposed Rulemaking, *Implementation of the Local Competition Provisions of the Telecommunications Act of 1996,* 15 F.C.C.R. 3696, 16 F.C.C.R. 1724 (1999); *rev'd and remanded,* United States Telecomm. Ass'n v. FCC, 290 F.3d 415 (D.C. Cir. 2002); *see also* Report and Order and Order on Remand and Further Notice of Proposed Rulemaking, *Review of the Section 251 Unbundling Obligations of Incumbent Local Exchange Carriers, Implementation of the Local Competition Provisions of the Telecommunications Act of 1996, Deployment of Wireline Services Offering Advanced Telecommunications Capability,* 18 F.C.C.R. 16,978 (2003), *corrected by* Errata, 18 F.C.C.R. 19,020 (2003), *vacated and remanded in part, aff'd in part,* United States Telecomm. Ass'n v. FCC, 359 F.3d 554 (D.C. Cir. 2004), *on remand,* Order on Remand, *Unbundled Access to Network Elements, Review of the Section 251 Unbundling Obligations of Incumbent Local Exchange Carriers,* 20 F.C.C.R. 2533 (2005), *aff'd,* Covad Commc'ns Co. v. FCC, 450 F.3d 528 (D.C. Cir. 2006).

31. 47 U.S.C. § 251
32. 525 U.S. 366, 119 S. Ct. 721(1999).
33. 535 U.S. 467, 122 S. Ct. 1646 (2002).
34. "The incumbent carriers here are just like the electric utilities in Duquesne in failing to present any evidence that the decision to adopt TELRIC [i.e., compulsory pricing of local exchange service elements on the basis of quite low Total Element Long Run Incremental Costs] was arbitrary, opportunistic, or undertaken with a confiscatory purpose. What we do know is very much to the contrary." Verizon Commc'ns Inc. v. FCC, 535 U.S. 467, 527–528 (2002).
35. 535 U.S. at 500.
36. *Id.*
37. *See* Federal Communications Commission, Industry Analysis and Technology Division, Wireline Competition Bureau, *Local Telephone Competition: Status as of June 30, 2007*, Table 4, p. 8 (Mar. 2008).
38. *Id.*
39. *See* Chevron U.S.A. v. Natural Resources Defense Council, 467 U.S. 837 (1984).
40. United States v. Mead Corp., 533 U.S. 218, 226 (2001).
41. In Skidmore v. Swift & Co., 323 U.S. 134 (1944), the Supreme Court stated that where Congress has not expressly delegated interpretive authority to an agency, courts should give only limited deference to agency interpretations, depending upon the persuasiveness of that interpretation and the agency's degree of expertise.
42. 512 U.S. 218 (1994).
43. 47 U.S.C. § 203(2007).
44. 406 F.3d 689 (D.C. Cir. 2005).
45. 373 F.3d 372 (2004).
46. 5 U.S.C. § 551 *et seq.*
47. 373 F.3d at 397.
48. *Id.* at 402.
49. Courts "need not determine that the [agency's] reading . . . is the best possible reading, only that it was reasonable." Am. Fed'n of Gov't Employees, Local 446 v. Nicholson, 475 F.3d 341, 355 (D.C. Cir. 2007).
50. Other cases overturning the FCC on flawed fact finding or failure to justify its decisions include BellSouth Telecomm. Inc. v. FCC (D.C. Cir. 2006) (court reversed and remanded FCC finding that volume discount plan favored incumbent telephone company's affiliate over unaffiliated competitors); AT&T Inc. v. FCC (D.C. Cir. 2006) (court reversed the FCC's denial of a forbearance petition filed by SBC before its merger with AT&T on the grounds that part of what SBC sought was hypothetical); Verizon Telephone Cos. v. FCC (D.C. Cir. 2004) (court reversed FCC determination that telephone company abandoned legal argument for a forbearance request by a letter filed in a parallel proceeding).
51. Comcast Corp. v. FCC, 579 F.3d 1 (D.C. Cir. 2009).

52. *Id.* at 7.
53. *Id.*
54. *Id.*
55. "The Cable Television Consumer Protection and Competition Act of 1992 directed the FCC, "[i]n order to enhance effective competition," 47 U.S.C. § 533(f)(1), to prescrib[e] rules and regulations . . . [to] ensure that no cable operator or group of cable operators can unfairly impede, either because of the size of any individual operator or because of joint actions by a group of operators of sufficient size, the flow of video programming from the video programmer to the consumer. *Id.* § 533(f)(2)(A).
56. Comcast Corp. v. FCC, 579 F.3d at 8.
57. Ad Hoc Telecommunications Users Committee v. FCC, 572 F.3d 903 (D.C. Cir. 2009) (citing EarthLink Inc. v. FCC, 462 F.3d 1, 12 (D.C. Cir. 2006)).
58. Pacific Bell Telephone Co. v. Linkline Commc'ns Inc., 129 S. Ct. 1109 (2009).
59. 540 U.S. 398 (2004) (when the FCC refuses to provide a regulatory remedy authorized by law for allegedly anticompetitive conduct, an appellate court has no legal basis on which to apply antitrust remedies).
60. "DSL now faces robust competition from cable companies and wireless and satellite services." Pacific Bell Telephone Co. v. Linkline Commc'ns Inc., 129 S. Ct. at 1115.
61. "The challenge here focuses on retail prices—where there is no predatory pricing—and terms of dealing where there is no duty to deal." 129 S. Ct. at 1118. "If there is no duty to deal at the wholesale level and no predatory pricing at the retail level, then a firm is certainly not required to price *both* of these services in a manner that preserves its rivals' margins." *Id.* at 1120.
62. *Id.* at 1123.
63. 545 U.S. 967.
64. *See* Rob Frieden, *Neither Fish Nor Fowl: New Strategies for Selective Regulation of Information Services,* 6 J. TELECOMM. & HIGH TECH. L. 373 (2008).
65. 489 F.3d 1232 (D.C. Cir. 2007).
66. 47 U.S.C. § 254(d). The court supported the FCC's interpretation of the law to permit the Commission to require contributions from providers of telecommunications, including ones combining telecommunication with other information services, rather than be limited solely to ventures that offer telecommunications or telecommunications services.
67. *See, e.g.,* North Carolina Utils. Comm'n v. FCC, 537 F.2d 787 (4th Cir. 1976), *cert. denied,* 429 U.S. 1027 (1976); North Carolina Utils. Comm'n v. FCC, 552 F.2d 1036 (4th Cir. 1977) *cert. denied,* 434 U.S. 874 (1977) (upholding FCC preemption of state regulation because it was not possible to separate the interstate and intrastate components of the asserted FCC regulation); New York State Comm'n on Cable Television v. FCC, 749 F.2d 804 (D.C. Cir. 1984) (affirming FCC order preempting state and local entry regulation of Satellite Master Antenna Television); Nat'l Ass'n of Regulatory Util. Comm'rs v. FCC, 525 F.2d 630 (D.C. Cir. 1976) *cert. denied,* 425 U.S. 992

(1976); Virgin Islands Tel. Co. v. FCC, 198 F.3d 921 (D.C. Cir. 1999) (federal preemption of states on the determination of what constitutes common carriage and whether non-common carriers may secure interconnection with common carriers).

68. In Verizon Commc'ns Inc. v. Law Offices of Curtis V. Trinko, 540 U.S. 398, 124 S. Ct. 872 (2004), the Supreme Court determined that the FCC's statutory authority to examine antitrust issues was so comprehensive that courts would not have any grounds to consider cases seeking greater regulatory intervention. *See also* Nicholas Economides, *Hit and Miss: Leverage, Sacrifice, and Refusal to Deal in the Supreme Court Decision in Trinko,* VAND. J. ENT. & TECH. L. 121 (2007); Daniel F. Spulber, *Mandating Access to Telecom and the Internet: The Hidden Side of Trinko,* 107 COLUM. L. REV. 1822 (2007); Spencer Weber Waller, *Microsoft and Trinko: A Tale of Two Courts,* 2006 Utah L. Rev. 741 (2006); Adam Candeub, *Trinko and Re-grounding the Refusal to Deal Doctrines,* 66 U. PITT. L. REV. 821 (2005).

69. Second Report and Order, *Truth-in-Billing and Billing Format, National Association of State Utility Consumer Advocates' Petition for Declaratory Ruling Regarding Truth-in-Billing,* 20 F.C.C.R. 6448 (2005), *partially reversed,* Nat'l Ass'n of State Utility Consumer Advocates v. FCC, 457 F.3d 1238 (11th Cir.2006)(conclude that the FCC exceeded its authority when it prevented the states from requiring or prohibiting the use of wireless carrier billing line items), *opinion modified on denial of rehearing,* Nat'l Ass'n of State Utility Consumer Advocates v. FCC, 468 F.3d 1272(11th Cir. 2006).

CHAPTER FOUR. CASE STUDIES IN WRONGHEADED POLICYMAKING

1. *See* Harvey Zuckman, Robert Corn-Revere, Rob Frieden & Charles Kennedy, MODERN COMMUNICATIONS LAW (West Group, 1999).
2. Administrative Procedure Act, 5 U.S.C. §§ 1001–1011.
3. Chevron U.S.A. Inc. v. Natural Res. Def. Council Inc., 467 U.S. 837 (1984). "If a statute is ambiguous, and if the implementing agency's construction is reasonable, *Chevron* requires a federal court to accept the agency's construction of the statute, even if the agency's reading differs from what the court believes is the best statutory interpretation." Nat'l Cable & Telecomm. Ass'n v. Brand X Internet Servs., 545 U.S. 967, 980 (2005) 980 (citing *Chevron,* 467 U.S. at 843–44, n.11).
4. Nat'l Cable & Telecomm. Ass'n v. Brand X Internet Servs., 545 U.S. at 982.
5. 47 U.S.C. § 151. *See* J. Steven Rich, *Brand X and the Wireline Broadband Report and Order: The Beginning of the End of the Distinction Between Title I and Title II Services,* 58 FED. COMM. L.J. 221 (2006).
6. "Ancillary jurisdiction may be employed, in the Commission's discretion, when Title I of the Act gives the Commission subject matter jurisdiction over the service to be regulated and the assertion of jurisdiction is 'reasonably ancillary to the effective performance of [its] various responsibilities.'" First Re-

port and Order and Notice of Proposed Rulemaking, *IP-Enabled Services; E911 Requirements for IP-Enabled Service Providers*, 20 F.C.C.R. 10,245, 10,261 (2005), *citing* United States v. Sw. Cable Co., 392 U.S. 157, 177–178 (1968); United States v. Midwest Video Corp., 406 U.S. 649, 667–668 (1972); FCC v. Midwest Video Corp., 440 U.S. 689, 700 (1979).

7. "Regulatory lag creates the danger that restrictions will persist long after the conditions that justified their imposition have dissipated." Christopher Yoo, *Beyond Network Neutrality*, 19 HARV. J. L. & Tech. 1, 11 (2005). Regulatory lag also can benefit regulated ventures when delays in regulatory adjustments allow firms to accrue excessive profits through the "inevitable delay that regulation imposes in the downward adjustment of rate levels that produce excessive rates of return and in the upward adjustments ordinarily called for if profits are too low." Alfred E. Kahn, THE ECONOMICS OF REGULATION: PRINCIPLES AND INSTITUTIONS, Vol. II, 48 (MIT Press, 1988).
8. *See* William Baumol, John Panzar & Robert Willig, CONTESTABLE MARKETS AND THE THEORY OF INDUSTRY STRUCTURE (Harcourt Brace Jovanovich, 1982). "In economic theory, a contestable market is one in which there are no sunk costs. A sunk cost is an initial investment that cannot be recovered if the firm decides to leave the market. In a contestable market, the mere threat of entry is sufficient to prevent monopolistic behavior—actual entry need not occur. Broadband access markets are not contestable because entrants must make substantial investments that may never be recovered. The mere possibility of entry, therefore, is unlikely to control market power fully. Instead, such control must occur as a result of actual entry, a credible investment-backed commitment to enter, or the possibility of entry by a competitor possessing some advantage over the incumbents." Jerry Brito & Jerry Ellig, *A Tale of Two Commissions: Net Neutrality and Regulatory Analysis*, 16 COMMLAW CONSPECTUS 1, 22 (2007).
9. Under the spectrum cap, no entity could control more than forty-five megahertz of spectrum used for commercial wireless telecommunications services in any single urban metropolitan area, or more than fifty-five megahertz in rural locales. In November 2001, however, the FCC decided to raise the spectrum cap to fifty-five megahertz in all markets effective February 13, 2002, and to eliminate the restriction entirely effective January 1, 2003. *See* Report and Order, *2000 Biennial Regulatory Review Spectrum Aggregation Limits for Commercial Mobile Radio Services*, 16 F.C.C.R. 22,668 (2001).
10. Memorandum Opinion and Order and Report and Order, *Applications for Consent to the Transfer of Control of Licenses XM Satellite Radio Holdings Inc. Transferor to Sirius Satellite Radio Inc. Transferee*, 23 F.C.C.R. 12,348 (2008).
11. Prometheus Radio Project v. FCC 373 F.3d 372, 415 (3rd Cir. 2004).
12. J. Scott Marcus & Dieter Elixmann, *Regulatory Approaches to NGNs: An International Comparison*, 69 COMM. STRATEGIES, 19, 34 (2008).
13. *See* Industry Analysis and Technology Division, Wireline Competition Bu-

reau, *Trends in Telephone Service,* Chapter 15, Revenues (Aug. 2008). *See also* Alexander Belinfante, Industry Analysis and Technology Division, Wireline Competition Bureau, *Telephone Subscribership in the United States (Data Through July 2008).*

14. *See, e.g.,* United States House of Representatives, Committee on Energy and Commerce, Majority Staff Report, *Deception and Distrust: The Federal Communications Commission Under Chairman Kevin J. Martin,* 110th Congress (Dec. 2008).
15. § 706(b) of the Telecommunications Act of 1996, Pub. L. 104-104, 110 Stat. 56 (1996) (1996 Act), *codified at* 47 U.S.C. § 1302.
16. The term "advanced telecommunications capability" is defined, "without regard to any transmission media or technology, as high-speed, switched, broadband telecommunications capability that enables users to originate and receive high-quality voice, data, graphics, and video telecommunications using any technology." *See* § 706(c) of the Telecommunications Act of 1996.
17. Center for Public Integrity v. FCC, 505 F.Supp.2d 106 (D.D.C. 2007), *recon. denied,* 515 F.Supp.2d 167 (D.D.C. 2007).
18. *See, e.g.,* S. Derek Turner, Free Press, *"Shooting the Messenger" Myth vs. Reality: U.S. Broadband Policy and International Broadband Rankings* (July 2007), http://www.freepress.net.
19. Notice of Inquiry, *Inquiry Concerning the Deployment of Advanced Telecommunications Capability to All Americans in a Reasonable and Timely Fashion, and Possible Steps to Accelerate Such Deployment Pursuant to Section 706 of the Telecommunications Act of 1996,* 22 F.C.C.R. 7816 (2007).
20. United States Department of Commerce, National Telecommunications and Information Administration, *Networked Nation: Broadband in America 2007* (Jan. 2008), http://www.ntia.doc.gov.
21. "This country needs a national goal for . . . the spread of broadband technology. We ought to have . . . universal, affordable access for broadband technology by the year 2007, and then we ought to make sure as soon as possible thereafter, consumers have got plenty of choices when it comes to [their] broadband carrier." President George W. Bush, *Promoting Innovation and Economic Security Through Broadband Technology* (2004).
22. *See* Report and Order and Further Notice of Proposed Rulemaking, *Deployment of Nationwide Broadband Data to Evaluate Reasonable and Timely Deployment of Advanced Services to All Americans, Improvement of Wireless Broadband Subscribership Data, and Development of Data on Interconnected Voice over Internet Protocol (VoIP) Subscribership,* 23 F.C.C.R. 9691 (2008); Fifth Report, *Development of Nationwide Broadband Data to Evaluate Reasonable and Timely Deployment of Advanced Services to All Americans, Improvement of Wireless Broadband Subscribership Data, and Development of Data on Interconnected Voice over Internet Protocol (VoIP) Subscribership,* 23 F.C.C.R. 9615 (2008) [hereinafter cited as Fifth Broadband Report to Congress].
23. Fifth Broadband Report to Congress at 9652.

24. Order on Reconsideration, *Review of Section 251 Unbundling Obligations of Incumbent Local Exchange Carriers; Implementation of the Local Competition Provisions of the Telecommunications Act of 1996; Deployment of Wireline Services Offering Advanced Telecommunications Capability*, 19 F.C.C.R. 20,293 (2004).
25. Report and Order and Further Notice of Proposed Rulemaking, *Implementation of Section 621(a)(1) of the Cable Communications Policy Act of 1984 as Amended by the Cable Television Consumer Protection and Competition Act of 1992*, 22 F.C.C.R. 5101 (2007).
26. Declaratory Ruling, *Time Warner Cable Request for Declaratory Ruling That Competitive Local Exchange Carriers May Obtain Interconnection Under Section 251 of the Communications Act of 1934, as Amended, to Provide Wholesale Telecommunications Services to VoIP Providers,* WC Docket No. 06–55, Memorandum Opinion and Order, 22 F.C.C.R. 3513 (2007).
27. *See, e.g.*, Link Hoewing, Verizon PolicyBlog, *More Americans Getting More and Better Broadband* (May 14, 2008), http://policyblog.verizon.com.
28. *See, e.g.*, George S. Ford, Thomas M. Koutsky & Lawrence J. Spiwak, Phoenix Center for Advanced Legal and Economic Public Policy Studies, *The Broadband Efficiency Index: What Really Drives Broadband Adoption Across the OECD?* Policy Paper No. 33 (May 2008), http://www.phoenix-center.org.
29. Federal Communications Commission, Media Bureau, *Report on the Packaging and Sale of Video Programming Services to the Public* (Nov. 18, 2004).
30. Federal Communications Commission, Media Bureau, *Further Report on the Packaging and Sale of Video Programming Services to the Public* (Feb. 9, 2006).
31. *Id.* at 3.
32. 47 U.S.C. § 612.
33. Comcast Corp. v. FCC, 579 F.3d 1 (D.C. Cir. 2009).
34. Public Notice, *FCC Adopts 13th Annual Report to Congress on Video Competition*, and Notice of Inquiry for the 14th Annual Report (Nov. 27, 2007).
35. *See* Letter from Kirk S. Burgee, Associate Bureau Chief, Wireline Competition Bureau, Federal Communications Commission, to Drew Clark, Senior Fellow and Project Manager, The Center for Public Integrity, Sept. 26, 2006, at 2, http://www.publicintegrity.org. A reviewing court affirmed the FCC's determination. Ctr. for Pub. Integrity v. Fed. Communications Comm'n., 515 F.Supp.2d 167 (D.D.C. 2007).
36. Report on Cable Industry Prices, *Implementation of Section 3 of the Cable Television Consumer Protection and Competition Act of 1992, Statistical Report on Average Rates for Basic Service, Cable Programming Service, and Equipment*, 21 F.C.C.R. 15,087 (2006). The average monthly charge for basic service increased by 3.3 percent, rising from $13.84 on January 1, 2004, to $14.30 on January 1, 2005. Over the same period, the average charge for expanded basic service rose from $27.07 to $28.74, an increase of 6.2 percent. The Commission reported that more than 84 percent of cable consumers subscribed to the expanded basic service.

37. Second Report and Order, *Implementation of Section 304 of the Telecommunications Act of 1996, Commercial Availability of Navigation Devices,* 20 F.C.C.R. 6794 (2005).
38. Second Report and Order, *Implementation of Section 621(a) (1) of the Cable Communications Policy Act of 1984 as Amended by the Cable Television Consumer Protection and Competition Act of 1992,* 22 F.C.C.R. 19,633 (2007).
39. Report and Order and Further Notice of Proposed Rulemaking, *Exclusive Service Contracts for Provision of Video Services in Multiple Dwelling Units and Other Real Estate Developments,* 22 F.C.C.R. 20,235 (2007) [hereinafter cited as Exclusive MDU Contract Bar].
40. 47 U.S.C. § 548. The FCC also invoked its ancillary jurisdiction under Title I of the Communications Act. "Although we believe that we have specific statutory authority to adopt this prohibition, as described above, we note that our ancillary authority, under titles I and III of the 1934 Act, also provides a sufficient basis to prohibit cable operators from enforcing or executing exclusivity clauses for the provision of video service to MDUs." Exclusive MDU Contract Bar, 22 F.C.C.R. at 20,260.
41. Exclusive MDU Contract Bar, 22 F.C.C.R. at 20,243.
42. *Id.* 22 F.C.C.R. at 20,248.
43. *Id.* 22 F.C.C.R. at 20,249.
44. *Id.* 22 F.C.C.R. at 20,251.
45. "(1) the economic impact of the regulation on the claimant; (2) the extent to which the regulation has interfered with distinct investment-backed expectations; and (3) the character of the governmental action." Connolly v. Pension Ben. Guaranty Corp., 475 U.S. 211, 224–225 (1986).
46. Exclusive MDU Contract Bar, 22 F.C.C.R. at 20,262.
47. Report and Order and Further Notice of Proposed Rulemaking, *Leased Commercial Access,* 23 F.C.C.R. 2909 (2008).
48. *Id.* at 68.
49. *Id.* at 71–73, *citing* Time Warner Entertainment Co., L.P. v. FCC, 93 F.3d 957 (D.C. Cir. 1996).
50. Time Warner Entertainment Co. v. FCC, 240 F.3d 1126 (D.C. Cir. 2001). The lawfulness of having a horizontal ownership cap passed muster with a reviewing court. *See* Time Warner Entertainment Co. v. United States, 211 F.3d 1313 (D.C. Cir. 2000).
51. Fourth Report and Order and Further Notice of Proposed Rulemaking, *The Commission's Cable Horizontal and Vertical Ownership Limits, MM 92–264,* 23 F.C.C.R. 2134 (2008) [hereinafter cited as Fourth Cable Horizontal and Vertical Ownership Cap Order], *vacated* Comcast Corp. v. FCC, 579 F.3d 1 (D.C. Cir. 2009).
52. Section 613(f) of the 1992 Cable Act, *codified at* 47 U.S.C. § 533(f) (2) (A), directs the FCC to conduct proceedings to establish reasonable limits on the number of subscribers a cable operator may serve ("horizontal limit") and

the number of channels a cable operator may devote to its affiliated programming networks ("vertical" or "channel occupancy" limit).

53. Fourth Cable Horizontal and Vertical Ownership Cap Order at 12.
54. *Id.* at 70.
55. *Id.* at 71.
56. Comcast Corp. v. FCC, 579 F.3d 1 (D.C. Cir. 2009).
57. *Id.* 579 F.3d at 7.
58. Report and Order and Further Notice of Proposed Rulemaking, *Implementation of Section 621(a) (1) of the Cable Communications Policy Act of 1984 as amended by the Cable Television Consumer Protection and Competition Act of 1992*, 22 F.C.C.R. 5101 (2007), Second Report and Order, 22 F.C.C.R. 19,633 (2007), *aff'd* Alliance for Community Media v. FCC, 529 F.3d 763 (6th Cir. 2008).
59. 47 U.S.C. § 541(a) (1).
60. Cable Franchise Preemption Order, 22 F.C.C.R. at 5102. The FCC also stated its belief "that, absent Commission action, deployment of competitive video services by new cable entrants will continue to be unreasonably delayed or, at worst, derailed. Accordingly, we adopt incremental measures directed to LFA-controlled franchising processes. . . ." *Id.* 22 F.C.C.R. at 5110.
61. *Id.* at 5103.
62. *Id. citing* USTA v. FCC, 359 F.3d 554, 579–80 (D.C. Cir. 2004).
63. "The Communications Act preserves a role for local jurisdictions in the franchise process. We do not believe that the rules we adopt today will hamper the franchising process." Cable Franchise Preemption Order 22 F.C.C.R. at 5132.
64. The section requires the Commission to "adopt regulations to assure the commercial availability, to consumers of multichannel video programming and other services offered over multichannel video programming systems, of converter boxes, interactive communications equipment, and other equipment used by consumers to access multichannel video programming and other services offered over multichannel video programming systems, from manufacturers, retailers, and other vendors not affiliated with any multichannel video programming distributor." 47 U.S.C. § 549(a).
65. Memorandum Opinion and Order, *Consolidated Requests for Waiver of Section 76.1204(a) (1) of the Commission's Rules*, 22 F.C.C.R. 11,780 (2007) *citing* S. REP. 104–230, at 181 (1996) (Conf. Rep.); Bellsouth Interactive Media Services, LLC, 19 F.C.C.R. 15,607, 15,608 (2004).
66. Order and Further Notice of Proposed Rulemaking, *Implementation of Section 304 of the Telecommunications Act of 1996: Commercial Availability of Navigation Devices*, 18 F.C.C.R Rcd 7924, 7926 (2003); Second Report and Order, 20 F.C.C.R. 6794, 6802–03 (2005) *pet. for review denied*, Charter Commc'ns Inc. v. FCC, 460 F.3d 31 (D.C. Cir. 2006).
67. CableCard users can deencrypt received content but cannot access features

such as EPGs, VOD, PPV, and other ITV capabilities provided by cable operators that require an upstream, bidirectional system. CableCard users typically have to order on-demand services via the telephone.

68. "OCAP is a middleware software layer (based on the Java Execution Engine), which allows software developers to write applications and programs that would run on any OCAP-enabled device." Third Further Notice of Proposed Rulemaking, *Implementation of Section 304 of the Telecommunications Act of 1996*, CS Docket No. 97–80, *Commercial Availability of Navigation Devices, Compatibility Between Cable Systems and Consumer Electronics Equipment*, 22 F.C.C.R. 12,024, 12,026 (2007).

69. *Id.*

70. Use of the Carterfone Device in Message Toll Telephone Service, 13 FCC 2d 420 (1968), *recon. denied*, 14 FCC 2d 571 (1968) [hereinafter cited as *Carterfone*]; *see also* Telerent Leasing Corp., 45 FCC 2d 204 (1974), *aff'd sub nom.* North Carolina Utils. Comm'n v. FCC, 537 F.2d 787 (4th Cir. 1976), *cert. denied*, 429 U.S. 1027 (1976); Mebane Home Telephone Co., 53 FCC 2d 473 (1975), *aff'd sub nom.* Mebane Home Telephone Co. v. FCC, 535 F.2d 1324 (D.C. Cir. 1976); Public Utility Comm'n of Texas v. FCC, 886 F. 2d 1325 (D.C. Cir. 1989) (noting long-established FCC policy that carriers and non-carriers alike have a federal right to interconnect to the public telephone network in ways that are privately beneficial as long as they are not publicly detrimental). Previous FCC opposition to this principle failed to pass muster with a reviewing court that interpreted the Communications Act as mandating the right of consumers to attach equipment to the network in ways that were privately beneficial but not publicly harmful. Hush-A-Phone Corp. v. U.S., 238 F. 2d 266 (D.C. Cir. 1956).

71. "Part 68 of the FCC rules (47 C.F.R. Part 68) governs the direct connection of Terminal Equipment (TE) to the Public Switched Telephone Network (PSTN), and to wireline carrier-owned facilities used to provide private line services. Part 68 also contains rules concerning Hearing Aid Compatibility and Volume Control (HAC/VC) for telephones, dialing frequency for automated dialing machines, source identification for fax transmissions, and technical criteria for inside wiring." Federal Communications Commission, *Part 68 Home Page*, http://www.fcc.gov/wcb/iatd/part_68.html. *See also* Second Report and Order, *Detariffing the Installation and Maintenance of Inside Wiring*, 51 Fed. Reg. 8498 (Mar. 12, 1986), *recon.*, 1 F.C.C.R. 1190 (1986), *further recon.*, 3 F.C.C.R. 1719 (1988), *partially remanded sub nom.* Nat'l Ass'n Reg. Utils. Comm'rs v. FCC, 880 F.2d 422 (D.C.Cir.1989); *on remand*, Second Further Notice of Proposed Rulemaking, *Detariffing the Installation and Maintenance of Inside Wiring*, 5 F.C.C.R. 3407 (1990), *partially modified*, 7 F.C.C.R. 1334 (1992).

72. Skype Communications S.A.R.L., *Petition to Confirm a Consumer's Right to Use Internet Communications Software and Attach Devices to Wireless Networks*, submitted Feb. 20, 2007.

73. Google's interest in wireless net neutrality appears to stem from its possible interest in using wireless spectrum and in offering a wireless handset to promote greater access to its Internet services. *See* Google Public Policy Blog, *Network Neutrality*, http://googlepublicpolicy.blogspot.com.
74. *Carterfone*, 13 F.C.C.R. at 14,778. "The competitive market for consumer equipment in the telephone context provides the model of a market we have sought to emulate in this proceeding. Previously, consumers leased telephones from their service provider and no marketplace existed for those wishing to purchase their own phone. The *Carterfone* decision allowed consumers to connect CPE to the telephone network if the connections did not cause harm. As a result of *Carterfone* and other Commission actions, ownership of telephones moved from the network operator to the consumer. As a result, the choice of features and functions incorporated into a telephone has increased substantially, while the cost of equipment has decreased." *Id.* 13 F.C.C.R. at 14,780.
75. "A shortsighted and often just plain stupid federal government has allowed itself to be bullied and fooled by a handful of big wireless phone operators for decades now. And the result has been a mobile phone system that is the direct opposite of the PC model. It severely limits consumer choice, stifles innovation, crushes entrepreneurship, and has made the U.S. the laughingstock of the mobile-technology world, just as the cellphone is morphing into a powerful hand-held computer. . . . That's why I refer to the big cellphone carriers as the 'Soviet ministries.' Like the old bureaucracies of communism, they sit athwart the market, breaking the link between the producers of goods and services and the people who use them." Walt Mossberg, All Things Digital Blog, *Free My Phone* (Oct. 21, 2007), http://mossblog.allthingsd.com.
76. "Cellphones and cellphone services made news with amazing frequency, making it clear that this service-we-love-to-hate is still in its crude Neanderthal age. . . . No matter how depressed you get about the state of the world, you have to have faith in one thing: when things swing out of control, the public has a way of setting things straight. . . . [T]he latest public pushback concerns evil cellphone-carrier greediness." David Pogue, Pogue's Posts Blog, *The Year of the Cellphone* (Dec. 13, 2007), http://pogue.blogs.nytimes.com.
77. "Of the 1.4 million iPhones sold so far (of which 1,119,000 were sold in the quarter ending Sept. 30), [Apple Chief Operating Officer Timothy] Cook estimated that 250,000 were sold to people who wanted to unlock them from the AT&T network and use them with another carrier." Saul Hansell, Bits Blog site, *Apple: $100 Million Spent on Potential iBricks*, NEW YORK TIMES (Oct. 22, 2007), http://bits.blogs.nytimes.com. "You bought the iPhone, you paid for it, but now Apple is telling you how you have to use it, and if you don't do things the way they say, they're going to lock it. Turn it into a useless 'brick.' Is this any way to treat a customer? Apparently, it's the Steve Jobs way.

But some iPhone users are mad as heck, and they're not going to take it anymore." Alexander Wolfe, Wolfe's Den Blog, *Apple Users Talking Class-Action Lawsuit over iPhone Locking,* http://www.information week.com.

78. "The benefits of competition have been observed in a great variety of markets through centuries of experience. We ourselves have observed such tangible benefits in telecommunications equipment markets after our Carterfone decision effectively opened such markets to competition. In Docket No. 20003—a broad fact-finding inquiry into the economic implications and relationships arising from regulatory policies and pricing practices for telecommunications services and facilities subject to competition—we concluded that 'consumer inter-connection has benefited the general public by speeding innovation and meeting needs that were unmet prior to the introduction of customer provided equipment.'" Report and Third Supplemental Notice of Inquiry and Proposed Rulemaking, *MTS and WATS Market Structure,* 81 F.C.C.2d 177, ¶ 106 (1980).
79. "The carrier retail channel still accounts for the large majority of wireless sales; however, the distribution support provided by indirect channel partners keeps getting stronger. . . . Verizon Wireless has been shifting focus to its own retail outlets that account for 65% of new sales." A. Greengart & B. Akyuz, Current Analysis, *Consumer Handsets, Mobile Devices—U.S.,* 2–3 (2006), http://www.currentanalysis.com.
80. For example, the major cable television companies own ventures creating video programming as well as ventures that distribute video programming to consumers. "Vertical relationships may have beneficial effects, or they may deter competitive entry in the video marketplace and/or limit the diversity of programming." Twelfth Annual Report, *Annual Assessment of the Status of Competition in the Market for the Delivery of Video Programming,* 21 F.C.C.R. 2503, 2575 (2006). "Beneficial effects can include efficiencies in the production, distribution, and marketing of video programming, and providing incentives to expand channel capacity and create new programming by lowering the risks associated with program production ventures." *Id.* at n.565. "Possible detrimental effects can include unfair methods of competition, discriminatory conduct, and exclusive contracts that are the result of coercive activity." *Id.* at n.566.
81. Report and Order and Notice of Proposed Rulemaking, *Implementation of the Cable Television Consumer Protection and Competition Act of 1992,* 22 F.C.C.R. 17,791 (2007).
82. "[W]e find that the exclusive contract prohibition continues to be necessary to preserve and protect competition and diversity in the distribution of video programming, and accordingly, retain it again for five years, until October 5, 2012." *Id.* at 17,792
83. "What is most significant to our analysis is not the percentage of total available programming that is vertically integrated with cable operators, but rather the popularity of the programming that is vertically integrated and

how the inability of competitive MVPDs to access this programming will affect the preservation and protection of competition in the video distribution marketplace. While there has been a decrease since 2002 in the percentage of the most popular programming networks that are vertically integrated, we find that the four largest cable MSOs (Comcast, Time Warner, Cox, and Cablevision) still have an interest in six of the Top 20 satellite-delivered networks as ranked by subscribership, seven of the Top 20 satellite-delivered networks as ranked by prime time ratings, almost half of all RSNs, popular subscription premium networks, such as HBO and Cinemax, and video-on-demand ("VOD") networks, such as iN DEMAND." *Id.* at 17,815.

84. "An exclusive arrangement between a cable-affiliated programmer and its affiliated cable operator will reduce the number of platforms distributing the cable-affiliated programming network and thus the total number of subscribers to the network. This results in a reduction in potential advertising or subscription revenues that would otherwise be available to the network. In the long term, however, the cable-affiliated programmer would gain from an increased number of subscribers as customers switch to the affiliated cable distribution service in order to receive the exclusive programming. Thus, an exclusive contract is a kind of 'investment,' in which an initial loss of profits from programming is incurred in order to achieve higher profits later from increased cable distribution. This type of arrangement is most profitable when the costs of the investment are low and its benefits are high." *Id.* at 17,821.
85. "We find that access to vertically integrated programming is essential for new entrants in the video marketplace to compete effectively. If the programming offered by a competitive MVPD lacks 'must have' programming that is offered by the incumbent cable operator, subscribers will be less likely to switch to the competitive MVPD. We give little weight to the claims by cable operators that recent entrants, such as telephone companies, have not experienced 'any trouble' to date in acquiring access to satellite-delivered vertically integrated programming." *Id.* at 17,819.
86. *Id.* "[W]e conclude that there are no good substitutes for some satellite-delivered vertically integrated programming and that such programming therefore remains necessary for viable competition in the video distribution market." *Id.* at 1810.
87. Leslie Cauley, *AT&T Eager to Wield Its iWeapon,* USA TODAY, May 21, 2007 http://www.usatoday.com (displaying statistics compiled by Forrester Research). In mid-2008, the top four carriers controlled 88.1 percent of the wireless telecommunications market. Verizon's acquisition of Alltel Wireless raised the total market penetration of the top four carriers to about 90 percent and over 54 percent for the top two carriers.
88. Digital subscriber lines provide Internet access via the copper wires initially used solely to provide narrowband telephone service. Telephone companies retrofit the wires to provide medium-speed broadband services by expanding

the available bandwidth by about fifteen hundred kilohertz. The FCC provides the following definition: "Digital Subscriber Line is a technology for bringing high-speed and high-bandwidth, which is directly proportional to the amount of data transmitted or received per unit time, information to homes and small businesses over ordinary copper telephone lines already installed in hundreds of millions of homes and businesses worldwide. With DSL, consumers and businesses take advantage of having a dedicated, always-on connection to the Internet." Federal Communications Commission, *FCC Consumer Facts: Broadband Access for Consumers,* http://www.fcc.gov/cgb/consumerfacts/dsl2.html.

89. Horizontal integration occurs when a single company develops, or acquires firms offering the capability of providing, two or more services that may compete in the same relevant market. For example, a major newspaper chain may diversify by developing cable television programming or acquire companies that produce such content. Horizontal integration also describes situations where a venture acquires an existing or potential competitor. While such a combination might reduce existing or potential competition, the FCC believes that the merger can diversify available content so that the acquiring firm can offer new, niche programming. "With respect to horizontal integration of a major and an emerging television network, the merger should have little or no adverse effect on competition or pricing in the market for television network advertising, since major and emerging networks compete in different strategic groups. To the extent that the emerging network continues to offer programming following the merger that targets niche or special interest audiences, then the welfare of viewers of both mass audience and niche programming should not be adversely affected by the merger and may indeed be advanced by the resulting efficiencies." Report and Order, *Amendment of Section 73.658(G) of the Commission's Rules—The Dual Network Rule,* 16 F.C.C.R. 11,114, 11,125 (2001).

90. Traditional phone companies "are primed to offer a 'triple play' of voice, high-speed Internet access, and video services over their respective networks." Notice of Proposed Rulemaking, *Exclusive Service Contracts for Provision of Video Services in Multiple Dwelling Units and Other Real Estate Developments,* 22 F.C.C.R. 5935, 5938 (2007).

91. A quadruple play is the combination of "video, broadband Internet access, VoIP and wireless service. . . ." Memorandum Opinion and Order, *AT&T Inc. and Bellsouth Corporation Application for Transfer of Control,* 22 F.C.C.R. 5662, 5735 (2007).

92. Alexander Belinfante, *Telephone Subscribership in the United States (Data Through November 2007),* Table 1, Household telephone subscribership in the United States (Mar. 2008), http://hraunfoss.fcc.gov/edocs_public/attachmatch/DOC-280980A1.pdf.

93. Roger Cheng, *Vonage's Loss Narrows but Subscriber Growth Slows,* THE WALL STREET JOURNAL, May 9, 2008, at B4.

94. *See* Rob Frieden, *Neither Fish Nor Fowl: New Strategies for Selective Regulation of Information Services,* 6 J. TELECOMM. & HIGH TECH. L., No. 2, 373 (2008).
95. Report and Order and Notice of Proposed Rulemaking, *Universal Service Contribution Methodology,* 21 F.C.C.R. 7518 (2006) (extending section 254(d) permissive authority to require interconnected VoIP providers to contribute to USF), *pet. for rev. denied and vacated in part on other grounds,* Vonage Holding Corp. v. FCC, 489 F.3d 1232 (D.C. Cir. 2007).
96. First Report and Order and Further Notice of Proposed Rulemaking, *Communications Assistance for Law Enforcement Act and Broadband Access and Services,* 20 F.C.C.R. 14,989, 15,001 (2005) (citations omitted), *aff'd,* American Council on Education v. FCC, 451 F.3d 226 (D.C. Cir. 2006).
97. First Report and Order and Notice of Proposed Rulemaking, *IP-Enabled Services; E911 Requirements for IP-Enabled Service Providers,* 20 F.C.C.R. 10,245 (2005), *aff'd,* Nuvio Corp. v. FCC, 473 F.3d 302 (D.C. Cir. 2006).
98. Report and Order, *IP-Enabled Services,* 22 F.C.C.R. 11,275 (2007).
99. For example, the FCC classified wireless broadband Internet access as a lightly regulated information service: "[W]e find that classifying wireless broadband Internet access service as an information service furthers the goals of sections 7 and 230(b) (2) of the Communications Act, and section 706 of the Telecommunications Act of 1996. As noted above, wireless broadband Internet access technologies continue to evolve at a rapid pace. Through this classification, we provide the regulatory certainty needed to help spur growth and deployment of these services. Particularly, the regulatory certainty we provide through this classification will encourage broadband deployment in rural and underserved areas, where wireless broadband may be the most efficient broadband option. Additionally, we believe that wireless broadband Internet access service can provide an important homeland security function by creating redundancy in our nation's communications infrastructure." Declaratory Ruling, *Appropriate Regulatory Treatment for Broadband Access to the Internet over Wireless Networks,* 22 F.C.C.R. 5901, 5911 (2007). Section 706 of the Telecommunications Act of 1976, *codified at* 47 U.S.C. § 1302, requires "[t]he Commission and each State commission with regulatory jurisdiction over telecommunications services . . . [to] encourage the deployment on a reasonable and timely basis of advanced telecommunications capability to all Americans (including, in particular, elementary and secondary schools and classrooms) by utilizing in a manner consistent with the public interest, convenience, and necessity, price cap regulation, regulatory forbearance, measures that promote competition in the local telecommunications market, or other regulating methods that remove barriers to infrastructure investment." Section 706(c) (1) defines advanced telecommunications capability "without regard to any transmission media or technology, as high-speed, switched, broadband telecommunications capability that enables users to originate and receive high-quality voice, data, graphics,

and video telecommunications using any technology." *See also* 47 U.S.C. § 230(b) (2) (stating that it is the policy of the United States "to preserve the vibrant and competitive free market that presently exists for the Internet").

100. *See* Report and Order, *DTV Consumer Education Initiative,* 23 F.C.C.R. 4134 (2008), *on recon.,* 23 F.C.C.R. 7272 (2008), *amended,* 23 F.C.C.R. 9833 (2008), *further modification,* 24 F.C.C.R. 2526 (2009), *on recon.,* 24 F.C.C.R. 3399 (2009), *clarified,* 24 F.C.C.R. 4186 (2009).
101. "According to an analysis by The Associated Press, the two telecom companies bid more than $16 billion, constituting the vast majority of the overall $19.6 billion that was bid in the FCC auction. With Verizon Wireless and AT&T dominating the auction so completely, hopes that the auction would allow for the creation of a new nationwide wireless service provider were dashed." W. David Gardner, *Verizon, AT&T Big Winners in 700 MHz Auction,* INFORMATIONWEEK, Mar. 20, 2008, http://www.informationweek.com; *see also* Saul Hansell, *Verizon and AT&T Win Big in Auction of Spectrum,* THE NEW YORK TIMES, Mar. 21, 2008; Federal Communications Commission, *Auction 73 700 MHz Band, Fact Sheet,* http://wireless.fcc.gov/auctions.
102. *See* http://www.usatoday.com/tech/news.
103. *See* Sascha Meinrath, New America Foundation, *White Space Devices and the Battle over Innovation: Public Access vs. Industry Control of the Airwaves,* Policy Backgrounder (June 2008), http://www.spectrumpolicy.org/.
104. *See* Federal Communications Commission, Office of General Counsel, Transaction Team, http://www.fcc.gov/transaction (containing links to FCC approved merger applications).
105. Federal Communications Commission, News Release, *FCC Approves Merger of AT&T Inc. and BellSouth Corporation, Significant Public Interest Benefits Likely to Result* (Dec. 29, 2006) [hereinafter cited as AT&T–BellSouth Merger News Release]. The deadlock resulted because Republican commissioner Robert McDowell recused himself in light of having served at two trade associations, Comptel, the Competitive Telecommunications Association, and America's Carriers Telecommunications Association, that advocated positions for competitive local and long-distance carriers at the FCC and Congress. Commissioner McDowell had received a legally contestable internal authorization to participate issued at the behest of FCC chairman Kevin Martin. *See* Office of the General Counsel, Memorandum, *Authorization to Participate in the AT&T/BellSouth Merger Proceeding* (Dec. 8, 2006).
106. *Joint Statement of Chairman Kevin J. Martin and Commissioner Deborah Taylor Tate Re: AT&T Inc. and BellSouth Corporation Application for Transfer of Control* (Dec. 29, 2006).
107. Letter from Robert W. Quinn, Jr., AT&T Sr. Vice President Federal Regulatory, Dec. 28, 2006, attached to the AT&T–BellSouth Merger News Release.
108. *See* Policy Statement, *Appropriate Framework for Broadband Access to the Internet over Wireline Facilities,* 20 F.C.C.R. 14,986 (2005).
109. Memorandum Opinion and Order, *Applications for Consent to the Assignment*

and/or Transfer of Control of Licenses, Adelphia Communications Corporation (and Subsidiaries, Debtors-in-Possession), Assignors, to Time Warner Cable Inc. (Subsidiaries), Assignees, 21 F.C.C.R. 8203 (2006).

110. Federal Communications Commission, *General Motors Corporation, Hughes Electronics Corporation, and The News Corporation Limited Transaction Page,* http://www.fcc.gov/mb/newsdirectv/.

CHAPTER FIVE. BEST AND WORST PRACTICES

1. 47 U.S.C § Sec. 254 (b) (3) Universal Service Principles, Access in Rural and High Cost Areas.
2. "Universal service was seen by [AT&T president Theodore] Vail as the delivery of all telephone through one 'system' guided by one 'policy.' Obviously he saw universal service as requiring a nationally integrated single system, managed by AT&T." Robert W. Crandall & Leonard Waverman, WHO PAYS FOR UNIVERSAL SERVICE? WHEN TELEPHONE SUBSIDIES BECOME TRANSPARENT, 6 (The Brookings Institution, 2000), http://brookings.nap.edu/books. "[T]o Vail, universal service was not merely a social goal but instead a sound corporate strategy for eliminating competition and establishing ubiquitous interconnection for the Bell System." Patricia M. Worthy, *Racial Minorities and the Quest to Narrow the Digital Divide: Redefining the Concept of "Universal Service,"* 26 HASTINGS COMM. & ENT. L.J., 1, 7–8 (Autumn 2003).
3. Heather E. Hudson, *Access to the Digital Economy: Issues in Rural and Developing Nations,* paper presented at Understanding the Digital Economy—Data, Tools and Research, conference organized by the United States Department of Commerce, Washington, D.C., May 25–26, 1999, http://mitpress.mit.edu/ude.html; *see also* http://www.ecommerce.gov.
4. *See, e.g.,* Ingo Vogelsang, *Micro-Economic Effects of Privatizing Telecommunications Enterprises,* 13 BOS. U. INT'L L.J. (Fall 1995); Robert J. Saunders, Jeremy J. Warford & Bjorn Wellenius, TELECOMMUNICATIONS AND ECONOMIC DEVELOPMENT, 2d ed. (Johns Hopkins University Press, 1994); Ben A. Petrazzini, THE POLITICAL ECONOMY OF TELECOMMUNICATIONS REFORM IN DEVELOPING COUNTRIES: PRIVATIZATION AND LIBERALIZATION IN COMPARATIVE PERSPECTIVE (Praeger, 1995); Walter T. Molano, THE LOGIC OF PRIVATIZATION: THE CASE OF TELECOMMUNICATIONS IN THE SOUTHERN CONE OF LATIN AMERICA (Greenwood Press, 1997). *See also* Christopher J. Sozzi, *Project Finance and Facilitating Telecommunications Infrastructure Development in Newly-Industrializing Countries,* 12 SANTA CLARA COMPUTER & HIGH TECH. L.J. 435 (1996).
5. "BroadbandInternet access could contribute substantially to economic growth. Consumers benefit from new ways to acquire information, enjoy audio and video entertainment, monitor remote locations, receive medical care, and buy items ranging from books to cars. A study in 2001 estimated that

universal broadband adoption could yield annual consumer benefits of $300 billion." Robert W. Hahn, Scott Wallsten, Robert W. Crandall & Robert E. Litan, American Enterprise Institute, *Bandwidth for the People,* Policy Review (Oct. 2004), http://www.aei.org.

6. When AT&T president Theodore Vail articulated the concept of universal service, he sought the "unification of telephone service under regulated local exchange monopolies." Milton L. Mueller, Jr., UNIVERSAL SERVICE: COMPETITION, INTERCONNECTION, AND MONOPOLY IN THE MAKING OF THE AMERICAN TELEPHONE SYSTEM 92 (American Enterprise Institute, 1997).
7. "There should be specific, predictable and sufficient Federal and State mechanisms to preserve and advance universal service." 47 U.S.C. § 254(b) (5).
8. "The Joint Board and the Commission shall base policies for the preservation and advancement of universal service on the following principles: (1) Quality and rates: Quality services should be available at: just, reasonable, and affordable rates. (2) Access to advanced services: Access to advanced telecommunications and information services should be provided in all regions of the Nation. (3) Access in rural and high cost areas: Consumers in all regions of the Nation, including low-income consumers and those in rural, insular, and high cost areas, should have access to telecommunications and information services, including interexchange services and advanced telecommunications and information services, that are reasonably comparable to those services provided in urban areas and that are available at: rates that are reasonably comparable to rates charged for similar services in urban areas. (4) Equitable and nondiscriminatory contributions: All providers of telecommunications services should make an equitable and nondiscriminatory contribution to the preservation and advancement of universal service." 47 U.S.C. § 254(b) (1)-(4).
9. *See* Federal Communications Commission, *Universal Service, Contribution Factor & Quarterly Filings,* http://www.fcc.gov/omd/contribution-factor.html. VoIP carriers that provide subscribers with access to wireline or wireless telephone subscribers via conventional public switched telecommunications networks must contribute to USF.
10. "Access to advanced telecommunications services for schools, health care, and libraries: Elementary and secondary schools and classrooms, health care providers, and libraries should have access to advanced telecommunications services as described in subsection (h)." 47 U.S.C. § 254(b) (6); "A telecommunications carrier shall, upon receiving a bona fide request, provide telecommunications services which are necessary for the provision of health care services in a State, including instruction relating to such services, to any public or nonprofit health care provider that serves persons who reside in rural areas in that State at rates that are reasonably comparable to rates charged for similar services in urban areas in that State." 47 U.S.C. § 254(h) (1) (A); "All telecommunications carriers serving a geographic area shall,

upon a bona fide request for any of its services that are within the definition of universal service under subsection (c) (3), provide such services to elementary schools, secondary schools, and libraries for educational purposes at rates less than the amounts charged for similar services to other parties. The discount shall be an amount that the Commission, with respect to interstate services, and the States, with respect to intrastate services, determine is appropriate and necessary to ensure affordable access to and use of such services by such entities." 47 U.S.C. § 254(h) (1) (B).

11. The USAC is a subsidiary of the National Exchange Carrier Association (NECA) and operates as a private, not-for-profit corporation. *See* http://www.usac.org/default.aspx; *see also* http://www.universalservice.org/default.asp.
12. Low-income qualification requires proof of income at or below 100 percent of the U.S. Census Bureau Poverty Level Guidelines or proof that the applicant currently receives welfare assistance and that no one claims the applicant as a dependent for tax purposes unless the applicant is sixty years of age or older.
13. Universal Service Administrative Company, *Federal Universal Service Support Mechanisms Fund Size Projections for the Second Quarter 2009*, at 3 (Jan. 30, 2009), http://www.usac.org [hereinafter cited as USAC 2008 Estimate].
14. USAC 2008 Estimate at 3.
15. *Id. See also* Fifth Report and Order and Order, *Schools and Libraries Universal Service Support Mechanism*, 19 F.C.C.R. 15,808 (2004). "Under the Commission's rules, eligible schools and libraries may receive discounts ranging from 20 percent to 90 percent of the pre-discount price of eligible services, based on indicators of need. Schools and libraries in areas with higher percentages of students eligible for free or reduced-price lunch through the National School Lunch Program (or a federally approved alternative mechanism) qualify for higher discounts for eligible services than applicants with low levels of eligibility for such programs. Schools and libraries located in rural areas also generally receive greater discounts. The Commission's priority rules provide that requests for telecommunications services, voice mail and Internet access for all discount categories shall receive first priority for the available funding (Priority One services). The remaining funds are allocated to requests for support for internal connections (Priority Two services), beginning with the most economically disadvantaged schools and libraries, as determined by the schools and libraries discount matrix." *Id.* 19 F.C.C.R. at 15,810 (footnotes omitted).
16. USAC 2008 Estimate at 3.
17. *Id.*
18. "Because fees or taxes imposed on the consumption of a service alter prices that consumers face, they distort consumers' choices: consumers will allocate their spending differently than they would have in the absence of a tax." United States Congress, Congressional Budget Office, *Financing Universal Telephone Service* at 19 (Mar. 2005), http://www.cbo.gov.

19. The FCC's truth-in-billing policies state, *inter alia,* "that it is misleading to represent discretionary line item charges in any manner that suggests such line items are taxes or charges required by the government." Second Report and Order, Declaratory Ruling, and Second Further Notice of Proposed Rulemaking, *Truth-in-Billing and Billing Format, National Association of State Utility Consumer Advocates' Petition for Declaratory Ruling Regarding Truth-in-Billing,* 20 F.C.C.R. 6448, 6449 1 (2005), *review granted,* Nat'l Assn. of State Util. Consumer Advocates v. FCC, 457 F.3d 1238 (11th Cir. 2006); *opinion modified,* 468 F.3d 1272 (11th Cir. 2006). Additionally, "the amount of a carrier's federal universal service line item will not exceed the relevant interstate telecommunications portion of the bill times the relevant contribution factor." Report and Order and Second Further Notice of Proposed Rulemaking, *Federal-State Joint Board on Universal Service,* 17 F.C.C.R. 24,952, 24,978 (2002).
20. *See* Allen S. Hammond IV, *Universal Service: Problems, Solutions, and Responsive Policies,* 57 FED. COMM. L.J. 187 (Mar. 2005); David B. Bender, *Everything That Rises Must Converge: The Case for IP Telephony Regulation After Vonage v. Minnesota Public Utilities Commission,* 36 RUTGERS L.J. 607 (Winter 2005); Sunny Lu, *Cellco Partnership v. FCC & Vonage Holdings Corp. v. Minnesota Public Utilities Commission: VoIP's Shifting Legal and Political Landscape,* 20 BERKELEY TECH. L.J. 859 (2005); Joseph Gratz, *Voice over Internet Protocol,* 6 MINN. J. L. SCI. & TECH. 443 (Dec. 2004); J. Scott Marcus, *Evolving Core Capabilities of the Internet,* 3 J. TELECOMM. & HIGH TECH. L. 121 (2004); Chérie R. Kiser & Angela F. Collins, *Regulation on the Horizon: Are Regulators Poised to Address the Status of IP Telephony?* 11 COMMLAW CONSPECTUS 19 (2003); Robert M. Frieden, *Dialing for Dollars: Should the FCC Regulate Internet Telephony?* 23 RUTGERS COMPUTER & TECH. L.J. 47 (1997).
21. *See* Rob Frieden, *Adjusting the Horizontal and Vertical in Telecommunications Regulation: A Comparison of the Traditional and a New Layered Approach,* 55 FED. COMM. L.J., No. 2, 207 (Mar. 2003); Richard S. Whitt, *A Horizontal Leap Forward: Formulating a New Communications Public Policy Framework Based on the Network Layers Model,* 56 FED. COMM. L.J. 587 (May 2004); Yochai Benkler, *From Consumers to Users: Shifting the Deeper Structures of Regulation Toward Sustainable Commons and User Access,* 52 FED. COMM. L.J. 561 (2000); Scott Marcus, Federal Communications Commission, Office of Plans and Policy, *The Potential Relevance to the United States of the European Union's Newly Adopted Regulatory Framework for Telecommunications,* Working Paper Series No. 36 (July 2002), http://www.fcc.gov/osp/workingp.html; Kevin Werbach, *A Layers Model for Internet Policy,* 1 J. ON TELECOMM. & HIGH TECH. L. 37 (2002); John T. Nakahata, *Regulating Information Platforms: The Challenge of Rewriting Regulation from the Bottom Up,* 1 J. ON TELECOMM. & HIGH TECH. L. 95 (2002); Philip J. Weiser, *Law and Information Platforms,* J. ON TELECOMM. & HIGH TECH. L. 1 (2002).

22. *See* Order and Notice of Proposed Rulemaking, *AT&T Corp. Petition for Declaratory Ruling Regarding Enhanced Prepaid Calling Card Services,* 20 F.C.C.R. 4826 (2005) (finding AT&T responsible for USF contributions from revenues derived from calling cards containing prerecorded information).
23. *See* Federal Communications Commission, Industry Analysis and Technology Division, Wireline Competition Bureau, *Trends in Telephone Service,* Table 3.2, Average monthly household telecommunications expenditures by type of provider (Feb. 2007).
24. "USAC administers the schools and libraries universal service support program under Commission oversight. Under this program, eligible schools, libraries, and consortia that include eligible schools and libraries may receive discounts for eligible telecommunications services, voice mail, Internet access, and internal connections. Prior to applying for discounted services, an applicant must conduct a technology assessment and develop a technology plan to ensure that any services it purchases will be used effectively. The applicant then must submit to the Administrator a completed FCC Form 470, in which the applicant sets forth, among other things, the services for which it seeks discounts. Once the school or library has complied with the Commission's competitive bidding requirements and entered into agreements for eligible services, it must file an FCC Form 471 application to notify the Administrator of the services that have been ordered, the service providers with whom the applicant has entered into an agreement, and an estimate of funds needed to cover the discounts to be given for eligible services." Fifth Report and Order and Order, *Schools and Libraries Universal Service Support Mechanism,* 19 F.C.C.R. 15,808, 15,809 (2004).
25. For insights on the procedural complexity of the USAC E-Rate funding process *see* John Noram, *E-Rate for Beginners,* Power point presentation (Sept. 27–29, 2004), http://www.sl.universalservice.org; *see also* Michigan Department of Education, *E-Rate Application Flow Chart,* http://www.michigan.gov.
26. *See, e.g.,* eRate Solutions, LLC, World Wide Web page, http://www.eratesolutions.com.
27. Federal Communications Commission, Office of Inspector General, *Semiannual Report* (Mar. 2008), http://www.fcc.gov/oig; *see also* Bob Williams, The Center for Public Integrity, *Phone Fund for Schools, Libraries Riddled with Fraud* (Jan. 9, 2003), http://www.public-i.org.
28. Notice of Proposed Rulemaking and Further Notice of Proposed Rulemaking, *Comprehensive Review of Universal Service Fund Management, Administration, and Oversight,* 20 F.C.C.R. 11,308 (2005); Report and Order, 22 F.C.C.R. 16,372 (2007).
29. The FCC has capped the amount of the USF subsidy for high-cost areas based on concerns for the future viability of the program. Order, *High-Cost Universal Service Support Federal-State Joint Board on Universal Service, Alltel Communications, Inc., et al.,* 23 F.C.C.R. 9232, 23 F.C.C.R. 8834 (2008); *see also* Alenco Commc'ns Inc. v. FCC, 201 F.3d 608, 620–21 (5th Cir. 2000)

("[t]he agency's broad discretion to provide sufficient universal service funding includes the decision to impose cost controls to avoid excessive expenditures that will detract from universal service").

30. Despite eight years of operation neither the FCC nor the USAC has established clearly articulated goals and a process for compiling reliable performance data. "The Commission is in the process of compiling USF performance measures, particularly for the Schools and Libraries program and the High Cost program, in order to comply with the Office of Management and Budget (OMB) Program Assessment Rating Tool (PART) requirements." Notice of Proposed Rulemaking and Further Notice of Proposed Rulemaking, *Schools and Libraries Universal Service Support Mechanism*, 20 F.C.C.R. 11,308, 11,319 (2005).
31. Recommended Decision, *Federal-State Joint Board on Universal Service*, 19 F.C.C.R. 4257 (2004) (recommended revisions to the ETC designation process). The Commission has tightened the requirements that existing and prospective ETCs must satisfy. Each applicant and incumbent must (1) provide a five-year plan demonstrating how high-cost universal service support will be used to improve its coverage, service quality, or capacity in every geographical area served by a switching facility known as a wire center; (2) demonstrate its ability to remain functional in emergency situations; (3) demonstrate that it will satisfy consumer protection and service quality standards; (4) offer a local usage plan, if it is a prospective ETC, comparable to those offered by incumbent local exchange carriers in the areas for which it seeks designation; and (5) acknowledge that it may be required to provide equal access if all other ETCs in the designated service area relinquish their designations. Report and Order, *Federal-State Joint Board on Universal Service*, 20 F.C.C.R. 6371 (2005).
32. Once certified, an eligible telecommunications carrier receives the same financial support on a line-by-line basis as the incumbent carrier receives, even though it might not serve the entire geographical area that the incumbent serves. "The potential for creamskimming, however, arises when an ETC seeks designation in a disproportionate share of the higher-density wire centers in an incumbent LEC's service area. By serving a disproportionate share of the high-density portion of a service area, an ETC may receive more support than is reflective of the rural incumbent LEC's costs of serving that wire center because support for each line is based on the rural telephone company's average costs for serving the entire service area unless the incumbent LEC has disaggregated its support. Because line density is a significant cost driver, it is reasonable to assume that the highest-density wire centers are the least costly to serve, on a per-subscriber basis. The effects of creamskimming also would unfairly affect the incumbent LEC's ability to provide service throughout the area since it would be obligated to serve the remaining high-cost wire centers in the rural service area while ETCs could target the rural incumbent LEC's customers in the lowest cost areas and also re-

ceive support for serving the customers in these areas." Report and Order, *Federal-State Joint Board on Universal Service*, 20 F.C.C.R. 6371, 6393 (2005).

33. Under the Commission's portability rules, a competitive ETC receives the same support for each line served that the incumbent carrier would receive, based on the incumbent carrier's costs. *See* 47 C.F.R. § 54.307. "Similar to other types of universal service support, interstate access support is portable to competitive ETCs. Consequently, because interstate access support is targeted to $650 million, when a competitive ETC receives interstate access support, there is a corresponding reduction in support available to incumbent carriers." Order, *Sprint Corporation*, 19 F.C.C.R. 22,663, 22,671 (2004).

34. *See, e.g.*, Public Notice, *FCC Proposes over $2 Million in Forfeitures for Universal Service Fund and Other Regulatory Program Violations* (July 25, 2005); Notice of Apparent Liability for Forfeiture and Order, *Carrera Communications, LP*, 20 F.C.C.R. 13,307 (2005).

35. "The FCC built assumptions based on existing, widespread models into its regulations, and thus required that new installations be 'more of the same'; this benefited incumbent companies. In particular, regulations prevented the use of funds for the purchase of external lines or wireless equipment, which would have been a low-cost, long-term solution for many schools and libraries. Schools and libraries were not given practical goals, but simply instructed to spend as much of other people's money as they could. In other words, their goal was to spend the available money on easily obtainable equipment, not necessarily to make the best possible use of the money. They had no encouragement to be creative. The law provided only telecom equipment and networking services. It did not consider other useful things one could ask for to achieve Internet access. Such as computers, for instance. Or trained teachers and staff." Andy Oram, O'Reilly Developer Weblogs, *Getting Universal Service to Work*, July 21, 2004, http://www.oreillynet.com.

36. Starting in 2004, the FCC compiles annually a list of eligible services available for discounting under the E-Rate program. "To be eligible for support, telecommunications services must be provided by an eligible telecommunications provider, that is, one who provides telecommunications on a common carriage basis." Public Notice, *Release of Funding Year 2005 Eligible Services List for Schools and Libraries Universal Service Mechanism*, 19 F.C.C.R. 20,221, 20,222 (2004).

37. *See* Heather E. Hudson, *Universal Access: What Have We Learned from the E-Rate?* 28 TELECOMM. POL'Y, Nos. 3–4, 309 (2004) (noting the prohibition on schools or libraries providing Internet access externally, and reporting on a highly conditioned FCC waiver granted for Alaska but not yet applied).

38. *See* United States Department of Agriculture, Rural Utilities Service, *Telecommunications Program* Web site, http://www.usda.gov/rus/telecom/index.htm.

39. *See, e.g.*, Rob Frieden, *Lessons from Broadband Development in Canada, Japan, Korea and the United States*, 29 TELECOMM. POL'Y, 595 (Sept. 2005).

40. Heretofore the FCC and a board comprising FCC and state regulatory commissioners have proposed only stopgap reforms. *See, e.g.*, Order, High-Cost Universal Service Support Federal-State Joint Board on Universal Service, 23 F.C.C.R. 9232 (2008) (reining in the explosive growth in high-cost universal service support disbursements by ordering an emergency cap on the amount of high-cost support that competitive eligible telecommunications carriers may receive).
41. *See* Eleventh Report and Order, *Access Charge Reform*, 15 F.C.C.R. 12,962 (2000) *aff'd in part, rev'd in part, and remanded in part*, Texas Office of Public Util. Counsel v. FCC, 265 F.3d 313 (5th Cir. 2001), *cert. denied*, Nat'l Ass'n of State Util. Consumer Advocates v. FCC, 535 U.S. 986 (2002), *on remand*, 18 F.C.C.R. 14,976 (2003). *See also* Order, *Cost Review Proceeding for Residential and Single-Line Business Subscriber Line Charge (SLC) Caps*, 17 F.C.C.R. 10,868 (2002), *aff'd*, Nat'l Ass'n of State Util. Consumer Advocates v. FCC, 372 F.3d 454 (D.C. Cir. 2004).
42. *See also* Further Notice of Proposed Rulemaking, *Developing a Unified Intercarrier Compensation Regime*, 20 F.C.C.R. 4685 (2005).
43. "[I]t does not appear that minutes-of-use are a significant determinant of costs given developments in telecommunications technologies. The Commission long ago recognized this with respect to loop costs, which are a function of subscriber density and choice of technology. For similar reasons, it appears that switching costs are primarily a function of the number of subscribers, rather than the number of calls or MOU [minutes of use], because a reduction in call minutes per subscriber would not substantially reduce the investment and operating cost of the switch serving those customers, at least in the case of wireline networks." Further Notice of Proposed Rulemaking, *Developing a Unified Intercarrier Compensation Regime*, 20 F.C.C.R. 4685, 4785–86 (2005).
44. 47 U.S.C. § 151 *et seq.*
45. Vonage Holdings Corp. v. Federal Commc'ns Com'n, 489 F.3d 1232 (D.C. Cir. 2007).
46. *See* Organisation for Economic Co-operation and Development, DAC Network on Poverty Reduction, *Leveraging Telecommunications Policies for Pro-Growth Universal Access Funds with Minimum-Subsidy Auctions (2004)* (Oct. 22, 2004), http://www.oecd.org.
47. *See, e.g.*, Second Report and Order, *Implementation of Section 309(j) of the Communications Act—Competitive Bidding*, 9 F.C.C.R. 2348 (1994); Ninth Report and Order, 11 F.C.C.R. 14,769 (1996); Dale N. Hatfield, *The Current Status of Spectrum Management*, in Robert M. Entman, Rapporteur, *Balancing Policy Options in a Turbulent Telecommunications Market: A Report of the Seventeenth Annual Aspen Institute Conference on Telecommunications Policy*, at 29 (2003), http://www.aspeninst.org; *see also* Omnibus Budget Reconciliation Act of 1993, Pub. L. 103–66, 107 Stat. 312 (1993) (*codified* at 47 U.S.C. § 309)

(authorizing the FCC to grant licenses "through a system of competitive bidding").

48. *See, e.g.*, Gregory L. Rosston & Jeffrey S. Steinberg, *Using Market-Based Spectrum Policy to Promote the Public Interest*, 50 FED. COMM. L.J. 87 (1997); Symposium, *The Law and Economics of Property Rights to Radio Spectrum*, 41 J.L. & ECON. 521 (1998); Peter Cramton, *The Efficiency of the FCC Spectrum Auctions*, 41 J.L. & ECON. 727 (1998); Pablo T. Spiller & Carlo Cardilli, *Towards a Property Rights Approach to Communications Spectrum*, 16 YALE J. ON REG. 53 (1999); D. Daniel Sokol, *The European Mobile 3G UMTS Process: Lessons from the Spectrum Auctions and Beauty Contests*, 6 VA. J.L. & TECH. 17 (2001); Thomas W. Hazlett, *The Wireless Craze, the Unlimited Bandwidth Myth, the Spectrum Auction Faux Pas, and the Punchline to Ronald Coase's "Big Joke": An Essay on Airwave Allocation Policy*, 14 HARV. J.L. & TECH. 335 (2001).

49. *See* Rob Frieden, *Balancing Equity and Efficiency Issues in the Management of Shared Global Radiocommunication Resources*, 24 U. PENN. J. INT'L ECON. L., No. 2, 289 (Summer 2003).

50. For background on Canada's broadband initiatives *see* http://www.ic.gc.ca; *see also* International Telecommunication Union, Workshop on Promoting Broadband, *Promoting Broadband: The Case of Canada* (Apr. 2003), http://www.itu.int/osg/spu/ni/promotebroadband.

51. *See, e.g.*, General Assembly of Pennsylvania, House Bill No. 30, An Act further providing for residential telephone service rates based on duration or distance of call and for local exchange service increases and limitations, Signed in the House and in the Senate, November 19, 2004, Approved by the Governor, November 30, 2004, http://www.legis.state.pa.us.

52. Harold Feld, Gregory Rose, Mark Cooper & Ben Scott, *Connecting the Public: The Truth About Municipal Broadband* (Apr. 2005), http://www.mediaaccess.org; Public Knowledge, *Principles for an Open Broadband Future* (July 6, 2005), http://www.publicknowledge.org. *Cf.* Adam Thierer, The Progress and Freedom Foundation, *Risky Business: Philadelphia's Plan for Providing Wi-Fi Service*, Progress on Point, Release 12.4 (Apr. 2005), http://www.publicknowledge.org; Thomas M. Lenard, The Progress and Freedom Foundation, *Wireless Philadelphia: A Leap into the Unknown*, Progress on Point, Release 12.3 (Apr. 2005), http://www.pff.org; New Millennium Research Council, *"Not in the Public Interest"—The Myth of Municipal Wi-Fi Networks* (Feb. 2005), http://newmillenniumresearch.org.

53. American Recovery and Reinvestment Act of 2009, Pub. L. 111–005 (signed into law, Feb. 17, 2009), http://frwebgate.access.gpo.gov.

54. *Id.* at 1.

55. Pub. L. No. 110-385, 122 Stat. 4097 (*codified at* 47 U.S.C. §§ 1301–04).

56. Section 103(b) requires the FCC to compare the extent of broadband service capability (including data transmission speeds and prices for broadband ser-

vice capability) in a total of seventy-five communities in at least twenty-five countries abroad and to choose communities for the comparison under this subsection in a manner that will offer, to the extent possible, communities of a population size, population density, topography, and demographic profile that are comparable to the population size, population density, topography, and demographic profile of the various communities within the United States.

CHAPTER SIX. UNDERSTANDING THE DOTCOM IMPLOSION

1. "The high tech bubble was inflated by myths of astronomical Internet traffic growth rates." Andrew M. Odlyzko, Proceedings of the Society of Photo-Optical Instrumentation Engineers, *Internet Traffic Growth: Sources and Implications* (2003), http://www.dtc.umn.edu.
2. "The original Moore's Law derives from a speech given by Gordon Moore, later a founder of Intel, in 1965, in which he observed that the number of microcomponents that could be placed in an integrated circuit (microchip) of the lowest manufacturing cost was doubling every year and that this trend would likely continue into the future. As this observation and prediction began to be frequently cited, it became known as Moore's Law. In later years, the Law was occasionally reformulated to mean that rate. The pace of change having slowed down a bit over the past few years, the definition has changed (with Gordon Moore's approval) to reflect that the doubling occurs only every 18 months." Whatis.com, *IT Encylopedia,* http://whatis.techtarget.com.
3. When every long-distance telephone company offers crystal-clear service via fiber-optic cables, no single carrier, such as AT&T or Sprint, can differentiate their service based on reliability ("genuine" AT&T) or quality ("you can hear a pin drop").
4. "Dense wavelength division multiplexing (DWDM) is a technology that puts data from different sources together on an optical fiber, with each signal carried at the same time on its own separate light wavelength. Using DWDM, up to 80 (and theoretically more) separate wavelengths or channels of data can be multiplexed into a lightstream transmitted on a single optical fiber. Each channel carries a time division multiplexed (TDM) signal. In a system with each channel carrying 2.5 Gbps (billion bits per second), up to 200 billion bits can be delivered a second by the optical fiber." SearchTelecom.com.
5. Peer-to-peer (P2P) computing refers to the ability of a group of computer users with the same networking program to connect with one another and directly access files from one another's hard drives. P2P enables the transfer of large files on a timely basis because each file is broken down into smaller portions sent to the recipient at the same time from multiple sources.
6. Background on the Netflix service is available at: http://www.netflix.com/.
7. The "greater fool" theory has been called the "[b]elief held by one who makes a questionable investment, with the assumption that he/she will be able to sell it later to a bigger fool." Investorwords.com, http://www.investorwords.com.

8. Section 271 of the Telecommunications Act of 1996, Pub. L. No. 104-104, 110 Stat. 56 (*codified at* 47 U.S.C. § 271 *et seq.*), provides that a Regional Bell Operating Company (RBOC) may provide long-distance service within its own territory (determined on a state-by-state basis) once it has met certain conditions, including those specified in a fourteen-point competitive checklist, and once the FCC has determined that granting the RBOC's application is consistent with the public interest. The FCC must act on an application within ninety days after its filing. It must consult with the U.S. Department of Justice, giving the department recommendation substantial but not preclusive weight. It must also consult with the public utility company for the state that is the subject of the application. In practice, the RBOC typically files its proposal with the state public utility company well in advance of a filing with the FCC, and files with the FCC only after the public utility company has endorsed the application.
9. United States v. Am. Tel. & Tel. Co., 552 F.Supp. 131 (D.D.C.1982), *aff'd,* 460 U.S. 1001, 103 S. Ct. 1240 (1983).
10. MCI Telecomm. Corp. v. FCC, 712 F.2d 517 (D.C. Cir. 1983); MCI Telecomm. Corp. v. FCC, 561 F.2d 365 (D.C. Cir. 1977), *cert. denied,* 434 U.S. 1040, 98 S. Ct. 781 (1978); MCI Telecomm. Corp. v. FCC, 580 F.2d 590 (D.C. Cir.), *cert. denied,* 439 U.S. 980, 99 S. Ct. 566 (1978).
11. Specialized Common Carrier Services, 29 F.C.C.2d 870 (1971), *aff'd sub nom.* Washington Utils. & Transp. Comm'n v. FCC, 513 F.2d 1142 (9th Cir.), *cert. denied,* 423 U.S. 836, 96 S. Ct. 62, 46 L.Ed.2d 54 (1975), paved the way for carriers offering services in competition with AT&T to enter the market for private lines. Subsequent FCC and appellate court decisions clarified that AT&T could not, through its subsidiaries, the Bell Operating Companies (BOCs), block competition by denying competitors interconnection. Decision, *Bell System Tariff Offerings,* 46 F.C.C.2d 413, *aff'd sub nom.* Bell Telephone Co. v. FCC, 503 F.2d 1250 (3d Cir.1974), *cert. denied,* 422 U.S. 1026, 95 S. Ct. 2620, 45 L.Ed.2d 684 (1975).
12. Pole Attachment Act of 1978, Pub. L. No. 95–234, 92 Stat. 33 (Feb. 21, 1978), *codified at* 47 U.S.C. § 224 (2002). The Pole Attachment Act requires the FCC to set reasonable rates, terms, and conditions for certain attachments made by cable television and other telecommunications service providers to telephone and electric utility poles. 47 U.S.C. § 224(b) (v). It requires the FCC to "regulate the rates, terms, and conditions for pole attachments to provide that such rates, terms, and conditions are just and reasonable, and shall adopt procedures necessary and appropriate to hear and resolve complaints concerning such rates, terms, and conditions." 47 U.S.C. § 224(b) (1). Background on the law is available at: S. Rep. No. 95–580, 1978 U.S.C.C.A.N. 109. Background on FCC enforcement actions is available at: http://www.fcc.gov/eb/mdrd/PoleAtt.html.
13. For example, in 2002 the Supreme Court upheld the FCC's authority to limit fees that cable telecommunications and wireless telecommunications service

providers pay to attach wires and other facilities to utility poles. The Court held that the Pole Attachment Act of 1978 provides for many types of attachments, including those used by cable television systems to provide high-speed Internet access in addition to conventional cable television services. Nat'l Cable & Telecomm. Ass'n v. Gulf Power Co., 534 US 327 (2002), 122 S. Ct. 782 (2002).

14. A partial summary of the Telecommunications Act identifies some of the pro-competitive requirements imposed on all telecommunications carriers: (1) to interconnect directly or indirectly with the facilities and equipment of other carriers; and (2) not to install network features, functions, or capabilities that do not comply with specified guidelines and standards. Specific requirements of local exchange carriers include the duty: (1) not to prohibit resale of their services; (2) to provide number portability; (3) to provide dialing parity; (4) to afford access to poles, ducts, conduits, and rights-of-way consistent with pole attachment provisions of the act; and (5) to re-establish reciprocal compensation arrangements for the transport and termination of telecommunications. Requirements of ILECs include the duty to: (1) negotiate in good faith the terms and conditions of agreements; (2) provide interconnection at any technically feasible point of the same quality they provide to themselves, on just, reasonable, and nondiscriminatory terms and conditions; (3) provide access to network elements on an unbundled basis; (4) offer resale of their telecommunications services at wholesale rates; (5) provide reasonable public notice of changes to their networks; and (6) provide physical collocation, or virtual collocation if physical collocation is impractical. *See* United States Congress, Telecommunications Act of 1996, Conference Report, 104–458 (Jan. 31, 1996), http://thomas.loc.gov.

15. For background on the formation of the WTO *see* World Trade Organization, *What Is the WTO?* http://www.wto.org.

16. World Trade Organization, Coverage of Basic Telecommunications and Value-Added Services, http://www.wto.org.

17. Report and Order, *Rules and Policies on Foreign Participation in the U.S. Telecommunications Market,* 11 F.C.C.R. 3873 (1997), Report and Order on Reconsideration, 12 F.C.C.R. 23,891 (1997). FCC orders implementing aspects of the Basic Telecommunications Agreement are available at: http://www.fcc.gov/ib/pd/pf/wto.html.

18. For an outline of the revenues generated by FCC spectrum auctions *see* Federal Communications Commission, *Completed Auctions,* http://wireless.fcc.gov/auctions/summary.html#completed.

19. For background on the scope of commitments made by RBOCs to secure FCC approval of major mergers and acquisitions *see* Federal Communications Commission, *Merger Compliance Oversight Team (MCOT),* http://www.fcc.gov/wcb/mcot/.

CHAPTER SEVEN. THE FUNDAMENTALS OF DIGITAL LITERACY

1. For background on the concept of digital literacy and efforts to promote widespread acquisition of necessary skills *see ICT Digital Literacy* Web site, http://www.ictliteracy.info/; University of Illinois at Urbana-Champaign, Library, *Digital Literacy Portal*, http://www.library.uiuc.edu/diglit/; European Commission, *Mastering ICTs to Promote Innovation*, http://ec.europa.eu; e-Inclusion Ministerial Conference and Expo, *Digital Literacy European Commission Working Paper and Recommendations from Digital Literacy High-Level Expert Group* (Nov. 2008), http://ec.europa.eu; Paul Glister, DIGITAL LITERACY (John Wiley and Sons, 1997).
2. *See* Forest Woody Horton, Jr., United Nations Educational, Scientific and Cultural Organization, *Understanding Information Literacy: A Primer* (2008), http://unesdoc.unesco.org; Anthony G. Wilhelm, *Digital Nation: Toward an Inclusive Information Society* (MIT Press, 2004); *see also* The World Bank, infoDev, *Access to ICT: Broadening the Reach and Affordability of ICTs*, http://www.infodev.org.

CHAPTER EIGHT. CHALLENGES AND CHOICES

1. Converging technologies and markets favors companies with the financial resources to serve an increasing array of services and thereby achieve efficiency gains, also known as economies of scale (size) and scope (market diversity). When markets consolidate, both regulators and the judiciary may have to examine instances of anticompetitive conduct, unfair trade practices and other market countervailing behavior. *See, e.g.*, Stacy L. Dogan & Mark A. Lemley, *Antitrust Law and Regulatory Gaming*, 87 TEX. L. REV. 685 (Mar. 2009). Others have little fear that concentration will diminish competitive benefits. *See, e.g.*, Paul Shoning, *Convergence and Competition: Why a Duopoly of Convergent Competitors Might Be Sufficient to Protect Broadband Consumers Without* Regulation, 7 J. TELECOMM. & HIGH TECH. L. 139 (Winter 2009).
2. "For decades, packet-switched data communications networks have been constructed around several fundamental organizing principles, including the "protocol layering" concept (networks employ different functional rules, or protocols, arranged in layered stacks) and the "end-to-end network" concept (dumb networks support intelligent applications). Together, protocol layering and end-to-end principles have become the building blocks of the Internet. In the resulting layered protocol stack, the IP resides in the "middle" logical layers, with physical network facilities at layers below and user applications and content at layers above. As technology has evolved, existing networks and markets have begun converging to common IP platforms. Key inherent aspects of this IP-centric New World Order include blurred distinctions between services, lack of relevant geographic boundaries, and a mesh of virtual interconnected networks. Moreover, this network architecture tends to shape and drive business fundamentals." Richard S. Whitt, *A Horizontal Leap For-*

ward: Formulating a New Communications Public Policy Framework Based on the Network Layers Model, 56 FED. COMM. L.J. 587, 590 (May 2004).

3. Robert D. Atkinson, *The Role of Competition in a National Broadband Policy*, 7 J. TELECOMM. & HIGH TECH. L. 1 (Winter 2009).
4. *See* Anthony E. Varona, *Toward a Broadband Public Interest Standard*, 61 ADMIN. L. REV. 1 (Winter 2009) (suggesting that public interest regulation remains necessary).
5. "A strong federal role is needed to support broadband investment, in part, because investment in broadband generates considerable positive network externalities that accrue not just to the individual consumer, but also to society as a whole. Market forces alone will not generate the socially optimal level of broadband, at least for the foreseeable future." Robert D. Atkinson & Daniel D. Castro, *A National Technology Agenda for the New Administration*, 11 YALE J.L. & TECH. 190 (2009).

CHAPTER NINE. THE IMPACT OF TECHNOLOGICAL AND MARKET CONVERGENCE

1. "A new . . . online survey of consumer digital media and entertainment habits shows audiences are more in control than ever and increasingly savvy about filtering marketing messages. The global findings overwhelmingly suggest personal Internet time rivals TV time. Among consumer respondents, 19 percent stated spending six hours or more per day on personal Internet usage, versus nine percent of respondents who reported the same levels of TV viewing. 66 percent reported viewing between one to four hours of TV per day, versus 60 percent who reported the same levels of personal Internet usage." *IBM Consumer Survey Shows Decline of TV as Primary Media Device*, Aug. 22, 2007, http://www.ibm.com.
2. Bill Gorman, TV by the Numbers, *Where Did the Primetime Broadcast Audience Go?—Ask Not Where the Broadcast Audience Went, It Went to Cable* (Apr. 16, 2008), http://tvbythenumbers.com.
3. Chris Anderson, THE LONG TAIL: WHY THE FUTURE OF BUSINESS IS SELLING LESS OF MORE (Hyperion, 2006); Anderson, *The Long Tail*, 12 WIRED, Oct. 2004, http://www.wired.com.
4. Anita Elberse, *Should You Invest in the Long Tail?* 86 HARVARD BUS. REV. Reprint R0807H (July–Aug. 2008).
5. *See* Rob Frieden, *Lessons from Broadband Development in Canada, Japan, Korea and the United States*, 29 TELECOMM. POL'Y, 595 (Sept. 2005).
6. *See, e.g.*, United Kingdom, Office of Communications, *Final Statements on the Strategic Review of Telecommunications, and Undertakings in Lieu of a Reference Under the Enterprise Act, 2002* (Sept. 22, 2005), http://www.ofcom.org.uk (discussing structural separation of British Telecom to achieve equal access between ventures affiliated with British Telecom and competitors).
7. United States Congress, 97th Cong., 2d Sess., Home Recording of Copyrighted Works, Hearing before the Subcomittee on Courts, Civil Liberties,

and the Adminstration of Justice of the Committee on the Judiciary House of Representatives, on H.R. 4783, H.R. 4794 H.R. 4808, H.R. 5250, H.R. 5488, and H.R. 5705, April 12, 13, 14, June 24, August 11, September 22 and 23, 1982, Testimony of Jack Valenti, http://cryptome.org/hrcw-hear.htm.

8. In Sony Corp. v. Universal City Studios Inc., 464 U.S. 417, 104 S. Ct. 774 (1984), the Supreme Court articulated this concept for noncommercial users of videocassette tape recorders. *See also* Jane C. Ginsburg, *Separating the Sony Sheep from the Grokster Goats: Reckoning the Future Business Plans of Copyright-Dependent Technology Entrepreneurs,* 50 ARIZ. L. REV. 577 (Summer 2008).
9. Digital Millennium Copyright Act, Sec. 1201, Circumvention of copyright protection systems, 17 U.S.C. § 1201.
10. *See, e.g.,* Perfect 10 v. Google Inc., 416 F. Supp. 2d 828 (C.D. Cal. 2006) (search engine reproduction of copyrighted photographs as small thumbnails deemed fair use).
11. *See, e.g.,* A&M Records v. Napster, 239 F.3d 1004 (9th Cir. 2001) (music-sharing service contributory to infringed copyrights); MGM Studios v. Grokster, 545 U.S. 913, 125 S. Ct. 2764 (2005); BMG Music v. Gonzalez, 438 F.3d 888 (7th Cir. 2005); Columbia Pictures Inc. v. Justin Bunnell, 245 F.R.D. 443 (C.D. Cal. 2007) (similar holding for movie file sharing).
12. Recent U.S. statistics show an overall increase in both television and Internet viewing. "Nielsen's findings show that screen time of the average American continues to increase with TV users watching more TV than ever before (127 hrs, 15 min per month), while also spending 9% more time using the Internet (26 hrs, 26 min per month) from last year. At the same time, a small but growing number of Internet and mobile phone users are watching video online (2 hrs, 19 min per month), as well as using their cell phones to watch video (3 hrs, 15 min per month)" Nielsen, *Nielsen Reports TV, Internet And Mobile Usage Among Americans* (July 8, 2008), http://nielsen.com.
13. *See* Frances Cairncross, THE DEATH OF DISTANCE: HOW THE COMMUNICATIONS REVOLUTION WILL CHANGE OUR LIVES (Harvard Business School Press, 1997).
14. Non-traffic-sensitive plant requires cost triggers that do not vary with the degree of use. For example, the costs of procuring and installing a telephone jack do not vary with the number of calls made via that particular component.
15. The FCC acknowledged the need to recover non-traffic-sensitive costs on a flat-rate basis. "[N]on-traffic-sensitive costs-costs that do not vary with the amount of traffic carried over the facilities should be recovered through flat-rate charges, and traffic-sensitive costs should be recovered through per-minute charges. This approach fosters competition and efficient pricing." Order on Remand, *Access Charge Reform Price Cap Performance Review for LECs,* 18 F.C.C.R. 14,976 (2003).
16. Implicit subsidies in telecommunications "result, in large part from rate averaging between rural and suburban/urban areas and the recovery of certain non-traffic-sensitive costs through traffic-sensitive per-minute rates,

which over-recovers costs from higher volume users, often business customers." Order on Remand, *Review of the Section 251 Unbundling Obligations of Incumbent Local Exchange Carriers*, CC Docket No. 01–338, 18 F.C.C.R. at 14,976.

17. The Telecommunications Act requires cost averaging to achieve universal service objectives: "Consumers in all regions of the Nation, including low-income consumers and those in rural, insular, and high cost areas, should have access to telecommunications and information services, including interexchange services and advanced telecommunications and information services, that are reasonably comparable to those services provided in urban areas and that are available at: rates that are reasonably comparable to rates charged for similar services in urban areas." 47 U.S.C. § 254(b) (3). Additionally, "the rates charged by providers of interexchange telecommunications services to subscribers in rural and high cost areas shall be no higher than the rates charged by each such provider to its subscribers in urban areas. Such rules shall also require that a provider of interstate interexchange telecommunications services shall provide such services to its subscribers in each State at rates no higher than the rates charged to its subscribers in any other State." 47 U.S.C. § 254(g).
18. For example, carriers typically still incur different mileage-based costs when they lease a dedicated line of varying distances. The line transport charges of a local exchange carrier is mileage-based when a single carrier leases a line instead of sharing it with other carriers.
19. ISPs initially offered unlimited Internet access to stimulate demand and considered unused network capacity as available for loading at little, if any, additional cost. Such promotional pricing does not burden heavy users with higher charges even though such rates could help ISPs recover fixed costs. Absent congestion, ISPs could consider the incremental cost of handling more traffic as near zero.
20. Notice of Proposed Rulemaking, *Developing a Unified Intercarrier Compensation Regime*, 16 F.C.C.R. 9610, 9623 (2001) [hereinafter cited as Bill and Keep Carrier Compensation Proposal]. The phrase "death of distance" comes from Cairncross, *supra* note 13.
21. Section 252(b) (5) of the Telecommunications Act of 1996, 47 U.S.C. § 252(b) (5), requires all local exchange carriers "to establish reciprocal compensation arrangements for the transport and termination of telecommunications." Examples of the quite small rates that ILECs charge for local facilities access is available at: Billy Jack Gregg, *A Survey of Unbundled Network Element Prices in the United States* (July 2003), http://nrri.org; and Jeffrey H. Rohlfs & J. Gregory Sidak, *Exporting Telecommunications Regulation: The United States–Japan Negotiations on Interconnection Pricing*, 43 HARV. INT'L L.J. 317 (2002).
22. For background on the international long-distance telephone toll revenue division process *see* Rob Frieden, MANAGING INTERNET-DRIVEN CHANGE IN INTERNATIONAL TELECOMMUNICATIONS, Chapter 9.1

(Artech House, 2001); Robert M. Frieden, *Falling Through the Cracks: International Accounting Rate Reform at the ITU and WTO*, 22 TELECOMM. POL'Y, 963 (Dec. 1998).

23. *See* Federal Communications Commission, *IMTS Accounting Rates of the United States 1985–2004* (July 1, 2004).
24. "If the U.S.-outbound call is terminating on the network of a mobile provider in the foreign country, there is an additional termination charge passed back through to the U.S. carrier, under 'calling party pays,' when the call is handed-off to the foreign mobile provider for termination. U.S. providers generally recoup these mobile termination costs from U.S. consumers through rate surcharges. Examples of the highest current per minute mobile surcharges [above the international long-distance charge] include: $0.28 for France; $0.22 for Haiti; $0.32 for Panama; $0.22 for the United Kingdom; and $0.33 for Uruguay." Notice of Proposed Rulemaking, *International Settlements Policy Reform* 17 F.C.C.R. 19,954, 19,979 (2002).
25. For example, before the FCC sought more carefully calculated and accurate cost allocations between interstate and intrastate jurisdictions, it used a "gross allocator" to split local exchange carriers' plant investments between the interstate jurisdiction (75 percent) and the intrastate jurisdiction (25 percent). Recommended Decision, *Jurisdictional Separations Reform and Referral to the Federal-State Joint Board*, 15 F.C.C.R. 13,160, 13,177 n.40 (2000).
26. Bill and Keep Carrier Compensation Proposal, 16 F.C.C.R. at 9610.
27. For example, universal service subsidies to any local exchange carrier operating in a high-cost, usually rural area benefits all subscribers of that carrier regardless of their individual financial status. "[A]ny policy that attempts to increase subscribership levels by reducing the price of customer access is likely to have only limited success, particularly if the program does not target specific beneficiaries." David L. Kaserman & John W. Mayo, *Cross-Subsidies in Telecommunications: Roadblocks on the Road to More Intelligent Telephone Pricing*, 11 YALE J. ON REG. 119, 140 (1994).
28. "With the passage of the [Telecommunications] Act [of] 1996, and its mandate for opening all telecommunications markets to competition, it is no longer clear that intercarrier compensation rules can serve all of these multiple goals. For example, Congress, in passing the 1996 Act, recognized that the implicit subsidies historically contained in access charges are not sustainable in competitive local telecommunications markets. Accordingly, Congress in the 1996 Act directed this Commission and the states to reform universal service, and in particular, to eliminate implicit subsidies contained in access charges and instead make all universal service support explicit." Bill and Keep Carrier Compensation Proposal, 16 F.C.C.R. at 9623.
29. "Interstate access charges are imposed by local exchange carriers (LECs) to recover the costs of providing access to their networks for interstate and long-distance service. The Commission has long recognized that, to the extent possible, interstate access costs should be recovered in the manner in which

they are incurred. In particular, non-traffic-sensitive costs—costs that do not vary with the amount of traffic carried over the facilities—should be recovered through flat-rate charges, and traffic-sensitive costs should be recovered through per-minute charges. This approach fosters competition and efficient pricing. The Part 69 rules governing access charges, however, have not been fully consistent with this goal. For example, the costs of the common line or loop that connects an end user to a LEC's central office should be recovered from the end user through a flat charge, because loop costs do not vary with usage. Yet the subscriber line charge (SLC), a flat monthly charge assessed directly on end users to recover interstate loop costs, has been capped since its inception due to affordability concerns. Historically, LECs recovered their remaining common line costs through per-minute carrier common line (CCL) charges imposed on interexchange carriers (IXCs), which, in turn, passed these charges on to their customers in the form of higher long distance rates. By making the end-user rate for long distance calls more expensive, CCL charges artificially suppressed demand for interstate long distance services. CCL charges also created significant implicit subsidies flowing from high-volume to low-volume users of interstate long distance services, which have a disruptive effect on competition in the markets for local exchange and exchange access services." Order on Remand, *Access Charge Reform, Price Cap Performance Review for LECs*, 18 F.C.C.R. 14,976, 14,977–78 (2003).

30. *See, e.g.*, Third Report and Order and Fourth Notice of Proposed Rulemaking, *Implementation of Local Competition Provisions in Telecommunications Act of 1996*, 15 F.C.C.R. 3696 (1999), *remanded sub nom.* U.S. Telecom Ass'n v. FCC, 290 F.3d 415 (D.C. Cir. 2002).

31. For example, an ISP might avoid facilities construction or line-leasing costs by handing off traffic to another ISP, which would then bear the burden of securing final delivery or at least carriage onward to the intended destination. This free-riding tactic is referred to as "hot potato routing": "Rather than lease lines throughout the nation and expand capacity, the free rider ISP may attempt to hand off traffic to a larger, better equipped ISP at the closest public peering point. The free rider ISP considers traffic a 'hot potato' and has a financial incentive to pass such traffic off to any other ISP who agrees to take it." Rob Frieden, *Without Public Peer: The Potential Regulatory and Universal Service Consequences of Internet Balkanization*, 3 VA. J.L. & TECH. 8, n.2 (1998); *see also* Michael Kende, *The Digital Handshake: Connecting Internet Backbones*, 11 COMMLAW CONSPECTUS 45, 60 (2003).

32. For example, if a carrier charges higher fees to deliver international traffic than domestic traffic, a foreign carrier seeking termination of traffic will attempt to interconnect with the terminating carrier in a manner that makes the traffic appear domestic or even local in origin. The term "refiling" refers to the physical reinsertion of distant traffic into a local or additional long-distance network to reduce fees borne by the sender.

33. For example, if two carriers agree to a zero-cost bill-and-keep interconnection arrangement, all traffic handed off from one carrier to the other involves no payment obligation. Carriers agree to this arrangement when they have roughly equal traffic volumes. However, the zero-cost arrangement may encourage carriers to collect traffic from diverse locations where an interconnection payment would be required and to route it to the carrier offering zero-cost interconnection.
34. The FCC believes that the existing "exchange of reciprocal compensation payments appears to have distorted the development of competition in the local exchange market." Bill and Keep Carrier Compensation Proposal, 16 F.C.C.R. at 9632.
35. A "long-recognized form of regulatory arbitrage is the ability of certain owners of private branch exchanges ('PBXs') to avoid paying access charges on long-distance calls (the 'leaky PBX' problem)." Bill and Keep Carrier Compensation Proposal, 16 F.C.C.R. at 9616.
36. "For over six decades a tariff regime was mandated by the Communications Act of 1934, which requires the FCC to review telecommunications carriers' tariffs to ensure their reasonableness [*citing* 47 U.S.C. §§ 201–202]. The Act requires carriers to file their tariffs with the FCC [*citing* 47 U.S.C. § 203(a)], and they are prohibited from charging consumers except as provided in the tariffs [*citing* 47 U.S.C. § 203(c)] (establishing what is popularly known as the 'filed-rate doctrine')." MCI WorldCom Inc. v. FCC, 209 F.3d 760, 762 (D.C. Cir. 2000). Starting in the early 1980s, the FCC tried to prohibit tariff filing by all IXCs but AT&T. *See* MCI Telecommunications Corp. v. FCC, 765 F.2d 1186 (D.C. Cir. 1985) (mandatory detariffing deemed inconsistent with the 1934 act). These efforts failed until Congress expressly authorized elimination of regulatory requirements based on changed circumstances and a public interest justification. *See* Communications Act of 1934, as amended, 47 U.S.C. § 160.
37. The "leaky PBX" problem arises where large end users that employ multiple PBXs in multiple locations lease private lines to connect their various PBXs. Although these lines were intended to permit employees of the large users to communicate between locations without incurring access charges, some large users permitted long-distance calls to leak from the PBX into the local public network, where they were terminated without incurring access charges. In order to address this problem, the Commission in 1983 imposed a $25 per month charge on each trunk that could "leak" traffic into the public switched network. Bill and Keep Carrier Compensation Proposal, 16 F.C.C.R. at 9616, n.21, *citing* 47 C.F.R. § 69.115; Memorandum Opinion and Order, *MTS and WATS Market Structure*, 97 F.C.C. 2d 682 (1983).
38. "[A]fter an investigation, AT&T was ordered by the FCC to remove all resale restrictions in its tariffs for Message Telephone Service (MTS). After the WATS resale went into effect, many resellers began to take advantage of the new opportunities. Through leasing WATS lines, both MCI and Sprint were

then able to connect their customers' calls to anywhere in the AT&T network." Richard E. Nohe, *A Different Time, a Different Place: Breaking Up Telephone Companies in the United States and Japan*, 48 FED. COMM. L.J. 307, 319 (1996).

39. Second Report and Order, *Regulatory Policies Concerning Resale and Shared Use of Common Carrier Services and Facilities*, 60 F.C.C.2d 261, 7 (1976).
40. "Simple Resale, or ISR, could introduce competitive forces on routes that would place downward pressure on U.S.-international settlement rates. ISR involves the provision of switched services over resold or facilities-based private lines that connect to the public switched network at either end-point. Instead of U.S. carriers paying for the use of half of a shared circuit to a foreign point through traditional settlement payments, U.S. carriers under ISR arrangements may connect or lease a complete or whole circuit end-to-end to the corresponding foreign carrier's network and pay a negotiated rate for termination of services on the foreign network." Notice of Proposed Rulemaking, *International Settlements Policy Reform International Settlement Rates*, 17 F.C.C.R. 19,954, 19,961 (2002).
41. "Call-back service allows a customer in a foreign country to use foreign facilities to dial a telephone number in the United States and receive dial tone at a switch at the reseller's U.S. location, which the customer can then use to place a call via an outbound switched service of a U.S. carrier. The through calls are billed at U.S.-tariffed rates." Order, Authorization and Certificate, *VIA USA, Ltd., Telegroup, Inc., Discount Call International Co.*, 9 F.C.C.R. 2288 (1994), *on recon.*, 10 F.C.C.R. 9540 (1995).
42. "We therefore find, as a matter of international comity, that the Commission should prohibit carriers authorized to provide call-back service utilizing uncompleted call signaling from providing this offering in countries where it is expressly prohibited. We would expect no less from foreign governments in a comparable context." Order on Reconsideration, *VIA USA, Ltd., Telegroup, Inc., Discount Call International Co.*, 10 F.C.C.R. 9540, 9557 (1995).
43. Order, *Enforcement of Other Nations' Prohibitions Against the Uncompleted Call Signaling Configuration of International Call-Back Service, Petition for Rulemaking of the Telecommunications Resellers Association to Eliminate Comity-Based Enforcement of Other Nations' Prohibitions Against the Uncompleted Call Signaling Configuration of International Call-Back Service*, 18 F.C.C.R. 6077 (2003).
44. "By no longer enforcing prohibitions against call-back in foreign countries, we are not rejecting the sovereign rights of any foreign government or limiting the ability of a foreign government to adopt and enforce policies to prohibit call-back within its jurisdiction. Rather, we are re-emphasizing our standing policy to encourage competition in all markets, both developed and developing. We will continue to work in various fora to promote network expansion and universal access. We encourage a pro-competitive call-back policy that extends to the international marketplace, embraces free and open competition, and benefits U.S. consumers as well as the global community

by ensuring lower prices, new and better products and services, and greater consumer choice. Indeed, we believe that eliminating call-back prohibitions enhances competition throughout the global marketplace." *Id.* 18 F.C.C.R. at 6081–82.

45. "Carriers are adopting nontraditional, more cost-efficient means of routing traffic, such as routing switched traffic over private lines and switched hubbing. Some experts predict that by 2005, the resale market will be worth ten times what it was in 1996. New technologies such as callback and Internet telephony are already putting significant pressure on international settlement rates and domestic collection rates." Report and Order and Order on Reconsideration, *Rules and Policies on Foreign Participation in the U.S. Telecommunications Market,* 12 F.C.C.R. 23,891, 23,895 (1997), *modified,* 13 F.C.C.R. 6219 (1998).
46. Conventional dial-up local and long-distance telephone service use dedicated links and line switching between caller and call recipient. The network architecture optimizes quality and reliability for voice communications. For background on telephony basics *see* Marshal Brain, *How Telephones Work,* http://electronics.howstuffworks.com.
47. The Internet uses a network architecture that splits traffic into units known as packets. Packets are switched and routed via any available network that provides a shared medium available to multiple senders and receivers of data traffic. For background on Internet architecture basics *see* Jeff Tyson, *How Internet Infrastructure Works,* http://computer.howstuffworks.com.
48. Bill and Keep Carrier Compensation Proposal, 16 F.C.C.R. at 9657.
49. Memorandum Opinion and Order, *Petition for Declaratory Ruling That Pulver .com's Free World Dialup Is Neither Telecommunications Nor a Telecommunications Service,* 19 F.C.C.R. 3307 (2004).
50. Report to Congress, *Federal-State Joint Board on Universal Service,* 13 F.C.C.R. 11,501, 11,541 (1998).
51. Vonage Holdings Corp. v. FCC, 489 F.3d 1232 (D.C. Cir. 2007).
52. Seventh Report and Order and Further Notice of Proposed Rulemaking, *Reform of Access Charges Imposed by Competitive Local Exchange Carriers,* 32 Communications Reg. (P&F) 576, 2001 WL 431685 (2001).
53. Notice of Proposed Rulemaking, *International Settlements Policy Reform International Settlement Rates,* 17 F.C.C.R. 19,954, 19,979 (2002).
54. *See* Rob Frieden, *Internet Packet Sniffing and Its Impact on the Network Neutrality Debate and the Balance of Power Between Intellectual Property Creators and Consumers,* 18 FORDHAM INTELL. PROP. MEDIA & ENT. L.J. 633 (2008).
55. Walter S. Mossberg, *Wireless Carriers' Veto over How Phones Work Hampers Innovation,* THE WALL STREET JOURNAL, June 2, 2005, at B1.
56. *How Old Media Can Survive in a New World of Technology,* The Journal Report, THE WALL STREET JOURNAL, May 23, 2005, at R1.

CHAPTER TEN. CAPTURING THE BENEFITS OF CONVERGENCE

1. "Over the last two decades, the communications industry has undergone rapid technological advancements leading to the convergence of services. New technological capabilities allow companies to compete in markets which previously had no competition. While potentially beneficial to the consumer, convergence within the communications industry has created a regulatory nightmare." Ryan K. Mullady, *Regulatory Disparity: The Constitutional Implications of Communications Regulations That Prevent Competitive Neutrality*, 2 PGH J. TECH L. & POL'Y 4 (Spring 2007).
2. For example, Verizon markets itself as a communications and entertainment company, not a telephone company.
3. For background on the Telecommunications Act of 1996 *see* Robert M. Frieden, *The Telecommunications Act of 1996: Predicting the Winners and Losers*, 20 HASTINGS COMM. & ENT. L.J., 11 (Fall 1997); Thomas G. Krattenmaker, *The Telecommunications Act of 1996*, 29 CONN. L. REV. 123 (1996); Michael I. Meyerson, *Ideas of the Marketplace: A Guide to the 1996 Telecommunications Act*, 49 FED. COMM. L.J. 251 (Feb. 1997); Michael Glover & Donna Epps, *Is the Telecommunications Act of 1996 Working?* 52 ADMIN. L. REV. 1013 (Summer 2000); John C. Roberts, *The Sources of Statutory Meaning: An Archaeological Case Study of the 1996 Telecommunications Act*, 53 SMU L. REV. 143 (Winter 2000); Aimee M. Adler, *Competition in Telephony: Perception or Reality? Current Barriers to the Telecommunications Act of 1996*, 7 J.L. & POL'Y 571 (1999).
4. The FCC has crafted a basic and enhanced services dichotomy with the former referring to telecommunications, typically regulated as essential public utility services, and enhanced services, typically unregulated in view of their nonessential nature. *See generally* Final Decision and Order, *Regulatory and Policy Problems Presented by the Interdependence of Computer and Communications Services and Facilities*, 28 F.C.C. 2d 267 (1971), *aff'd in part sub nom.* GTE Service Corp. v. FCC, 474 F.2d 724 (2d Cir. 1973), *decision on remand*, Order, 40 F.C.C. 2d 293 (1973); Final Decision, *Amendment of Section 64.702 of the Commission's Rules and Regulations (Second Computer Inquiry)*, 77 FCC 2d 384 (1980), *on recon.*, Memorandum Opinion and Order, 84 F.C.C. 2d 50 (1980), Memorandum Opinion and Order on Further Reconsideration, 88 F.C.C. 2d 512 (1981), *aff'd sub nom.* Computer and Communications Indus. Ass'n v. FCC, 693 F.2d 198 (D.C. Cir. 1982), *cert. denied*, 461 U.S. 938 (1983); Report and Order, Memorandum Opinion and Order on Further Reconsideration, *Amendment of Section 64.702 of the Commission's Rules and Regulations (Third Computer Inquiry)*, 104 F.C.C. 2d 958 (1986), *on recon.*, 2 F.C.C.R. 3035 (1987), Memorandum Opinion and Order on Reconsideration, 3 F.C.C.R. 1135 (1988), Memorandum Opinion and Order on Further Reconsideration and Second Further Reconsideration, 4 F.C.C.R. 5927 (1989), *vacated in part*, California v. FCC, 905 F.2d 1217 (9th Cir. 1990); Report and Order, 2 F.C.C.R. 3072 (1987), *on recon.*, Memorandum Opinion and Order on Recon-

sideration, 3 F.C.C.R. 1150 (1988), *vacated in part,* California v. FCC, 905 F.2d 1217 (9th Cir. 1990); Report and Order, *Computer III Remand Proceedings,* 5 F.C.C.R. 7719 (1990), *on recon.,* Memorandum Opinion and Order on Reconsideration, 7 F.C.C.R. 909 (1992), *pet. for review denied,* California v. FCC, 4 F.3d 1505 (9th Cir. 1993); Report and Order, *Computer III Remand Proceedings: Bell Operating Company Safeguards and Tier I Local Exchange Company Safeguards,* 6 F.C.C.R. 7571 (1991), *vacated in part and remanded,* California v. FCC, 39 F.3d 919 (9th Cir. 1994), *cert. denied,* 514 U.S. 1050 (1995); Report and Order, *COMPUTER III Further Remand Proceedings: Bell Operating Company Provision Of Enhanced* Services 14 F.C.C.R. 4289 (1999), *on recon.,* Order, 14 F.C.C.R. 21,628 (1999). On several occasions, the court presiding over the federal government's antitrust lawsuit against AT&T created service definitions, including definitions of regulated telecommunications and unregulated information services. *See* United States v. Western Electric Co., 673 F. Supp. 525 (D.D.C. 1987), and 714 F. Supp. 1 (D.D.C. 1988), *rev'd in part,* 900 F.2d 283 (D.C. Cir. 1990). The modification of final judgment that established the terms and conditions for the divestiture of the local Bell Operating Companies from AT&T defined "telecommunications" as "the transmission, between or among points specified by the user, of information of the user's choosing, without change in the form or content of the information as sent and received, by means of electromagnetic transmission, with or without benefit of any closed transmission medium, including all instrumentalities, facilities, apparatus, and services (including the collection, storage, forwarding, switching, and delivery of such information) essential to such transmission." 552 F. Supp. at 229, *aff'd sub nom.* Maryland v. United States, 460 U.S. 1001 (1983). The modification of final judgment defines "information service" as the "offering of a capability for generating, acquiring, storing, transforming, processing, retrieving, utilizing, or making available information which may be conveyed via telecommunications . . ."; "information" is defined as "knowledge or intelligence represented by any form of writing, signs, pictures, sounds, or other symbols." *Id.*

5. *See, e.g.,* Commission of the European Communities, *Proposal for a Directive of the European Parliament and of the Council on a Common Regulatory Framework for Electronic Communications Networks and Services,* COM (2000) 393 final (Brussels, July 12, 2000).
6. Telephone companies incur federal and state common carrier economic regulation based initially on their monopoly market share. "The decree [divesting the AT&T Bell System of its local operating companies] did nothing, however, to increase competition in the persistently monopolistic local markets, which were thought to be the root of natural monopoly in the telecommunications industry." Verizon Commc'ns Inc. v. FCC, 535 U.S. 467, 475, 122 S. Ct. 1646, 1654 (2002).
7. Public utility regulation, like that applied to telephone companies, applies, because of the view that government must intervene, in the absence of com-

petition, to ensure fair prices, universal access, and high-quality service. "Until the 1990's, local phone service was thought to be a natural monopoly. States typically granted an exclusive franchise in each local service area to a local exchange carrier (LEC), which owned, among other things, the local loops (wires connecting telephones to switches), the switches (equipment directing calls to their destinations), and the transport trunks (wires carrying calls between switches) that constitute a local exchange network. Technological advances, however, have made competition among multiple providers of local services seem possible, and Congress recently ended the longstanding regime of state-sanctioned monopolies." AT&T Corp. v. Iowa Utilities Bd., 525 U.S. 366, 371, 119 S. Ct. 721, 726 (1999).

8. Mass media regulation derives, in part, from its perceived reach and social impact. "[A]t least one set of competing claims to the protection of . . . [the First] Amendment derives from the fact that, because of the limited number of broadcast frequencies available and the potentially pervasive impact of the electronic media, 'the people as a whole retain their interest in free speech by radio and their collective right to have the medium function consistently with the ends and purposes of the First Amendment.'" Columbia Broadcasting System Inc. v. Democratic Nat. Committee, 412 U.S. 94, 182–83, 93 S. Ct. 2080, 2126 (1973), *citing* Red Lion Broadcasting Co. v. FCC, *supra,* 395 U.S. at 390, 89 S. Ct. at 1806.
9. "Consider the following scenario: A federal regulator walks into a room and is confronted with five television sets, each displaying the same program. The show features a steamy sex scene between a man and a woman, complete with nudity, adult language, and lots of sweat. Although transparent to the viewer, each television is fed via a different transmission source. The first television is receiving a terrestrial broadcast transmission, the second obtains the images by coaxial cable, the third is connected to a fiber optic common carrier network, the fourth is hooked to a VCR, and the fifth is receiving a direct broadcast satellite (DBS) feed. Leaving aside any questions of federal versus local jurisdiction and assuming that the images are not obscene, what is the regulator's constitutional authority to control these images? The answer is, it depends." Robert Corn-Revere, *New Technology and the First Amendment: Breaking the Cycle of Repression,* 17 HASTINGS COMM. & ENT L.J. 247, 249 (1994).
10. *See* Rob Frieden, *Whither Convergence: Legal, Regulatory and Trade Opportunism in Telecommunications,* 18 SANTA CLARA COMPUTER & HIGH TECH. L.J., No. 2, 171 (2001).
11. Common carriers provide essential public utility services on a nondiscriminatory basis, typically subject to extensive economic regulation to ensure just and reasonable rates. Section 153(44) of the Communications Act of 1934, as amended, 47 U.S.C. § 153(44), defines "telecommunications carrier" as a carrier offering "telecommunications service," and 47 U.S.C. § 153(46) states that "telecommunications services" are common carrier services. For

extensive background on the history of common carriage *see* James B. Speta, *A Common Carrier Approach to Internet Interconnection,* 54 FED. COMM. L.J. 225 (Mar. 2002).

12. The FCC defined "enhanced services" as "any offering over the telecommunications network which is more than a basic transmission service," or—more specifically—as "combin[ing] basic service with computer processing applications that act on the format, content, code, protocol or similar aspects of the subscriber's transmitted information, or provide the subscriber with additional, different, or restructured information, or involve subscriber interaction with stored information." Final Decision, *Amendment of Section 64.702 of the Commission's Rules and Regulations (Second Computer Inquiry),* 77 F.C.C.2d 384, 387 (1980). Practically speaking, the FCC's enhanced services definition is compatible with the information services classification contained in the Telecommunications Act of 1996: "The Commission has determined that information services consist of all services that the Commission previously considered to be enhanced services. However, the Commission also has determined that while all enhanced services are information services, not all information services are enhanced services." Robert Cannon, *Where Internet Service Providers and Telephone Companies Compete: A Guide to the Computer Inquiries, Enhanced Service Providers and Information Service Providers,* 9 COMMLAW CONSPECTUS 49, 55 (2001).
13. Even prior to the current acceleration of technological and marketplace convergence, some commentators objected to nonuniform and inconsistent regulation and jurisprudence as between, for example, the print and broadcast media. *See* Thomas G. Krattenmaker & L. A. Powe, Jr., *Converging First Amendment Principles for Converging Communications Media,* 104 YALE L.J. 1719 (1995); Mark Nadel, *A Technology Transparent Theory of the First Amendment and Access to Communications Media,* 43 FED. COMM. L.J. 157, 182 (1991).
14. *See* James H. Lister, *The Rights of Common Carriers and the Decision Whether to Be a Common Carrier or a Non-regulated Communications Provider,* 53 FED. COMM. L.J. 91 (Dec. 2000).
15. "A regulatory model based on who provides the services is no longer an appropriate model in the broadband world." Antonia M. Apps & Thomas M. Dailey, *Non-regulation of Advanced Internet Services,* 8 GEO. MASON L. REV. 681, 682 (Summer 2000).
16. Data networks, including the Internet fit well into a horizontal model for purposes of understanding the structure and technical interfaces needed to achieve connections. The Open Systems Interconnection (OSI) model provides a helpful example of horizontal modeling. It is a "standard description or 'reference model' for how messages should be transmitted between any two points in a telecommunication network. Its purpose is to guide product implementors so that their products will consistently work with other products. The reference model defines seven layers of functions that take place at

each end of a communication. Although OSI is not always strictly adhered to in terms of keeping related functions together in a well-defined layer, many if not most products involved in telecommunication make an attempt to describe themselves in relation to the OSI model. It is also valuable as a single reference view of communication that furnishes everyone a common ground for education and discussion." Searchnetworking.com.

17. *Directive 2002/21/EC of the European Parliament and of the Council of 7 March 2002 on a Common Regulatory Framework for Electronic Communications Networks and Services (Framework Directive)*, Council Directive 2002/21 art.5, 2002 O.J. (108/33).
18. *Id.* at art. 27.
19. 47 U.S.C. § 160.
20. "Congress enacted the safe harbors in response to concerns expressed by online service providers about their potentially overwhelming liability for copyright infringement committed by their users." Mark A. Lemley & R. Anthony Reese, *Reducing Digital Copyright Infringement Without Restricting Innovation,* 56 STAN. L. REV. 1345, 1369 (May 2004).
21. Report and Order and Notice of Proposed Rulemaking, *Universal Service Contribution Methodology,* 21 F.C.C.R. 7518 (2006) (extending section 254(d) permissive authority to require interconnected VoIP providers to contribute to the Universal Service Fund), *partially aff'd and partially reversed,* Vonage Holdings Corp. v. FCC, 489 F.3d 1232 (D.C. Cir. 2007).
22. First Report and Order and Notice of Proposed Rulemaking, *IP-Enabled Services,* 20 F.C.C.R. 10,245 (2005), *aff'd,* Nuvio Corp. v. FCC, 473 F.3d 302 (D.C. Cir. 2006).
23. Report and Order, *IP-Enabled Services,* 22 F.C.C.R. 11,275 (2007).
24. Declaratory Ruling, Order on Remand, and Notice of Proposed Rulemaking, *Telephone Number Requirements for IP-Enabled Services Providers,* 22 F.C.C.R. 19,531, 23 F.C.C.R. 1647 (2007).
25. Sec. 103(a) of the Communications Assistance for Law Enforcement Act (CALEA), *codified at* 47 U.S.C. § 1002(a), requires, *inter alia,* that "a telecommunications carrier shall ensure that its equipment, facilities, or services that provide a customer or subscriber with the ability to originate, terminate, or direct communications are capable of—(1) expeditiously isolating and enabling the government, pursuant to a court order or other lawful authorization, to intercept, to the exclusion of any other communications, all wire and electronic communications carried by the carrier within a service area to or from equipment, facilities, or services of a subscriber of such carrier concurrently with their transmission to or from the subscriber's equipment, facility, or service, or at such later time as may be acceptable to the government. However Sec. 103(b) (2) (A) explicitly exempts providers of information services from having to provide wiretapping assistance. "The requirements of subsection (a) do not apply to—(A) information services." CALEA defines information service as "the offering of a capability for generating, acquiring,

storing, transforming, processing, retrieving, utilizing, or making available information via telecommunications; and (B) includes—(i) a service that permits a customer to retrieve stored information from, or file information for storage in, information storage facilities; (ii) electronic publishing; and (iii) electronic messaging services; but (C) does not include any capability for a telecommunications carrier's internal management, control, or operation of its telecommunications network." 47 U.S.C. § 1001 (6).

26. *See* Memorandum Opinion and Order, *United Power Line Council's Petition for Declaratory Ruling Regarding the Classification of Broadband over Power Line Internet Access Service as an Information Service,* WC Docket No. 06–10, 21 F.C.C.R. 13,281 (2006) (extending the information service deregulatory safe harbor to broadband-over-power-line networks).
27. *See* Declaratory Ruling, *Appropriate Regulatory Treatment for Broadband Access to the Internet over Wireless Networks,* 22 F.C.C.R. 5901 (2007) (extending the information service deregulatory safe harbor to wireless broadband networks).
28. Report and Order and Notice of Proposed Rulemaking, *Appropriate Framework for Broadband Access to the Internet over Wireless Facilities,* 20 F.C.C.R. 14,853 (2005) [hereinafter cited as Appropriate Framework for Broadband Access to the Internet over Wireless Facilities].
29. "[T]his Order encourages the ubiquitous availability of broadband to all Americans by, among other things, removing outdated regulations. Those regulations were created over the past three decades under technological and market conditions that differed greatly from those of today." *Id.* at 14,855.
30. "[T]he framework we adopt in this Order furthers the goal of developing a consistent regulatory framework across platforms by regulating like services in a similar functional manner, after a transitional period." *Id.*
31. "[T]he actions we take in this Order allow facilities-based wireline broadband Internet access service providers to respond to changing marketplace demands effectively and efficiently, spurring them to invest in and deploy innovative broadband capabilities that can benefit all Americans. . . ." *Id.*
32. "[T]he record before us demonstrates that the broadband Internet access market today is characterized by several emerging platforms and providers, both intermodal and intramodal, in most areas of the country." *Id.* at 14,856. But curiously the Commission also forecasts competition resulting from its decision: "We are confident that the regulatory regime we adopt in this Order will promote the availability of competitive broadband Internet access services to consumers, via multiple platforms, while ensuring adequate incentives are in place to encourage the deployment and innovation of broadband platforms consistent with our obligations and mandates under the Act." *Id.*
33. Section 706(d) of the Telecommunications Act of 1996 defines "advanced telecommunications capability . . . without regard to any transmission media or technology, as high-speed, switched, broadband telecommunications capability that enables users to originate and receive high-quality voice, data,

graphics, and video telecommunications using any technology." 47 U.S.C. § 1302(d).

34. "Finally, the directives of section 706 of the 1996 Act require that we ensure that our broadband policies promote infrastructure investment, consistent with our other obligations under the Act." Appropriate Framework for Broadband Access to the Internet over Wireless Facilities, 20 F.C.C.R. at 14,865.
35. "Wireline broadband Internet access service, for purposes of this proceeding, is a service that uses existing or future wireline facilities of the telephone network to provide subscribers with Internet access capabilities." *Id.* at 14,860.
36. "Applying the definitions of 'information service,' 'telecommunications,' and 'telecommunications service,' we conclude that wireline broadband Internet access service provided over a provider's own facilities is appropriately classified as an information service because its providers offer a single, integrated service (*i.e.,* Internet access) to end users. That is, like cable modem service (which is usually provided over the provider's own facilities), wireline broadband Internet access service combines computer processing, information provision, and computer interactivity with data transport, enabling end users to run a variety of applications (*e.g.,* e-mail, web pages, and newsgroups). These applications encompass the capability for 'generating, acquiring, storing, transforming, processing, retrieving, utilizing, or making available information via telecommunications,' and taken together constitute an information service as defined by the Act." *Id.* at 14,863–64 (footnotes omitted).
37. *Id.* at 14,864 (footnote omitted).
38. "Based on the record before us, we expect that facilities-based wireline carriers will have business reasons to continue making broadband Internet access transmission services available to ISPs without regard to the *Computer Inquiry* requirements. The record makes clear that such carriers have a business interest in maximizing the traffic on their networks, as this enables them to spread fixed costs over a greater number of revenue-generating customers. For their part, cable operators, which have never been required to make Internet access transmission available to third parties on a wholesale basis, have business incentives similar to those of incumbent LECs to make such transmission available to ISPs, and are continuing to do so pursuant to private carriage arrangements." *Id.* at 14,887 (footnotes omitted).
39. "Based on the record before us, it is not necessary to make a finding of market non-dominance as to the incumbent LECs in the provision of broadband Internet access transmission, as some parties have asked us to do, before we may eliminate the *Computer Inquiry* obligations. We decline to do so. Nor do we think it necessary or appropriate to make findings about dominance or non-dominance with respect to the retail market for broadband Internet access." *Id.* at 14,897–98 (footnotes omitted).
40. "The previous market environment differs markedly from the dynamic and evolving broadband Internet access marketplace before us today where the current market leaders, cable operators and wireline carriers, face competi-

tion not only from each other but also from other emerging broadband Internet access service providers. This rapidly changing market does not lend itself to the conclusions about market dominance the Commission typically makes to determine the degree of regulation to be applied to well-established, relatively stable telecommunications service markets. On the contrary, any finding about dominance or non-dominance in this emerging broadband Internet access service market would be premature." *Id.* at 14,898 (footnotes omitted).

41. The FCC proposes to provide still-essential consumer protection safeguards under a common framework for all broadband services. "This framework necessarily will be built on our ancillary jurisdiction under Title I; as we explain in the Order, this jurisdiction is ample to accomplish the consumer protection goals we identify below, and we will not hesitate to exercise it." *Id.* at 14,929–30 (footnotes omitted).
42. "The Commission may exercise its ancillary jurisdiction when Title I of the Act gives the Commission subject matter jurisdiction over the service to be regulated and the assertion of jurisdiction is 'reasonably ancillary to the effective performance of [its] various responsibilities.' We recognize that both of the predicates for ancillary jurisdiction are likely satisfied for any consumer protection, network reliability, or national security obligation that we may subsequently decide to impose on wireline broadband Internet access service providers." *Id.* at 14,913–14 (quoting United States v. Sw. Cable Co. 392 U.S. 157, 178 (1968)) (other footnotes omitted).
43. 5 U.S.C. § 706(2) (A).
44. In their objection to interconnection requirements imposed by the Telecommunications Act, incumbent telephone companies used the term "confiscatory" to characterize the burden created. These carriers objected to the FCC's statutory interpretation of the terms, conditions, and scope relating to the carriers' obligation to lease facilities and services to competitors on rates below what the incumbent carriers would require in direct negotiations with market entrants. The Supreme Court on two occasions endorsed the FCC's implementation of a congressional mandate to promote competition by requiring significant cooperation between incumbents and market entrants. In AT&T Corp. v. Iowa Utilities Board, 525 U.S. 366, 119 S. Ct. 721 (1999), the Supreme Court largely upheld the Commission's implementation of section 251 as a reasonable exercise of its rulemaking authority, including its requirement that incumbent carriers unbundle various network elements and offer market entrants the opportunity to pick and choose from an à la carte menu or platform of services and functions. The Court also ruled that in identifying which network elements ILECs should unbundle, the Commission not limit the set of network elements to those necessary to promote competition whose absence from the list might impair market entrants' ability to compete. In other words, the Court did not deem unconstitutional the congressional mandate of requiring incumbent carriers to unbundle their

networks and make each element available to competitors. The Court also largely deferred to the FCC's determination on how to price such access. In Verizon Commc'ns Inc. v. FCC, 535 U.S. 467, 122 S. Ct. 1646 (2002), the Court rejected incumbent local exchange carrier arguments that using a theoretical cost-efficient model, instead of actual historical costs, constituted a taking that violated the Fifth Amendment. The Court noted that no party had disputed any specific rate established by the TELRIC pricing model and concluded that "regulatory bodies required to set [just and reasonable] rates . . . have ample discretion to choose methodology." Verizon Commc'ns Inc. v. FCC, 535 U.S. at 500, 122 S. Ct. at 1667.

45. Not just the safe harbor but also the largely unregulated Commercial Mobile Radio Service classification for wireless networks helped remove government oversight. Communications Act § 332(A) (i)–(iii), *amended by* 47 U.S.C. § 332(A) (i)–(iii) (authorizes the FCC to forbear from applying most of the Title II common carrier regulations to commercial mobile radiotelephone service providers, such as cellular radiotelephone carriers, if "(i) enforcement of such provision is not necessary in order to ensure that the charges, practices, classifications, or regulations for or in connection with that service are just and reasonable and are not unjustly or unreasonably discriminatory; (ii) enforcement of such provision is not necessary for the protection of consumers; and (iii) specifying such provision is consistent with the public interest").

CHAPTER ELEVEN. WHAT GOVERNMENT SHOULD DO

1. "The capacity of countries and firms to develop and manage knowledge assets has become a major determinant of economic growth and competitiveness. . . . [I]nvestment in and exploitation of knowledge remains a key driver of innovation, economic performance and social well being. Over the last decade, investments in knowledge—as measured by expenditures on research and development (R&D), higher education, and information and communication technologies (ICTs)—grew more rapidly than gross fixed capital formation." Organisation for Economic Co-operation and Development, *Towards a Knowledge-Based Economy—Recent Trends and Policy Directions from the OECD,* Background Paper for the OECD-IPS Workshop on Promoting Knowledge-Based Economies in Asia, at 3 (2002), http://www.oecd.org; *see also Science, Technology and Industry Scoreboard 2009,* http://www.oecd.org.
2. "Knowledge is now recognized as the driver of productivity and economic growth, leading to a new focus on the role of information, technology and learning in economic performance. The term '*knowledge-based economy*' stems from this fuller recognition of the place of knowledge and technology in modern . . . economies." Organisation for Economic Co-operation and Development, *The Knowledge-Based Economy,* Forward at 3 (1995).
3. *See also World Summit on the Information Society and the Role of ICT in Achieving the Millennium Development Goals* Web site, http://topics.development

gateway.org/ict/sdm/previewDocument.doactiveDocumentId=815843; *ICT for Development* Web site, http://topics.developmentgateway.org/ict; International Telecommunication Union, *The World Summit on the Information Society* Web site, http://www.itu.int/wsis/.

4. In a joint venture with Siemens the China Academy of Telecommunications Technology has developed the TD-SCDMA mobile radio standard for third-generation mobile radiotelephones. This is the first telecommunications standard proposed by the Chinese industry and accepted as one of several standards by international forums.
5. Rick Petree, Radoslav Petkov & Eugene Spiro, *Technology Parks—Concept and Organization*, Columbia International Affairs Online Working Paper (June 1999).
6. For extensive research and reports on ICT issues in Korea and elsewhere *see* the Korea Informatization Promotion Committee Web site, http://www.ipc.go.kr/intra/HPEnglish.nsf; and the Korea Information Strategy Development Institute Web site, http://www.kisdi.re.kr/.
7. *See* Prime Minister of Japan and His Cabinet, *Information Technology* Web site, http://www.kantei.go.jp/foreign/it_e.html. "We will strive to establish an environment where the private sector, based on market forces, can exert its full potential and make Japan the world's most advanced IT nation within five years by: 1) building an ultra high speed Internet network and providing constant Internet access at the earliest date possible, 2) establishing rules on electronic commerce, 3) realizing an electronic government and 4) nurturing high-quality human resources for the new era." *e-Japan Strategy*, Jan. 2001, http://www.kantei.go.jp.
8. *See* Japan Ministry of Internal Affairs and Communications, u-Japan Policy Web site, http://www.soumu.go.jp.
9. The Korean government offers several vehicles for expediting broadband deployment and use. *See* United Kingdom Department of Trade and Industry and Brunel University, *Investigating Broadband Deployment in South Korea—Broadband Mission to South Korea* (Oct. 2002), http://www.broadbanduk.org.
10. "The Pew Internet study also explores the reasons why many Americans—either dial-up users or non-internet users—do not have high-speed internet connections at home. Among the 10% of Americans (or 15% of home internet users) with dial-up at home: 35% of dial-up users say that the price of broadband service would have to fall; 19% of dial-up users said nothing would convince them to get broadband; and 10% of dial-up users—and 15% of dial-up users in rural America—say that broadband service would have to become available where they. Overall, 62% of dial-up users say they are not interested in switching from dial-up to broadband." Pew Internet and American Life Project, Press Release, *55% of Adult Americans Have Home Broadband Connections* (July 2, 2008).
11. For background on how the Internet evolved from a government-underwrit

ten project to a privatized and commercialized medium *see* Rob Frieden, *Revenge of the Bellheads: How the Netheads Lost Control of the Internet*, 26 TELECOMM. POL'Y, No. 6, 125 (Sept.–Oct. 2002).

12. For example, the FCC determined that Comcast deliberately blocked subscribers' use of peer-to-peer networking services even in the absence of congestion. Memorandum Opinion and Order, *Formal Complaint of Free Press and Public Knowledge Against Comcast Corporation for Secretly Degrading Peer-to-Peer Applications*, 23 F.C.C.R. 13,028 (2008).
13. "As a consequence of these changes, the share of costs for international connectivity for Australian ISPs has fallen from around 70% to about 10%." John Hibbard, John de Ridder, Dr. George R. Barker & Professor Rob Frieden, *International Internet Connectivity and Its Impact on Australia: Final Report on an Investigation for the Department of Communication Information Technology and the Arts* at 4 (May 31, 2004), http://www.dcita.gov.au. *See also* Australian Competition Commission, *Internet Interconnection Service* (Apr. 2003), http://www.accc.gov.au.
14. *See* Rob Frieden, New America Foundation, *Wireless Carterfone—A Long Overdue Policy Promoting Consumer Choice and Competition*, Wireless Future Program, Working Paper No. 20 (Jan. 2008), http://www.newamerica.net; Tim Wu, New America Foundation, *Wireless Net Neutrality: Cellular Carterfone and Consumer Choice In Mobile Broadband*, Wireless Future Program, Working Paper No. 17 (Feb. 2007), http://www.newamerica.net; Robert W. Hahn, Robert E. Litan & Hal J. Singer, AEI-Brookings Joint Center for Regulatory Studies, *The Economics of "Wireless Net Neutrality* (Apr. 2007).
15. "Now what they would like to do is use my pipes free, but I ain't going to let them do that because we have spent this capital and we have to have a return on it. So there's going to have to be some mechanism for these people who use these pipes to pay for the portion they're using. Why should they be allowed to use my pipes? The Internet can't be free in that sense, because we and the cable companies have made an investment and for a Google or Yahoo! or Vonage or anybody to expect to use these pipes [for] free is nuts!" Ed Whitacre, quoted in *At SBC, It's All About "Scale and Scope,"* BUSINESSWEEK, Online Extra, Nov. 7, 2005, http://www.businessweek.com.
16. For background on the economics and logistics of peering *see* Geoff Huston, *Where's the Money?—Internet Interconnection and Financial Settlements* (Jan. 2005); Steve Gibbard, *Economics of Peering* (Oct. 2004).
17. "So Enron was also responsible for some of California's power crisis! What was then a profoundly corrupt enterprise manipulated the Golden State's power market to help create artificial shortages that would jack up prices. A particularly repellent example of this enterprise was Enron's so-called Death Star strategy, which, as a company memo put it, let Enron be paid 'for moving energy to relieve congestion without actually moving any energy or relieving any congestion.' In one case, Enron bought power in California at a capped price of $250 a megawatt hour and resold it in Oregon for $2,500.

The company also 'laundered' electricity to avoid federal price caps." PROVIDENCE JOURNAL-BULLETIN, May 22, 2002 (retrived from Lexis-Nexis Academic Universe).

CHAPTER TWELVE. UNRESOLVED ISSUES

1. A well-regarded telecommunications business analyst has expressed doubt about whether any other broadband technology will offer a competitive alternative to DSL and cable modem service. "Prospects for the long-heralded 'third pipe' appear dim and dimming." Blair Levin, Stifel Nicolaus Corp., quoted in Ed Gubbins, *Broadband Competition: Is This as Good as It Gets?* TELEPHONY ONLINE, Aug. 21, 2008, http://telephonyonline.com.
2. FCC, Industry Analysis and Technology Division, Wireline Competition Bureau, *High-Speed Services for Internet Access: Status as of December 31, 2007* (rel. Jan 16, 2009).
3. *Id.* at 4.
4. *Id.*
5. Federal Communications Commission, *Annual Report and Analysis of Competitive Market Conditions with Respect to Commercial Mobile Services,* WT Docket No. 07–71, Twelfth Report and Order, 1 (rel. Feb. 4, 2008).
6. "One of the underhanded tactics increasingly being used by telecom companies is 'Astroturf lobbying'—creating front groups that try to mimic true grassroots, but that are all about corporate money, not citizen power." Common Cause, *Wolves in Sheep's Clothing: Telecom Industry Front Groups and Astroturf* (Aug. 10, 2006), http://www.commoncause.org.

RECOMMENDED READINGS

BROADBAND ICT DEVELOPMENT AND POLICY

Robert D. Atkinson, The Information Technology and Innovation Foundation, *The Case for a National Broadband Policy* (June 2007), http://www.itif.org/files/CaseForNationalBroadbandPolicy.pdf.

Leonard M. Baynes, *"The Mercedes Divide?"—American Segregation Shapes the Color of Electronic Commerce,* 29 W. NEW ENG. L. REV. 165 (2006).

Benjamin W. Cramer, *"The Nation's Broadband Success Story": The Secrecy of FCC Broadband Infrastructure Statistics,* 31 HASTINGS COMM. & ENT L.J. 339 (Spring 2009).

Rob Frieden, *Lies, Damn Lies and Statistics: Developing a Clearer Assessment of Market Penetration and Broadband Competition in the United States,* 14 VA. J.L. & TECH. 100 (Summer 2009), http://www.vjolt.net/vol14/issue2/v14i2_100%20-%20Frieden.pdf.

International Telecommunication Union, *Measuring the Information Society—The ICT Development Index* (2009).

Jennifer A. Manner, *Achieving the Goal of Universal Access to Telecommunications Services Globally,* 13 COMM. L. CONSPECTUS 85 (2004).

Philip M. Napoli, *Toward a Federal Data Agenda for Communications Policymaking,* 16 COMMLAW CONSPECTUS 53 (2007).

Organisation for Economic Co-operation and Development, Directorate for Science, Technology and Industry, *OECD Broadband Portal,* http://www.oecd.org/sti/ict/broadband.

Organisation for Economic Co-operation and Development, *The Future of the Internet Economy: A Statistical Profile* (June 2008), http://www.oecd.org/dataoecd/44/56/40827598.pdf.

Tramanh Phi, *Duopolies, Restrictions, and Content Regulation: How Much Access Are We Really Getting from Broadband Internet Access?* 47 SANTA CLARA L. REV. 347 (2007).

Edward J. Sholinsky, *Blocking Access to the Information Superhighway: Regulating the Internet Out of the Reach of Low-Income Americans,* 38 RUTGERS L.J. 321 (Fall 2006).

Hannibal Travis, *Of Blogs, Ebooks, and Broadband: Access to Digital Media as a First Amendment Right,* 35 HOFSTRA L. REV. 1519 (Spring 2007).

Richard S. Whitt, *Evolving Broadband Policy: Taking Adaptive Stances to Foster Optimal Internet Platforms* 17 COMMLAW CONSPECTUS 417 (2009).

John Windhausen, Educause, *A Blueprint for Big Broadband* (Jan. 2008), http://net.educause.edu/ir/library/pdf/EPO0801.pdf.

COMPARATIVE INTERNET AND TELECOMMUNICATIONS STUDIES

Junseong An, *Korean DSL Policy: Implications for the United States,* 20 J. MARSHALL J. COMPUTER & INFO. L. 417 (Spring 2002).

Bob Bell, *Broadband Deregulation—Similar Legislation, Different Results: A Comparative Look at the United States and the European Union,* 10 TUL. J. TECH. & INTELL. PROP. 77 (Fall 2007).

Timothy J. Brennan, *Skating Toward Deregulation: Canadian Developments,* 60 FED. COMM. L.J. 325 (Mar. 2008).

Susan P. Crawford, *Transporting Communications,* 89 B.U. L. REV. 871 (June 2009).

Nicholas P. Dickerson, *What Makes the Internet So Special? And Why, Where, How, and By Whom Should Its Content Be Regulated?* 46 HOUS. L. REV. 61 (2009).

Donna Coleman Gregg, *Lessons Learned from the Spectrum Wars: Views on the United States' Effort Going Into and Coming Out of a World Radiocommunication Conference,* 17 COMMLAW CONSPECTUS 377 (2009).

Sandra C. Lee, *WIMAX in Africa: A New Frontier,* 15 COMMLAW CONSPECTUS 517 (2007).

Tilman Lüder, *The Next Ten Years in E.U. Copyright: Making Markets Work,* 18 FORDHAM INTELL. PROP. MEDIA & ENT. L.J. 1 (Autumn 2007).

Patrick S. Ryan, *European Spectrum Management Principles,* 23 J. MARSHALL J. COMPUTER & INFO. L. 277 (Winter 2005).

D. Daniel Sokol, *The European Mobile 3G UMTS Process: Lessons from the Spectrum Auctions and Beauty Contests,* 6 VA. J. L. & TECH. 17 (Fall 2001).

Oliver Solano, *Challenges to the Effective Implementation of Competition Policy in Regulated Sectors: The Case of Telecommunications in Mexico,* 26 NW. J. INT'L L. & BUS. 527 (2006).

COMPETITION AND ANTITRUST POLICY

Ashutosh Bhagwat, *Unnatural Competition? Applying the New Antitrust Learning to Foster Competition in the Local Exchange,* 50 HASTINGS L.J. 1479 (Aug. 1999).

Timothy J. Brennan, *Bundled Rebates as Exclusion Rather Than Predation,* 4 J. COMPETITION L. & ECON. 335 (June 2008).

Adam Candeub, *Trinko and Re-grounding the Refusal to Deal Doctrine*, 66 U. PITT. L. REV. 821 (Summer 2005).

Gregory S. Cooper, *A Tangled Web We Weave: Enforcing International Speech Restrictions in an Online World*, 8 U. PITT. J. TECH. L. & POL'Y 2 (Fall 2007).

Daniel A. Crane, *Technocracy and Antitrust*, 86 TEX. L. REV. 1159 (May 2008).

Stacey L. Dogan & Mark A. Lemley, *Antitrust Law and Regulatory Gaming*, 87 TEX. L. REV. 685 (Mar. 2009).

William J. Drake & Ernest J. Wilson III, eds., *Governing Global Electronic Networks—International Perspectives on Policy and Power* (MIT Press, 2008).

Nicholas Economides, *Hit and Miss: Leverage, Sacrifice, and Refusal to Deal in the Supreme Court Decision in Trinko*, 10 VAND. J. ENT. & TECH. L. 121 (Fall 2007).

David S. Evans, *Antitrust Issues Raised by the Emerging Global Internet Economy*, 102 NW. U. L. REV. 285 (Apr. 28, 2008).

Brett Frischmann, *Revitalizing Essential Facilities*, 75 ANTITRUST L.J. 1 (2008).

Damien Geradin, *The Concurrent Application of Competition Law and Regulation: The Case of Margin Squeeze Abuses in the Telecommunications Sector*, 1 J. COMPETITION L. & ECON. 355 (June 2005).

Erik N. Hovenkamp & Herbert Hovenkamp, *The Viability of Antitrust Price Squeeze Claims*, 51 ARIZ. L. REV. 273 (Summer 2009).

Michel Kerf & Damien Geradin, *Controlling Market Power in Telecommunications: Antitrust vs. Sector-Specific Regulation—An Assessment of the United States, New Zealand and Australian Experiences*, 14 BERKELEY TECH. L.J. 919 (Fall 1999).

Marina Lao, *Networks, Access, and "Essential Facilities": From Terminal Railroad to Microsoft*, 62 SMU L. REV. 557 (Spring 2009).

Paul W. MacAvoy, *An Oligopoly Analysis of At&T's Performance in the Wireline Long-Distance Markets After Divestiture*, 61 FED. COMM. L.J. 31 (Dec. 2008).

A. Douglas Melamed, *Exclusionary Conduct Under the Antitrust Laws: Balancing, Sacrifice, and Refusals to Deal*, 20 BERKELEY TECH. L.J. 1247 (Spring 2005).

Michele Polo, *Price Squeeze: Lessons from the Telecom Italia Case*, 3 J. COMPETITION L. & ECON. 453 (Sept. 2007).

Glen O. Robinson, *On Refusing to Deal with Rivals*, 87 CORNELL L. REV. 1177 (July 2002).

Frank X. Schoen, *Exclusionary Conduct After Trinko*, 80 N.Y.U. L. REV. 1625 (Nov. 2005).

Daniel F. Spulber, *Mandating Access to Telecom and the Internet: The Hidden Side of Trinko*, 107 COLUM. L. REV. 1822 (Dec. 2007).

Maurice E. Stucke, *Should the Government Prosecute Monopolies?* 2009 U. ILL. L. REV. 497.

Hannibal Travis, *Wi-Fi Everywhere: Universal Broadband Access as Antitrust and Telecommunications Policy*, 55 AM. U. L. REV. 1697 (Aug. 2006).

Spencer Weber Waller, *Areeda, Epithets, and Essential Facilities*, 2008 WIS. L. REV. 359.

Tim Wu, *Why Have a Telecommunications Law? Antidiscrimination Norms in Communications*, 5 J. TELECOMM. & HIGH TECH. L. 15 (2006).

COPYRIGHT AND DIGITAL RIGHTS MANAGEMENT

Andrew William Bagley, *Fair Use Rights in a World of the Broadcast Flag and Digital Rights Management: Do Consumers Have a Chance?* 18 U. FLA. J.L. & PUB. POL'Y 115 (Apr. 2007).

Dan L. Burk, *Legal and Technical Standards in Digital Rights Management Technology,* 74 FORDHAM L. REV. 537, (2005).

Julie E. Cohen, *Creativity and Culture in Copyright Theory,* 40 U.C. DAVIS L. REV. 1151 (2007).

Michael A. Einhorn, *Digitization and Its Discontents: Digital Rights Management, Access Protection, and Free Markets,* 51 J. COPYRIGHT SOC'Y U.S.A. 279 (Winter 2004).

Rob Frieden, *Internet Packet Sniffing and Its Impact on the Network Neutrality Debate and the Balance of Power Between Intellectual Property Creators and Consumers,* 18 FORDHAM INTELL. PROP. MEDIA & ENT. L.J. 633 (Spring 2008).

Brett M. Frischmann, *An Economic Theory of Infrastructure and Commons Management,* 89 MINN. L. REV. 917 (2005).

James Gibson, *Once and Future Copyright,* 81 NOTRE DAME L. REV. 167 (Nov. 2005).

Dave Hauser, *The DMCA and the Privatization of Copyright,* 30 HASTINGS COMM. & ENT L.J. 339 (Winter 2008).

Bill D. Herman, *Breaking and Entering My Own Computer: The Contest of Copyright Metaphors,* 13 COMM. L. & POL'Y 231 (Spring 2008).

Amy Kapczynski, *The Access to Knowledge Mobilization and the New Politics of Intellectual Property,* 117 YALE L.J. 804 (Mar. 2008).

Hyangsun Lee, *The Audio Broadcast Flag System—Can It Be a Solution?* 12 COMM. L. & POL'Y 405 (Autumn 2007).

Mark A. Lemley, *Property, Intellectual Property, and Free Riding,* 83 TEX. L. REV. 1031 (2005).

Mark A. Lemley & R. Anthony Reese, *Reducing Digital Copyright Infringement Without Restricting Innovation,* 56 STAN. L. REV. 1345 (2004).

Mark A. Lemley & Philip J. Weiser, *Should Property Rules or Liability Rules Govern Information?* 85 TEX. L. REV. 783 (2007).

Jessica Litman, *Lawful Personal Use,* 85 TEX. L. REV. 1871 (June 2007).

Brette G. Meyers, *Filtering Systems or Fair Use? A Comparative Analysis of Proposed Regulations For User-Generated,* 26 CARDOZO ARTS & ENT. L.J. 935 (2009).

Neil Weinstock Netanel, *Temptations of the Walled Garden: Digital Rights Management and Mobile Phone Carriers,* 6 J. TELECOMM. & HIGH TECH. L. 77 (Fall 2007).

Henry H. Perritt, Jr., *New Architectures for Music: Law Should Get Out of the Way,* 29 HASTINGS COMM. & ENT L.J. 259 (Spring 2007).

Joel Reidenberg, *The Rule of Intellectual Property Law in the Internet Economy,* 44 HOUS. L. REV. 1073 (2007).

Joseph D. Schleimer, *Protecting Copyrights at the "Backbone" Level of the Internet,* 15 UCLA ENT. L. REV. 139 (Summer 2008).

Rebecca Tushnet, *User-Generated Discontent: Transformation in Practice,* 31 COLUM. J.L. & ARTS 497 (Summer 2008).

Molly Shaffer Van Houweling, *Communications' Copyright Policy*, 4 J. TELECOMM. & HIGH TECH. L. 97 (Fall 2005).
Molly Shaffer Van Houweling, *Distributive Values in Copyright*, 83 TEX. L. REV. 1535 (May 2005).
John M. Williamson, *Rights Management in Digital Media Content: A Case for FCC Intervention in the Standardization Process*, 3 J. TELECOMM. & HIGH TECH. L. 309 (Spring 2005).
Brian T. Yeh, Congressional Research Service, *Copyright Protection of Digital Television: The Broadcast Video Flag*, CRS Report to Congress (Jan. 11, 2007), http://ipmall.info/hosted_resources/crs/RL33797-070111.pdf.
Christopher S. Yoo, *Copyright and Public Good Economics: A Misunderstood Relation*, 155 U. PA. L. REV. 635 (Jan. 2007).
Peter K. Yu, *The Escalating Copyright Wars*, 32 HOFSTRA L. REV. 907 (Spring 2004).
Peter K. Yu, *P2P and the Future of Private Copying*, 76 COL. L. REV. 653 (Summer 2005).

INTERCONNECTION, ACCESS PRICING, AND UNBUNDLING

Robert C. Atkinson, *Telecom Regulation for the 21st Century: Avoiding Gridlock, Adapting to Change*, 4 J. TELECOMM. & HIGH TECH. L. 379 (Spring 2006).
William P. Barr, *The Gild That Is Killing the Lily: How Confusion over Regulatory Takings Doctrine Is Undermining the Core Protections of the Takings Clause*, 73 GEO. WASH. L. REV. 429 (Apr. 2005).
T. Randolph Beard, *Why ADCO? Why Now? An Economic Exploration into the Future of Industry Structure for the "Last Mile" in Local Telecommunications Markets*, 54 FED. COMM. L.J. 421 (May 2002).
Gerald W. Brock, *Interconnection Policy and Technological Progress*, 58 FED. COMM. L.J. 445 (June 2006).
Stuart Buck, *TELRIC vs. Universal Service: A Takings Violation?* 56 FED. COMM. L.J. 1 (Dec. 2003).
Adam Candeub, *Network Interconnection and Takings*, 54 SYRACUSE L. REV. 369 (2004).
Jim Chen, *The Death of the Regulatory Compact: Adjusting Prices and Expectations in the Law of Regulated Industries*, 67 OHIO ST. L.J. 1265 (2006).
Jim Chen, *The Nature of the Public Utility: Infrastructure, the Market, and the Law*, 98 NW. U. L. REV. 1617 (Summer 2004).
Eric R. Claeys, *The Telecommunications Act of 1996, The Takings Clause, and Tensions in Property Theory*, 22 YALE J. ON REG. 205 (Summer 2005).
Robert W. Crandall, *The Remedy for the "Bottleneck Monopoly" in Telecom: Isolate It, Share It, or Ignore It?* 72 U. CHI. L. REV. 3 (Winter 2005).
Robert W. Crandall & Leonard Waverman, *The Failure of Competitive Entry into Fixed-Line Telecommunications: Who Is at Fault?* 2 J. COMPETITION L. & ECON. 113 (Mar. 2006).
Nicholas Economides, *Hit and Miss: Leverage, Sacrifice, and Refusal to Deal in the Supreme Court Decision in Trinko*, 10 VAND. J. ENT. & TECH. L. 121 (Fall 2007).

Jerry Ellig, *Costs and Consequences of Federal Telecommunications Regulations,* 58 FED. COMM. L.J. 37 (2006).

Jerry Ellig, *What Did the Unbundled Network Element Platform Cost?* 14 COMMLAW CONSPECTUS 1 (2005).

Richard A. Epstein, *Takings, Commons, and Associations: Why the Telecommunications Act of 1996 Misfired,* 22 YALE J. ON REG. 315 (Summer 2005).

Gerald R. Faulhaber, *Cross-Subsidy Analysis with More Than Two Services,* 1 J. COMPETITION L. & ECON. 441 (Sept. 2005).

Gerald R. Faulhaber, *Will Access Regulation Work?* 61 FED. COMM. L.J. 37 (Dec. 2008).

George S. Ford & Lawrence J. Spiwak, The Phoenix Center for Advanced Legal & Economic Public Policy Studies, *The Positive Effects of Unbundling on Broadband Deployment,* Policy Paper No. 19 (2004), http://www.phoenix-center.org/pcpp/PCPP19Final.pdf.

David Gabel & David I. Rosenbaum, *Who's Taking Whom? Some Comments and Evidence on the Constitutionality of TELRIC,* 52 FED. COMM. L.J. 239 (Summer 2000).

Douglas A. Galbi, *Transforming the Structure of Network Interconnection and Transport,* 8 COMMLAW CONSPECTUS 203 (Summer 2000).

David Gilo, *A Market-Based Approach to Telecom Interconnection,* 77 S. CAL. L. REV. 1 (Nov. 2003).

Jerry A. Hausman & J. Gregory Sidak, *A Consumer-Welfare Approach to the Mandatory Unbundling of Telecommunications Networks,* 109 YALE L.J. 417 (Dec. 1999).

Jerry Hausman & J. Gregory Sidak, *Did Mandatory Unbundling Achieve Its Purpose? Empirical Evidence from Five Countries,* 1 J. COMP.L. & ECON. 173 (2005).

Thomas Hazlett, *Rivalrous Telecommunications Networks With and Without Mandatory Sharing,* 58 FED. COMM. L.J. 477 (2006).

Michael A. Heller, *The UNE Anticommons: Why the 1996 Telecom Reforms Blocked Innovation and Investment,* 22 YALE J. ON REG. 275 (Summer 2005).

Allan T. Ingraham, *Mandatory Unbundling, UNE-P, and the Cost of Equity: Does TELRIC Pricing Increase Risk for Incumbent Local Exchange Carriers?* 22 YALE J. ON REG. 389 (Summer 2003).

Michael J. Legg, *Verizon Communications, Inc. v. FCC—Telecommunications Access Pricing and Regulator Accountability Through Administrative Law and Takings Jurisprudence,* 56 FED. COMM. L.J. 563 (May 2004).

Nirali Patel, *FCC Broadband Policy: More Power for the Bell Monopolies,* 55 ADMIN. L. REV. 393 (Spring 2003).

Tramanh Phi, *Duopolies, Restrictions, and Content Regulation: How Much Access Are We Really Getting from Broadband Internet Access?* 7 SANTA CLARA L. REV. 347 (2007).

Harvey Reiter, *The Contrasting Policies of the FCC and FERC Regarding the Importance of Open Transmission Networks in Downstream Competitive Markets,* 57 FED. COMM. L.J. 243 (May 2002).

J. Steven Rich, *Brand X and the Wireline Broadband Report and Order: The Beginning of the End of the Distinction Between Title I and Title II Services*, 58 FED. COMM. L.J., No. 2, 221 (Apr. 2006).
Howard A. Shelanski, *Adjusting Regulation to Competition: Toward a New Model for U.S. Telecommunications Policy*, 24 YALE J. ON REG. 55 (Winter 2007).
James B. Speta, *Deregulating Telecommunications in Internet Time*, 61 WASH. & LEE L. REV. 1063 (Summer 2004).
Daniel F. Spulber, *Access to Networks: Economic and Constitutional Connections*, 88 CORNELL L. REV. 885 (May 2003).
Daniel F. Spulber, *Network Regulation: The Many Faces of Access*, 1 J. COMPETITION L. & ECON. 635 (Dec. 2005).
John Thorne, *Discounted Bundling by Dominant Firms*, 13 GEO. MASON L. REV. 339 (Winter 2005).
Kevin Werbach, *The Federal Computer Commission*, 84 N.C. L. REV. 1 (Dec. 2005).
Keven Werbach, *Only Connect*, 22 BERKELEY TECH. L.J. 1233 (Fall 2007).

INTERNET HISTORY AND TECHNOLOGY

Barry M. Leiner, Vinton G. Cerf, David D. Clark, Robert E. Kahn, Leonard Kleinrock, Daniel C. Lynch, Jon Postel, Larry G. Roberts & Stephen Wolff, *A Brief History of the Internet* (Internet Society, 2003), http://www.isoc.org/internet/history/brief.html.
Jonathan Zittrain, *A History of Online Gatekeeping*, 19 HARV. J.L. & TECH. 253 (Spring 2006).
Ethan Zuckerman & Andrew McLaughlin, *Introduction to Internet Architecture and Institutions* (Aug. 2003), http://cyber.law.harvard.edu/digitaldemocracy/internetarchitecture.html.

INTERNET POLICY AND GOVERNANCE

Steven Aronowitz, *Brand X Internet Services v. FCC: The Case of the Missing Policy Argument*, 20 BERKELEY TECH. L.J. 887 (2005).
Julie E. Cohen, *Cyberspace as/and Space*, 107 COLUM. L. REV. 210 (Jan. 2007)
Rob Frieden, *Neither Fish Nor Fowl: New Strategies for Selective Regulation of Information Services*, 6 J. TELECOMM. & HIGH TECH. L., No. 2, 373 (2008).
Brett Frischmann, *Cultural Environmentalism and the Wealth of Networks*, 74 U. CHI. L. REV. 1083, 1096 (2007).
William D. Rahm, *Watching Over the Web: A Substantive Equality Regime for Broadband Applications*, 24 YALE J. ON REG. 1 (Winter 2007).
Kevin Werbach, *The Centripetal Network: How the Internet Holds Itself Together, and the Forces Tearing It Apart*, 42 U.C. DAVIS L. REV. 343 (Dec. 2008).
Jonathan L. Zittrain, *The Generative Internet*, 119 HARV. L. REV. 1974 (2006).

LIABILITY OF INTERNET INTERMEDIARIES

Jeffrey Cobia, *The Digital Millennium Copyright Act Takedown Notice Procedure: Misuses, Abuses, and Shortcomings of the Process*, 10 MINN. J.L. SCI. & TECH. 387 (Winter 2009).

Amanda Groover Hyland, *The Taming of the Internet: A New Approach to Third-Party Internet Defamation*, 31 HASTINGS COMM & ENT.L.J. 79 (Fall 2008).

Matthew G. Jeweler, *The Communications Decency Act of 1996: Why § 230 Is Outdated and Publisher Liability for Defamation Should Be Reinstated Against Internet Service Providers*, 8 U. PITT. J. TECH. L. & POL'Y 3 (Fall 2007).

Seth F. Kreimer, *Censorship by Proxy: The First Amendment, Internet Intermediaries, and the Problem of the Weakest Link*, 155 U. PA. L. REV. 11 (Nov. 2006).

Mark A. Lemley, *Rationalizing Internet Safe Harbors*, 6 J. TELECOMM. & HIGH TECH. L. 101 (Fall 2007).

Tara E. Lynch, *Good Samaritan or Defamation Defender? Amending the Communications Decency Act to Correct the Misnomer of Section 230 Without Expanding ISP Liability*, 19 SYRACUSE SCI. & TECH. L. REP. 1 (Fall 2008).

Robert G. Magee, *Information Conduits or Content Developers? Determining Whether News Portals Should Enjoy Blanket Immunity from Defamation Suits*, 12 COMM. L. & POL'Y 369 (Autumn 2007).

Wolfgang McGavran, *Picking Roommates on the Internet: Matching Roommates Online and Losing Communications Decency Act Immunity in the Process*, 11 TUL. J. TECH. & INTELL. PROP. 139 (Fall 2008).

Aaron K. Perzanowski, *Rethinking Anticircumvention's Interoperability Policy*, 42 U.C. DAVIS L. REV. 1549 (June 2009).

Rebecca Tushnet, *Power Without Responsibility: Intermediaries and the First Amendment*, 76 GEO. WASH. L. REV. 986 (June 2008).

Colette Vogele & Ilana Sabes, *Attention Web Site Operators: Be Certain You Qualify for § 230 Protection*, 5 J. INTERNET L. 1 (Nov. 2008).

Cecilia Ziniti, *The Optimal Liability System for Online Service Providers: How Zeran v. America Online Got It Right and Web 2.0 Proves It*, 23 BERKELEY TECH. L.J. 583 (2008).

MEDIA CONCENTRATION AND ACCESS

Enrique Armijo, *Public Airwaves, Private Mergers: Analyzing the FCC's Faulty Justifications for the 2003 Media Ownership Rule Changes*, 82 N.C. L. REV. 1482 (May 2004).

C. Edwin Baker, *Media Concentration: Giving Up on Democracy*, 54 FLA. L. REV. 839 (2002).

C. Edwin Baker, *Viewpoint Diversity and Media Ownership*, 61 FED. COMM. L.J. 651 (June 2009).

Jerome A. Barron, *Access to the Media—A Contemporary Appraisal*, 35 HOFSTRA L. REV. 937 (Spring 2007).

Sandra Braman, *The Ideal v. the Real in Media Localism: Regulatory Implications*, 12 COMM. L. & POL'Y 231 (Summer 2007).

Sandra Braman, *Where Has Media Policy Gone? Defining the Field in the Twenty-first Century*, 9 COMM. L. & POL'Y 153 (Spring 2004).

Adam Candeub, *Media Ownership Regulation, The First Amendment, and Democracy's Future*, 41 U.C. DAVIS L. REV. 1547 (Apr. 2008).

Daniel A. Farber, *Access and Exclusion Rights in Electronic Media: Complex Rules for a Complex World*, 33 N. KY. L. REV. 459 (2006).

Ellen P. Goodman, *Media Policy out of the Box: Content Abundance, Attention Scarcity, and the Failures of Digital Markets*, 19 BERKELEY TECH. L.J. 1389 (2004).

Daniel E. Ho & Kevin M. Quinn, *The Role of Theory and Evidence in Media Regulation and Law: A Response to Baker and a Defense of Empirical Legal Studies*, 61 FED. COMM. L.J. 673 (June 2009).

Daniel E. Ho & Kevin M. Quinn, *Viewpoint Diversity and Media Consolidation: An Empirical Study*, 61 STAN. L. REV. 781 (2009).

Sean Michael McGuire, *Media Influence and the Modern American Democracy: Why the First Amendment Compels Regulation of Media Ownership*, 4 CARDOZO PUB. L. POL'Y & ETHICS J. 689 (Aug. 2006).

Christa Corrine McLintock, *The Destruction of Media Diversity, or: How the FCC Learned to Stop Regulating and Love Corporate Dominated Media*, 22 J. MARSHALL J. COMPUTER & INFO. L. 569 (Spring 2004).

Philip M. Napoli & Sheea T. Sybblis, *Access to Audiences as a First Amendment Right: Its Relevance and Implications for Electronic Media Policy*, 12 VA. J.L. & TECH 1 (2007).

Maria Simone & Jan Fernback, *Invisible Hands or Public Spheres? Theoretical Foundations for U.S. Broadcast Policy*, 11 COMM. L. & POL'Y 287, No. 2 (2006).

John F. Sturm, *Time for Change on Media Cross-Ownership Regulation*, 57 FED. COMM. L.J. 201 (2005).

Adam Thierer, *Why Regulate Broadcasting? Toward a Consistent First Amendment Standard for the Information Age*, 15 COMMLAW CONSPECTUS 431 (2007).

Anthony E. Varona, *Out of Thin Air: Using First Amendment Public Forum Analysis to Redeem American Broadcasting Regulation*, 39 U. MICH. J.L. REFORM 149 (1995–1996).

NETWORK NEUTRALITY

Marvin Ammori, *Beyond Content Neutrality: Understanding Content-Based Promotion of Democratic Speech*, 61 FED. COMM. L.J. 273 (Mar. 2009).

Dan G. Barry, *The Effect of Video Franchising Reform on Net Neutrality: Does the Beginning of IP Convergence Mean That It Is Time for Net Neutrality Regulation?* 24 SANTA CLARA COMPUTER & HIGH TECH. L.J. 421 (Jan. 2008).

T. Randolph Beard, *Network Neutrality and Industry Structure*, 29 HASTINGS COMM. & ENT L.J. 149 (Winter 2007).

Jerry Brito, *A Tale of Two Commissions: Net Neutrality and Regulatory Analysis*, 16 COMMLAW CONSPECTUS 1 (2007).

Barbara A. Cherry, *Misusing Network Neutrality to Eliminate Common Carriage Threatens Free Speech and the Postal System*, 33 N. KY. L. REV. 483 (2006).

Larry F. Darby, *Consumer Welfare, Capital Formation and Net Neutrality: Paying for Next Generation Broadband Networks,* 16 MEDIA L. & POL'Y 122 (Summer 2007).

Rob Frieden, *Internet 3.0: Identifying Problems and Solutions to the Network Neutrality Debate,* 1 INT'L J. OF COMM., 461 (2007), http://ijoc.org/ojs/index.php/ijoc/article/view/160/86.

Rob Frieden, *Network Neutrality or Bias?—Handicapping the Odds for a Tiered and Branded Internet,* 29 HASTINGS COMM. & ENT. L.J., No. 2, 171 (2007).

Brett Frischmann & Barbara van Schewick, *Yoo's Frame and What It Ignores: Network Neutrality and the Economics of an Information Superhighway,* 47 JURIMETRICS J. 383 (2007).

Bill D. Herman, *Opening Bottlenecks: On Behalf of Mandated Network Neutrality,* 59 FED. COMM. L.J. 103 (Dec. 2006)

Justin (Gus) Hurwitz, *Neighbor Billing and Network Neutrality,* 11 VA. J.L. & TECH. 9 (Fall 2006).

William G. Laxton, Jr., *The End of Net Neutrality,* 2006 DUKE L. & TECH. REV. 15 (July 18, 2006).

Mark A. Lemley & Lawrence Lessig, *The End of End-to-End: Preserving the Architecture of the Internet in the Broadband Era,* 48 UCLA L. REV. 925 (2001).

Lawrence Lessig, *In Support of Network Neutrality,* I/S: J. L. & POL'Y FOR INFO. SOC'Y 185 (Spring 2007).

Robert E. Litan, *Unintended Consequences of Net Neutrality Regulation,* 5 J. TELECOMM. & HIGH TECH. L. 533 (Spring 2007).

Christopher T. Marsden, *Net Neutrality: The European Debate,* 12 J. INTERNET L. 1 (Aug. 2008).

Randolph J. May, *Net Neutrality Mandates: Neutering the First Amendment in the Digital Age,* I/S: J. L. & POL'Y FOR INFO. SOC'Y 197 (Spring 2007).

Craig McTaggart, *Was the Internet Ever Neutral?* Paper presented at the 34th Research Conference on Communication, Information and Internet Policy, George Mason University School of Law, Arlington, Virginia (Sept. 30, 2006), http://web.si.umich.edu/tprc/papers/2006/593/mctaggart-tprc06rev.pdf.

Sascha D. Meinrath & Victor W. Pickard, *Transcending Net Neutrality: Ten Steps Toward an Open Internet,* 12 J. INTERNET L., No. 6, 1 (Dec. 2008).

Jennifer L. Newman, *Keeping the Internet Neutral: Net Neutrality and Its Role in Protecting Political Expression on the Internet,* 31 HASTINGS COMM. & ENT. L.J. 153 (Fall 2008).

Amit M. Schejter, *"Justice, and Only Justice, You Shall Pursue": Network Neutrality, the First Amendment and John Rawls's Theory of Justice,* 14 MICH. TELECOMM. & TECH. L. REV. 137 (Fall 2007).

Howard A. Shelanski, *Network Neutrality: Regulating with More Questions Than Answers,* 6 J. TELECOMM. & HIGH TECH. L. 23 (Fall 2007).

J. Gregory Sidak, *A Consumer-Welfare Approach to Network Neutrality Regulation of the Internet,* 2 J. COMP. L. & ECON., No. 3, 349 (2006).

Adam Thierer, *Are "Dumb Pipe" Mandates Smart Public Policy? Vertical Integration,*

Net Neutrality, and the Network Layers Model, 3 J. TELECOMM. & HIGH TECH. L. 275 (2005).

Barbara van Schewick, *Towards an Economic Framework for Network Neutrality Regulation*, 5 J. ON TELECOMM. & HIGH TECH. L. 329 (2007).

Tim Wu, *Network Neutrality, Broadband Discrimination*, 2 J. TELECOMM. & HIGH TECH L. 141 (2005), http://ssrn.com/abstract=388863.

Tim Wu & Christopher S. Yoo, *Keeping the Internet Neutral? Tim Wu and Christopher Yoo Debate*, 59 FED. COMM. L.J. 575 (June 2007).

Christopher S. Yoo, *Beyond Network Neutrality*, 19 HARV. J.L. & TECH. (Fall 2005).

Christopher S. Yoo, *Network Neutrality and the Economics of Congestion*, 94 GEO. L.J. 1847 (June 2006).

Christopher S. Yoo, *Would Mandating Broadband Network Neutrality Help or Hurt Competition? A Comment on the End-to-End Debate*, 3 J. ON TELECOMM. & HIGH TECH. L. 23 (2004).

NEXT-GENERATION NETWORK REGULATION AND REGULATORY REFORM

Robert D. Atkinson, *Framing a National Broadband Policy*, 16 COMMLAW CONSPECTUS 145 (2007).

Yochai Benkler, *Freedom in the Commons: Towards a Political Economy of Information*, 52 DUKE L.J. 1245 (Apr. 2003).

Jim Chen, *The Authority to Regulate Broadband Internet Access over Cable*, 16 BERKELEY TECH. L.J. 677 (Spring 2001).

Robert W. Crandall, *The Empirical Case Against Asymmetric Regulation of Broadband Internet Access*, 17 BERKELEY TECH. L.J. 953 (Summer 2002).

Robert W. Crandall & Leonard Waverman, *The Failure of Competitive Entry into Fixed-Line Telecommunications: Who Is at Fault?* 2 J. COMPETITION LAW & ECONOMICS 113 (Mar. 2006).

Susan P. Crawford, *The Internet and the Project of Communications Law*, 55 UCLA L. REV. 359 (Dec. 2007).

Susan P. Crawford, *Internet Think*, 5 J. TELECOMM. & HIGH TECH. L. 467 (Winter 2007).

James Crowe, *The Digital Broadband Migration Regulation and Free Markets Redux: Additional Insights on Regulating the Telecommunications Industry in the New Economy*, 5 J. TELECOMM. & HIGH TECH. L. 487 (Winter 2007).

Rob Frieden, *Adjusting the Horizontal and Vertical in Telecommunications Regulation: A Comparison of the Traditional and a New Layered Approach*, 55 FED. COMM. L.J. 207 (Mar. 2003).

Rob Frieden, *Regulatory Arbitrage Strategies and Tactics in Telecommunications*, 5 N.C. J. L. & TECH. 227 (Spring 2004).

Rob Frieden, *What Do Pizza Delivery and Information Services Have in Common? Lessons from Recent Judicial and Regulatory Struggles with Convergence*, 32 RUTGERS COMPUTER. & TECH. L.J., No. 2, 247 (2006).

Justin P. Hedge, *The Decline of Title II Common-Carrier Regulations in the Wake of Brand X: Long-Run Success for Consumers, Competition, and the Broadband Internet Market,* 14 COMMLAW CONSPECTUS 427 (2006).

Reed E. Hundt, *Communications Policy for 2006 and Beyond,* 58 FED. COMM. L.J. 1 (Jan. 2006).

International Telecommunication Union, *ITU New Initiatives Programme: The Regulatory Environment for Future Mobile Multimedia Services,* World Wide Web site, http://www.itu.int/osg/spu/ni/multimobile/index.html.

Sascha D. Meinrath & K.C. Claffy, *The Commons Initiative: Cooperative Measurement and Modeling* 16 COMMLAW CONSPECTUS 407 (2008).

Thomas B. Nachbar, *The Public Network,* 17 COMMLAW CONSPECTUS 67 (2008).

Philip M. Napoli, *Paradoxes of Media Policy Analysis: Implications for Public Interest Media Regulation,* 60 ADMIN. L. REV. 801 (Fall 2008).

Susan Ness, *The Law of Unintended Consequences,* 58 FED. COMM. L.J. 531 (June 2006).

Jonathan E. Nuechterlein & Philip J. Weiser, DIGITAL CROSSROADS—AMERICAN TELECOMMUNICATIONS POLICY IN THE INTERNET AGE (MIT Press, 2005).

William D. Rahm, *Watching Over the Web: A Substantive Equality Regime for Broadband Applications,* 24 YALE J. ON REG. 1 (Winter 2007).

Ed Rosenberg, The National Regulatory Research Institute, *Assessing Wireless and Broadband Substitution in Local Telephone Markets,* Publication No. 07–06 (June 2007), http://nrri.org/pubs/telecommunications/07–06.pdf.

Amit M. Schejter, ed., . . . AND COMMUNICATIONS FOR ALL—A POLICY AGENDA FOR A NEW ADMINISTRATION (Lexington Books, 2009).

Howard A. Shelanski, *Adjusting Regulation to Competition: Toward a New Model for U.S. Telecommunications Policy,* 24 YALE J. ON REG. 55 (Winter, 2007).

Philip J. Weiser, *Law and Information Platforms,* J. ON TELECOMM. & HIGH TECH. L., 1 (2002).

Philip J. Weiser, *Toward a Next Generation Regulatory Strategy,* 35 LOY. U. CHI. L.J. 41 (2003).

Kevin Werbach, *Breaking the Ice: Rethinking Telecommunications Law for the Digital Age,* 4 J. TELECOMM. & HIGH TECH. L. 59 (Fall 2005).

Kevin Werbach, *The Federal Computer Commission,* 84 N.C. L. REV. 1 (Dec. 2005).

Richard S. Whitt, *Adaptive Policymaking: Evolving and Applying Emergent Solutions for U.S. Communications Policy,* 61 FED. COMM. L.J. 483 (June 2009).

Richard S. Whitt, *A Horizontal Leap Forward: Formulating a New Communications Public Policy Framework Based on the Network Layers Model,* 56 FED. COMM. L.J. 587 (May 2004).

Richard S. Whitt & Stephen J. Schultze, *The New "Emergence Economics" of Innovation and Growth, and What It Means for Communications Policy,* 7 J. TELECOMM. & HIGH TECH. L. 217 (Spring 2009).

Tim Wu, *Why Have a Telecommunications Law? Antidiscrimination Norms in Communications,* 5 J. TELECOMM. & HIGH TECH. L. 15 (2006).

Christopher S. Yoo, *The Rise and Demise of the Technology-Specific Approach to the First Amendment,* 91 GEO. L.J. 245 (2003).

SPECTRUM MANAGEMENT

Stuart Minor Benjamin, *The Logic of Scarcity: Idle Spectrum as a First Amendment Violation,* 52 DUKE L.J. 1 (Oct. 2002).
Stuart Minor Benjamin, *Spectrum Abundance and the Choice Between Private and Public Control,* 78 N.Y.U. L. REV. 2007 (Dec. 2003).
Jerry Brito, *The Spectrum Commons in Theory and Practice,* 2007 STAN. TECH. L. REV. 1 (2007).
Kenneth R. Carter, *Policy Lessons from Personal Communications Services: Licensed vs. Unlicensed Spectrum Access,* 15 COMMLAW CONSPECTUS 93 (2006).
Susan P. Crawford, *The Ambulance, the Squad Car, and the Internet,* 21 BERKELEY TECH. L.J. 873 (Spring 2006).
Gerald R. Faulhaber, *The Question of Spectrum: Technology, Management, and Regime Change,* 4 J. TELECOMM. & HIGH TECH. L. 123 (Fall 2005).
Gerald R. Faulhaber, *Wireless Telecommunications: Spectrum as a Critical Resource,* 79 S. CAL. L. REV. 537 (2006).
Harold Feld, *From Third Class Citizen to First Among Equals: Rethinking the Place of Unlicensed Spectrum in the FCC Hierarchy,* 15 COMMLAW CONSPECTUS 53 (2006).
Rob Frieden, *Balancing Equity and Efficiency Issues in the Management of Shared Global Radiocommunication Resources,* 24 U. PA. J. INT'L ECON. L. 289 (Summer 2003).
Ellen P. Goodman, *Spectrum Auctions and the Public Interest,* 7 J. TELECOMM. & HIGH TECH. L. 343 (Spring 2009).
Ellen P. Goodman, *Spectrum Equity,* 4 J. TELECOMM. & HIGH TECH. L. 217 (Fall 2005).
Ellen P. Goodman, *Spectrum Rights in the Telecosm to Come,* 41 SAN DIEGO L. REV. 269 (Feb.–Mar. 2004).
Thomas W. Hazlett, *A Law and Economics Approach to Spectrum Property Rights: A Response to Weiser and Hatfield,* 15 GEO. MASON L. REV. 975 (June 2008).
Thomas W. Hazlett, *Property Rights and Wireless License Values,* 51 J.L. & ECON. 563 (Aug. 2008).
Thomas W. Hazlett, *Spectrum Tragedies,* 22 YALE J. ON REG. 242 (Summer 2005).
Thomas W. Hazlett & Matthew L. Spitzer, *Advanced Wireless Technologies and Public Policy,* 79 S. CAL. L. REV. 595 (Mar. 2006).
Jeremiah Johnston, *The Paradise of the Commons or Privileged Private Property—What Direction Should the FCC Take on Spectrum Regulation?* 4 J. TELECOMM. & HIGH TECH. L. 173 (2004).
John S. Leibovitz, *The Great Spectrum Debate: A Commentary on the FCC Spectrum Policy Task Force's Report on Spectrum Rights and Responsibilities,* 6 YALE J. L. & TECH. 390 (2003–2004).
Travis E. Litman, *Cognitive Radio: Moving Toward a Workable Framework for Com-*

mercial Leasing of Public Safety Spectrum, 4 J. TELECOMM. & HIGH TECH. L. 249 (Fall 2005).

R. Paul Margie, *Can You Hear Me Now? Getting Better Reception from the FCC's Spectrum Policy,* 2004 STAN. TECH. L. REV. 5 (2004).

New America Foundation, THE CARTOON GUIDE TO FEDERAL SPECTRUM POLICY (2006), http://www.newamerica.net/publications/policy/the_cartoon_guide_to_federal_spectrum_policy.

Patrick S. Ryan, *Application of the Public-Trust Doctrine and Principles of Natural Resource Management to Electromagnetic Spectrum,* 10 MICH. TELECOMM. TECH. L. REV. 285 (2004).

Daniel Sineway, *What's Wrong with Wireless? An Argument for a Liability Approach to Electromagnetic Spectrum Regulation,* 41 GA. L. REV. 671 (Winter 2007).

James B. Speta, *Making Spectrum Reform "Thinkable,"* 4 J. TELECOMM. & HIGH TECH. L. 183 (Fall 2005).

Pablo T. Spiller, *Towards a Property Rights Approach to Communications Spectrum,* 16 YALE J. ON REG. 53 (Winter 1999).

Lindsey L. Tonsager, *Increasing E-Quality in Rural America: U.S. Spectrum Policy and Adverse Possession,* 90 MINN. L. REV. 1506 (May 2006).

Scott Wallsten, *Reverse Auctions and Universal Telecommunications Service: Lessons from Global Experience,* 61 FED. COMM. L.J. 373 (Mar. 2009).

Joseph M. Ward, *Secondary Markets in Spectrum: Making Spectrum Policy as Flexible as the Spectrum Market It Must Foster,* 10 COMMLAW CONSPECTUS 103 (2001).

Philip J. Weiser, *Communicating During Emergencies: Toward Interoperability and Effective Information Management,* 59 FED. COMM. L.J. 547 (June 2007).

Philip J. Weiser, *Policing the Spectrum Commons,* 74 FORDHAM L. REV. 663 (Nov. 2005).

Philip J. Weiser & Dale Hatfield, *Spectrum Policy Reform and the Next Frontier of Property Rights,* 15 GEO. MASON L. REV. 549 (Spring 2008).

Kevin Werbach, *Supercommons: Toward a Unified Theory of Wireless Communication,* 82 TEX. L. REV. 863 (Mar. 2004).

UNIVERSAL SERVICE

Colin R. Blackman, *Universal Service: Obligation or Opportunity?* TELECOMM. POL'Y 19 (1995).

Jim Chen, *Standing in the Shadows of Giants: The Role of Intergenerational Equity in Telecommunications Reform,* 71 U. COLO. L. REV. 921 (Fall 2000).

Jim Chen, *Subsidized Rural Telephony and the Public Interest: A Case Study in Cooperative Federalism and Its Pitfalls,* 2 J. TELECOMM. & HIGH TECH. L. 307 (Fall 2003).

Rob Frieden, *Killing with Kindness: Fatal Flaws in the $6.5 Billion Universal Service Funding Mission and What Should Be Done to Narrow the Digital Divide,* 24 CARDOZO ARTS & ENT. L.J. 447 (2006).

Farid Gasmi, Jean-Jacques Laffont & William W. Sharkey, *Competition, Universal*

Service and Telecommunications Policy in Developing Countries, 12 INFO. ECON. & POL'Y, No. 3, 221 (2000).

Allen S. Hammond, IV, *Universal Service: Problems, Solutions, and Responsive Policies*, 57 FED. COMM. L.J. 187 (Mar. 2005).

Krishna P. Jayakar & Harmeet Sawhney, *Universal Service: Beyond Established Practice to Possibility Space*, 28 TELECOMM. POL'Y., Nos. 3–4, 339 (2004).

Jonathan Meer, *Highway Robbery Online: Is E-Rate Worth the Fraud?* 2006 BYU EDUC. & L.J. 323 (2006).

Milton L. Mueller, UNIVERSAL SERVICE: COMPETITION, INTERCONNECTION, AND MONOPOLY IN THE MAKING OF THE AMERICAN TELEPHONE SYSTEM (MIT Press, 1997).

Milton L. Mueller, *Universal Service in Telephone History: A Reconstruction*, 17 TELECOMM. POL'Y, 352 (1993).

Mira Burri Nenova, *The New Concept Of Universal Service in a Digital Networked Communications Environment*, 3 I/S: J. L. & POL'Y FOR INFO. SOC'Y 117 (Spring 2007).

Caio M. Silva Pereira Neto, *Development Theory and Foundations of Universal Access Policies*, 2 I/S: J. L. & POL'Y FOR INFO. SOC'Y 365 (Spring–Summer 2006).

Kevin Werbach, *Connections: Beyond Universal Service in the Digital Age*, 7 J. TELECOMM. & HIGH TECH. L. 67 (Winter 2009).

Ramsey L. Woodworth, *Camp Runamuck: The FCC's Troubled E-Rate Program*, 14 COMMLAW CONSPECTUS 335 (2006).

Xinzhu Zhang, Jean-Jacques Laffont & Antonio Estache, UNIVERSAL SERVICE OBLIGATIONS IN DEVELOPING COUNTRIES, World Bank Policy Research Working Paper Series No. 3421 (2004).

VOICE OVER INTERNET PROTOCOL

Stephen E. Blythe, *The Regulation of Voice-over-Internet-Protocol in the United States, the European Union, and the United Kingdom*, 5 J. HIGH TECH. L. 161 (2005).

Robert Cannon, *State Regulatory Approaches to VoIP: Policy, Implementation, and Outcome*, 57 FED. COMM. L.J. 479 (May 2005).

Mark C. Del Bianco, *Voices Past: The Present and Future of VoIP Regulation*, 14 COMMLAW CONSPECTUS 365 (2006).

Jared S. Dinkes, *Rethinking the Revolution: Competitive Telephony in a Voice over Internet Protocol Era*, 66 OHIO ST. L.J. 833 (2005).

R. Alex DuFour, *Voice over Internet Protocol: Ending Uncertainty and Promoting Innovation Through a Regulatory Framework*, 13 COMMLAW CONSPECTUS 471 (2005).

Jerry Ellig & Alastair Walling, *Regulatory Status of VoIP in the Post-Brand X World*, 23 SANTA CLARA COMPUTER & HIGH TECH. L.J. 89 (No. 2006)

Daniel B. Garrie & Rebecca Wong, *Regulating Voice over Internet Protocol: An E.U./U.S. Comparative Approach*, 22 AM. U. IN'TL L. REV. 549 (2007).

Chérie R. Kiser & Angela F. Collins, *Regulation on the Horizon: Are Regulators Poised to Address the Status of IP Telephony?* 11 COMMLAW CONSPECTUS 19 (2003).

Sunny Lu, Note, *Cellco Partnership v. FCC & Vonage Holdings Corp. v. Minnesota Public Utilities Commission: VoIP's Shifting Legal and Political Landscape*, 20 BERKELEY TECH. L.J. 859 (2005).

Linda A. Rushnak, *Is Voice over Internet Protocol (VoIP) Subject to Regulation Under the Telecommunications Act of 1996?* 17 ALB. L.J. SCI. & TECH. 213 (2007).

Jimar Sanders, *Voice over Internet Protocol: An International Approach to Regulation*, 35 GA. J. INT'L & COMP. L. 575 (Spring 2007).

Mark L. Silverstein, *VoIP and Pay-To-Play: Broadband's Attempt to Push Away Direct Competition*, 155 U. PA. L. REV. 1305 (May 2007).

Konrad L. Trope, *Voice over Internet Protocol: The Revolution in America's Telecommunications Infrastructure*, 22 COMPUTER & INTERNET LAW, No. 12, 1 (Dec. 2005).

Melissa Winberg, *Calling All Angles: Perspectives on Regulating Internet Telephony*, 10 VAND. J. ENT. & TECH. L. 241 (Fall 2007).

WIRELESS REGULATION

Randolph Beard, *Developing a National Wireless Regulatory Framework: A Law and Economics Approach*, 16 COMMLAW CONSPECTUS 391 (2008).

Yochai Benkler, *Some Economics of Wireless Communications*, 16 HARV. J.L. & TECH. 25 (Fall 2002).

Adam Clay, *Unlocking the Wireless Safe: Opening Up the Wireless World for Consumers*, 61 FED. COMM. L.J. 715 (June 2009).

Rob Frieden, *Hold the Phone: Assessing the Rights of Wireless Handset Owners and Carriers*, 69 U. PITT. L. REV. No. 4, 675 (2008).

Robert W. Hahn, *The Economics of "Wireless Net Neutrality,"* 3 J. COMPETITION L. & ECON. 399 (Sept. 2007).

Thomas Hazlett, *The Wireless Craze, the Unlimited Bandwidth Myth, the Spectrum Auction Faux Pas, and the Punchline to Ronald Coase's "Big Joke": An Essay on Airwave Allocation Policy*, 14 HARV. J.L. & TECH. 335 (Spring 2001).

Thomas W. Hazlett & Matthew L. Spitzer, *Advanced Wireless Technologies and Public Policy*, 79 S. CAL. L. Rev. 595 (Mar. 2006).

Patrick S. Ryan, *Wireless Communications and Computing at a Crossroads: New Paradigms and Their Impact on Theories Governing the Public's Right to Spectrum Access*, 3 J. TELECOMM. & HIGH TECH. L. 239 (Spring 2005).

Kevin Werbach, *Supercommons: Toward a Unified Theory of Wireless Communication*, 82 TEX. L. REV. 863 (Mar. 2004).

INDEX